کائنات

پروفیسر محمد غلام حسین صاحب دلیل

KAYINATH

PROF. M. GHULAM HUSSAIN DALEEL

ENGLISH TRANSLATION & COMMENTARY: G.Z RAZIA BEGUM ABDUL AZEEZ, B.A

DQJ Foundation

For Literature and Philanthropy

ISBN

Hardcase: 979-8-88909-907-9
Paperback: 979-8-88883-969-0

DEDICATION

I consecrate this commentary to the memory of my beloved father Alijanab M.Ghulam Hussain Sahib, Daleel who confronted with, and amounted all notes of hardship in introducing female education in the Muslim Society of Madurai. By Almighty Allah's grace and Daleel Sahib's perseverant endeavours innumerable beautiful flowers have been blooming in the literary field of Madurai.

– G.Z. RAZIA BEGUM ABDUL AZEEZ

(Servant of Islam)

ACKNOWLEDGEMENT

I am highly thankful to Almighty Allah for having granted the courage and aptitude to undertake the task of writing this commentary and for having blessed me with the fulfilment of my ambition.

I am highly obliged to Dr.P.M. Ajmal Khan Sahib for having taken the trouble of scrutinizing the whole literature and for having written a splendid and lengthy foreword for my commentary with the touch of Islamic Culture. I am bound to be grateful to Dr.P.Nisar Ahmed Sahib for having written a commendable preface with sincere appreciation for my commentary and appreciable criticism on the text Nazm-e-Kayinat, authored by my father Late Prof.M.Ghulam Hussain Sahib Daleel. I acknowledge the intense and keen interest, evinced by Dr.Syed Safiullah Sahib in writing my profile with brotherly affection. I am all prayers for the peace of the soul of Late Dr.S.A.Q.Hussaini Sahib for his short, sweet and unparalleled criticism written for my father's Nazm-Kayinat during their life time.

A great deal of obligations are due to my revered husband Janab M.Abdul Azeez Sahib for his continuous cooperation every way throughout my literary endeavours. My fervent prayers and ample gratitude are due to my beloved nephew Mr.Usman Fayaz for having voluntarily and most sincerely lending his helping hand in the initial processing's of the book with great zeal, enthusiasm and love for Islam. I offer my whole-hearted thankfulness to my sisters and brothers for their moral support, loving gestures and encouragement to me.

I am specially grateful to the readers of this book.

– G.Z. RAZIA BEGUM

Servant of Islam

THE CHOSEN ONE

By

Dr.G.V. Suraiya Begum

Retd. Dean
Madras medical college and government general hospital
Secretary, Daleel Qateel Jameel foundation, Chennai.

———ol◠ ♦ ◠lo———

"Gratitude" is a feeling, the intensity and depth of which can neither be expressed in words nor fathomed. We are immensely grateful to God for having blessed our revered father Late Prof. Ghulam Hussain Daleel with a daughter like Razia Begum Abdul Azeez, my younger sister. She is the author of this book 'Islamic Spiritualism', whichis based on our father's book "Kayinat" (Universe), a long poem in Urdu with Sophistic Philosophy, written in his last days.

While all the other six children of Daleel Saheb underwent regular formal education in medicine, science, art and technical courses, God did not allow Razia to complete her final year in school or collage course, either due to her eye problem or father's illness or some indisposition or the other. Perhaps, God had 'Chosen' her for something great as our father prophesised then. Quite undeterred, her amazing courage, determination, dexterity, sincerity of purpose and her strong Imaan, enable to her take up Urdu Literature and appear for private examination in Northern Universities, after passing the Entrance Examination of Madras University privately. Our benevolent Uncle Late Janab Mohammed Hussain Jameel (to whom we owe everything we are) took her to Aligarh University to write the intermediate examination and subsequently to Nagpur, University to write B.A. Urdu examinations. She had also registered for M.A Urdu in Nagpur, but by that time our father was seriously ill. She preferred to be by her father's side and nurse him, rather than be away for higher studies. Throughout her study period, Razia was by the side of our father who taught her everything she needed. It was a l : l teacher -student ration and patient – nurse ration. Hence the education and nursing care were superb. At last the inevitable happened and our beloved father expired in 1957. Razia was married the following year to Mr.Abdul Azeez, a relative and an old student of our father in American Collage, Madurai.

In this book Islamic Spiritualism, Razia has translate "Kayinat" into English and made elaborate commentary with reference from Quran and Ahadis-e-Nabavi. It is quite evident that she must have done an exhaustive study in Urdu and Islamic literature. By translating it in English, Razia has presented this enlightening book to a wider public in a more assimilative form. This indeed is a treasure to our families.

Apart from this book, Razia's works include an English translation of Jaffar Barmaki (Prime Minister of Khalifa Haroon -ur-Rasheed), an Urdu drama written by Qateel Saheb, our father's younger brother. She also has on the anvil for publication the following works:

A series of lectures on 94 topics about Islam and its culture;

Excerpts of interesting verses from Daleel Saheb's Thohfa-e-Darwesh, Naghma-e-Darwesh and Nara-e-Darwesh, with due translation, meanings and explanation of the underlying sublime sufistic Philosophy;

1. Daleel Saheb's Biography and Genealogy;

2. Excerpts of important verses from Quran with an in-depth analysis.

Her greatest contribution is retrieving and reconstructing the tattered manuscript of our father and Uncle Qateel, which were kept safe and passes on to her by our beloved Uncle Jameel saheb. She has done all these works not only within the four walls of her house at Madurai, but also on the four legs of her sick bed. Very often she could be seen propped up in bed with a light desk across her legs. This surprisingly matched with our father's condition when he wrote "Kayinat"

It is due to the persistent request by Razia that a family organization "Daleel Qateel Jameel Foundation" was established, in the Pen Names of our father and his two younger brothers, by our beloved elder brother Dr.Anwar Hussain(15.3.1929-6.8.1993),

Under the guidance of our esteemed Uncle Jameel saheb and with the co-operation of all the children of Daleel Saheband Jameel saheb.

1. Prof. Ghulam Hussain Daleel (16.3.1895-2.8.1957)

2. Janab Ahmed Hussain Qateel (29.10.1907-24.5.1940)

3. Janab Mohammed Hussain Jameel (14.6.1912-9.5.1995)

Daleel saheb was a Sufi Poet. Qateel Saheb and Jameel Saheb were Urdu poets, dramatists and story writers.

The eligibility for membership and the responsibility for expenses involved in this foundation are confined to the members of Daleel Saheb's and Jameel Saheb's families (Qateel Saheb died as bachelor at the age of 32.) this foundation was inaugurated in the year 1992 and Razia's first book, the English Translation of Jaffar Barmaki was released.

Thereafter the anniversary function of the foundation are conducted and the books of the three brothers are published and released. Mushairas are also being conducted. It is also proposed to widen the activities in the literary and social fields. The following books have so far been published by the children of Daleel Saheb and Jameel Saheb and released at the annual functions.

I.   Daleel Saheb's Poetic Compositions:
1.   Thohfa-e-Darwesh
2.   Naghma-e-Darwesh
3.   Nara-e-Darwesh
4.   Kayinat

II. Qateel Saheb's Works:
1.   Jaffar Barmaki (a Drama)
2.   Khyaban-e-Qateel(Poetic Compositions)

III. Jameel Saheb's Works :
1.   Nava-e-Jameel (Poetic Composition)
2.   Nava-e- Jameel in Hindi
3.   Gharib Ma-a drama
4.   Aseer Shahzadi -a drama
5.   Parchayen-one act plays.

The Urdu dramas Gharib Ma and Aseer Shahzadi were staged in the 1960s by Muslim Organizations to raise funds for poor students.

IV. Razia's personal publications:

1. English Translation of Qateel Saheb's drama Jaffar Barmaki.

2. Islamic Spiritualism (an English translation and commentary on Daleel saheb's Kayinat).

We are immensely grateful to Razia's husband Janab Abdul Azeez Saheb for all his co-operation in her literary work. But for our revered Uncle Jameel Saheb's love and care with which he safe-guarded the manuscripts of his brothers, Razia could not have retrieved and complied them. Jameel Saheb had also published Daleel Saheb's Nagma-e-Darwesh in 1960s. our heartfelt gratitude to him. it was our beloved brother Dr.Anwar Hussain who established the Foundation and had all the manuscripts calligraphed. Our profound thanks for his boundless love. He was the live wire of the Daleel and Jameel families and instilled enthusiasm in every member of the foundation including the children. It is our great misfortune that Jameel Saheb and Dr.Anwar Hussain who were the main pillars of the joint family of Daleel and Jameel Saheb are no more with us. May their souls rest in peace.- Ameen

Razia's arduous task for over a decade in aligning together the tits and bits of manuscripts in faded ink, and filling up the missing words, has saved these great literary works from going to dust and has enabled the children of Daleel Saheb and Jameel Saheb to Publish the books of the three brothers.

Our heartfelt gratitude to Dr. Syed Safiullah Saheb for taking up the responsibility of the arduous task of scrutinizing, verifying and correcting the proof in bringing out this publication. But for his real concern and affection such an undertaking would not have been possible.

I am thankful to Mr.Syed sultan Basha, Azra Printers, Chennai-5 for the love and dedication with which he has taken up this work foe publication.

How I wish that our revered grandfather late Janab Muhammed Ibrahim Zabeh's literary works were also available, Razia would have retrieved them also and we could have had the pleasure of publishing them.

May God Bless you Razia with good health, long and peaceful life to enable you to continue your priceless service - Ameen.

Razia, we salute you for keeping alive this literary treasure of our elders against all storms and floods.

You are indeed the CHOSEN ONE.

– G.V.SURAIYA BEGUM

17-6-2001

RAZIA BEGUM ABDUL AZEEZ

A PROFILE

I will be right, if I say that Mrs. Razia Begum is the real heir to the intellectual property of her father, late Professor Ghulam Husain Daleel who was a great poet of his time. I assert this because it is she who resurfaced her father's poetic wealth-lying in the form of worn-out manuscripts and scattered papers with her paternal uncle Janab Mohammed Husain Jameel. She got them under different collections. Her other sisters and brothers too are well educated and had full respect to their father's works, but technically they were unable to join her in this matter as they belong to the disciplines other than literature and were either doctors or teachers. Even Mrs. Razia Begum wanted to have her education on similar lines. But due to one reason or other, she could neither opt for medicine nor could continue in any other professional or humanity courses.

It is a fact that when God thinks of using a person for some particular work, He Creates circumstances accordingly. It might be this reason that prevented Mrs.Razia Begum somehow or other from taking professional courses. Secondly, she was provided with more and more chance of her staying with father and thus getting attached to literature. It was she who had to stay with her father in later part of his life and thus had to have frequent chances to see his father composing verses, to read and interact with them.

Two of her paternal uncle, the younger brothers of professor Daleel, were also good poets. Ahmad Husain Qateel died in his young age leaving behind a number of short stories, a historical play and collection of poems, all of which were later edited by Mrs.Razia Begum. The other uncle Janab Mohammed Husain Jameel was a poet and a dramatist. Many of their works have now been published by "Daleel Qateel Jameel Foundation" founded by sons and daughters, their families and the in-laws of Prof.Daleel and Jameel.

After the death of Prof.Daleel, his works and the works of Janab Qateel went into the custody of his younger brother Jameel Sahib who preserved them with utmost care and love. Most of these works were in the from of manuscripts and scattered papers.

Around 80s Mrs. Razia Begum thought of saving this literary wealth of her father and uncle from going into oblivion. She wanted to get them published at early as possible otherwise too would have met the same fate as her grand father's poetry. Her grant father Hazrath Zaabeh was a Sufi poet but his poetical collection is not traceable now. Her uncle Jameel Sahib appreciated her plans and handed over all the manuscript and printed material of his brothers which he had carefully preserved. As the brought them home and opened, she was shocked to see them in a very bad condition. The ravages of time had left its imprints on the paper leaves. All her plans seemed to be melting like ice. Most of the sheets were so weak that even a finger touch was enough to turn them into powder or broken pieces. Some pages were not in order. At some places the words were not decipherable. Some parts found eaten by worms.

For a moment she felt that Heaven had collapsed over her head. But she was Razia, the second in the history! A few moments, no doubt, swept her in the darkness of disappointment. But soon, she rose up and picked up courage. Her pale eyes turned bright and she stood vowing that her plans will see the success.

After coming across lot of hurdles, hardship, disappointment and testing moments, a day came when Mrs.Razia begum Abdul Azeez declared that most of the works were ready for publication. Soon 'Daleel Qateel Jameel Foundation' was founded. Her brother Dr.Anwer Husain took the responsibility of getting the manuscripts calligraphed. Thus in 1993 'Kayinat' the long mystic and philosophically poem of professor Daleel appeared under the foundation as its second publication.

Mrs. Razia Begum was happy and satisfied to the extent that the most prestigious work of her father had seen the light of the day.

But her task would not end here!

Kayinath is a poem of very high standards. The author, Professor Daleel was a poet, philosopher and guide. He was a contemporary of Allama Iqbal. But when he started writing, Iqbal's fame was at its peak. Almost all his contemporaries were influenced by Allama Iqbal's poetry. Professor Daleel was not exception to it. But after studying professor Daleel my conclusion is that this influence worked on him only to the extent of inspiration. Otherwise Professor Daleel's thoughts and Allama Iqbal's philosophy run parallel to each other. Their approaches may be similar but not the same.

Professor Daleel had earlier produced three collections of his poems. But this long poem is the essence of his all previous works. It was the product of his study, observation and ideals, his maturity of thoughts and expression. Further, it is a philosophical, mystical and thought-provoking poem containing lot of references to political, social and scientific topics, Quranic verses and saying of Prophet. Some very basic Islamic ideals have been dealt with here. Above all the contents are presented from an Islamic perspective. The subject of the poem is so pregnant, wide and deep that it demanded longer time and more attention from the poet. But we know that Professor Daleel Sahib composed this poem at the fag end of his life. His health condition then was so poor that he could not withstand this requirement. He himself has admitted that due to ill health and old age he could not devote the time it required, neither he had the chance to revise and elaborate the subject matter in order to give more clarity and better shape to expression. His health condition during that period was such that he never hoped that he would be completing this poem before he breathed his last.

These facts raised concern in Mrs.Razia Begum's mind that unless these verses are not explained in their proper perspective, given in detail the social, political, philosophical, scientific and sufistic aspects and also quoting Quranic Texts and sayings of the Prophet which have been referred to in plenty, her reader will not be abled to reach the depth of the meaning and the poem will not establish its validity. The poet had also expressed his desire in his 'Testament to the poem' that "even if a single heart gets filled up to the brim with love to Allah after reading the poem. I shall deem it a remunerative success". This could only be achieved by making the poem as understandable as possible. This too could have enthused her to write the present commentary on the poem. She, therefore decided to uncap the pen and fulfil the last wish of her father.

Pen is mightier than sword. When this mightier pen goes under the grip of a still mightier hand, the result cannot be less than priceless and voluminous book like this. Primarily Mrs.Razia Begum would have sat with the idea of translating the poem "Kayinath" with necessary commentary. But when she started penning down the commentary, the flow of thoughts started flooding the pages. It may be perhaps due to this reason that in most of the places the renderings are explanatory and inclined towards religion and other metaphysical sciences and she finally had to present this volume under the title of "Islamic Spiritualism"

I wonder how she could have brought the whole world of knowledge in this single volume. Her maturity of mind, her craftmanship of carving beautiful sentences and her integrated thoughts have scattered many gems and pearls throughout the book. They shine as stars shine in a clear sky. Just two of them may be quoted here as examples.

" According to Islamic Principle, the peace of the society is permanent consideration. Religion should be directed towards maintenance of peace, harmony, cohesion, unity and religious tolerance". (p.213)

"Islamic brotherhood is one which binds man to man, family, society to society, nation to nation, state to state and finally country to country. (p.215)

Her capacity to understand the most difficultverses of the poem, their poetic explanation and logical interpretations, the wonderful power of explaining the problems, her vast and advanced scientific knowledge, her know-how of the world affairs, deep study of religious sciences and Islamic mysticism, her convincing arguments and style of presenting the supportive material to her arguments, her flow of thought and command over the language are a few of her qualities that web the book in a master blend, and prove herself a proud daughter of a great father.

– PROF.SYED SAFIULLAH

Vice Chairman

Tamil Nadu Government Urdu Academy Chennai

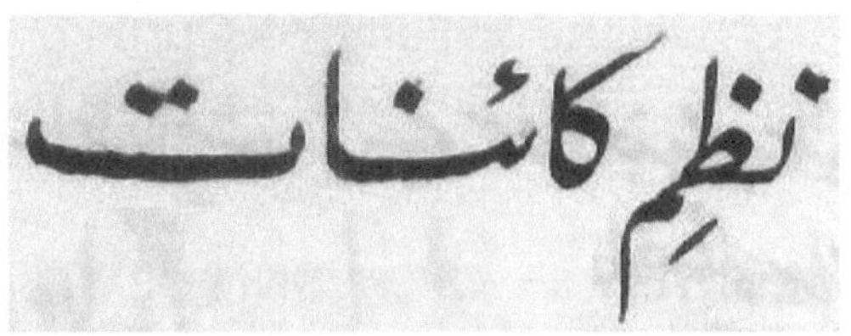

NAZM-E-KAYINAT

(long urdu poem)

By
PROF. M.GHULAM HUSSAIN, DALEEL
&
English Translation and Commentary
By
G.Z. RAZIA BEGUM ABDUL AZEEZ, B.A.,
(Daughter of the poet)

———◦◦◦ ✦ ◦◦◦———

The Urdu poet late Prof.M.Ghulam Hussain Sahib, Daleel, has left behind him four books of spiritualism. Nazm-e-Kayinat is his master piece. This poem consists nothing else than the essence of some Quranic Verses and sayings of Prophet Muhammed (PBUH) regarding the Divine Laws and tenets of Islam.

Quran has dealt with all aspects of life man and all branches of studies. Quran has provided date and has left ample scope for researches in all sciences and technology. In the commentary hundreds of Quranic Verses (in Arabic and their translation in English) and considerable number of Ahadis-e-

Nabavi have been quoted which prove the accuracy and precision of the poet's assertions. Maximum attempts have been made to prove the validity of Quranic verses by the arguments of the scientific discoveries, their modern devices and inventions in fields of technology.

THIS COMMENTARY IS OF A UNIQUE NATURE AS IT A COMBINATION OF THE ESSENCE OF HOLY QURAN, AHADIS-E-NABAVI ALONG WITH SOME REFERENCES OF IMPORTANT AND INTERESTING EVENTS OF ISLAMIC HISTORY AND PRE-ISLAMIC HISTORY.

The purpose of composing this poem was to persuade the believers to adhere to Divine Laws and to love Almighty Allah more and more which will lead to spiritual perfection. He has attempted to convince the readers about the supremacy, absolute Sovereignty and Greatness of Allah, by mentioning the Wonderous and Astounding deeds (Qudrat) of Allah.

SOME IMPORTANT TOPICS WHICH INCLUDE ALL OTHER TOPICS DEALTH WITH IN THIS COMMENTARY: -

1. Quran and Unity of God and Unity of Creations.
2. Quran and divinity
3. Articles of Faith
4. Quran and Mysticism.
5. Quran and Spiritiuralim. Islamic Codes of Ethics
6. Quran and Divine Administration through Angels.
7. Quran and Ahadees-e-Nabavi
8. Quran and Physical Sciences.
9. Quran and Biological Sciences.
10. Quran and Space Science.

11. Quran and Fine Arts.

12. Quran and Technology.

13. Quran and Social Sciences.

14. World Society and Arabian Society before the Advent of Islam.

15. Purity of Islamic Society.

16. Revolution of Islam.

17. Aims of Islam.

18. Evolution of Islam.

19. Social Reforms. Human rights and Human Dignity.

20. Primacy of Knowledge: Haqiqat, Maarifat, Shariat and Tariqat.

21. Islamic Concept of Jihad. General concept of Jihad. Dignity of Labour.

22. Islamic Socialism.

23. Islamic Democracy. Systems of Governments, acceptable to Islam.

24. Day of the Doom and Day of Resurrection.

25. Islamic teachings.

26. Achievements of Islam.

27. Character of ideal Prophet (PBUH).

28. SOME Special Prestige's of Prophet Muhammad (PBUH) over other Prophets.

Commentator : **G.Z. Razia Begum Abdul Azeez**

Residential Address : 135, K.K. Nagar,

Madurai-625 020.

Tamil Nadu South India.

INTRODUCTION FOR THE TRANSLATION AND COMMENTARY FOR NAZM-E-KAYINAT

The Urdu poem Kayinat was composed by my father late Professor M. Ghulam Hussa Daleel. He was a sufi poet. When he started writing this poem, he was suffering from disease. He expired in 1957 A.D. soon after completing this poem.

This poem has been entitled "Kayinat" which means the Universe because this consists of the description of the universe, information about the creation of the universe. ex of the universe, a few natural and physical phenomenan, active in the universe, destruction of the universe and recreation of the universe, all of which have been revealed in the Holy Quran and which were quite unknown to the people of those days. This book is the combination the essence of some important Quranic verses and some Ahadis-e-Nabvi which mean the sayings of Prophet Muhammad (PBUH).

The book Nazm-e-Kayinat is totally an Islamic literature and Sufism (spiritualism) of my father. As my father was seriously ill in his last days, he had to complete this poem in a hurry without his satisfaction. Hence, he has touched the main aspects of life and universe mentioned in Quran. Perhaps Almighty Allah wished so and ordained that I should write the detailed explanation which is within the scope of my little knowledge. Some professors of Madras University and several Urdu scholars of India persuaded me to translate the poem and write the commentary in English. Thus, encouraged by all, I took up this tough and tedious mission of doing research and writing the commentary with great zeal and enthusiasm. The Quranic verses and their few relevant Ahadis have been quoted in the commentary in order to prove the validity of the sophistic arguments of my father.

Some ninety-nine beautiful names of Allah Asma-ul-Husna have been mentioned in Quran, denoting His Attributes. These attributes reveal some injunctions and prohibitions of Islam for human beings. Allah expects His worshippers to acquire some of His attributes, such as mercy, generosity, doing favour, forgiveness, honouring others etc. Allah only has got the rights and powers of possessing some attributes such as anger, giving punishment, defaming. taking life etc. There are some other kinds of attributes of Allah which can never be possessed by human beings. Some unique attributes of Allah have been discussed in the following:

1. **ALLAH IS OMNIPOTENT**: (Allah is Almighty) Human being can never be so. God grants him a minute fraction of His potency needed to lead the life.

2. **ALLAH IS OMNI PRESENT**: (Allah is All Pervading) In other words Allah is present everywhere in the universe. We cannot be present everywhere. We are where we are. We occupy a very little place.

3. **ALLAH IS OMNI SCIENT:** (Allah is All knowing) Human being can never be so. He grants us a very little knowledge which is indispensable for the welfare of human beings.

4. **ALLAH IS ETERNAL:** It means Allah is the First and the Last. The corporeal body of human being is temporal. After all the existence of creations whether animate or inanimate are transitory in this world. Nothing can be eternal except Allah.

These four main attributes of Allah namely His Omni Potence, His Omni Presence, His Omni Science and Eternity are the distinguishing features between the Worshipped and the worshippers. All the ninety-nine attributes of Allah have been incorporated in the classification of four main Attributes, mentioned above. All the attributes of Allah have been interpreted and brought to light in some way or other in Daleel Sahib's Nazm Kayinat.

The classification of Unity of Allah, Unity of Creations and Unity of Religions is as follows:

1. **THE UNITY OF GOD:** It means God is only one.

2. **UNITY AND DUALITY:** It means unity in two things i.e., Creator and creations as a whole.

3. **UNITY AND DIVERSITY:** or unity in diversity i.e. (in different things) because every creation was created with the effulgence of ONE GOD.

4. **UNITY IN RELIGIONS:** This concept aims at teaching religious tolerance and universal brotherhood, as all true religions were descended from ONE AND THE SAME GOD. But, except Islam, all other religions have undergone adulteration. More details are given in the commentary with Quranic verses and its proofs.

The above-mentioned classifications have been explained in commentary in different places. For the easy comprehension, I have given details about the subjects dealt with in this poem. I have quoted several Quranic verses and Ahadis-e-Nabvi in support of the arguments, presented by the poet in his poem.

Kayinat is a book of high standard of sufistic philosophy, language and a variety of original, sociological and scientific topics from an Islamic perspective. This book can be considered one of the authoritative books of devotion and sufism. The poet has interpreted the significance and impact of the verses from many chapters of Quran mostly from Al-Baqara. He has also interpreted the essence of some complete Suras such as Sura-e-Fatiha, Sura-e-Ikhlas, Sura-e-Asr etc. The poet has proved the validity of Quranic verses by wonderfully applying his sufistic philosophy. In Kayinat the part has dealt with the touch of divine principles, the topics such as creation, existence, evolution, change in matter, radiation, galaxies, action and life, retribution of action, electronics, fine arts, Islam, Islamic concepts, Angels, good and evil, equality. differences between caste and creed, piety, purity, foundation of hope, religion and politics, democracy, economics, system of government, Islamic socialism, faith and love. The poet has explained the necessity of creating Iblis (Satan), mysterious administration of God, importance number of topics, this a great of 220 stanza, poem of true faith and true love for God. For such each containing six lines, is very short. Hence the poet has dealt with the topics briefly, conveying the main essence of respective topics which really required immense talents.

In the sub-topics, he has touched many more issues. It can be noted that this poem comprises of topics from the fertilization of ovum, Allah's providence for the development of the corporeal body (Jism-e-Khaki) in this world, astral (immaterial) body (Jism-e-Misali) in the hereafter, spiritual evolution, spiritual perfection which is the destination is the destination of man's sojourn in this world and in the hereafter. The pleasant consequences of selflessness for the sake of God have been mentioned.

There were numerous controversies between the Muslims and the Non-Muslims regarding several revelations from Allah in the Holy Quran. Prophet Muhammad (PBUH) was able to answer only some of the questions, and on many occasions, he said that only Allah knew the substance of the verses and that the secret of the verses would be disclosed later. As he told so, many verses are being proved to be valid one by one with the advance of science.

In his Nazm-e-Kayinat. Daleel Sahib has mentioned some of the modern scientific discoveries, especially discoveries relating to space science mentioned in the Quran, quite unknown in those days. He has dealt with economic, politics and many other social aspects beneficial to humanity. He has also described the revolutionary and evolutionary aspects of Islam. Thus, with sincere efforts, he has attempted to highlight the tenets of Islam. He has described the Holy Quran as the best scripture, expounding and advocating hard strife, a book of decisive pronouncement and permanent guide till the Day of Reckoning, Quran is a holy book which is unique in its substance, uncorrupted and unadulterated. He has proved the unity of God in the chapter "Tawheed" (to believe in the unity of God) by his sufistic interpretations. He has described Prophet Muhammad (PBUH) as the ideal prophet and has urged people to follow his example if they want to lead a contented successful, noble and accomplished life. With his wonderful arguments and splendid sufism, he has disproved the anti-Islamic concept of rebirth in this world. He has given most attractive and impressive definitions for the Beauty of effulgence and refulgence of Allah in the Chapter 'Husn (Beauty) in marvelous and novel style. After a concentrated study of Nazm-e-Kayinat, an individual can reorient his attitude to life from one of selfishness to one of dedication to God. The wavered mind can be disciplined by prayers and worship to Omnipotent Allah. All the basic principles of a noble and successful life are incorporated and summarized in this book. It brings the efficacy of the law of righteousness.

In the Holy Quran data are available for all sciences and all branches of studies. The Europeans and other foreigners availed the advantages of those data and went on and go on making new discoveries and inventions. Now the scientists of the world are convinced that the Holy Quran was the real revelation from God.

Some people are atheists who do not believe in any religion at all. Some people express their doubts about the existence of God and want evidence for it. In his own foreword for his poem 'Kayinat' Daleel Sahib has expressed his purpose of composing this poem. At the outset he wants to convince such people about the existence of God, strengthen the faith of the believers, teach the Islamic ways of life, lead them in the path of righteousness and finally fill their minds and hearts with love for Almighty Allah.

For this purpose, the poet has adopted the interesting, gradual, steady impressive and beautifully regulated sufistic method of interpretations. In the first chapter of his poem, the poet has taken the first step in which he has described a landscape and some creations which have been created by the effulgence of Allah and which are nothing but the manifestations of God. He has done this to explain that when there are creations, there must be a Creator.

In the second step, the poet has strived hard to strengthen the faith of the believers and to prove the validity of some important Quranic verses by mentioning a few physical and natural phenomena active in the universe and by mentioning recent scientific discoveries. revealed in the Holy Quran more than 1425 years ago.

In the third step. the poet has explained the advantages of the ways of life, moral, economic, political, social, educational, ethical and religious, advocated by Islam. He has laid emphasis on fear of God which is the prime basis for a virtuous and righteous life. Fear of God is a powerful and efficacious factor which can promote restraint and evade all sorts of vices and sins.

Finally, he has attempted to enlighten the minds of the readers with the maximum love for God and to instill it into the hearts of the believers. In his concluding lines, the poet has mentioned four attributes of Allah, which connote especially His Omni Presence and Eternity which can never be obtained by His creations.

We can note how tactfully and in what an interesting manner, the poet has taken us to the lanes and labyrinths of love for Allah by creating in our minds the indelible impressions of the astounding deeds (Qudrat) of Allah.

SOME IMPORTANT TOPICS WHICH INCLUDE ALL OTHER TOPICS DEALT WITHIN THIS COMMENTARY:

1. Quran and Unity of God and Unity of Creations. (2) Quran and Divinity (3) Articles of Faith (4) Quran and Mysticism. (5) Quran and Spiritualism. (6) Islamic Codes of Ethics. (7) Quran and Divine Administration through Angels. (8) Quran and Ahadis-e-Nabvi. (9) Quran and Physical Sciences. (10) Quran and Biological Sciences. (11) Quran and Space Science. (12) Quran and Fine Arts. (13) Quran and Technology: (14) Quran and Social Sciences. (15) World Society and Arabian Society before the Advent of Islam. (16) Purity of Islamic Society. (17) Revolution of Islam. (18) Aims of Islam. (19) Evolution of Islam. (20) Social Reforms. (21) Human Dignity. (22) Human Rights. (23) Primacy of Knowledge: Haqiqat, Marrifat, Shariat and Tariqat. (24) Islamic Concept of Jihad. (25) General Concept of Jihad. (26) Dignity of Labour. (27) Islamic Socialism. (28) Islamic Democracy. Systems of Governments, acceptable to Islam. (29) Day of the Doom and day of Resurrection. (30) Islamic Teachings. (31) Achievements of Islam. (32) Character of Ideal Prophet (PBUH). (33) Some Special Prestige's of Prophet Muhammad (PBUH) over other Prophets.

It is my bounden duty to acknowledge the help I received from the wonderful works, authored by eminent scholars for my references. I made use of the commentary on Quran by Moulana Abdullah Yusuf Ali, commentary on Quran by Moulana Ashraf Ali, translation by Muhammad Marmaduke Pickthal and Moulana Fathe Muhammad, Moulana Fath-ul-

Hameed, 'Ideal Prophet' by Khwaja Kamal-ud-din, 'Muhammad The Prophet' by M.R.M. Abdurraheem, "Teachings of Islam" published by Munshi Anis Ahmed, Islamic History by Moulana Shwkat Ali Fahmi different books of Ahadis, "Islamic Voice" a monthly magazine, "Radiance" a weekly magazine, "Din Dunya" a monthly magazine, Daily read magazine and many other religious books.

I am highly obliged to my revered husband Janab M. Abdul Azeez Sahib, for his generous and substantial co-operation in helping me financially, morally and physically. But for his assistance, I would never have succeeded in my endeavour of achieving my end.

I am satisfied with the duty which a have discharge to the best of my ability.

May Allah fulfill Daleel Sahib's noble desire in attaining his objective of enlightening the minds of the believers- Ameen.

– G.Z. RAZIA BEGUM ABDUL AZEEZ

PREFACE

Professor Mohammed Ghulam Husain Sahib Daleel was a living legend in the field of Urdu language and Literature of his period. He was born in the city of Madurai, the great center of Tamil language and literature, in the last decade of Nineteenth century A.D. He belonged to the noble soul of Sufi family which has descended from the North India and settled in the Southern part of Tamil Nadu. The fore-fathers of this family certainly have come to this part of the country to preach Islam with Sufistic tendencies. Later on, they became the part of modern society serving the people as teachers, doctors, social workers etc. His poetry resembles the contents and style of the works of the great and eminent poets Ghalib and Iqbal. We find in his poetry the essence of sufistic thoughts of Ghalib and the desire for the revival of Islamic, moral and spiritual values as presented by Allama Iqbal in his poems 'Bal-e-Jibrael' and 'Zaboor-e-Ajam'.

Professor Daleel Sahib had his early education at American School and later on this school was converted into a college and he had his collegiate education also in this college and got the appointment as Lecturer in Urdu in this college. He started his career as Govt. Employee at an early age. Later on, he continued his studies, left the Govt job and got lectureship.

He was the eldest son of Hazrat Zabih who was a Scholar and also a poet and had good command over Arabic, Persian and Urdu languages. Hazrat Zabih was very popular among the people of Madurai, Muslims and Non-Muslims alike for his righteousness and erudite scholarship.

Hazrat Zabih trained his sons on Islamic lines and provided them best education. Due to his personal care and training all his children both sons and daughters reached the Zenith with higher education and a good place in society. This family was settled in the Qazi Mohallah of Madurai city which is the Island of Urdu speaking Muslims in the ocean of Tamil Culture.

Modern education was considered as Taboo for women in the conservative families of this locality. Professor Daleel had to struggle a lot but with dignity and nobility to educate his children who are now the leading personalities of the modern society and his grandchildren are working in U.S.A. and Gulf countries etc., as doctors and teachers etc.

Mrs. Razia Begum had edited, translated many compositions of her father Prof. Daleel Sahib. She has translated and published the Urdu Drama "Jafar Barmaki" written by her uncle Janab Ahmed Husain Qateel.

"Kayinat" is the master piece of Urdu Poetry composed by Professor Daleel Sahib. This work is published by Daleel Qateel Jameel Foundation, an Association established by the members of this family, like Dr. G.M. Anwar Hussain, Dr. Suraiya Begum and Mrs. Razia Begum. Mrs. G.Z. Razia Begum, daughter of late Prof. Daleel Sahib has written a commentary in English on "Kayinat" quoting numerous Quranic verses and sayings of Prophe (peace be upon him). This work of poetry does not contain Sentiments of Love and Romance but we find a reflection of human thinking about God, the Creator of the

Universe, origin and evolution of the cosmos, Creation of Adam the first man and the First Prophet and the Vicegerent of God on planet earth and numerous mysteries and realities of the Universe He has discussed the latest scientific theories about Electrons, Protons, galaxies and the final resurrection etc.

Also, we find in this work the description of basic tenets of Islam and the traditions of Prophet of Islam. This commentary reveals the minds of both the father and the daughter Father is the author and the daughter is the commentator who now has crossed 63 years of age, living with her dignified and noble husband, son and daughter-in-law peacefully. This family is famous for their prosperity, generosity and more important point is, their interest to promote literature and education. This commentary on "Nazm-e-Kayinat" composed by Hazrat Daleel Sahib is a monumental work and perhaps the first of its kind in the field and history of Urdu literature in modern times, that is, published in the evening of twentieth century, a century when man is turned to be a mechanical Animal who with all his scientific developments is about to collapse totally. This work calls man and humanity towards love, value-based life system, mutual cooperation, Service to poor etc. It is nothing but a description of Islamic teachings and spiritual values evolved, practised and preached by the great personalities of "Muslim Ummah". One can get himself acquainted with high spirit of spiritual values and modern thinking by reading this work.

– Dr. P. NISAR AHMED

Head, Dept. of Arabic Persian & Urdu

Director, Oriental Research Institute

UNIVERSITY OF MADRAS Chennai - 600 005.

FOREWORD

Islam is a major world religion which has swayed the minds and hearts of a large section of mankind. The fascinating elements of Islam are the passionate belief in one God without a second and one who is the Creator of the universe, full of power, mercy and goodness and the mystic elements found in Al-Quran, Mysticism is the eternal yearning of the human soul to have direct experience of the Ultimate Reality. In this basic quest the mystical experience is common to all religions. The birth and growth of the mystic ideal in Islam were due to several factors.Mysticism as practiced by the followers of Islam has had a chequered history.

Islamic mysticism was a reaction against excess intellectualism, formalism and hair-splitting theology. Islamic mysticism is otherwise known as "Tasawwuf' or Sufism. Sufism traces its origin to the Quranic revelation and the Sunnah of the Prophet. "Surely this (the Revelation) is a Reminder; so, let him who will, take unto his Lord a way" (Al-Quran 48:19). Islam is spoken in general throughout the Quran is "Way of God", that is the path ordained by God, which may be said to include both esoterism and exoterism. But the way to God is clearly the esoteric path.

The Quran is really the first and the foremost mystical text of Islam and that the Prophet Mohamed Nabi (SAW) is the first and the greatest of the Sufi sages and saints, even though the term Sufi is of later origin. Sufism teaches how to purify one's self, improve one's morals, and build up one's inner and outer life in order to attain perpetual bliss. Its subject matter is the purification of the soul and its end or aim is the attainment of eternal felicity and blessedness.

In this sense Sufism is a purely Islamic discipline which builds up the character and inner life of the Muslims by imposing certain ordinances and duties, obligations and impositions which may not be abandoned in any way by any man. So, the end and aim of a Sufi's life is God alone, he loves God alone; his thinking, meditation and prayer are to God alone; He is ever ignorant of everything save God and when he thinks of God alone, his mind is purified. A Sufi is totally captivated by God alone. But any way, experience of the Sufi vary according to their spiritual growth.

When one peeps into the history of Sufism, one finds that the contribution of Quranic versions and sayings of Prophet Mohammed Nabi (SAW) Occupy a distinguished place. In later periods Muslim mystics are characterized equally by literacy charm of their own country and by their ethical spiritual values.

During the medieval period Sufi poets spread all over the world. As Sufism spread in Tamil Nādu, the Muslim mystic poets have not lagged behind. Sufistic literature in Tamil, Urudu, Persian etc. began to appear in large number. The Sufism of Tamil Nādu is said to be the mixture of Arabic, Persian and Indian mysticism. It is also said to be an attempt to unify or reconcile different schools of philosophical thoughts as rivers flow into a sea. This is also called syncretism. Their devotional songs impregnated with the highest truth of theosophy, constituted a significant part of their own literature. In this way, a large number of Sufi poets have lived in Tamil Nādu enriching the Islamic culture and Tamil and Urdu languages. One of the prominent Sufi poet of Tamil Nādu is the Urdu poet late Prof. M. Ghulam Hussain Sahib' Daleel of Madurai (1895-1957 A.D.), son of Sufi poet Muhammad Ibrahim. Ghulam Hussain Sahib contributed four books of Spiritualism in Urdu namely,

1. Tuhfa-e-Darwesh (Gift from Darwesh)

2. Naghma-e-Darwesh (Songs of Darwesh)

3. Nara-e-Darwesh (Slogan of Darwesh)

4. Nazm-e-Kayinat (Poem Universe)

The poet himself has stated in his foreword to the book Kayinat that "I am a Dan. (Lover of God) and Son of Darwesh... It is only a cry of Darwesh...". This statement author Prof. Ghulam Hussain Sahib Daleel is a true statement if anyone can go through his poems. Among these, Nazm-E-Kayinat is his master piece. This book consists of nothing than the essence of some Quranic verses and sayings of Prophet Mohammed (SAWA regarding the Divine laws and tenets of Islam.

His Nazm-E-Kayinat contains twenty-nine chapters with different titles. All are in poetic compositions on spiritual knowledge. Most of them are his spiritual experiences. He has strictly followed the Urdu literary traditions in his verse. The total number of verses in Nazm-E. Kayinat is 220. In all the verses, the author stresses the unity of God and unity of Creations. The omnipresence of Allah is mentioned in most of the verses. Another theosophical truth that devout men who have comprehended 'self-attuned to Divine Grace and have no wish other than to immerse themselves in the love of God, have been enlightened by the poet. Let me conclude with the hope that it is left to the present and future generations to know about a great poet's contributions and to live up to them. This book which happens to be the first commentary fulfils the requirement of a qualitative one which will serve the purpose of Sufism. Even a layman will find it easy to accommodate with the book and assimilate the contents therein.

In this juncture Mrs. G.Z. Razia Begum Abdul Azeez, daughter of the poet has made an attempt to bring out a beautiful commentary to her father's mystic contribution i.e., Nazm-E-Kayinat. Mrs. Razia Begum Abdul Azeez belongs to Madurai and she is very much interested in Islamic theology and mysticism. She has translated and published many books in English and Urdu. A Urdu drama, Jaffer Barmaki of Qateel Sahib compiled by her has been selected for Ph.D. research in Delhi University. The Urdu Ghazals and poems of Daleel Sahib compiled by Mrs. G.Z. Razia Begum Abdul Azeez have been prescribed for college courses of Madras University. She is a well-known public speaker in social organization and educational institutions. Since May 1992 she has been working as the Editor of "Daleel, Quateel, Jameel Foundation", Madras, established by her elder brother Dr. Anwar Hussain and her elder sister Dr. Suraiya Begum after the pen names of Prof. Ghulam Hussain Daleel and his younger brothers Janab Ahmed Hussain Qateel and Janab Muhammad Hussain Jameel. This Foundation is a literary and educational organization with broad based objectives of promoting literature and education; National integration and Harmony; International concord and World Peace. Hence anyone can easily say that Mrs. Razia Begum Abdul Azeez is a qualified person to bring out the translation and commentary for the Sufistic Urdu literature Nazm-E-Kayinat.

For the benefit of this intellectual world, Mrs. Razia Begum took up the tough and tedious mission by way of translating the Urdu poem Nazm-e-Kayinat and made an attempt to bring out a wonderful commentary, with great enthusiasm. But for her translation and commentary, one cannot easily get the benefit of the book Nazm-e-Kayinat. We ought to thank and encourage Mrs. Razia Begum for her hard work and valuable commentary.

The commentator of Nazm-e-Kayinat has strictly followed the Islamic traditions in her commentary. The Quranic verses and their few relevant Hadis have been quoted in the commentary in order to prove the validity of the Sufistic arguments of the author of the book Nazm-e-Kayinat. The commentator has discussed all the unique powers of Allah by way of discussing His Omnipotence, His Omnipresence, His Omniscience and Eternity. In Chapter three Allah's Effulgence has been interpreted and brought to light in detailed way by the commentator as follows: "The seventh stanza of Kayinat says that heavens and earth and all things sandwiched between them are nothing but the effulgence of God. A true Muslim must believe in the attribute of Allah's Omni-presence (pervading everywhere), as well as unity in duality (Oneness in the Creator and Creation)". (Chapter III - Commentary)

In this way the commentator has incorporated each and every word of the poet Ghulam Hussain Daleel in detailed manner. The above-mentioned classifications have been explained in commentary in different places. For the easy comprehension the commentator has given the details about the subject dealt in the poems. In support of her arguments, she has quoted several Quranic verses and Hadis. These arguments found in commentary stand as the evidences for the critical exposition of the commentator.

Nazm-e-Kayinat is a book of high standard of Sufistic philosophy with chaste language and variety of original, sociological and scientific topics from an Islamic perspective. For instance, let us quote here the commentary found in Chapter Fourteen in Kayinat. This particular chapter is entitled "Life and Action". The poet describes the administration of the universe depending upon the eternal activity of God, the beginning of whom is not known. (Chapter XIV, Stanza - 37). Here the commentator clearly explains that "Islam emphasizes both faith and action (Amal) to lead a noble life. In Islam action is the test of faith. Faith must be coupled or backed by action. All Muslims are bound to progress and promote goodness and dispel evil for the uplift of a good society" (Commentary - Chapter XIV). This is one example of how the commentator has interpreted the significance and impact of the verses from many chapters of Quran.

In many instances the commentator Mrs. Razia Begum has interpreted the essence of some complete Surahs such as "Sura-e-Fatiha, Sura-e-Ikhlas, Sura-e-Asr" etc. The commentator has proved her good knowledge of Quranic verses by applying her thoughts with Sufistic philosophy.

In almost all the commentary in twenty-nine chapters found in Kayinat the commentator has touched many more issues like Existence and Non-Existence (Chp.VI), Creation (Chp.VII). Investigated Truth (Chp.XII), the Concept of Jihad (Chp.XVII). Love for God and Service to Humanity (Chp. XXVI), Providence and Religion (Chp. XXVI)etc. in detailed way. One cannot understand the exact meaning and significance of the topics found in Nazm-e-Kayinat without the help of the informations given by the commentator definitely.

Finally, I wish to show one more example for the vast knowledge on in Islamic religion. She has attempted to highlight various aspects of y-six with sincere efforts. In this chapter, the Commentator Janaba Razia Begum has empted to bring out various new information's from various sources. For instance, at one place under the title of "Best Propagator of Islam" she has given the photo cop Etters of the Holy Prophet Mohammed Nabi (SAW) which were written to various persons for the propagation of Islam. This was described by the Commentator as, to prove the efforts taken by Mohammed (SAW) for the propagation of Islam. In her commentary she has described Prophet Mohammed (SAW) as the Ideal Prophet.

In all the places the Commentator has proved her intelligence in and involvement with Islamic philosophy by way of her wonderful and simple way of her presentation.

After a deep study of Nazm-e-Kayinat with this commentary of Mrs. Razia Begum Abdul Azeez, an individual can reorient his attitude to life, from one of selfishness to one of dedication to God. With these few words, I pray God to give a good and fortunate life to the Commentator Mrs. Razia Begum Abdul Azeez. May Allah the Great and Merciful fulfil the desires of Mrs. Razia Begum Abdul Azeez. Amen.

– Dr. P.M. Ajmal Khan
Professor & Head Co-Ordinator School of Religions Philosophy, & Humanist Thought Department of Islam and Islamic Tamil Studies. Madurai Kamaraj University,

APPRECIATION BY
DR. SYED ABDUL QADIR HUSSAINI

NOTE - Late Dr. Syed Abdul Quadir Hussaini, M.A.Ph.D., was the Professor of Islamiat in the University of Dhaka. He was eminent scholar and author of eleven books of high repute. He was the first cousin of my late father Janab M. Ghulam Hussain Daleel, who composed this poem and authored three more books of spiritualism. Dr. Hussaini wrote a short but provoking criticism in Urdu for the poem Kayinat in 1957 when both of them were alive, and before this long poem was published. The following is my English translation of the critical appreciation of Dr. Syed Abdul Qadir Hussaini.

– G.Z. RAZIA BEGUM ABDUL AZEEZ

In my opinion, "Kayinat" is the best Urdu poem of exalted standard. I do not know in which place and in which language, a poem of such a high ranking has been composed. The efficacious impression, created in my mind by this poem can never vanish. I have absolute confidence, that this matchless poem will ever be reckoned as the sublime one in the society of literary scholars. This is not just a poem. this is a unique miracle and amorous marvel of the Mysterious Inspirer (God). Any amount of pride for South India, is less than this invaluable literary gift deserves. As appropriate commendation for this poem is impossible, silence is better.

– Dr. SYED ABDUL QADIR HUSSAINI, M.A.Ph.D

TRANSLATION OF THE TESTAMENT OF LATE PROF. M. GHULAM HUSSAIN DALEEL FOR HIS OWN POEM KAYINAT COMPLETED IN 1957

Kayinat is a poem presented in your service by a Darwesh. When my very existence has no significance, how can my poem have any worth? Even then, it is comprised of the essence of some important Quranic verses and Ahadis-e-Nabavi (sayings of Prophet Muhammed PBUH) so that the readers may not have any complaint that nothing substantial is contained in the poem. Darwesh also must have some satisfaction that something beneficial, contains in the poem. I have done nothing wonderful or applaudable. I am a Darwesh (lover of God) and son of a Darwesh. Composing poem is not my profession but it is the mode of my worship to Allah. To worship Allah through my compositions is my natural and unavoidable habit. Worshipping through poetic composition is meant neither for popularity nor for commercial benefit nor for contribution to Urdu literature. It is only a cry of Darwesh. It is the expression of perfect belief that success and prosperity in this world and the hereafter depend upon the love for God. This poem was written during my severe ailment. How could I have got such enormous strength which was required to complete this poem? My firmness of faith, desire for service to humanity and timely divine help made me successful in achieving this goal. My life has always been at risk which made me think that I might die even before writing a single verse of this poem. Time is the most valuable factor for all. I have made a great attempt so that the readers of this poem might not complain that their time was wasted. I like them to remember me with their sincere prayers. This poem was written with great struggle. Every moment I was feeling that I was nearing my end. With Allah's name on my lips, I reached my desired destination. Knowingly I have used some words in this poem which are out of date. I thought it advisable to leave them as they are, because, I felt that any change might affect the expression of thoughts. Because of the brevity, the subject dealt with, may seem dry, the interpretations for which may require hundreds, of pages in prose. Intentionally, the poetic imagination was avoided. The charm of the beauty of thoughts may be a little. But I have strived hard to point the real picture of Truth.

Composing this poem is not meant for displaying talent. I have presented the Truth with maximum sincerity. After completing this poem, I felt a sort of mental relief. This mental relief is not a remuneration for my strife. Even if a single heart gets full to the brim with love for Allah after reading the poem, I shall deem it a remunerative success, I think that this poem may be. published after my expiry. I wish that the copies of this book may be gifted to Urdu institutions and college libraries free of cost.

At present I am helpless. Allah only knows His schemes. I thank from the depth of my heart, my respected and literate friends and relatives for having whole heartedly applauded and appreciated this poem. It is only due to their tendency and traits of humanity and love for God. Their appreciations may induce the readers to love God and study the poem with perfect faith and may enable to understand it. No words are adequate to describe my thankfulness to God. If the readers acquaint me with the defects in the poem, it will be a great favour on their part. It will be duly considered over in the future editions.

– M. GHUILAM HUSSAIN DALEEL

ABBREVIATIONS USED IN THIS BOOK

Q:- Quran

S:- Sura

S:-   Stanza

H:- Hadith

Tr:- Translation

C:- Commentary

N:- Note

No:- Number

K:- Kayinat

A.D:- Anno Domini, The year of Christian Calendar

A.H:- Anno Hijrat, the year of the Hijrat

Viz:- Videlicet or namely

i.e:- Id est or that is

e.g:- Example gratia, for example

Pg:- Page

Ex:- Explanation

INTERPRETATION FOR BISMILLAHIR – RAHMANIR – RAHIM

Every Muslim utters the Holy Phrase "Hismillahir-Rahmanir-Rahim" which means the name of Allah, the most beneficent, the most Merciful", before starting to do anythina According to this religious conversion, I have also written this phrase at the top before proceeding to comment on Daleel Sahib's poem, Nazm-e-Kayinat. I feel the essentiality of interpreting the impact and importance of this phrase at the outset.

The world "Ism" means "name" and "Asma" means names i.e. plural of "Ism" - "Husna means beautiful. In our religious book "Asma-ul-"Husna" means the beautiful names of God. There are ninety-nine names of God, mentioned in the Quran. Allah's names imply his attributes Among all His names "Rahman" which means "Beneficent or Benevolent" has the first importance. Allah's Rahmaniat or Beneficence is that Allah has created human being in the best form and has granted the position of being the highest of all His creations even higher than the angels. Another Beneficence of Allah is that he has gifted human beings with soul which has not been gifted to other creatures of this world. Because of his Rahmaniat His Khallaguiat (Creative Power) became active. Khaliq means Creator and Khallaquiat means Allah's attribute of Create Power.

There is one more evidence for Allah's name "Rahman" for possessing the greatest and first importance. Sureah Ar Rahman (55th Chapter in Quran) starts with four small Aayaat 55 1-4.i.e; These four Aayaats comprise of four factors which are best and highest. Rahman is the best and most importance name of Allah. Quran is the best guiding Book ever revealed. Insan (human being is the highest creation of Allah. Bayan (Power of speech) is the unique faculty of man which the other creatures of this world are not blessed with. Thus the 55th chapter of Quran proves the great importance of Allah's name "Rahman".

Allah's name "Rahim" which means Merciful or Compassionate has got the second importance. Due to his Rahimiat, attribute of compassion. He created everything needed by all the living creatures for their physical development. As Allah has gifted soul of human beings. it is also his responsibility to provide the necessities for the spiritual elevation and evolution. For spiritual evolution, there are three requisites namely (1) Preceptor (2) Guide and (3) Goal.

Preceptor means the teacher who preaches the commands of Allah. Guide means the scripture revealed by Allah which is pregnant of all the religious tenets and codes of ethics. The goal is "Allah". The first two requisites for the development of the soul namely Preceptor and Guide have been provided with, by Allah by sending numerous Prophets and revealing several scriptures in different nations and different parts of the world. To attain the third requisite the Goal (Allah), is the responsibility of people by seeking the pleasure of Allah with their noble deeds.

(Rubb) is one of the names of Allah. Rubb means Allah, the Sustainer, or the Fosterer or the Cherisher. Rububiath or Providence is one of Allah's attributes which becomes active due to His compassion towards the creatures. Through Allah's Providence, physical and spiritual development is attained. Development means evolution. In this sense, Allah's Providence is His attribute of evoling our souls also.

This my explanation about the impact and significance of "Bismillahir-Rahmanir-Rahim", within the scope of my little knowledge. That is why, the believers repeat this phrase on every occasion.

– G.Z. RAZIA BEGUM ABDUL AZEEZ

NAZM-E-KAYINAT
TRANSLATION AND COMMENTARY

INDEX

بِسْمِ اللَّهِ الرَّحْمَنِ الرَّحِيمِ

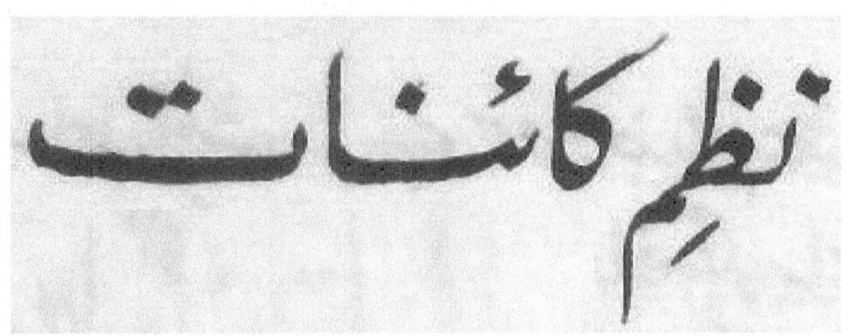

CHAPTER – I

NAZM-E-KAYINAT

Landscape: The large sandy tract of Rameshwar Island and sea. The appearance of full moon at midnight. Stanza:

١۔منظر: جزیرہ رامیشور کا ریگستان اور سمندر
آدھی رات کا سماں اور ماہِ کامل کا جلوہ

STANZA: 1

١۔ ماہ کامل ہے کمال شوق سے جلوہ فشاں
نور کے سیلاب سے دھویا ہوا ہے آسماں
اگر جس کا نام ہے کوسوں نہیں اس کا نشان
یہ شب دنیا ہے یا رب یا کوئی صبح جناں
ہے سراپا نور اس قندیل قدرت کا وجود
اس کی تابانی میں ہے شان جمالی کی نمود

Tr: The full moon diffuses and strews its beauty with perfect eagerness. The sky is washed with the flood of its effulgence.

For miles together there is no sign of any cloud. Oh God: Is this the night of this world or the dawn of the heavens? The existence of this divine lantern (moon) is full of effulgence (of God). The splendor of beauty of God is manifest by the light of the moon.

Stanza: 2

2۔ محفل انجم ردائے نور میں روپوش ہے

بادۂ تنویر سے ساری فضا مدہوش ہے ہے

ہے فسون خواب کا عالم جہاں خاموش ہے

سینۂ مہتاب میں لیکن بلا کا جوش ہے

مائل گفتار ہے یہ عظمت حق کا نقیب

آسماں سے آچکا ہے یہ بہت دل کے قریب

Tr:- The group of stars is hidden behind the curtain of effulgence (of moon). The whole atmosphere is unconscious with sedating effect of the light. The whole world is silent due to the magical effect of the sleep. But there is wonderful emotion inside the moon. The emissary (moon) which is a pride of God has come near my heart and is engaged in conversation with me (gives informations).

Stanza: 3

3۔ چاندنی سے جھلملاتی ہے بساط بحر و بر

موج مضطر ہے کہیں رقص تجلّی سر بسر

ہے فضائے نیم شب میں جلوہ نور سحر

دور تک پھیلا ہوا ہے اس تجلّی کا اثر

کیا نہاں تنویر میں ہوتے ہیں اسرار حیات

ہیں نمایاں ریت کے ذروں سے حیات

Tr: The sea and Land glimmering in conjunction and the dance of the brilliant flood of light (on the waves) is elsewhere. The beauty of the light of dawn is felt in the atmosphere of mid-night (due to moon-light). The effect of this effulgence is spread far and wide. Are there any secrets of life concealed in this light? The evidences of life is manifest in the sand.

Stanza: 4

4۔ میں ہو ریگستان ہے اور ساحل رامیشور

ہے سمندر جذبہ ماہتاب۔ سے زیرو زبر

شورشوں سے اسکی انداز جنوں ہے جلوہ گر

ہائے رے وارفتگی ساحل سے ٹکراتا ہے سر

شوق سے ابھرا ہوا سینہ ہے دل بے تاب ہے

کیا اسے منظور ہم آغوشی مہتاب ہے

Tr:I am on the shore of Rameshwar and in its sandy tract. Because of the in the moon-light, the waves of the sea rise high and come down. The frenzy of love of for God can be assessed by the noise of the sea produced by its active waves). Ha dashes against the shore in its unconscious state (due to its deep devotion to God). The swelled and is restless. Does it wish to unite with the moon?

Stanza : 5

5۔ اندرون بحر بھی یہ ماہ مہر آثار ہے

اس کا جلوہ اک نرالا حسن کا بازار ہے

آب کے ذروں سے پیدا اک تجلّی زار ہے

ایک ادائے غیب سے ذوق نگہ سرشار ہے

آہ وہ سینے جو نور ذات سے معمور ہیں

آہ وہ دل عشق سے جلتے ہوئے جو طور ہیں

Tr: The light of the moon which is illuminated by the sun, is still manifest into the depth of the sea. The appearance of the moon creates a world of beauty. The very atoms of war reveal a world of effulgence (of God). With a single divine deed, the fervor of vision is satisfied Ha: Those chests which are full of effulgence of God and those hearts which are alike M Senai, due to love for God and really applaudable.

Commentary:. In the first chapter of Nazm-e-Kayinat, the poet Daleel Sahib bas attempted to convince about the existence of God, to the atheists and those who express doubts, by mentioning some of Allah's creations and some physical phenomena active in the nature and by describing different landscapes. He says that the full-moon strews her bright light. The waves of the sea rise high at nights due to the gravitational pull of the moon. Moon itself is not luminous. It looks bright due to its exposure to sun-light.

Q:- Bani Isra-il -:17:44

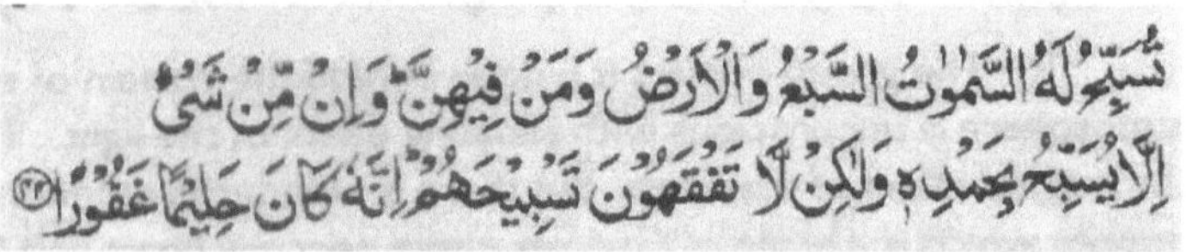

Tr:- The seven heavens and the earth and all beings there in, declare His God's glory There is not a thing but celebrates His praise; and yet ye understand not how they declare His glory. Verily He is Oft-Forgiving". Both heavens and earth and all creations glorify Allah

S. Al-Baqara 2:29:

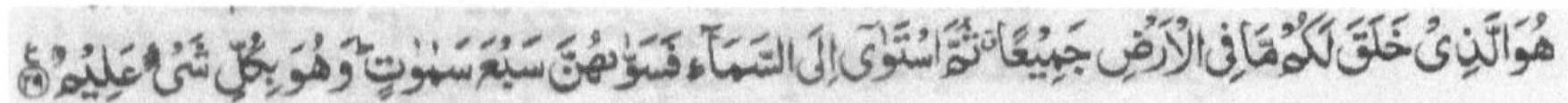

Tr:-:It is He who has created for you all things that are on earth. More over His design comprehended the heavens. For He gave order and perfection to the seven firmaments and of all things. He hath perfect knowledge. (All creations benefit man).

S. Saffa 37:6:

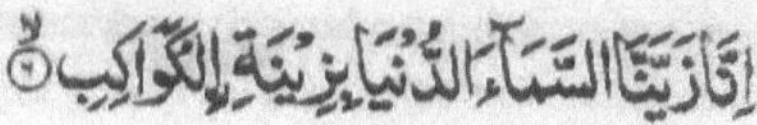

Tr: "We have indeed decked the lower heaven with beauty (in) the stars". (Beautification)

C - This mysterious universe and its wonders are clear testimonials of God's love towards man. This universe is created and packed with things that supply the want of man, His supreme creation.

This vast panorama with its charm and beauty, the sky with its shining stars and waning moon and the surprising harmony of these things in the nature proclaim the boundless love of Allah towards mankind.

The purpose of the poet in composing the five Stanzas of the first chapter is same as Allah's purpose of revealing the Surah Ar-Rahman, namely convincing the readers about the existence of God by mentioning some of His creations which are nothing but the manifestations of Allah. When there are creations, there should be a Creator. The second purpose is to inculcate love of Allah in the hearts of the believers by mentioning a few bounties of God through which Allah expresses His love for humanity. When all creations whether animate or inanimate glorify Allah, it is the first and foremost duty of man to extol the glory of Allah. All His creations and the beautification of the sky by heavenly bodies are meant for the benefit of man. They satisfy the different needs of man.

Q: S: Ar-Rahman. 55:62-63:-

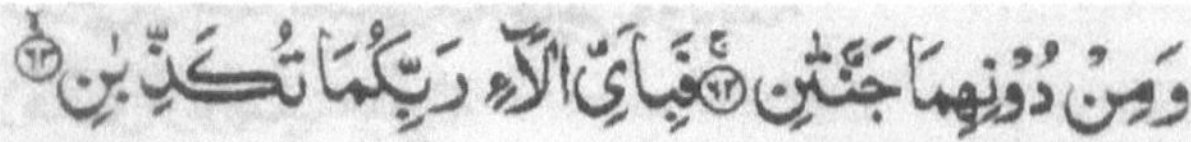

Tr:- "And besides these two, there are two other gardens. Which of the favours of your Lord will ye deny?"

Quran itself is revealed in the poetic style which produces musical note while reciting, and leaves indelible impressions in the hearts of the readers. The Qir'at of Quran can be defined as the musical recitation of Quran. That is why Daleel Sahib has preferred to compose, then to write in prose. In Surah Ar-Rahman, Allah has mentioned a few of His creations and interrogates the reader as to which of His bounties will he deny. In order to lay maximum emphasis on His existence and bounties, Allah has adopted the method of interrogation. It bears more effect that assertion. In this Surah, he has repeated the question thirty-one times. In the beginning of this Sura Allah has made mention of His best name (Rahman).

His best scripture (Quran). His highest creation (man) and his unique faculty (speech). lend extraordinary beauty to it. Its composition greatly facilitates a sweet musical recitation which procures the esthetic satisfaction of the readers. For all such reasons, this Surah is described as "The Jewel or Beauty of Quran".

I have given the above explanation with a view of prove that the purpose of composing the first chapter of Kayinat and the revelation of Surah Ar-Rahman is identical (Physical Science and Spiritualism)

CHAPTER – II

MOON

——◦ı◠~◆~◠ı◦——

Stanza: 6

2 /مہتاب

6- اے قتیل شیوہ تسلیم اے ماہ مبین

ہے منور جلوہ خورشید سے تیری جبیں

تو چراغ بزم قدرت ہے ز روز اولین

تیری صورت سے عیاں ہے نور عرفان و یقیں

فاش کر اپنی زبان سے کچھ رموز کائنات

جستجوئے راز قدرت ہے مرا سوز حیات

Tr:- Mh. the lustrous Moon, a sincere devout to the total submission to the of God. you are illuminated by the brilliance of the sun. You are the divine lantern since the creation of the universe. The light of discernment (knowledge) and the light of certainty are revelated through your appearance.

beacuse am in quest of the purpose of life.

Q : -S. Anbiyaa-21.33:-

وَهُوَ الَّذِىْ خَلَقَ الَّيْلَ وَالنَّهَارَ وَالشَّمْسَ وَالْقَمَرَ كُلٌّ فِىْ فَلَكٍ يَّسْبَحُوْنَ ۝

It is He who created Day and the Night, and the sun and the moon. All the celestial bodies swim along each in its rounded course.

S. Luqmaan - 31:20:-

اَلَمْ تَرَوْا اَنَّ اللّٰهَ سَخَّرَ لَكُمْ مَّا فِى السَّمٰوٰتِ وَمَا فِى الْاَرْضِ وَاَسْبَغَ عَلَيْكُمْ نِعَمَهٗ ظَاهِرَةً وَّبَاطِنَةً وَمِنَ النَّاسِ مَنْ يُّجَادِلُ فِى اللّٰهِ بِغَيْرِ عِلْمٍ وَّلَا هُدًى وَّلَا كِتٰبٍ مُّنِيْرٍ ۞

Tr:- Do you not see that God has subjected to your (use) all things in the heavens and on earth and has made His bounties flow to you in exceeding measure (both) seen and unseen"

S. Ar-Rahmaan. 55:5:-

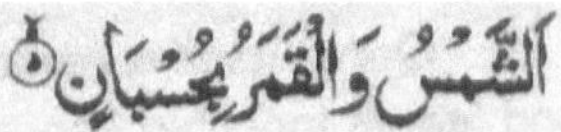

الشَّمْسُ وَالْقَمَرُ بِحُسْبَانٍ ۞

Tr:- The Sun and Moon follow the course exactly computed.

S. Yunus (Jonah) 10:5:

هُوَ الَّذِىْ جَعَلَ الشَّمْسَ ضِيَآءً وَّالْقَمَرَ نُوْرًا وَّقَدَّرَهٗ مَنَازِلَ لِتَعْلَمُوْا عَدَدَ السِّنِيْنَ وَالْحِسَابَ مَا خَلَقَ اللّٰهُ ذٰلِكَ اِلَّا بِالْحَقِّ يُفَصِّلُ الْاٰيٰتِ لِقَوْمٍ يَّعْلَمُوْنَ ۞

Tr:- It is He who made the sun to be a shining glory and moon to be a light (of beauty) and measured out stages for her that ye might know the number of years and time.

C:- At the outset. the poet addresses the moon as a beautiful creation of God, which carries out the divine commands and discharges its duty regularly with sincere devotion and total submission to Allah. He has hinted at the physical phenomenon that the sun focuses Its light on the moon in order to illuminate it. The moon by itself is dark. Its shining is due to its exposure to sun-light. He has also hinted at the "Big Bang" theory which expounds that thewhole universe was created by the explosion of a big mass of smoke and all things in the universe were created simultaneously. Hence the poet has described the moon a divine lantern from the first day of the creation of the universe. By its very appearance. its certainty and divine discernment are evident. As the celestial bodies extol the glory of God, carry out His commands and render service to humanity. untiringly and unceasingly. the poet expects the moon to have acquired more divine knowledge than he has done.

The poet is not satisfied with his little knowledge granted by God and acquired through his own intellect. Now, he proceeds to request the moon to disclose some secrets about the universe as the purpose of life is the unending quest of divine secrets.

The purposes of life are different in the different categories of people. The Holy Quran is an exhaustive and comprehensive Book which is comprised of not Only the principles of belief but also the basic tenets of social welfare and level precepts. It contains both injunctions and prohibitions. Human birth and his life are meant for the realization Of God's existence and attaining the goal of merging with Him. By determining the real purpose of life, Quran has enlightened humanity to achieve the goal (God). Quran has spoken about the people whose purpose of life is worldly pleasures and comforts, whose instincts are to aggravate trouble. mischief. chaos and causing torture to humanity and also those who practice the divine dogma and doctrines. The people who adhere to religious tenets and codes of ethics, purify their own soul and lead mankind towards the path of righteousness and illumine the entire world with divine knowledge. The Poem Kayinat describes Daleel Sahib's purpose of life as the love for God and desire for realization of God.

This chapter has been entitled "Moon". There is no chapter entitled "Sun" as such. Because of the significance of heavenly bodies and their services to humanity. the words "Sun" and "Moon' are mostly used jointly in the Quranic verses. Likewise. the word "Sun" is also used in the chapter "Moon". Hence it is proper to explain their significance jointly. The sun emits its bright rays of light during the day while the moon strews its lustrous light during the nights for the benefit of the man especially in guiding the way-farer. The Muslims start the Ramazan fasting at the sight of the ninth crescent (new moon) of the year and celebrate the Ramazan festival after sighting the tenth crescent.

Sun-light and sun heat are some of the most important elements for the existence of organisms. Neither a blade of grass, nor a microscopic organism nor a single protoplasm can be vital without sun heat and sun-light. It emits its ray's night and day without taking any rest and renders substantial service to humanity.

Before the discovery of the regulated revolutions of the sun and the moon, time was calculated by observing the position of these planets. After the discovery of their revolutions, the number of days, months and years could be calculated by observing their stages from their appearances and disappearances.

Christian Era/Birth of Jesus (Christ) started with the introduction of solar calendar, calculated by the revolution of the sun. Islamic Era (date of Hijrat) started with the introduction of lunar calendar by the revolution of the moon. Man has been successful in landing on moon. Its soil and stones were brought and found to be very rich in minerals. At present we cannot envisage the exploitation of these properties of its earth crust and how they are going to be beneficial to man. As the moon has a broad pit of diametrical circumference, it serves as a clear testimony of the miracle of splitting the moon wrought by Prophet Muhammed (PBUH) (Physical science and spiritualism)

CHAPTER - III

HEAVENS AND EARTH ARE ALLAH'S EFFULGENCE

Stanza: 7

3/اللہ زمین و آسماں کا نور ہے .

7۔ بزم قدرت میں نظر کی حد نہو چرخ بریں

ہے تیری تنویر کا ایک رہ گزر مہر مبیں

اس کے جلوہ کا بھی ہوگا کوئی منبع یا نہیں

کیا کہوں کس کی ضیاء سے ہے مری روشن جبیں

دیکھ اس کو جو زمین و آسماں کا نور ہے

دیکھنے والوں کو دنیا جلوہ گاہ طور ہے

Tr:-Oh. sublime sky the expanse of the realm of God is beyond one's visionary power. The brilliant sun which the manifestation of God's effulgence is the traveler in your splendor Can't there be any source or cause of its existence? What should say about the light contained in my face? Just behold the effulgence contained in the heavens and the earth. For those who realise the truth. the world (all the creations) is like Mount of Senai.

QS: "An'am: - (Part of the Sura):-

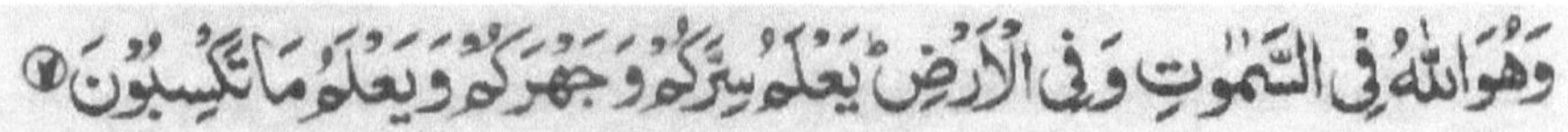

وَهُوَ اللَّهُ فِى السَّمٰوٰتِ وَفِى الْأَرْضِ يَعْلَمُ سِرَّكُمْ وَجَهْرَكُمْ وَيَعْلَمُ مَا تَكْسِبُوْنَ

Tr:- "And He is God in the heavens and on earth"

S:- Al-baqara:-2: 164

اِنَّ فِىۡ خَلۡقِ السَّمٰوٰتِ وَالۡاَرۡضِ وَاخۡتِلَافِ الَّيۡلِ وَالنَّهَارِ وَالۡفُلۡكِ الَّتِىۡ تَجۡرِىۡ فِى الۡبَحۡرِ بِمَا يَنۡفَعُ النَّاسَ وَمَآ اَنۡزَلَ اللّٰهُ مِنَ السَّمَآءِ مِنۡ مَّآءٍ فَاَحۡيَا بِهِ الۡاَرۡضَ بَعۡدَ مَوۡتِهَا وَبَثَّ فِيۡهَا مِنۡ كُلِّ دَآبَّةٍ وَّتَصۡرِيۡفِ الرِّيٰحِ وَالسَّحَابِ الۡمُسَخَّرِ بَيۡنَ السَّمَآءِ وَالۡاَرۡضِ لَاٰيٰتٍ لِّقَوۡمٍ يَّعۡقِلُوۡنَ

Tr:- Behold In the creations of the heavens and the earth; in the alternation ofthe night and the day. in the ships through the ocean of the profit of mankind: in the rain which God sends down from the skies; and the life which He gives there with to the earth that is dead; in thebeasts of all kinds that He scatters through the earth; in the change of the winds and the clouds which they trail like their slaves. between the sky and the earth (here) indeed are Signs for the that are Wise".

S: Ha-

Mim: 41:53:-

سَنُرِيۡهِمۡ اٰيٰتِنَا فِى الۡاٰفَاقِ وَفِىۡ اَنۡفُسِهِمۡ حَتّٰى يَتَبَيَّنَ لَهُمۡ اَنَّهُ الۡحَقُّ اَوَلَمۡ يَكۡفِ بِرَبِّكَ اَنَّهُ عَلٰى كُلِّ شَىۡءٍ شَهِيۡدٌ

Tr- "Soon We Will show them our signs to the (farthest) regions (of the earth) and in their own soul. unit it becomes manifest to them that this is the Truth. Is it not enough that Thy Lord doth Witness all things?

S:-Al-Baqara 2:26. •

اِنَّ اللّٰهَ لَا يَسۡتَحۡىٖ اَنۡ يَّضۡرِبَ مَثَلًا مَّا بَعُوۡضَةً فَمَا فَوۡقَهَا فَاَمَّا الَّذِيۡنَ اٰمَنُوۡا فَيَعۡلَمُوۡنَ اَنَّهُ الۡحَقُّ مِنۡ رَّبِّهِمۡ وَاَمَّا الَّذِيۡنَ كَفَرُوۡا فَيَقُوۡلُوۡنَ مَاذَآ اَرَادَ اللّٰهُ بِهٰذَا مَثَلًا يُضِلُّ بِهٖ كَثِيۡرًا وَّيَهۡدِىۡ بِهٖ كَثِيۡرًا وَمَا يُضِلُّ بِهٖ اِلَّا الۡفٰسِقِيۡنَ

Tv:- "God disdains not to use the similitude of things, lowest as well as highest. Those who believe know that is truth from their Lord. But those who reject Fatth say "what does God means by this similitude?"

C:- The seventh Stanza Of Kayinath says that heavens and earth, and all things sandwiched between them are nothing but the effulgence of God. A true Muslim must believe in the attribute Of Allah's Omni-presence (Pervading everywhere) as well as Unity in duality (Oneness in the Creator and creations and unity in diversity (Oneness in the Creator and His different creations).

In Quran Allah has been described as Omni-Potent (Almighty or All Powerful), Omni-Present (All pervading) and Omni-Scient (All Knowing). He is not described as having a physical structure. His presence does not require any material space. His presence is incorporeal. In the Quranic verse 6:3, the line "God is in the heavens and the earth" means that His effulgence exists in each and everything and in other worlds God created everything by His effulgence.

Quranic verse 2: 164 persuades the reader to realise Allah's actions in the daily activities of the people and the natural phenomena. We must realise that the roaring of the beasts. chirping of birds and utterances of the devotees are nothing but the Voice of God. The beautyin the nature is definitely the beauty of God. Now, it is clear that Allah's effulgence resides in all His creations. Except human being no other creation in this world has been bestowed with uniquegift of God. Hence our soul also is the residence of Allah.

The verse 2:26 explains why God does not feel shy or disdain to make mention of His smallest creations like insects. Allah does not distinguish between high and low, small and big.dark and bright because all creations are His manifestations which consist of His own effulgence.

Besides the above interpretations two of Allah's names viz: "Al-Batin" and "Al-Zahir"expounded the proof that it is Allah's effulgence which pervades the universe. Al-Batin means invisible and that which is inside. Al-zahir means perceptible and that which is outside. By these two names it is evident that

Allah exists inside everything and outside everything and that the heavens and earth are nothing the effulgence of Allah. (Islam and spiritualism)

CHAPTER –IV

LIMITATION OF WISDOM

—◦।ᗡ ◆ ᗡ।◦—

Stanza: 8

4 /خرد کی مجبوری

8۔ ہیں یہ موجودات یک بے مثل قوت کی ادا

عالم ایجاد کی ہے ہر جہت بے انتہا

فرق ہے موہوم ماضی حال و استقبال کا

کب میسر ہو تصور حق کے سانچے میں ڈھلا

ہے خرد وابستہ تیری عالم تشبیہ سے

ہے حقیقت کا تعلق عالم تنزیہہ سے

نوٹ : انسان کا سارا علم اضافی ہے

Arabic

Tr:- The present creations are the results of the deeds of unparalleled Power (God) The direction and dimensions of the scope of creations are limitless. Regarding our imagination about God and His creations the difference between the past. present and future is unreal and meaningless. Neither could we see the real picture of God in the past. nor do we see it nor we imagine in the future. While your wisdom is based on the comparison ofcreations, the truth is concerned with the purification of creations.

Note by Daleel Sahib: The wisdom of man is based on comparison or on the theory of relativity.

Stanza: 9

9۔ ایک دنیائے تصور چاہیے بالکل نئی

عقل کو حاجت ہے الہامی تخیل کی بڑی

نور ایماں سے حقیقت میں ہو چشم آدمی

دہر میں آثار کا ادراک ہے مشکل ابھی

ذہن انسان میں حقیقت کی کہاں تصویر ہو

ہے بہت قاصر زبان تقریر ہو تحریر ہو

نوٹ : ماہیت

کسی طرف بعض اوقات آثار کا ادراک بھی مشکل ہے ۔ مثلاً روشنی کی رفتار فی سیکنڈ ۱۸۶۰۰۰ میل ہے۔ بعض ستارے دنیا سے اس قدر دور ہیں کہ ان کی روشنی کو یہاں تک آنے کیلئے لاکھوں کروڑوں برس گزر جاتے ہیں اور بعض اس قدر دور ہینکہ ابھی تک انکی روشنی دنیا کو نہیں آئی

Tr.-A quite new scope for imagination is needed at all times and our wisdom requires a lot of inspired imagination for new discoveries. The human vision must be able to discover the truth by the help of enlightened faith. Yet the comprehension of signs are difficult. How can the human intellect be pregnant of the picture of Truth? Our capacity of vocabulary, our power of speech and ability of writing are extremely deficient in order to portray the real picture of

Note by Daleel Sahib about Nature

Maahiat:-Somewhere or sometimes human comprehension of available signs in the nature (Maahiat) is difficult. For example, the speed of light per second is I miles which perplexes the human intellect. Some stars are so high above the earth that it takes Lakhs and crores of years for their light to reach here and some stars are so high that their light has not yet reached this world.

Quran : Surah : Anaam : 6:59:

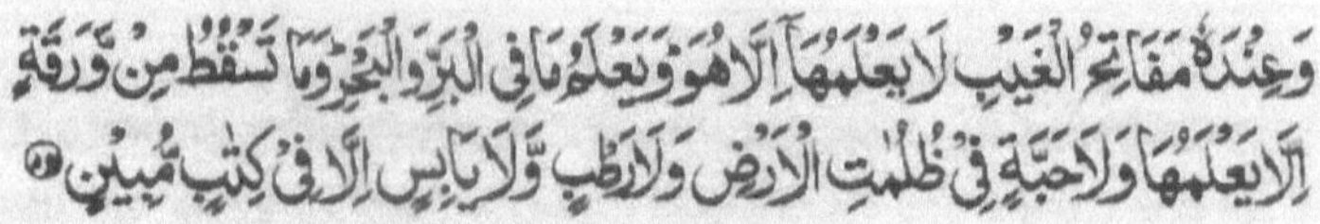

Tr.- "With Him are keys of the unseen, the treasures that none knoweth but He. He knoweth whatever there is on the earth and in the sea. Not a leaf doth fall but with His knowledge. There is not a grain in the darkness (or depths) of the earth, nor anything fresh or dry (green or withered) but is (inscribed) in a Record, clear (to those who can read)"

S: Al.Baqara: 2:31'.

Tr:. "And He taught Adam the names of all things. then He placed them before the Angels and said "Tell Me the nature of these if ye are right".

S:Alk.Baqarah: 2:32:

Tr: "They (Angels) said, "glory to Thee; of knowledge. we have none save what Thou has taught us; in truth it is Thou who are perfect in knowledge and wisdom".

H:- The ink of the pen of the scholar is holier than the blood of the martyr.

H:- The acquisition of knowledge is compulsory for Muslim men and Muslim women.

Hadith: Acquire knowledge because it enables you to distinguish between lawful and unlawful and persuades you to tread the path which leads to Paradise. It inculcates mutual love. It is a companion in loneliness. It is a guide at times of both prosperity and adversity. It is the deadliest weapon against the enemies and a unique companion for the friends. Because of knowledge. one becomes the leader of the noble people who follow his foot-steps and have confidence in his opinions.

H:- "Prophets did not leave material wealth behind them. They left only knowledge. Hence only learned people are the real inheritors of their property".

C:- Sura-e-Alaq. the first Sura revealed to Prophet Muhammad (PBUH) starts with the word "Iqra" (Read) which expounds the primacy of knowledge. Now. it is clear that Islam is a religion which has placed knowledge in the highest level of human endeavor which strengthens the faith and makes the people good citizens and God-fearing. Every piety, culture. civilization and nobility comes through pure knowledge. Learning promotes wisdom and thus diminishes the deficiency in the wisdom. Islam repeatedly urges the acquisition of knowledge. so much so that the word "I'm" is most used after the word Allah. The sentence. "Allah is All knowing" is used at the end of several verses Of Quran. The Omni-Science of Allah indirectly connotes that man knows very little.

The matter related in the Quran is a very small fraction of the knowledge Allah has. Allah has granted man a limited acquisition of knowledge. He has reserved an unimaginable amount of knowledge for Himself He has granted that amount of knowledge to man, which is indispensable to lead life in this world and which is quite necessary to attain spiritual perfectionAllah does not impart that sort of knowledge which is either useless for man or harmful for human life. Even Prophets did not know the language, Allah speaks with the Angels because this information is not at all advantageous to human life. Even Prophets did not know as to when the Day of the Doom would occur because this knowledge is harmful to human life in many ways and is in no way beneficial. In case man is able to acquire the entire divine knowledge. there will be no distinction between the worshipper and the worshipped. It will also degrade the dignity of Divinity.

CHAPTER -V

LIVING CREATIVE POWER

Stanza: 10

5 /خلاقیت

10۔بزم قدرت کے عجائب ہیں بہت حیرت فزا

ہر زماں اُن کے نئے ہوتے ہیں جلوے رونما

ابتدا انکی ازل سے ہے ابد میں انتہا

چشم بینا کے لئے حیرت حیرت ہے سدا

زندہ جاوید حق کی سب ہیں کہ لا فانی صفات

نغمہائے کن سے ہے معمور بزم کائنات

نوٹ

بَدِيعُ السَّمَاوَاتِ وَالْأَرْضِ ۔ وَإِذَا قَضَىٰ أَمْرًا فَإِنَّمَا يَقُولُ لَهُ كُن فَيَكُونُ (قرآن)

وہ آسمان و زمین کا صناع ہے۔ وہ جب کسی کام کا ارادہ کر لیتا ہے تو اُسے کسی

مددگار کی ضرورت ہوتی نہ وسائل و ذرائع کی۔ بس وہ حکم دیتا ہے کہ ہو جا جیسا

اس نے حکم دیا ویسا ہی ظہور میں آ جاتا ہے (البقرہ)

Tr : - The wonderous Divine deeds cause unaccountable surprise. With the march of time the astounding deeds Of God display new manifestations. Neither the time of the Of creations is known nor the time Of their termination is known. The vision Which sees the truth reahses the wonders of God continuously. The attributes of God are external just as His existence is external. In compliance with God's wish and single command, anything comes into beng.

Q : Surah : Al - Baqara:2: 1:7:-

بَدِيْعُ السَّمٰوٰتِ وَالْاَرْضِ ۚ وَاِذَا قَضٰى اَمْرًا فَاِنَّمَا يَقُوْلُ لَهٗ كُنْ فَيَكُوْنُ ۝

Tr:-"To Him is due. the primal origin of the heavens and the earth. When He decreeth a matter, He sajth to it "Be" and it is".

Surah : Ha-Mim:41 :11

ثُمَّ اسْتَوٰۤى اِلَى السَّمَاۤءِ وَهِىَ دُخَانٌ فَقَالَ لَهَا وَلِلْاَرْضِ ائْتِيَا طَوْعًا اَوْ كَرْهًا ۚ قَالَتَاۤ اَتَيْنَا طَاۤئِعِيْنَ ۝

Tr:- "Moreover He comprehended in His design the sky and it had been as smoke. He said to it and to the earth "come ye together willingly or unwillingly ". They said. "We do come (together) in willing obedience".

C: -Surely all praises belong to Allah for (he brought all creations into existence with hissingle command "Be". Without any previous model. Nor did the seek anybody's help in the

Now. the poet has hinted about the law of changes and the economic theory that man can neither create a matter nor can he destroy it. It is not within the power of man to destruct anything created by Allah. Man can only change the shapes of things. The existence of matter is everlasting Both the Creator and the Destructor is Allah. The matter created by God undergoes changes with the march of time and new things come into being. For example. if a piece of wood IS burnt, it gets disappeared and converted into smoke and fire. The smoke exists in the atmosphere to be changed into another thing later

The fire. when cooled down. becomes coal. Thus, the new manifestations of God come into being the poet expresses his wonder at the eternity of creative power of God and Hisand His most astounding deed of creating the whole universe with HIS single command"be" (Eternal Creative Power and eternity of matter).

CHAPTER - VI

EXISTENCE AND NON-EXISTENCE

Stanza:11

6/وجود و عدم

11۔ ریت کے خاموش ٹیلوں پر طاری ہے یک جمود

باعث حیرت بنی یک بیک اُن کی نمود

یک ہوائے تند سے اُن کی ہے بود و نبود

ہے یہ ریگستان ہی ان کا عدم اُن کا وجود

ہے صفات رب کا جلوہ یہ ظہور کائنات

یہ مشیّت میں نہاں تھے یا عیاں ہیں ممکنات

Tr:- A sort of inertness, inactivity and state of suspension are prevailing over the silent hillocks of sand. The sudden appearance of these hillocks has become a great matter of surprise for me. A strong and furious storm is the cause for the existence of some hillocks in one place and their non-existence as well in another place. This desert is the place for their appearance and disappearances. This universe is the manifestation of the attributes of God. It is the intention or pleasure of God that His attributes may be sometimes concealed and sometimes manifested, facilitating the feasibility and practicability of the phenomena of nature.

Q: Sura-e-Murslaat- 77: 1-4:

وَالْمُرْسَلٰتِ عُرْفًا ۙ فَالْعٰصِفٰتِ عَصْفًا ۙ وَّالنّٰشِرٰتِ نَشْرًا ۙ فَالْفٰرِقٰتِ فَرْقًا ۙ

Tr:- "By the (Winds) sent forth, one after another (to man's profit); which then blow violently in tempestuous gusts and scatter things far and wide; then separate them one from another"

C:- Geological theory expounds that the surface of the earth is not even and the ups and downs of earth have been undergoing changes by the fury of nature such as volcanic eruptions. erosion by wind and water, earth quakes and manual exploitations, the ultimate cause being the supreme Power of Allah.

In this verse, the poet has described a desert with hillocks of sands in the state of suspended activities. Then he expresses his surprise at the violent sand-storm which tremendously changes previous scenery and the positions of the sand hillocks. As the vegetation can hold the soil by its roots, is rarely seen in the desert. The sand is loose and susceptible to be raised by the forceful wind from one place to another. Hence the sand-hillocks disappear from their previous spots and appear in other spots. The poet describes the desert as the place for the existence and non-existence of the sand-hillocks. The poet has attempted to explain the reason for Allah's pleasure to conceal His power for sometime (hint at the inertness of the nature) and then to reveal His Potency (hint at the fury of nature) over the whole universe.

The reason is Allah wishes that every believer should have firm faith that there is a supreme Force or Being which prevails over the universe and which can control the inertness and activities of the universe. The purpose of the poet in composing this verse is to interpret, that if this criterion is absent, a person cannot be devoted to Truth (Haq). (Geology and natural phenomena)

CHAPTER – VII

MODERN AND ANCIENT OLD AND NEW CREATIONS

—◦⊙◦—◆—◦⊙◦—

Stanza: 12

7/حدوث و قدم

12ہے جہاں یک شان نو میں ہر زماں جلوہ نماں

محفل کون و مکان حادث نہ ہو کیونکر بھلا

یاں یہی عالم کہ ہے اس کی مشیّت برملا

اصلیت میں ہے قدیم اپنی مگر اے ہم نوا

یہ حدا ثت اور قدامت چیز ہے کیا کچھ نہیں

جب زمانہ ایک ہے یا 'ہم میں ہے' یا کچھ نہیں

نوٹ : تصور زماں ہے کہ انسان کی قیام اس کی حرکت اس کے احساس اور حالت دل سے بہت کچھ وابستہ ہے " ہممیں ہے" ایک بلیغ فقرہ ہے

Tr:- With every advance of time, the universe strews its new splendour. This world is never a fresh creation. It is evident that the universe was created by the will and pleasure of God. The quintessence of the world is not new but ancient. The idea about the freshness of life and ancientness is meaningless.

Surah : Al-e-Imraan-3: 109:

وَلِلّٰهِ مَا فِى السَّمٰوٰتِ وَمَا فِى الْاَرْضِ ۚ وَاِلَى اللّٰهِ تُرْجَعُ الْاُمُوْرُ ۞

Tr:- "To God belongs all that is in the heavens and on earth. To Him, all things (His belongings) will return (for decision)".

S: Hajj-22:76:

يَعْلَمُ مَا بَيْنَ أَيْدِيْهِمْ وَمَا خَلْفَهُمْ وَإِلَى اللهِ تُرْجَعُ الْأُمُوْرُ ۞

T:- "He (God) knows what is before them and what is behind them. All things will go back to God (for decision)".

C:- All will be knowing well the theory that man can neither create matter nor destruct it but he can only change its shape. For example, he can make furniture out of a tree. Another theory explains that Law of changes is always active in the natural phenomena by the will of God. New things appear after the disappearance of the previous things. For example, a small seed grows into a tree and gives fruits. They are seemingly new creations. By His wonderous deeds Allah annihilates one matter till it totally disappears and then He brings into existence another thing using the same matter. Because of the changes in the shape of matter, the things appear to be fresh creations. In fact, the basic substance and quintessence of these creations have antiquity and ancientness about which man can never know. The imagination about new creation is false. The word "Return" in Quran 3:109 and the words "Go back" in 22:76 prove that the matter is ancient in nature and Allah had created it before it was transformed into different things. This means Allah had the matter and it will return to Him. In case any matter has no ancientness, the words "Will go" would have been used in Quran. The words "Return or Go back" are enough to understand the essence of the 12th Stanza in the poem Kayinath. It is the pleasure of God that the locations of things also change. Hence the universe seems to strew new splendour. Now, it is vivid that no matter is freshly created but it is ancient.

Notes given by Daleel Sahib:

Tr: "It is imagined by people that the station of man is influenced by his mentality, his feelings and activity".

C: "Though man uses his discretion about the location of his settlement, it ultimately depends on the will and pleasure of Almighty Allah"

CHAPTER – VIII

WORLD IS A TRUTH

Stanza: 13

8/عالم حقیقت ہے

13۔ کیا حقیقت سے کہیں ہوتی ہے باطل کی نمود ؟

کس کی ہستی ہے عدم معدوم ہو کیونکر وجود ؟

ہے تصور کونسا جس میں ہے یک بود و نبود؟

غیب کا اقرار کیا ہوتا ہے انکار شھود ؟

زندگی ہے بحر ہے پایاں نہیں موج سراب

زندگی ہے عین بیداری نہیں افسون خواب

نوٹ: دنیا تخلیق با الحق ہے ، ہر وجود ایک شان حقیقت ہے جو کبھی باطل نہیں ہوتا ،
صرف انسان کے خیالات اور اوہام ارتقاء فہم کے ساتھ کبھی بدلتے ہیں اور کبھی
باطل نظر آتے ہیں۔

Tr:- The topic of this chapter means the declaration that the creation of the universe by God is a truth.

When there is "Truth". falsehood can never have splendour. No matter is non-existent. No present things can go out of existence. The imagination of existence and non-existence is meaningless. The Divine declaration can never be a falsehood and negation. The life of man is an endless ocean and not at all a mirage. Life is not the effect of a dream, but it is full of consciousness.

Daleel Sahib's Notes:

Tr:- "The creation of the World is a Truth. The existence of each and every thing implies the pomp, splendour, glory and dignity of Truth which never negates. Sometimes the doubts and thoughts of human beings change with the evolution of their intellect. Sometimes their thoughts seem to be false and incorrect",

Q.S: Fathiha-1:1:

$$\text{اَلْحَمْدُ لِلّٰهِ رَبِّ الْعٰلَمِیْنَ}$$

Tr:- "Praise be to God, the Cherisher and Sustainer of the Worlds".

S. Al-Baqar-2: 107:

$$\text{اَلَمْ تَعْلَمْ اَنَّ اللّٰهَ لَهٗ مُلْكُ السَّمٰوٰتِ وَالْاَرْضِ وَمَا لَكُمْ مِّنْ دُوْنِ اللّٰهِ مِنْ وَّلِیٍّ وَّلَا نَصِیْرٍ}$$

Tr:- "Knowest thou not that to God belonged the dominion of the Heavens and the earth? And besides Him ye have neither patron or helper".

Al-Baqara-2: 17:-S.

$$\text{بَدِیْعُ السَّمٰوٰتِ وَالْاَرْضِ وَاِذَا قَضٰۤی اَمْرًا فَاِنَّمَا یَقُوْلُ لَهٗ کُنْ فَیَکُوْنُ}$$

Tr:- "To Him is due to primal origin of the Heavens and the Earth. When He decreeth a matter, He said to it "Be" and there it is".

S- Al-Mulk-67:

$$\text{الَّذِیْ خَلَقَ سَبْعَ سَمٰوٰتٍ طِبَاقًا مَا تَرٰی فِیْ خَلْقِ الرَّحْمٰنِ مِنْ تَفٰوُتٍ فَارْجِعِ الْبَصَرَ هَلْ تَرٰی مِنْ فُطُوْرٍ}$$

Tr:- "He Who created the seven heavens one above another; no want of proportion will thou see in the creation of

God Most Gracious. So, turn thy vision again. Seest thou any flaw?"

S. Nabaa-78:6:7.

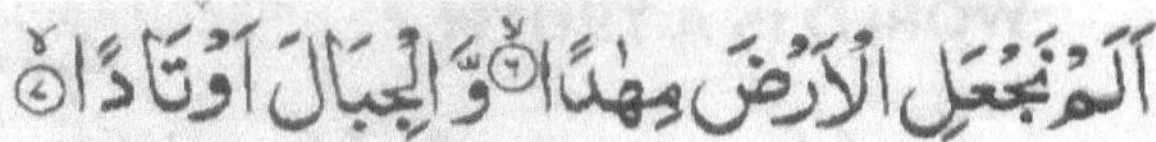

Tr:- "Have We not made the earth as a wide expanse; and the mountains as pegs?"

C:- It is the duty of every believer to believe in every word of Quran and the mystic knowledge it imparts. The above-mentioned Quranic quotations disclose the secrets of Divinity and explains that the creation of the universe by God is a truth. Again, the poet has referred to the economic theory that man can neither create matter nor destruct it. In Quranic Verse 2:117. God has commanded His already created matter to transform itself as the universe. This connotes the ancientness of the matter, the origin of which can never be discovered Divine declarations never come without proof. Allah has repeatedly declared in Quran that the heavens and earth were created by Him. His creations we see, serve as the doubtless and definite proof for His declarations. His creations are not without purpose. He has made the life of be unreal like the mirage. Man's life is full of consciousness which can enable man to make the best use of the bounties of Merciful Allah. As the universe is the creation of Allah, it is His duty to provide the sustenance for all His creations in the Universe. The first verse in Quran itself declares that Allah is the Cherisher of the Worlds. The above-mentioned Quranic quotations have proved the validity of the topic of this chapter which conveys the information that the creation of the universe by Almighty God is a Truth. (Truth about God and His Creations).

CHAPTER - IX

SPLENDOUR OF UNITY AND UNITY OF CREATIONS

Stanza: 14

9 /شان وحدت اور وحدت عالم

14۔ ایک ذرہ کی اگر سری حقیقت ہو عیاں

تُجھ پہ کھل جائیں گے اسرار زمین و آسمان

تو نہ بیگانہ رہے اپنی حقیقت سے یہاں

تُجھ سے پوشیدہ نہو راز خداوند جہاں

دہر کی ہر چیز یک گنجینہ اسرار ہے

یہ جہاں تنویر وحدت سے تجلی زار ہے

Tr:- If the whole truth about an atom is revealed, all the secrets of heavens and the earth will be disclosed to you. You should not be unaware of the truth of your existence in this world. The realization of the existence of the unseen God Who created the universe, should not be kept in secrecy from you. Everything in this world is a treasure-house of secrets and this universe is a vast expanse of refulgence due to the light of the unity of God.

Stanza: 15

15۔ کیا زمین کیا آسمان کیا سارے اجرام فلک

کیا شجر کیا سنگ کیا حیوان کیا جن و ملک

رشتہِ وحدت میں ہے سارا زمانہ منسلک

ایک ہی جلوہ کی ہر شئے میں نمایاں ہے جھلک

جو بھی تھے اور جو بھی ہیں اور جو بھی ہونگے تا ابد

دیکھتے ہیں اُن سے وابستہ تُجھے اہلِ خرد

نوٹ : رشتہِ وحدت ۔ موجوداتِ عالم میں ازلی اور ابدی تعلق۔

Tr:- Whether they are heavens or earth or heavenly bodies or tree or stone, or animal or Jinn or angels, all are related and bound by the unity of God. Beauty of everything is conspicuous owing to the one Beauty of God. People possessing true knowledge and wisdom see you connected with all creations which were in the past which are at present and which will be in the future.

S, Al-Baqara-2: 15:

وَبِّهِ الْمَشْرِقُ وَالْمَغْرِبُ فَاَيْنَمَا تُوَلُّوْا فَثَمَّ وَجْهُ اللّٰهِ إِنَّ اللّٰهَ وَاسِعٌ عَلِيْمٌ

Tr:- "God belongs to the East and the West Whithersoever you turn, there is the presence of God for God is all-Pervading and All-Knowing."

S:- Anna'am 6:3:-

وَهُوَ اللّٰهُ فِى السَّمٰوٰتِ وَفِى الْاَرْضِ يَعْلَمُ سِرَّكُمْ وَجَهْرَكُمْ وَيَعْلَمُ مَا تَكْسِبُوْنَ ۝

Tr:- "And He is God in heavens and the earth. He knows what ye hide and what ye reveal and knoweth the (recompense) which ye earn by your deeds."

S: Al-Sajda-32:6:

ذٰلِكَ عٰلِمُ الْغَيْبِ وَالشَّهَادَةِ الْعَزِيْزُ الرَّحِيْمُ

Tr:- "Such is He, the knower of all things, hidden and open, the (Exalted in Power), the Merciful."

S; Yunus- 10:61:

وَمَا تَكُوْنُ فِيْ شَأْنٍ وَّمَا تَتْلُوْا مِنْهُ مِنْ قُرْاٰنٍ وَّلَا تَعْمَلُوْنَ مِنْ عَمَلٍ اِلَّا كُنَّا عَلَيْكُمْ شُهُوْدًا اِذْ تُفِيْضُوْنَ فِيْهِ وَمَا يَعْزُبُ عَنْ رَّبِّكَ مِنْ مِّثْقَالِ ذَرَّةٍ فِى الْاَرْضِ وَلَا فِى السَّمَاءِ وَلَا اَصْغَرَ مِنْ ذٰلِكَ وَلَا اَكْبَرَ اِلَّا فِيْ كِتٰبٍ مُّبِيْنٍ ۝

Tr:- "Nor is hidden from thy Lord (so much as) the weight of an atom on the earth heaven. And not the least and not the greatest of these things but are recorded on a class Record."

S. Ann'aam 6:59:

وَعِنْدَهٗ مَفَاتِحُ الْغَيْبِ لَا يَعْلَمُهَا اِلَّا هُوَ وَيَعْلَمُ مَا فِى الْبَرِّ وَالْبَحْرِ وَمَا تَسْقُطُ مِنْ وَّرَقَةٍ اِلَّا يَعْلَمُهَا وَلَا حَبَّةٍ فِيْ ظُلُمٰتِ الْاَرْضِ وَلَا رَطْبٍ وَّلَا يَابِسٍ اِلَّا فِيْ كِتٰبٍ مُّبِيْنٍ

Tr:- "With Him are the keys of the unseen, the treasures that none knoweth but He. He knoweth whatever there is on the earth and in the sea. Not a leaf doth fall but with his knowledge. There is not a grain in the darkness (or depths) of the earth, nor anything fresh on dry (green or withered) but is inscribed in a Record, clear (to those, who can read)."

S:- Al-Baqara:2:33:

قَالَ يٰاٰدَمُ اَنْبِئْهُمْ بِاَسْمَائِهِمْ ۚ فَلَمَّا اَنْبَاَهُمْ بِاَسْمَائِهِمْ قَالَ اَلَمْ اَقُلْ لَّكُمْ اِنِّيْ اَعْلَمُ غَيْبَ السَّمٰوٰتِ وَالْاَرْضِ وَاَعْلَمُ مَا تُبْدُوْنَ وَمَا كُنْتُمْ تَكْتُمُوْنَ ۝

Tr:- "He said: Oh Adams! Tell them (angels) their (Things) nature." When, he told them. God said: "Did I not tell you that I know the secrets of heaven and earth and I know what reveal and you conceal?"

S: Al-Baqara-2:179 :

وَلَكُمْ فِى الْقِصَاصِ حَيٰوةٌ يّٰاُولِى الْاَلْبَابِ لَعَلَّكُمْ تَتَّقُوْنَ ۝

Tr:- "In the Law of equality, there is (saving of) Life of you O ye men of understanding, that ye may restrain yourself."

S. Al-Qasas-28:88:

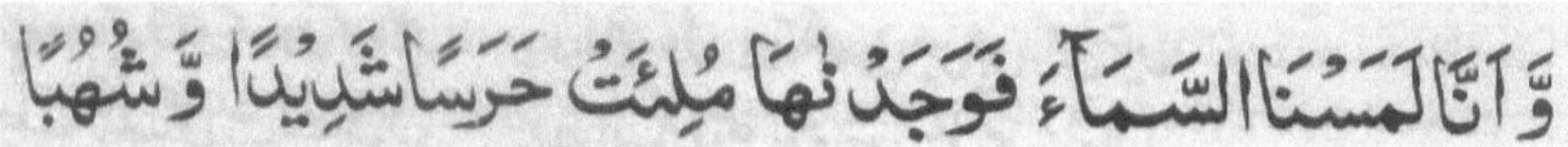

Tr:- "Except His own Face, will perish. To Him belongs the Command and to Him will ye (all) be brought back."

Hadis:-Allah, the Exalted and Glorious would fold the heavens on the Day of Judgement and then He would place them on His right hand and say, "I am the Lord, where are the naughty and where are the proud (today)?" (Muslim)

C:- The topic of this chapter "The glory of unity of God and unity in Diversity:" itself

The space technology and space exploration are encouraged by Islam for both Jinns and human race. The participation in this research by the scientists must be highly appreciated and Jauded. Men or Jinns cannot acquire the whole divine knowledge. Allah will grant Jinns and only a limited power to fly upto a little height in the vast expanse of the universe. Jinns can faster and higher than the man. Like the human beings Jinns also have interest in probing into the heavens.

Q: S:Jinn 72:8:

وَّ أَنَّا لَمَسْنَا السَّمَاءَ فَوَجَدْنٰهَا مُلِئَتْ حَرَسًا شَدِيدًا وَّ شُهُبًا

Tr:"And we (inns) pried into the secrets of heaven, but we found it filled with stern guards and flaming fire."

It is evident by this Stanza that the Jinns know space technology and had reached a very high level long ago and they have said in Quran which was revealed in the 7th century A.D. They have said that they could go up only to a certain height above which they found that the boundary had stern guards and flaming fire. This means that Allah does not want to impart the whole divine knowledge of the universe. Otherwise, there will be no difference between the worshippers and the worshipped. The degree of culture and civilization of the Jinns is not described in Quran.

It is said that the Jinns were in the service of Prophet (King) Solomon who had control over them. The believer Jinns cooked food for the poor in a very large scale, impossible for human beings, in response to the command of Sulaiman (A.S.). There is an interesting story entitled "King Soloman and Queen of Sheeba". The name of the great Jinn was Ifrit who brought the heavy golden throne of Bilquis, the Queen of Saba, a city in Yamen, to the court of King Solomon in the single wink of the eye. She was surprised to witness this miracle and decided to embrace Soloman's true religion after consulting her courtiers. All of them along with their Queen accepted Solomon's religion and shunned their own religion of worshipping the sun. In converting the Queen Bilquis and the people of Yamen to true faith, the believer Jinn Ifrit offered considerable cooperation to Prophet Solomon.

The Jinns can reach our earth but we can neither reach nor locate their habitation. Inspite of their super natural powers and extraordinary faculties. Allah has proclaimed in Quran that human being is the highest of His creations and He has created him in the best form. Jinns had become the servant of human beings but we do not serve them (Jinn and men).

Daleel Sahib has used the word "Angels" with the word 'Jinn' in the 15th Stanza of his Poem. This topic will be discussed in the 23rd chapter of his book Nazm-e-Kayinath.

Stanza. 16.

16۔ فصل گل کا غنچہء اول ہو کب جلوہ نما

جب زمین گردش میں یک پہلو بدلتی ہے نیا

تاکہ اس پر تیز تر ہو مہر روشن کی ضیاء

کاٹتے چکر ہیں جب مہر و مہہ و انجم جدا

نغمہ زن ہے غنچہء گل کے تبسّم کی بہار

عرش سے اسباب کا ایک سلسلہ ہے ہمکنار

Tr: The first bud begins to blossom in the season of Spring caused by the revolution of the earth. When the sun, moon and stars rotate and revolve, separately, the earth also changes its position so that its different parts may receive more heat and more light in different times. With the occurrence of Spring season, the bud begins to smile and blossom into flower, which is a cause related to the "Law of causes and Effects" which starts from the Arsh (Throne of God).

Stanza. 17.

17۔ کس طرح رنگیں ہے گل جب رنگ ہی اس میں نہیں

جذب ہوتا ہے اس میں جلوہ مہر مبین

منعکس کرتا ہے وہ کچھ خاص کرنوں کو وہیں

یہ دماغ و دل سے آنکھوں میں ہے رنگ دل نشین

کس طرح اللہ جانے رنگ گل سے ہے عیاں

ربط انسان و گل و خورشید میں کی ہے نہاں

نوٹ: ہر چیز اپنی ذات سے بے رنگ ہوتی ہے

Tr:-The flower is so colourful when there is no original colour in it. During the phenomena of radiation of the rays of the sun, the flower absorbs particular colour from the rays of the sun. But we think that the attractive colour of the flower is its original colour. Allah only knows how the colour of the flower speaks out the secret of the hidden connection among human being, flower and sun.

Stanza. 18.

18۔ سنگریزہ جو ہے ساحل پر وہ ہے کیونکر ہے وہاں

غور کر اسباب کی زنجیر جاتی ہے کہاں

بحر کی موجیں ہوا کا زور دور آسمان

ہے خدا ہی کو خبر گردش میں تھے کتنے جہاں

سنگریزہ یہ ذرا ہٹ کر کہیں ہوتا اگر

اور ہوتا قصہ کون و مکاں ہی سر بسر

Tr.Probing is required to find out the fact as to why the particular pebble is lying on the shore. Ponder over, from where the chain of causes and effects starts. Had there been a change in the position of a pebble, the level of the surface of the world would have been different.

S: Yasin-36:40:

لَا الشَّمْسُ يَنْبَغِى لَهَا أَن تُدْرِكَ الْقَمَرَ وَلَا الَّيْلُ سَابِقُ النَّهَارِ وَكُلٌّ فِى فَلَكٍ يَسْبَحُونَ ۞

Tr: It is not permitted to the sun to catch up the Moon, nor can the night outstrip the Day. Each (just) swims along in (its own) orbit (According to law)

S: Yasin-36:38:

وَالشَّمْسُ تَجْرِى لِمُسْتَقَرٍّ لَّهَا ذَٰلِكَ تَقْدِيرُ الْعَزِيزِ الْعَلِيمِ ۞

Tr:- And the sun runs its course for a period determined for it. That is the decree of (Him), the exalted in Might, the All-Knowing.

S: Zumar-:39:5

خَلَقَ السَّمَٰوَٰتِ وَالْأَرْضَ بِالْحَقِّ يُكَوِّرُ الَّيْلَ عَلَى النَّهَارِ وَيُكَوِّرُ النَّهَارَ عَلَى الَّيْلِ وَسَخَّرَ الشَّمْسَ وَالْقَمَرَ كُلٌّ يَجْرِى لِأَجَلٍ مُّسَمًّى أَلَا هُوَ الْعَزِيزُ الْغَفَّارُ ۞

Tr: "He created the Heavens and the earth in true (proportions). He makes the night overlap the day and the day overlap the night. He has subjected the sun and the moon (To His law). Each one follows a course for a time appointed. Is not He the exalted in power-He Who forgives again and again?"

S.Anbiyaa-21:33.

وَهُوَ الَّذِى خَلَقَ الَّيْلَ وَالنَّهَارَ وَالشَّمْسَ وَالْقَمَرَ كُلٌّ فِى فَلَكٍ يَسْبَحُونَ ۞

Tr." It is He who created the night and the day and the sun and the moon. All the celestial bodies) swim along, each in its rounded course."

S: Al-Baqara-2:164- (Quoted in ch:3)

Tr:- "Behold! In the creation of heaven and the earth; in the alternation of night and day in the sailing of the ships in the ocean; for the profit of mankind; in rain which God sends down from the skies, and the life which He gives therewith to an earth which is dead, in the beasts of all kinds that He scatters through the earth and the clouds which they trail like their slaves, between the sky and the earth - (here) indeed are the signs for a people that are wise". (purpose of creations)

S Yunus- -10:52

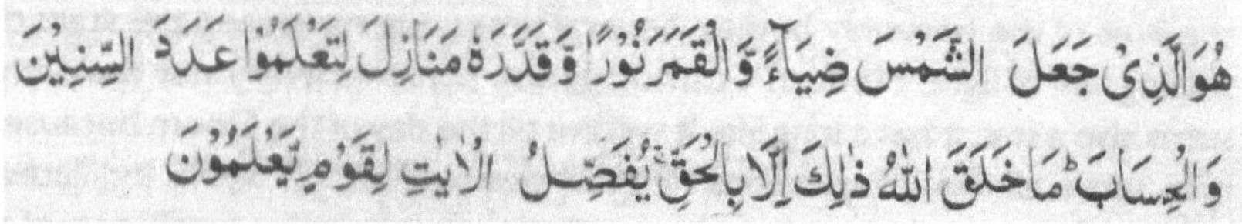

Tr:- It is He who made the sun to be a shining glory and the moon to be a light (of beauty), and measured out stages for her, that ye might know the number of years and the count of time). No wise that God created this but in truth and righteousness. (Thus)doth He explain His signs in detail for those who understand."

S:Anbiyaa:21:30

Tr:- Do not the unbelievers see, that the heavens and the earth were joined together (as one unit of creation) before We clove them as under? We made from water every living thing; Will they not then believe." (Things connected)

C:- One of the four seasons is the season of spring when the vegetation becomes fresh and green and the bud begins to blossom. These seasons are caused by the rotations and revolutions of the earth,sun, moon and stars.

Abeliever should have faith that there is a Supreme Force (God) controlling the activities of the universe. He should also have belief in the theory of causes and effects the chain of which will last forever. This theory governs the succession of events and natural phenomena in the universe. We must realis that the ultimate cause of this chain is Allah or the pleasure of Allah in creating this universe, where this Law is active.

"The theory of cause and effect, the "Law of Changes", Theory of inter-dependence of things and activities" the "Law of Eternity of matter" the "Theory of Eternal connection of matter" are inter-related. During its two movements namely rotation and revolution, the earth, exposes its different parts to the sun so that its different parts may receive more light and more heat from the sun. Its movements cause the alternation of day and night which facilitates to calculate the time and years. The revolution of the heavenly bodies results in the change of seasons and explains the validity of the Theory of cause and effect which starts from the (The throne of God). To start with, let me describe two short chains. The creation of soul Allah is the first cause. The creation of Adam was also the pleasure of God which can also called the first cause. His progeny is the effects of the first cause. Birth is the warrant for death. Now death becomes the effect of birth. New birth becomes cause which was previously the effect of the ultimate cause namely the pleasure or Will of Allah. Islam clearly explains through the Theory of Cause and effect that both happiness and misery are the consequences of one deed, and man has to reap the fruits of his actions. This theory of Retribution will be discussed. in detail later. The change in the position of a single pebble speaks out a long chain of causes and effects. The poet expresses his surprise to note the waves of the ocean, force of the wind and revolutions of the heavenly bodies, and says that Allah only knows the number of worlds which existed in the past and went out of existence. In Quran, a time limit has been hinted for the lives of the heavenly bodies. Several times, we have seen the stars disappear after giving a shining line of light. Modern Cosmology also says that every star has a limited life-time. Though sun is also a star, it has a long life. It will live till the day of the Doom because Allah has commanded it to serve all the living beings till their destruction. Q. 36:40 indicates that the sun and the moon revolve in their own orbits without any clash in compliance of the Divine command. 36:38 reveals that the life-span is determined by God. 21:30 reveals that all the creations in the universe have eternal connections in the universe, have eternal connections with each other as the heavens and the earth were joined together before they were split up. 39:5 reveals that Allah does not allow the night and day to overlap each other because light and darkness cannot exist simultaneously and because the time and year can never be calculated. 2:164 reveals that Allah created the universe for the benefit of man and it hints about the chain of causes and effects regarding clouds, change of winds, rain, fertilization of earth etc. 10:5 explains that besides the service of the sun and moon they render to humanity by giving heat and light they act as the medium for the calculation of time and years. Before the advent of Islam, the Christian Solar Calendar was in vogue which was invented according to the revolution of the sun and was calculated by A.D. which means after Birth of Christ (Anno Domini, the French Words) and B.C. i.e. before Christ.

Sura No. 10 Yunus was revealed in I Makkah before Hijrat (migration of Prophet Muhammad, (SAW) from Makkah to Madina). The Islamic Era started from the date of His arrival at Madina. Before this event, it was hinted in the Meccan Sura Yunus, that the stages of moon were measured by Allah and that Lunar Calendar could be invented and time and years could be calculated according to the revolution of the moon. Even before starting the Islamic Era, the Arabs were calculating months and years according to the revolution of moon. After the arrival of our Prophet at Madina there was a great and lengthy discussion about the introduction of the Islamic Calendar. At last, it was decided that Islamic Era should be started from the date of migration and that time and years should be calculated according to the revolution of the moon. The Muslims could have started the Islamic Era from the date of birth of Prophet Muhammad (SAW) or from the date of obtaining Prophethood. But they preferred the date of migration because Islam was strengthened to a great extent, got more recognition and got spread in different tribes and nations only after the Hijrat.

The creations of Allah in this world are colourless by themselves. Allah has created all the colours in the rays of the sun it emits. During the process of radiation of the rays of the sun, the different creations absorb different colours. Likewise flower also absorbs some particular rays which make it colourful. But the human mind does not realise the presence of the attractive coloured rays of the sun in the colourful flower. Again, at the end of the 17th stanza of Kayinat, the poet has pointed out the connection among the creations of Allah. In this couplet he has mentioned the connection among three things namely moon, flower and sun because he has explained about man's idea about the colour of the flower absorbed from the sun. 21:30 also proves the connection of creations by explaining that the whole universe was created as one unit of big mass of smoke before its explosion which the scientists call "The Big Bang". This explosion of the huge mass of smoke, scattered the splinters of the matter which formed the earth, sun, moon and all the heavenly bodies. The theory of original unity of the matter explains the theory of eternal connection of different creations in the universe. The essence of the above quoted Quranic Stanzas is contained in the 16th, 17th and 18th stanza of the poem Kayinat. (Quran, cosmology, space science, physical science and Big Bang Theory)

Stanza. 19.Arabic

19۔ زندگی ہو یا کوئی شئے وہ عیاں ہو یا نہاں

ہو نہیں سکتی عمل پیرا کبھی تنہا یہاں

ہے اثر ہر ایک کہ ہر دوسرے پر ہر زماں

یوں بہم وابستہ آئیں ہیں اشیاء جہاں

ایک ہی زندہ حقیقت ہے وجود کائنات

موجزن ہر رنگ میں ہے ایک ہی بحر حیات

آہ وہ تاروں کی دنیا جو ہے ذروں میں نہاں۔

Tr:- Whether it is life or a thing; whether it is manifest or concealed, nothing can be active on its own accord without the help of another thing. Each and everything is always influenced by another thing. All the creations in the universe are always bound by the "Law of Eternal Connection of matter". The existence of the universe and the creations in it are clear evidences of the existence of one big ocean of life which means the existence of God.

S: Anbiyaa-21:32:

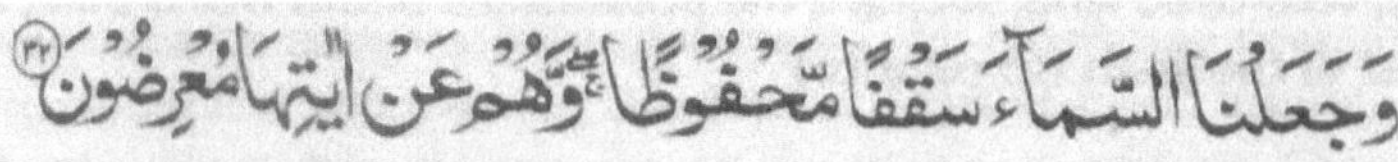

Tr:- "We have made the heavens as a canopy well-guarded; yet do they turn away from the signs which these things point to!"

S:Luqmaan-31:20:

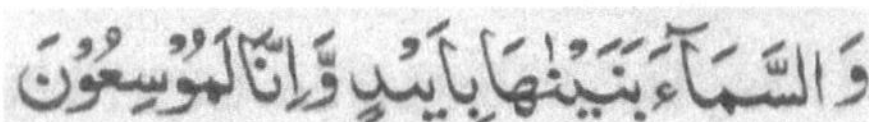

Tr:- "Oye not see that God has subjected to your (use) all things in the heavens and on earth and has made His bounties flow to you in exceeding measure, both seen and unseen. Yet there are among men, those who dispute about God without knowledge and without guidance and without a Book to enlighten them".

S:Zariyaat-51:47:

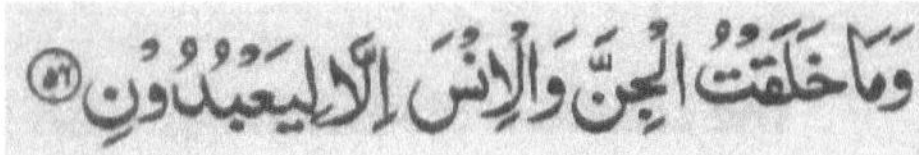

Tr:- "With power and skill did We construct the firmaments! For, it is We who created the vastness of space."

S:Zariyaat-51:56

Tr:- "I have only created Jinns and men that they may serve Me.

S:Anbiyaa - 21:16:

وَمَا خَلَقْنَا السَّمَاءَ وَالْأَرْضَ وَمَا بَيْنَهُمَا لَاعِبِينَ ۞

Tr.- "Not for (idle) sport did we create the heavens and the earth and all that is between.

S Ale-Imran - 3:185

كُلُّ نَفْسٍ ذَائِقَةُ الْمَوْتِ وَإِنَّمَا تُوَفَّوْنَ أُجُورَكُمْ يَوْمَ الْقِيَامَةِ فَمَنْ زُحْزِحَ عَنِ النَّارِ وَأُدْخِلَ الْجَنَّةَ فَقَدْ فَازَ وَمَا الْحَيَاةُ الدُّنْيَا إِلَّا مَتَاعُ الْغُرُورِ

Tr:- "Every soul shall have a taste of death and only on the Day of Judgement shall you be paid of your full recompense. Only he who is saved far from the Fire and admitted to the garden, would have attained the object (of life of this world, is but goods and chattels of deception."

Hadis - A chunk of Paradise equal to a yard is better than the earth and what is in it"

S:Al-e-Imraan;- 3:14

زُيِّنَ لِلنَّاسِ حُبُّ الشَّهَوَاتِ مِنَ النِّسَاءِ وَالْبَنِينَ وَالْقَنَاطِيرِ الْمُقَنْطَرَةِ مِنَ الذَّهَبِ وَالْفِضَّةِ وَالْخَيْلِ الْمُسَوَّمَةِ وَالْأَنْعَامِ وَالْحَرْثِ ذَلِكَ مَتَاعُ الْحَيَاةِ الدُّنْيَا وَاللَّهُ عِنْدَهُ حُسْنُ الْمَآبِ ۞

Tr:- "Hair in the eyes of men is the love of things they cover women and sons; heaped up hoards of gold and silver: horses branded for (blood and excellence) and (Wealth) of cattle und well-tilled land, such are the possessions of this world's life; but in nearness to God is the best of the goals (to refer to)

S:Muhammad (The Prophet) 47:12

إِنَّ اللَّهَ يُدْخِلُ الَّذِينَ آمَنُوا وَعَمِلُوا الصَّالِحَاتِ جَنَّاتٍ تَجْرِي مِنْ تَحْتِهَا الْأَنْهَارُ وَالَّذِينَ كَفَرُوا يَتَمَتَّعُونَ وَيَأْكُلُونَ كَمَا تَأْكُلُ الْأَنْعَامُ وَالنَّارُ مَثْوًى لَهُمْ ۞

Tr:- "Verily God will admit those who believe and do righteous deeds to Gardens beneath which rivers flow, while those who reject God will enjoy this World) and eat as cattle eat; and the fire will be their abode."

C:- In this stanza the poet has attempted to explain the purpose of creations, purpose of man's life, realisation of God's existence, realisation of human life and Law of interdependence."

Any life or anything cannot act independently. It needs the help of another thing for its activity. Food is required for the metabolism in our body. Sun heat, Sun light and water are necessary for all living beings including vegetation to grow. As all things are interdependent to continue their activities, God has created diverse things which are helpful to one another. Every creation of God has its influence over other things which are bound by the "Law of Inter-dependence". The existence of Life" namely God. It is a notable poin " The existence of the universe is itself a living proof for the "One Big Ocean Holy God. It is a notable point why this Ocean of Life is referred to in this context. It is because the ultimate dependence lies with God.

The sub-title of this chapter is "Existence of universe and Life". These needs elaborate mation about purpose of creation, realisation of God's existence and realisation of human life.

In Ouran 21:16 Allah says that he did not create the universe playfully in idle sports. But we did it with some keen and particular purpose. Regarding the purpose of creation of man Allah says in 51:56 that He created Jinns and men that they might worship Him. In 21:32,31:20 Allah reveals His purpose of creating diverse things so that man can realise His existence through His manifestations in them. In 3:185 and 47:12 Allah persuades man to understand the purpose of Human life, self-realization and eternal spiritual life.

Allah has some serious purpose of creating different things in the universe. Each creature is given the opportunity to develop and progress through His Providence. He persuades man to worship Him. He has given man the special faculty to subdue the natural forces and obtain salvation by His Mercy. The favours of Allah are all around man who has benefit from other creations because Allah has subdued them to his service.

Soil, sunlight, sun heat, air and water are the basic elements for the survival of all the living creatures including man. All the heavenly bodies such as sun, stone or soil can exist independently but living beings are dependent on other things. It is the irony of universal law that the highest and best creation of Allah (man) cannot have an independent existence. For example, the sun does not need the help of man but man's survival depends on sunlight. In several Stanzas of Quran, the role of water is indicated in all its dimensions as the most vital ingredient of life on earth.

The purpose of a believer must be attaining his goal namely God. He should seek the pleasure of God by adhering to divine law and treading the path of righteousness. Inspite of enlightenment from Quran, some people are only interested in eating and drinking. Quran has compared such people with irrational animals. They are more interested in acquiring and hoarding up temporal and transitory belongings in this mundane life.

Some people accept and realise the existence of God without any hesitation. Before they could realise the Truth, some people want proof for the existence of God though they witness astounding phenomena of nature. The existence of God can be realised through power of reasoning, intellectual education and religious practices. We can promote our intellect and acquire knowledge about the facts. The existence of God can be realised by reposing faith in the teachings of the prophets, spiritual practices and spiritual discipline. The observation of spiritual discipline despite great impediments on the path of righteousness will definitely enable us to steer safely through our life's voyage. In several Quranic Stanzas especially in Sura-eRahman. God has mentioned about His creations in order to convince humanity about His existence. Allah has provided humanity with facts and proofs for His existence through the mysterious natural phenomena. For the realisation of God's existence, a simple theory is enough which explains "When there are creations there must be a Creator". For those who demand more evidences, it is only his lack of faith in Allah's signs in His creations. For those who cannot of reasoning, intellectual education and religious practices. We can promote our intellect and acquire knowledge about the facts. The existence of God can be realised by reposing faith in the teachings of the Prophets, spiritual practices and spiritual discipline. The observation of spiritual discipline despite great impediments on the path of righteousness will definitely enable us to steer safely through our life's voyage. In several Quranic Verses especially in Sura-e. Rahman. God has mentioned about his creations in order to convince human paity about His existence. Allah has provided humanity with facts and proofs for His existence through the mysterious natural phenomena. For the realisation of God's existence, a simple theory is enough which explains "When there are creations there must be a Creator". For those who demand more evidences, it is only his lack of faith in Allah's signs in His creations. For those who cannot appreciate the Grand Designs of Creative Power of Allah, we need not tax our mind over the imagination on the physical concept of Allah.

Self-realisation of man and the eternity of spiritual life have been interpreted in the scriptural texts. Man is born innocent in this world. Generally, man identifies himself with his perishable body and never realises that his spiritual life is eternal. In Quran Allah has repeatedly mentioned about the Resurrection of man, Day of Reckoning, and retribution for his deeds during his corporeal life in this world. Man must realise and be thankful to Allah that He has created him in the best form and given him the highest status with true potential nature i.e. Effulgence of God. A wise man realises his true self, does not attach undue importance to his perishable body, and he is conscious of his immortal spiritual life. Enlightened by divine knowledge, he adheres to all Divine Laws. These noble deeds enable him to attain spiritual perfection which must actually be his life's goal namely God. It is meant that spiritual perfection can be obtained only through Union with God. The substance of the 19th stanza of Kayinat has been elaborately explained. (Purpose of creations, Law of Interdependence, potential nature of man. Mysticism).

CHAPTER - X

ELECTRICITY

—◦।◦~ ♦ ~◦।◦—

Stanza: 20

20۔اس قدر حیرت فزا ہے محفل انجم کہاں
قوت برقی ہے ان تاروں کی صورت میں عیاں
دیکھ اُن کی گردشوں میں عزم حکمت کے نشاں
دم بخود ہے آستانے غیب پر عقل سلیم
ذرہ ناچیز میں یہ جلوہ راز قدیم

Tr:- It is really wonderful that the world of stars is concealed in the atoms. The group of stars is extremely surprising. The electric energy is manifest in the form of stars. The Signs of divine Wisdom and Divine Resolve can be realised by the revolutions of the stars. A single atom which seems to us to have no significance at all, has in it the secret of ancientness. Even our perfect wisdom becomes dumb to note the astounding deeds of God in the realm or divinity.

C:- In this Stanza the poet has dealt with the original quintessence of electricity.

Revolutions of the heavenly bodies without clash, ancientness and eternity of matter have already been discussed in the previous chapters and Quranic verses have been quoted for them.

Every matter whether it is in the form of solid, liquid or gas, is composed of atoms. Every atom contains electric energy, generated from and emitted by stars especially the rays of the sun. The presence of electric energy can be explained by examples. When we rub our two palms together, we feel the heat. It is due to the presence of electricity in our body. When a granite stone is struck on the other, we can see the spark which is caused by electricity contained in the atoms of the stone. Sometimes we see the flames in the forest without the interference of man. How is the forest set ablaze? It is nothing else than electricity, produced by the rubbing and abrasion of the branches of the trees caused by stormy wind. The dashing of forceful winds against the saturated clouds produces electricity the light of which can be seen by us in the sky.

As the sub-topic of this chapter, the poet has mentioned the important contents of electricity as Electrons, Protons and Neutrons.

Electron is the negative element of electricity. Proton is the positive element of electricity. Neutron is the element which neutralizes the harmful effect of electricity and that which balances the negative effect and positive effect of electricity. It protects the matter from being burnt. These three elements of electricity revolve in their own orbits around the nucleus in each and every atom without clashing with each other. The heavenly bodies also revolve in their own orbits without any clash. The Signs of Divine Wisdom and Divine Designs are wonderful when we realis that the characteristics of the revolutions of the heavenly bodies and the revolutions of the elements of electricity are similar. By such interpretations, the poet proves that stars are composed of atoms and revolve without any clash just as the electrons, protons and neutrons do.

At the end the poet expresses his surprise over the Divine Designs and says that it is beyond human capacity to understand the secrecy of ancientness of the atom which is known only to God. (Quran and physical science)

CHAPTER XI

MATCHES

—◦١◦ ♦ ◦١◦—

Stanza: 21

11/دیا سلائی ۔ ماچس

21 ۔ لاٹ جو کبریت کی ماچس میں ہے جلتی ہوئی (سلفر)

اصلیت میں ایک ہے وہ اور کرن مریخ کی   (کبریت)

آگ ہو برق و کشش ہے رنگ ہو یا روشنی

ابر ہو آب و ہوا ہو خاک ہو یا زندگی

فی الحقیقت ایک ہی قدرت کے جلوے ہیں تمام   (وحدت اشیاء

یہ وہی قوت ہے کی رب کی مشیت لا کلام

Tr-The original quintessence of the chief element of Sulphur which burns in the matches is same as the ray emitted by the star Mars. Whether it is flame, or electricity, or gravitational pull, or colour or light or cloud or water or wind or mud or life, are all the manifestations of one Supreme Energy. It is an undisputed fact that this Energy contained in the creations is the consequence of the Will of Allah, the Provident Who provides and creates diverse things which are inter-dependent.

C:- Sulphur is a yellow mineral which is highly inflammable, feasible and brittle. Red Sulphur is rarely available. Brimstone is mainly composed of Sulphur.

It has been discovered by scientific research that the stones and soil are enriched with the meteors and the rays of heavenly bodies. By the process of metamorphosis, they are converted as minerals. These meteors have enough energy to travel through different spheres of the spaces and reach the earth for the benefit of humanity. When the huge heavenly bodies stay in their own spaces and have their own gravitational attractions, their small particles have enough strength to come out from their gravitational pull and enter into the atmosphere of the earth the gravitation of which pulls those particles towards it. This Divine Designs and Providence of Allah are Wonderful. The star Mars is said to be rich in Sulphur, the rays of which enrich the soil and the brimstones are formed by them. The extracted Sulphur is used in manufacturing the matches which are in their turn used for the purpose of inflaming other things. This Sulphur is also used for manufacturing crackers and gun powder. Hence the poet says that the Sulphur contained in the matches and the rays of the star Mars are similar. The poet concludes by saying that all the creations in the universe are the manifestations of Allah and the energy they contain is provided by the One Supreme Power and Will of Allah. Several times the poet has laid emphasis on the Unity of Creations of Allah which is the main requisite of a true Faith. (Unity of creations and chemical science).

CHAPTER - XII

INVESTIGATED TRUTH

Stanza: 22

12/دریافت شدہ حقیقت

22۔ ہے مشیت ہی کا جلوہ قوتِ عزم بشر

خارجی دنیا میں اعجاز آفریں اس کا اثر

ہو چکا ہے چاک اس کی زد سے خود میرا جگر

ہے ضمیر آدمی سر الہی سر بسر

ہو اگر پابندِ احکام خداوند جہاں

شان خلاقی ہو انساں کے ارادوں سے عیاں

نوٹ :

تو کیا وہ اپنے اوپر آسمان کو نہیں دیکھتے ہم نے کس طرح بنایا اور زینت دی اور
اس میں کوئی خلل نہیں۔(الملک 67-3)

باب نمبر 12 یعنی دریافت شدہ حقیقت کے لئے نوٹ

حدیث : جو بندہ نوافل کے ذریعے میرا قرب حاصل کرتا ہے یہاں تک کہ میں اس
سے محبت کرتا ہوں پس جب میں اس سے محبت کرتا ہوں تو میں اس کا کان ہوتا ہوں
جس سے وہ سنتا ہے اور۔ اس کی آنکھ ہوتا ہوں جس سے وہ دیکھتا ہے اور اس کا
ہاتھ ہوتا ہوں جس سے وہ پکڑتا ہے ۔

Tr:- The power of determination of man is the result of the Will of God. The effect of the Will of God on man's intention is appreciable and miraculous in this insignificant and transitory world. I myself have devoted my life to the submission of Allah's Will. The conscience of man is nothing else than the secret of God's Will. If the conscience of man abides by the

Laws or Commands of God, the glory of His creative Power is manifested in the intentions of man.

C:- In the 22nd Stanza of the text the poet explains Allah's Power in creating man which is manifest through man's intention. In fact the firm determination of man depends upon the Will of God. The poet points out the influence of the Will of God on the determination of man in this transitory world. Of course, a single blade of grass cannot shake without the command of God. Some people are completely resigned to the Will of God. Their total submission persuades them to adhere to all Divine Laws. The poet says that he is one among them. Whether fortunes or misfortunes, the true lover of God accepts them and remains absolutely calm and contented. Some people act truly to their conscience and some against their conscience. The latter category of people are not bothered about the life hereafter. There is an unknown secret which is the cause for the use of conscience in different ways.

The whole lot of man's life is pre-destined. His destiny is concealed in his intentions. He must be contented with the Will of God. At the same time, he is permitted by Islam to try to overcome the difficulties and to strive hard to achieve progress in every aspect of life and has got rights to pray Allah to grant him success. Of course, Allah hears the sincere prayers of the true believers. (Divine decision, hard endeavor, humanity and destiny).

Stanza: 23

23۔ جذبہائے دل بھی ہوتے ہیں ارادوں میں نہاں

ہے مشیت میں بھی رب کی صفات جاوداں

ہے صفت اللہ کی ہر ایک صورت میں عیاں

اس نے انسان کو خلافت کا دیا منصب گراں

جلوہ گر اس میں نہ ہو کیونکر صفات ایزدی

عقل آزادی ارادہ اختیار و آگہی

T:- The concealed emotions of man result in his intentions. Likewise, the eternal Attributes of God are contained in the Will of God. The Attribute of Allah is manifested in every form. He granted to human being the highest status of vicegerent in this world. It is but natural that Allah's Attributes such as wisdom, sense of liberty, intention, power of discretion and awareness are also present in human nature.

Stanza: 24

24۔کن فضاؤں میں نہ جانے وہ ستارے ہیں رواں

روشنی جن کی ہزاروں سال میں پہنچے یہاں

برق رفتاری میں بھی جو ہیں حدوں میں ہر زماں

ہے زمین یک سنگریزہ وہ ہے گر کوہ گراں

عظمت خلاق عالم پر جو ہوتی ہے نظر

ڈوب جاتا ہے یم حیرت میں ادراک بشر

Tr.- The atmospheres are not known to man where the stars are orbiting the light of which requires thousands of years to reach this world. The speed by which they are passing are always within boundaries of their own atmospheres. When this earth is compared to those stars, this earth is a pebble while those stars are big mountains. When the greatness of the

Creator of this universe is imagined or pondered over, the intellect of man gets submerged in the ocean of surprise.

Stanza: 25

25 ۔ سارے اجرام فلک گرم سفر ہیں سر کے بل

حسن ترتیب و توازن سے مزین ہے عمل

ہو جہاں برہم جو گردش ایک بھی ہو بے محل

ہے وہ نا بینا جو دیکھے نظم قدرت میں خلل

چاہیے ہر چیز کی تکمیل و خلقت پر نظر

چاہیے ہر شئے کی تقدیر و ہدایت پر نظر

نوٹ : پروردگار نے ہر چیز پیدا کی ، پھر اسے درست کیا، پھر ہے وجود کیلئے ایک اندازہ ٹھہرایا اور پھر اس پر راہ عمل کھول دی۔ (الاعلی ۔87-2-3-4-5)

Tr:- All the heavenly bodies are busily engaged in their journey (revolution). Their activity is beautified by the beauty of Divine arrangement and proportion. If a single revolution is out of place or out of the correct orbit, the whole universe will be upset and disordered. The person who sees any defect in the Divine Administration is blind to the truth. We must see the perfection of the creations and must realise the same Divine administration.

Q:S: Alaa-87:2,3,4,5

الَّذِیْ خَلَقَ فَسَوّٰی ۪ۙ وَالَّذِیْ قَدَّرَ فَهَدٰی ۪ۙ وَالَّذِیْۤ اَخْرَجَ الْمَرْعٰی ۪ۙ فَجَعَلَهٗ غُثَآءً اَحْوٰی ۪ؕ

Tr:- "Who hath created, and further given order and proportion; Who hath ordained law and granted guidance; and Who bringeth out the (green and lucious) pastures, and then doth make it (but) swarthy stubble"

S: Al-Baqara- 2:30

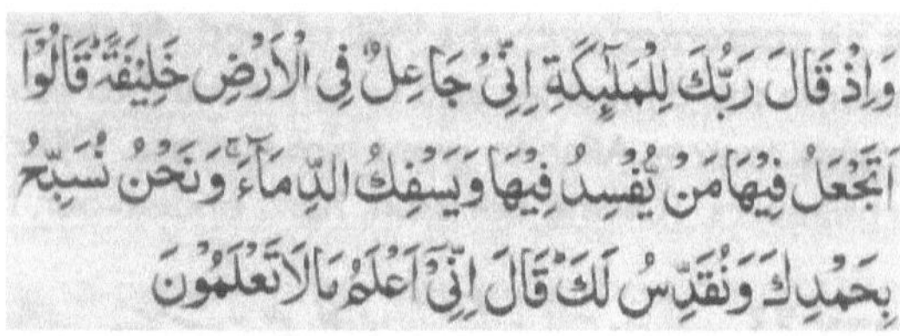

Tr:- "Behold, thy Lord said to the angels "I will create a Vicegerent on earth (Adam the first man)"

Al-Baqara :5 2:34

Tr:- "And behold, We said to the angles "Bow down to Adam" and they bowed down. Not so Iblis, he refused and was haughty he was of those who reject Faith."

C:- In the 23rd Stanza of the text the poet has explained the similarities between the decision and attributes of Allah and the emotions and intentions of man. The Eternal Attributes of Allah and His Will is manifested in every form because man is created with the effulgence of God like other creations. But unlike other irrational animals, Allah has bestowed on human being the soul, best bodily structure, wisdom, power of reasoning and discrimination between good and bad.

Sura Tinn-95:4:

Tr:- "We have indeed created man in the best of moulds". In the verse 2:31,32,33 (already quoted in the previous chapters) it is said that Allah has granted man the highest position of all Allah's creations. Allah asked the angels to bow before Adam in order to make it known that man is superior to Angels. In the verse 2:30 Allah informs the Angles that He would send a Vicegerent (Adam, the first man) on earth. The verse 2:31 explains that Allah taught Adam all things. In 2:33 Allah asked Adam to tell the nature of the things which the Angels did not know.

In this same stanza the poet has said that the Attributes of God are manifested in the faculties of man. In the following a few Attributes of Allah and the faculties of man have been enumerated which are similar, and a very few Ahadis (sayings of the Prophet) have been quoted to prove the validity of the explanation.

Some ninety-nine beautiful names of God have been mentioned in Quran indicating His Attributes. These Attributes reveal some injunctions and some prohibitions of Islam for human beings. There are four Attributes of Allah which can never be acquired by man. The classification of these four Attributes includes all other Attributes. They are:

1. **Allah is Omnipotent :**

   (Allah is Almighty and Powerful) Human being can never be so. God grants him a minute fraction of His potency needed to lead the life.

2. **Allah is Omni Present:**

   (Allah is All Pervading. In other words Allah is present everywhere in the universe). We are where we are. We occupy a very little space.

3. Allah is Omni Scient :

(Allah is all Knowing) Human being can never be so. Allah grants us a very little knowledge which is indispensable for the welfare of human beings.

4. Allah is Eternal :

(It means Allah is the First and Allah is the Last. He has no death and He will be for ever) Qyyum is the name of Allah Who is Eternal. We are but the travellers of this transitory world. The corporeal body of human being is temporal. After all, the existence of all the creations whether animate or inanimate are temporary in this world. Nothing can be eternal except Allah.

In the following, some names of Allah have been mentioned which connote His Attributes Man can acquire these faculties, but Allah and His Prophet have prohibited man to utilize these faculties. Man must abstain from exercising these powers. Allah has preserved these powers for Himself.

Qahhaar:- Allah Who is angry and furious. But in Islam, anger is considered to be one of the greatest sins for human being.

Hadith: "The strongest man is he who keeps his anger in check".

Al-Muzzil:

Allah who lowers and degrades other human being is commended by Islam to from abusing his fellow being.

Hadith:- The evil ones among you are those who go about telling tales about people spoil relationship between intimate friends and who seek to bring affliction to innocent people (Bukhari, Al-Adab, Al-Mufrad, Ahmed, Baihaqui)

Hadith:- "When two persons indulge in hurling (abuses) upon one another, it would be the first one who would be the sinner so long as the oppressed does not transgress the limite (Muslim).

Al-Muntaquim :- Allah Who retaliates or awards punishment for man's evil deeds. B. Allah has promised ample rewards for those who do not avenge the afflictions caused by others.

Hadith: "In response to the question of Moses, Allah affirmed to him that the man is dearest to Him who has the power to take revenge, yet forgives."

Al-Mumeet : Allah Who takes back life i.e. the giver of death. Allah has preserved this right for himself. Man is prohibited to kill a person without proper reasons. Islam itself has proclaimed death sentence for certain offences. 35th Stanza of Sura-e-Ma'ida says that to kill a single innocent man amounts to killing the whole humanity and to save a single man's life would mean to save the whole humanity.

Hadith :-"A poor man among my people is he who will bring on the day of Resurrection, prayers, fasting, zakat, but came having reviled a man, aspersed another, devoured a property of another, shed the blood of some and beaten others. Then the people, he harmed will be given some of his good deeds. If taken and cast upon him and he will be cast into Hell.(Muslim).

Hadith:- "The first thing that will be decided among people on the Day of Judgement will pertain to bloodshed". (Muslim). The above-mentioned Ahadis explain that nobody is permitted to afflict harm on others or shed his blood or murder him.

Allah expects His worshippers to acquire some of His attributes which are indispensable for the refined society, and to utilize them lawfully.

Hadith:- "The best among you are those whose appearance reminds you of Allah." (Bukhari, Al-Adab, Al-Mufrad Ahmed, Baihaqui)

In the following, there are a few names of God Whose Attributes. His worshippers should acquire.

Ar-Rahmaan: Allah who is Most Gracious and Most Benevolent. The values of life of a man can be realised only when it is advantageous and beneficial to humanity. A man should not be selfish. He must be helpful and gracious towards others.

Hadith - Charity is due to every joint in each person every day. The appearance of the sun to act Justly between two people is a charity. To help a man with his mount. lifting him unto ring up his belongings unto it is a charity: a good word is a charity and removing harmful thing from the road is a charity (Al-Bukhari, Muslim).

Al-Adl:- God Who is just, Allah wants his worshippers to be just towards all the people irrespective of colour, cast, creed, social status or relationship.

During the life time of Prophet Muhammad (PBUH), a lady from respectable family e something. Her hand had to be amputated for this offence. Her family members roached the Prophet and requested him to hush up the matter, spare her from the Punishment and infamy. This meant transgressing the justice. Our Prophet replied, "By Allah. had it been my daughter Fatima, I would have had her hand cut".

Hadith:- (A part of it): - "The man who possesses three qualities, takes advantage of Faith. This sort of person is he who loves most Allah and His Prophet; he who loves his other fellow beings in order to seek Allah's pleasure and he who rules with absolute justice (Bukhari).

Hadith:- None of you should judge between two persons when you are angry (Muslim).

Hadith:- When a judge gives a decision having tried his best to decide correctly and is right, there are two rewards for him, and if he gives the judgement after having tried his best to arrive at a correct decision, but errs, there is one, reward for him. (Muslim).

Al-Ghafoor:- Allah Who forgives. Allah wishes men to forgive one another in order to maintain peace. At the end of several Stanzas of Quran it is stated that Allah will forgive the sinner after he repents. Every time, the idolators of Makkah, teased, embarrassed or persecuted our Holy Prophet, he used to forgive them without any retaliation. On one such occasion, his companions asked him to curse them but he refused and replied:

Hadith:- "I have not been sent by God as a curse or imprecation to humanity but I have been sent as blessing or divine favour to humanity." Prophet's supplication- Hadith:- "You are my Lord and I am your servant. I have wronged myself and I do acknowledge my wrong action only. You forgive wrong actions. My Lord forgive me" (Bukhari).

As-Shakoor:- Allah Who acknowledges or thanks. It is one of the injunction of Islam that one must thank his benefactor.

Hadith:- "He who does not thank men is ungrateful to Allah." (Al-Bukhari, Al-Adab. AlMufrad, Ahmed, Abu Dawood, Tirmizi, Ibn-e-Maja).

Hadith:- "If a man favours his fellow being, he must thank him. If he fails to thank him, he fails to thank Allah." (Al-Bukhari).

Hadith:- "If a man favours his fellow being, it is essential for him to repay the favour in case it is within his capacity. If it is not possible for him, he may praise his benefactor which amounts to thanking him. If he conceals his favour, it amounts to ungratefulness. Remember! The man who cannot thank man, cannot thank God." (Tirmizi).

As-Salaam:- Allah Who gives peace. Name of Islam. Injunction of Islam Islam enjoins the believers to live in peace. It expects the Muslims to bring about reconciliation between two men or two factions or two communities. Islam is a peace-loving religion and it is the dun of the Muslims to adhere to its law.

Al-Ghani - Allah Who is self-sufficient. Islam does not encourage begging. Those who are strong enough to work must earn by honest means and become self-sufficient Peonia who are considered to be wealthy though they may be poor.

Hadith:- "To earn an honest living is a duty next to the principal duties of Iman" (Baihaquil).

Islam ennobled labour. Prophet Muhammad (SAW) himself was a worker and so were his early disciples. He instructed them to strive hard to earn their livelihood and become self-sufficient (Ghani). Begging was permitted only to the helpless and disabled people.

Al-Karim - Allah who is Generous and Charitable. His generosity is evident by the abundance of His Bounties. It is quite essential for a man to acquire the quality of this Attribute of Allah and always be generous and prepared to pay the poor dues.

Ar-Rahim:- Allah Who is Merciful. The Law of God is Law of Mercy. While reading on writing or doing something, we start with the phrase "In the name of God, the Beneficent, the Most Merciful." Out of His Mercy. He has created other things which are indispensable for the well-being and survival of other creations especially man. Out of His Mercy He has provided the sustenance for the bodily development. Out of His Mercy He sent several Prophets in different nations and revealed Books for the guidance of people and for their spiritual evolution which can ultimately result in the attainment of Goal i.e. God.

Q: S:Anbiyaa-21-107:

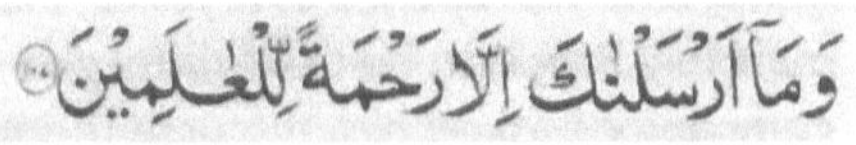

وَمَآ أَرْسَلْنَٰكَ إِلَّا رَحْمَةً لِّلْعَٰلَمِينَ ۝

Tr:- "We sent thee not, but as a Mercy for all creatures."

Though one of the Attributes of Allah is Anger; though Allah has admonished His worshippers against sins; though He has threatened people with punishment. torments and torture of Hell, He out of His Mercy seeks pretexts to forgive His worshippers. Even the prick of a thorn, the bite of an ant, even pain, pangs of grief, adversity, piety, physical ailment and patience are some of the pretexts for Allah for the salvation of that much of sins for His worshippers.

Q-Sura: Al-e-Imraan-3:31

قُلْ إِن كُنتُمْ تُحِبُّونَ ٱللَّهَ فَٱتَّبِعُونِى يُحْبِبْكُمُ ٱللَّهُ وَيَغْفِرْ لَكُمْ ذُنُوبَكُمْ وَٱللَّهُ غَفُورٌ رَّحِيمٌ

Tr:- "Say: if ye do love Allah, follow me (Prophet). Allah will love you and forgive you your sins, for Allah is oft-Forgiving, Most Merciful."

Hadith:- "Allah is compassionate (Rahim) and generous (Karim). He likes compassion and generosity. Allah is not compassionate towards the man who is not compassionate towards others." (Mashariq)

Hadith: "Allah •s not Merciful to the person who does not show mercy to His other creations: (Bukhari, Muslim),

By the above interpretations it is clear that man has a little of the faculties of Allah's Attributes which Allah expects him to put into practice which are advantageous both to himselfas well as to other creations of Allah.

In the last line of the 23rd Stanza of the text. the poet is right in saying that the Attributes are present in the faculties of man such as wisdom, liberty, intention, power of discresion and awareness-

In the 24th Stanza of the text, the poet has made mention about the scientific discovery of different atmospheres. in the vast expanse of the universe.

Q-SZaariyaat - 5 1 :47 (already quoted in the 9th Chapter) says, "With power and skin did We construct the firmaments, for it is We Who createth the vastness of space:

In this Stanza the poet has briefly dealt with space science which requires some explanation for the easy comprehension of the young readers. The poet has expressed his ignorance about the atmospheres where innumerable stars are in motion, the light of which requires thousands of years to reach the earth. In fact, all the stars are not Visible. By the data. given in the Quranic Stanzas. the scientists have discovered that there are several atmospheres in the Vast expanse of the universe with their own galaxies. The nature of atmosphere and the intensity of the power of gravitation depend on the size of the planets.

Islam is a religion which combines matter with spirit and urges for the exercise of reasons. research in all branches Of studies including the study of astronomy and space technology so that man can admire the creations of Allah which would strengthen the faith of the believer-s.In the following Stanza Allah permits the Jinns and men to make advance in space science.

Q-S-Ar-Rahmaan-55:33 (Already quoted in chapter:9): "O ye assembly ofJinns and men! If it be, ye can pass beyond the zones of the heavens and the earth, pass ye! Not without authority shall ye be able to pass."

Astronomy the study of heavenly bodies is the oldest among all other studies. Such striking phenomena as the rising and setting of the sun, phases of the moon, appearance and disappearance of the comets have been studied from the infancy of human race. It was believed by the ancient people chat human affairs in all Walks of life were controlled by the revolution rotation and changing positions of sun, moon, planets and stars. In the early period people began to worship them. But it was Islam which explained that they were only the creations of Allah and they are ever controlled by Him. (It must be remembered that all the Prophets brought the same messages as Islam did)

Sometimes (Of course, with the permission of Allah), the astrologers foretold the impending events correctly. For example, an astrologer, in the court of the unbelieving and cruel Pharaoh, the King of Egypt, foretold that a boy (Prophet Moses) was to be born in Egypt who would oppose him and bring about his destruction. Likewise, another astrologer. in the court of Namrood, the King of Iraq foretold that a boy (Prophet Abraham) was to be born who would oppose idolatry and defeat him.

Modern science has discovered that our earth is one of the planets (Worlds swim around a medium sized star called the sun. Some planets have moons which swim them. This system is called the solar system. Our solar system is an extremely small fraction other systems, operating in the universe.

In this current century (20th century) the exploration of space enabled men to the moon. Some space crafts have taken the photographs of other planets like Mars and which facilitated man to acquire a fund of knowledge. Some space crafts passed by Mars and Saturn.

The first Quranic verse in Sura-e-Fatiha and several other Stanzas reveal that Cherisher of several worlds. The worlds inhabited by people have not yet been discovered but Quranic verses have clearly revealed that there is a world inhabited by Jinns (head people) whom Allah created with smokeless fire. Allah has revealed in Quran that created several suns and several moons in the universe. Every world requires the heat of and light of a moon. Allah only knows the number of worlds He has created. Till the Day of the Doom man can never acquire whole knowledge of Divine secrets, Man's knowledge granted by Allah is very limited.

In the previous centuries, it was believed that excluding the sun and the moon, there were only seven planets in our solar system by name, Mercury, Venus, Mars, Earth. Jupiter Saturn, and Neptune. Later two more planets were discovered and were given the name Uranus and Pluto. An Indian astronomer Dr. J. Rawal who is working at Nehru Planetarium Bombay has discovered two more planets in addition to nine planets mentioned above. He made his discovery public in 1978. The National Aeronautics and Space Administration (NASA) of U.S. confirmed Rawal's 9th planet in 1987 and his 10th planet is expected to be confirmed in the near future.

Allah only knows the fact. But these discoveries tempt us to speculate that they have some connections with the dream of Yusuf Alaihis-Salam (Prophet Joseph) the great grandson of Ibrahim Alaihis-Salam and the grandson of Prophet Isaaq (PBUH). Less than three thousand years back, in his boyhood, Yusuf Alaihis-Salam informed his father Yaqoob Alaihis-Salam (Prophet Jacob) about his dream which has been quoted in Quran.

S-Yusuf-12:4:

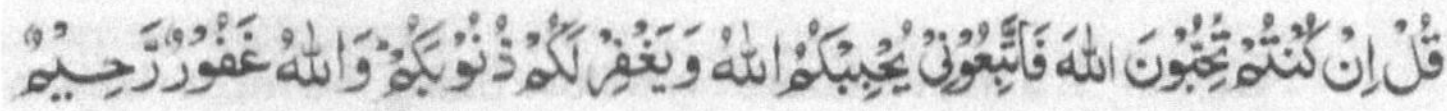

Tr:- "Behold! Joseph said to his father! I did see eleven stars and the sun and the moon: I saw them prostrate themselves to me."

Prophet Yaqoob prophesied Yusuf's exalted status in the future and said that the eleven stars were his own brother Benjamin and ten step brothers who were extremely jealous of Yusuf. He said that the prostration of the planets meant that his brothers would be humbled before him by Allah. He added the sun and the moon were Yusuf's father and mother and that the prostration of sun and the moon meant that Yusuf would become Prophet.

The sun is said by the scientists to be the medium size star. It means that there are billions of billion stars (The number of stars can never be estimated by the scientists) which are much bigger than the sun which is a million time bigger than the earth. In this Stanza, the poet compares the sizes of the earth and the stars and says that the earth is a pebble while the stars are huge mountains.

Q.S. Mumin-40:57

Tr:- "Assuredly, the creation of the heavens and the earth is greater (Matter) than the creation of men. Yet most men understand not."

Now the statements of the poet have been proved by Quran and science that there are innumerable stars and planets (worlds) having their own atmospheres in the universe and the electricity's passing through are ever in the limits of their own atmospheres.

In the last couplet, the poet admires the greatness of the Creator. He confesses his ignorance and says that the human intellect submerges into the ocean of surprise while pondering over the mighty creations of Allah and the astonishing phenomena active in the nature.

S:Al-Baqara-2:32

(Already quoted in the 4th chapter):- "They (Angels) said "Glory to thee; of knowledge we have none save Thou has taught us, in truth, It is Thou Who are perfect in knowledge and Wisdom."

S:An-aam:6:103:

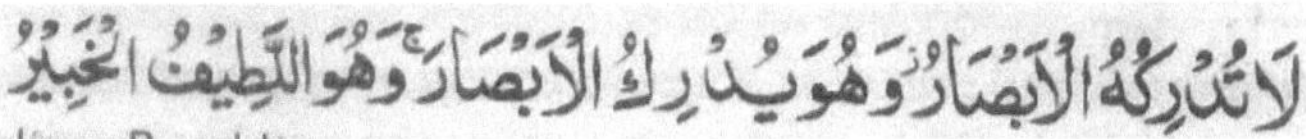

Tr:- No vision can grasp Him. But His grasp is over all vision: He is above all comprehension; yet is acquinted with all things.

After making mentions of astounding deeds of Allah, the poet has concluded this Stanza by confessing human ignorance about the Divine secrets and by glorifying the greatness of Allah.

In the 25th Stanza of the text, the poet has referred to the measured and regulated revolution of the heavenly bodies, beautified by the proper proportion and Divine arrangements. In case the heavenly bodies are a bit out of place or transgress the orbital limits, they may collide and make a mess of the universe. The Quranic Stanza 87:2-5 already quoted in this Chapter describe the above mentioned wonders of God. The person who remarks defect in the Divine administration is unfortunate for having submerged themself into bigotry. The Quranic Stanza 2:29 (already quoted in the first chapter) describes the design and order given to Allah's creations by Him.

Q-S:Al-Baqara-2:29:- "It is He Who has created for you all things that are on earth. Moreover, His design comprehended the heavens, for He gave order and perfection to the seven firmaments and of all things He has perfect knowledge.

It is a great blunder to doubt any defect in the regulated arrangements of the creation of Allah. It is our bounden duty to realise the inestimable bounties of Allah, comprehend the perfection of creations and admire the Divine Administration.

Stanza: 26.

26- بزم ہستی سے ابھی واقف بہت کم ہیں بشر

وسعت کونین ہے کب اس کی محسوب نظر

مصلحت ذرہ کی وابستہ شمس و قمر

ہے خدائے پاک ہی کو سارے عالم کی خبر

اور ہی جلوے حقیقت کے ہوں انسان پر عیاں

وہ نگاہ رب سے گر دیکھے زمین و آسماں

Tr:- Human beings are very little aware of the facts or secrets of the universe. Man can never calculate the expansive extension of heavens and earth. The sun and the moon connections with atom which is pregnant of God's prudence. Allah only knows the complete truth about the whole universe. If human beings explore the heavens and the earth acquiring a little of Divine Wisdom and Divine Knowledge, the truth about the universe appear to be different.

C - In this Stanza, the poet has pointed out the limitations of human knowledge. Om Science of Allah (All knowing) and the importance of the atom.

Scientists have made several discoveries pertaining to the natural phenomena, the creation of heavens and earth and still have in their schemes several discoveries to be made. Of course, with permission of Allah man has acquired a fund of knowledge. But it is nothing when compared to the Divine knowledge. This universe is a huge reservoir of Divine knowledge.

Inspite of numerous discoveries and advancement of science, no scientist has yet attempted and will never attempt to measure the expanse of the universe, because, he knows that it is beyond human capacity.

Sun, moon and all other matters are composed of atoms which consist of electricity (electrons and protons) Electric energy is required for each and every activity of all the creations of Allah. Without electric energy the whole phenomena of nature will come to a standstill. Hence the poet lays emphasis on the importance which is full of advisability and Divine prudence.

Islam urges us to acquire as much knowledge as possible and also explore the scope for acquiring knowledge by hard studies and hectic researches.

The poet also exhorts us to acquire a little of the Divine knowledge which will disclose a few secrets of the universe and make things appear to be different. This knowledge is sure to persuade us to extol the glory and greatness of Allah.

Stanza: 27

27 ۔ ذرہ ذرہ حکمت کامل کا ہے آئینہ دار

مصلحت کی بجلیاں ہر چیز میں ہے بیقرار

کونسی سے شئے میں نہیں بیتاب مقصد کے شرار

میں جدھر دیکھوں ادھر ہے جلوہ پروردگار

دیدہ کوتاہ بیں پر کفر کی بنیاد ہے

نور ایماں سے دلِ اہل نظر آباد ہے

بند نمبر 27 کیلئے فٹ نوٹس-:

پورب ہو یا پچّھم ساری دنیا اللہ ہی کے لئے ہے ۔ جہاں کہیں بھی تم اللہ کی طرف رخ کر لو تو اللہ تمہارے سامنے ہے ۔ بلا شبہ اس کی قدرت کی سمائی بڑی ہی سمائی ہے اور وہ سب جاننے والا ہے ۔(البقرہ :2 :115)

Tr: - Every atom is a proof for the perfect wisdom of Allah. In everything the lights of advisability are restless to be displayed. Nothing is devoid of the sparks of some or other restless purpose. Where ever I see, I see the presence of Allah. The wrong vision which does not see the truth is based on infidelity. The enlightened vision which sees the truth, is based on the light of true faith.

C:- In these stanzas the poet has described the Omni-Presence of Allah and the perfect wisdom of Allah which is proved by every atom contained in the matter. There is some purpose or other in every creation and every deed of Allah which man cannot understand. Allah has said in Quran that He did not create things for idle sports but He did it with some definite purpose. Manifestations of Allah are seen in all directions which disclose the fact that Allah is Omni-Present, ie. All-Pervading.

Q. S:Al-Baqara-2:115 (already quoted in the 9th chapter) explains that Allah is seen in all directions "To Allah belongs the East and the West; withersoever you turn, there is the presence of Allah. For, Allah is All-Pervading, All-knowing."

The acquisition of Divine knowledge and realisation of facts enlighten the true faith. Strengthening of the faith of the worshippers is one of the purposes of Allah in creating distanza things and leaving scope for the realisation of Allah's Potency. More and more enlightenment of faith is essential for all believers at all times.

Stanza: 28.

28 ۔ یک تصور ہے خدا کا یہ جہان سنگ و خشت

ایک روحانی حقیقت ہے ہر یک شئے کی سرشت

ہر اشارہ ہے ریاض دہر کا سوئے بہشت

ہے حسین سارا جہاں ناپید ہے ناخوب و زشت

حکمت کامل پہ قائم دہر کی بنیاد ہے

جلوہ مقصد سے ہر سینہ یہاں آباد ہے

Tr:- This material world composed of stones and bricks is only imaginary. The nature or essence of everything which is transitory speaks about the truth that it is created by the effulgence of Allah. Anything repulsive or ugly is absent in this beautiful world. Every sign in the garden of this world shows us the direction of paradise. The foundation or origin of this world is the result of the perfect Wisdom of God. The heart of every man is full of desires to achieve its goal namely God or the pleasure of God.

C:- This material world made of stones and bricks and created by God for a limited time has no significance at all. As this universe is transitory and the span of its life is very short, its importance is only imaginary. Though the significance of the creations is temporary, it must be remembered, that the main essence incorporated in the creations are nothing but the effulgence of God. Though Allah has decreed a certain period of life for his creations, He is Eternal. By saying that the signs in this world show direction of paradise, the poet means to say that the march of time and the development of every creation explain the end of everything. Every creation has death or destruction. The short span of its life is decreed by God. We have seen several comets disappear after giving a streak of light. Sura-e-Infitaar is full of descriptions of the Day of the Doom (Qiyamah) and the Day of Judgement (Hashr). The Day of Doom will be dealt with in detail in the 16th chapter.

In this world some creations will appear to be beautiful and some ugly. But for the vision which sees the truth, every creation appears to be beautiful in its own place, the reason being that every creation contains the beauty of the effulgence of God. The origin of this universe owes only to the perfect wisdom of Allah. The Goal (Allah) or His pleasure can be obtained only through love for and glorification of Allah. Allah has revealed in Quran that the heavens, the earth and all the creations (both) animate and inanimate glorify Him.

S: Bani Israil-17:44:- "The seven heavens and the earth and all beings in between them declare His (God's) glory. There is not a thing but celebrate His praise; and yet ye understand not how they declare His Glory. Verily He is often forgiving." Hence the poet says that every creation is prone to reach the stage of perfection by achieving the Goal through love for and glorification of God.

When even inanimate things declare the glory of God, it is the first and foremost duty of human being whom God has created in the best form, to glorify God and attain the spiritual perfection by merging with God. In Quran Allah has reminded man of His special blessings showered on him.

S: Infitaar-82:6-8:

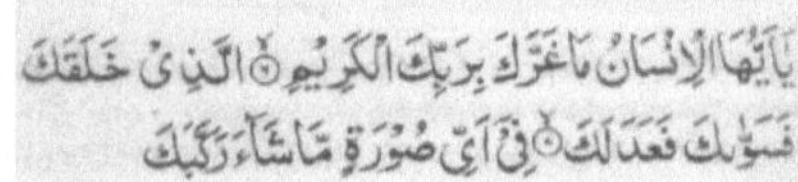

Tr:-O Man! What has seduced thee from thy Lord, Most Beneficent-Him Who created thee; fashioned thee in the proportion and gave thee a just bias; in whatever form He wills does He put thee together."

Allah reminds man of His first act of grace towards him, namely His moulding in such an upright, perfectly proportioned shape. Allah would have given him any form he wished. Yet man is ungrateful. The address of Allah, appeals to man's noble quality, his humanity, his power of reasoning, rationality, power of speech which distinguish him from all other creations, and assigns to him the highest position among them. The highest position of man represents the greatest blessing to man and his abundant generosity to him.

The miraculous aspects in man's constitution are far greater than he sees all around him and what he can imagine. Perfection and the right balance are easily evident in man's physical, mental and spiritual constitution. For having showered unique bounties on man having the power of speech, Allah expects him to extol His glory more than the speechless creations. Having received from Allah, the precious gift of soul, man can obtain spiritual perfection, and can get absorbed in God, his final goal.

Stanza: 29

29 عقل ہی وہ کیا نہیں جو عاشق رب کریم

عشق ہی وہ کیا جو سر تاپا نہیں عقل سلیم

عشق ہے خود معرفت سرچشمہ خلق عظیم

عشق و حکمت کا ہے جلوہ نور قرآن حکیم

دین بے حکمت جنون خام ہے اوہام ہے

پر تو الہام میں تنویر عقل تام ہے۔

Tr:- It is not 'wisdom' which is devoid of love for the magnanimous Cherisher namely Allah. It is not at all love which is devoid of perfect wisdom. Love itself is the fountain of Divine knowledge for the highest creation namely human being. The real love and perfect wisdom could only be realised through the philosophical scripture, Quran. Any religion without wisdom is nothing but wrong and insane notions and superstitions. The light of inspiration produces the light of perfect knowledge.

C:- Love is of two kinds. Firstly, the love for lust and unlawful desires. Secondly the love for God which is enjoined upon human beings by religion. The real love for God is most beneficial to humanity in this world and hereafter. Love for God is the fountain for Divine knowledge for human being which has been bestowed by God with power of reasoning 5:17 Quran has been called Kitaabum-Mubeen i.e. Light of Guidance Quran itself provides. the light and clear interpretations for love and wisdom. Hence this Holy Book has been defined Quran-e-HakimWhich means a philosophical Scripture or a Book of Wisdom. Now it is which indispensable to explain why it is called so.

Some Definitions of Quran:

Surah-e-Huud-11:1:

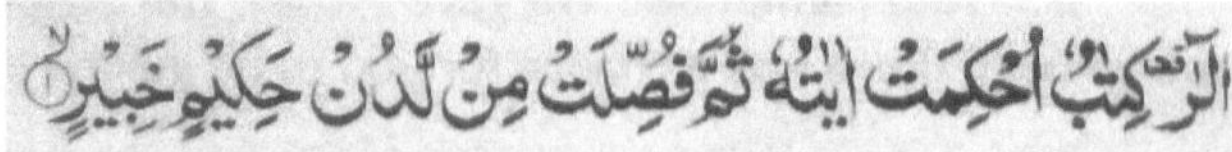

Tr:- A.L.Ra. "This is a book with Further explained in detail This is a book with Stanzas basic or fundamental (of established meaning) in detail from One Who is Wise and Well-acquainted with all things)."

b. Sura-e-Furqaan-25:1:

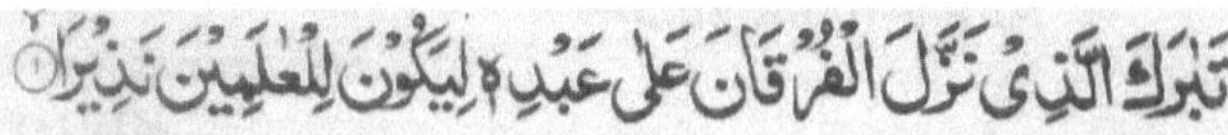

Tr:-"Blessed is He Who sent down the Criterion to his servant (Prophet Muhammed)that may be an admonition to all creatures."

In this verse Quran has been defined as Furqaan which means criterion.

c. Sura-e-Ibrahim-14:0:

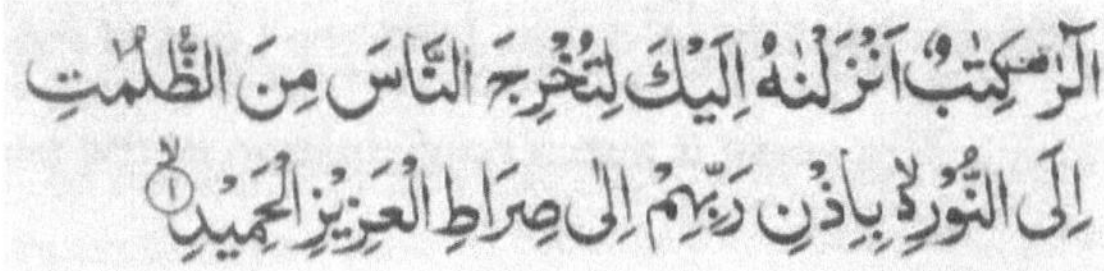

Tr:-B Book which we have revealed unto thee, in order that thou mightest lead mankind out of the depths of darkness into light-by the leave of their Lord to the Way of (Him) exalted in Power worthy of all praise."

The above mentioned verses describe Quran by its definitions. Now the Divine as incorporated in the Holy Quran must be confirmed. For such confirmation, the following Quranic verses is presented.

d. Sura-e-Nisaa- 4:82:

Tr:- "Do they not consider the Quran with care? Had it been from other than Allah, they would surely have found therein much discrepancy."

Now the purposes of Allah in revealing the Quran must be enumerated.

a. Sura-e-A'raaf-7:2

كِتَابٌ اُنْزِلَ اِلَيْكَ فَلَا يَكُنْ فِيْ صَدْرِكَ حَرَجٌ مِّنْهُ لِتُنْذِرَ بِهِ وَذِكْرٰى لِلْمُؤْمِنِيْنَ ۞

Tr:- "A book revealed unto thee-so let thy heart be oppressed no more by difficulty on that account that with it thou mightest warn the (erring) and teach the believers."

The above verse elucidates the purpose of Allah in revealing the Quran as benefiting, admonishing and enlightening the minds of human beings.

b. One of the purposes of Allah in revealing Quran was confirmation of the and previous scriptures.

Sura-e-Baqara-2:53:

وَاِذْ اٰتَيْنَا مُوْسَى الْكِتٰبَ وَالْفُرْقَانَ لَعَلَّكُمْ تَهْتَدُوْنَ ۞

Tr.- "And remember, We gave Moses, the Scripture and the Criterion (he and wrong): there was a chance for you to be guided aright."

The above quoted verse confirms the prophethood of Moosa-Alaihissalam scripture Torah revealed to him by Allah.

c. Sura-e-Yunus- 10:37:

وَمَا كَانَ هٰذَا الْقُرْاٰنُ اَنْ يُّفْتَرٰى مِنْ دُوْنِ اللهِ

Tr:- "This Quran is not such as can be produced by other than Allah. On the cont is a confirmation of (revelations) that went before it, and a fuller explanation of the wherein there is no doubt-from the Lord of the worlds."

This verse is also a confirmation of the previous scriptures.

Al-Baqara-2:253-Part of the Verse:

تِلْكَ الرُّسُلُ فَضَّلْنَا بَعْضَهُمْ عَلَىٰ بَعْضٍ مِّنْهُم مَّن كَلَّمَ اللَّهُ وَرَفَعَ بَعْضَهُمْ دَرَجَاتٍ وَآتَيْنَا عِيسَى ابْنَ مَرْيَمَ الْبَيِّنَاتِ وَأَيَّدْنَاهُ بِرُوحِ الْقُدُسِ

Tr:- "Those Apostles, We endowed with gifts, some above others. To one of them Allah spoke; others He raised to degrees (of honour); to Jesus, the son of Mary we gave clear (signs) and strengthened him with the Holy Spirit."

This verse is the confirmation for having sent previous Apostles including Jesus Christ.

Sura -e-Nisaa - 4:163:

إِنَّا أَوْحَيْنَا إِلَيْكَ كَمَا أَوْحَيْنَا إِلَىٰ نُوحٍ وَالنَّبِيِّينَ مِن بَعْدِهِ وَأَوْحَيْنَا إِلَىٰ إِبْرَاهِيمَ وَإِسْمَاعِيلَ وَإِسْحَاقَ وَيَعْقُوبَ وَالْأَسْبَاطِ وَعِيسَىٰ وَأَيُّوبَ وَيُونُسَ وَهَارُونَ وَسُلَيْمَانَ وَآتَيْنَا دَاوُودَ زَبُورًا

Tr:- "We have sent inspiration as we sent it to Noah and the messengers after him. We sent inspiration to Abraham, Isma'il, Issac, Jacob and the tribes; to Jesus, Job, Jonah, Aaron and Solomon and to David We gave the Psalms."

This verse serves as confirmation for sending past prophets and some Apostles to whom Books were revealed, and for revealing Psalms i.e. Zaboor to Apostle Dawood Alaihis-Salam.

Another purpose of Almighty Allah is to correct His messages revealed in Bible and The Christians and the Jews adulterated, and corrupted, the wordings according to whims and fancies. Their undesirable activities were the root causes for their split into ant sects having diverse religious concepts. There are several omissions and additions in their scriptures.

Sura e-Maaida 5:15.- (Only part of the verse)

وَمِنَ الَّذِينَ قَالُوٓا إِنَّا نَصَارَىٰٓ أَخَذْنَا مِيثَاقَهُمْ فَنَسُوا حَظًّا مِّمَّا ذُكِّرُوا بِهِۦ فَأَغْرَيْنَا بَيْنَهُمُ الْعَدَاوَةَ وَالْبَغْضَآءَ إِلَىٰ يَوْمِ الْقِيَامَةِ ۚ وَسَوْفَ يُنَبِّئُهُمُ اللَّهُ بِمَا كَانُوا يَصْنَعُونَ ۝

Tr- "From those too who call themselves Christians, We did take a covenant, but they forgot a good part of the message that was sent to them."

The above-mentioned Verse clearly informs us that there are several omissions from the Divine messages revealed for Bible.

Sura-e-Maaida: - 5:16-

يَٰٓأَهْلَ الْكِتَٰبِ قَدْ جَآءَكُمْ رَسُولُنَا يُبَيِّنُ لَكُمْ كَثِيرًا مِّمَّا كُنتُمْ تُخْفُونَ مِنَ الْكِتَٰبِ وَيَعْفُوا عَن كَثِيرٍ ۚ

Tr: "O People (Christians and Jews) of the Book, there hath come to you our Apostle (Prophet Muhammad), revealing to you much that ye used to hide in the book, and passing over much that is now unnecessary)".

This verse hints at both the omissions and additions in Bible and Torah.

Sura-e-Maaida -5:17

قَدْ جَآءَكُم مِّنَ اللَّهِ نُورٌ وَكِتَٰبٌ مُّبِينٌ ۝

Tri- "There has come to you from Allah a (new) light and a perspicuous Book (Quran)."

This verse means to explain that Quran was revealed to ward off and dispel the adulterations and corruptions undergone in Bible and Torah.

Some of the most important purposes of Allah in revealing Quran were to reform the world society, complete His messages through the last Prophet Muhammad, establish the permanent and last religion and grant the prayers of Ibrahim Alaihis-Salaam for the revival of their religion Islam and rehearsal of Allah's signs through their progeny.

Sura-e-Baqara-2:127:

وَإِذْ يَرْفَعُ إِبْرَٰهِمُ الْقَوَاعِدَ مِنَ الْبَيْتِ وَإِسْمَٰعِيلُ رَبَّنَا تَقَبَّلْ مِنَّا إِنَّكَ أَنْتَ السَّمِيعُ الْعَلِيمُ ۝

Tr:- "And remember Abraham and Isma'il raised the foundation of the House (Kabathullah) with this prayer "O Lord! Accept (this service) from us for thou art the All-Hearing and All-Knowing".

This verse gives us information about their supplication to Allah to accept their services of constructing Ka'bathullah

Sura-e-Baqara-2: 128

رَبَّنَا وَاجْعَلْنَا مُسْلِمَيْنِ لَكَ وَمِن ذُرِّيَّتِنَا أُمَّةً مُّسْلِمَةً لَّكَ

Tri "Our Lord! Make us Muslims bowing to Thy (Will) and of our progeny a Muslims bowing to Thy (Will), and show us our places for the celebration of due) turn unto us (in Mercy) for Thou art the oft-returning and Most Merciful."

In this verse Abraham and his son have requested Allah to name their religion Islam that their progen might be called

Muslims. They have also requested Allah to teach the method of solemnizing the religious rites.

Sura-e-Baqara-2:129:

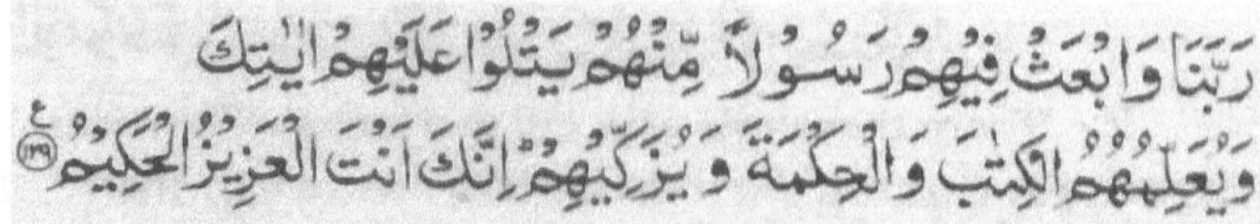

Tr:- "Our Lord! send among them (Muslim) an Apostle of their own, who shall rehearse Thy signs to them and instruct them in scripture and Wisdom and sanctify them for Thou a the Exalted in Might the Wise."

The above quoted verse informs us that Abraham prayed to Allah along with his elder son Isma'il to send an Apostle from among the Muslims, their progeny and reveal to him a scripture for the revival of Islam and the rehearsal of Allah's signs.

Al-Baqara-2:132:

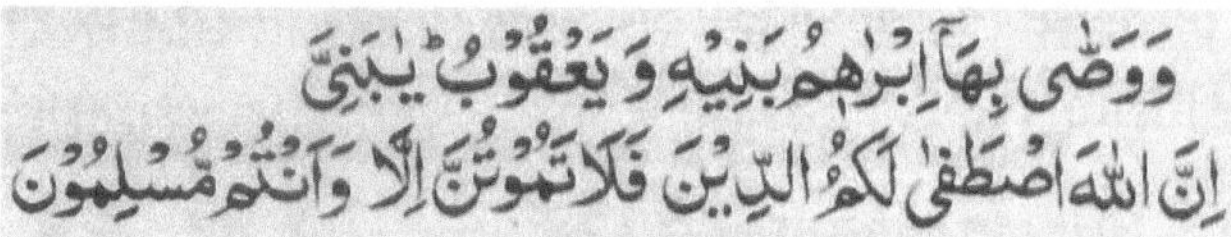

Tr: "And this was the legacy that Abraham left to his sons and so did Jacob "O my sons! Allah hath chosen the faith for you. Then die not except in the faith of Islam."

This verse reveals that Allah had complied with the request of Ibrahim Alaihis-Salaam and Isma'il Alaihis-Salaam by naming their religion Islam and its followers Muslims. In this verse Yaqoob Alaihis-Salaam advised his sons to be Muslims and die as Muslims. Yaqoob AlaihisSalaam was the son of Ishaq Alaihis-Salaam (Isaac), son of Ibrahim Alaihis-Salaam. The word 'Islam' for their religion lasted till the expiry of Yusuf

Alaihis-Salaam, son of Yaqoob AlaihisSalaam, because all the twelve tribes of Bani Israil had to suffer a lot under the suppression, oppression, tyranny and despotism of the Pharaos of Egypt. They could not call their religion as Islam and thus this word went out of usage.

In compliance of the desires of Ibrahim Alaihis-Salaam and Isma'il Alaihis-Salaam, Allah chose Prophet Muhammad (PBUH) from among the progeny of Ismail Alaihis-Salaam and revealed to him Quran for the revival of Islam and rehearsal of Allah's signs. Now the great purpose of Allah in revealing Quran is quite clear.

To sum up, the purposes of Allah in revealing the Quran are the confirmation about the truth of its own revelation, confirmation of the past prophets, confirmation of the previous scriptures, warding off and dispelling of the adulterations and corruptions in the previous scriptures and fulfilling the desires of Ibrahim Alaihis-Salaam and Isma'il Alaihis-Salaam by sending the last prophet from among their progeny and establishing the permanent religion Islam.

After acquiring some knowledge about specific definitions of Quran and specific purposesof its revelation, it is necessary to have some general knowledge about Quran in order to judge the reasonability of calling it a Book of Wisdom.

The first Sura revealed for Quran, Sura-e-Alaq was revealed in the cave of Hira on the 6th of August 610 A.D.. i.e. 27th night of Ramzan, twelve years before Hiirat.

Al-Baqara-2:185:- (part of the Stanza):-

شَهْرُ رَمَضَانَ الَّذِىٓ اُنْزِلَ فِيهِ الْقُرْاٰنُ هُدًى لِّلنَّاسِ وَ
بَيِّنٰتٍ مِّنَ الْهُدٰى وَالْفُرْقَانِ

T:-"Ramadhan is the (month) in which was sent down the Quran as a guide to mankind,also clear (signs) for guidance and judgement (between right and wrong)".

prophet Muhammad (PBUH) obtained prophethood and received the first revelation 6 months after he had completed the age of forty years according to lunar calendar and he just begun his 40th year according to solar calendar Quran contains 114 suras which have classified as Makki suras, revealed in Makkah and Madani Suras, revealed in Madinah after Hijrat (Migrations).

The first chapter Sura-e-Fatiha makes the readers to supplicate with Allah to lead them the path of righteousness. In the last Sura An-Naas, He makes the readers request Him to protect them from evil. It must be noted that the Holy Quran starts and ends with supplications and requests of man which interpret the injunctions and prohibitions of Islam.

The suras were revealed by Allah according to the urgent need and emergency of the situations. In Quran the suras have been arranged according to the instructions of our Holy Prophet in view of the continuity of subject matter. For example, Sura-e-Alaq was the first one revealed in Makkah, the serial number of which in Quran is 96. Sura-e-Malaida was the last one revealed both in Madinah and Makkah in 10 A.H. three months before the expiry of Holy Prophet. Its serial number in Quran is 5. Consequently the Makkhi suras revealed before Hiirat and the Madani suras revealed after Hijrat have been mixed up. The last Stanza was revealed to our Prophet at

Makkah in 10 A.H. during his last pilgrimage (Hajjatu -Wida) informing him that Allah has completed the bounties, and His messages and chosen the name "Islam" for this religion.

Sura-e-Ma'aida-5:3:- (part of the verse):--

حُرِّمَتْ عَلَيْكُمُ الْمَيْتَةُ وَالدَّمُ وَ لَحْمُ الْخِنْزِيرِ وَمَا أُهِلَّ لِغَيْرِ اللهِ بِهِ وَالْمُنْخَنِقَةُ وَالْمَوْقُوذَةُ وَالْمُتَرَدِّيَةُ وَالنَّطِيحَةُ وَمَا أَكَلَ السَّبُعُ إِلَّا مَا ذَكَّيْتُمْ وَ مَا ذُبِحَ عَلَى النُّصُبِ وَأَنْ تَسْتَقْسِمُوا بِالْأَزْلَامِ ذَلِكُمْ فِسْقٌ الْيَوْمَ يَئِسَ الَّذِينَ كَفَرُوا مِنْ دِينِكُمْ فَلَا تَخْشَوْهُمْ وَ اخْشَوْنِ الْيَوْمَ أَكْمَلْتُ لَكُمْ دِينَكُمْ وَأَتْمَمْتُ عَلَيْكُمْ نِعْمَتِي وَرَضِيتُ لَكُمُ الْإِسْلَامَ دِينًا فَمَنِ اضْطُرَّ فِي مَخْمَصَةٍ غَيْرَ مُتَجَانِفٍ لِإِثْمٍ فَإِنَّ اللهَ غَفُورٌ رَحِيمٌ

Tr:- "This day I have perfected your religion for you; completed my favour upon you and have chosen for you Islam as your religion".

This last verse revealed in Makkah has been included in Sura-e-Ma'aida revealed in Madina.

An interesting fact has to be observed here. During the course of constructing Kabathullah Ibrahim Alaihis-Salaam and Isma'il Alaihis Salaam had requested Allah to name their religion Islam and send a Messenger from among their progeny for revival of Islam and for the rehearsal of Allah's signs. Ibrahim Alaihis Salaam got ready to sacrifice his only son Ismail who was fully prepared to sacrifice his life for the sake of Allah. Allah loved them dearly. In compliance with their request, Allah bestowed prophethood on Muhammad (PBUH) who was the descendant of Ismail Alaihis-Salaam, revived their true religion Islam for the rehearsal of His signs. It is a notable point that Ibrahim Alaihis Salaam and Isma'il Alaihis-Salaam requested Allah that their religion should be called Islam and its followers be called Muslims. The verse 5:4 clearly says that the name Islam for the religion of Prophet Muhammad (PBUH) was chosen by Allah on His own accord without the request of our Prophet. This was because Allah wished to satisfy the desires of his beloved messengers Ibrahim (A.S.) and Ismail (A.S.).

Our Prophet is the preceptor while the guidance contained in the Holy Quran is the Divine Law (Shari'at). Quran promises success in this world and hereafter to those people who follow its Divine principles. Quran has exclusively prescribed codes of conduct, codes of morality, human ethics which include injuctions and prohibitions. It has provided data for studies which facilitate the scope for all sorts of researches, discoveries and inventions Quran provides information's, from the creation of soul, fertilization of Ovum, development of the foetus in the mother's Woinb (Embryology), life in this world and life hereafter ie the complete sojourn of temporary life in this world and the eternal spiritual life hereafter. Quran has not omitted any message which is necessary for the successful life of man and other creations. The scrutiny of the following two verses will prove the fact.

Sura Am'aam-6:38:

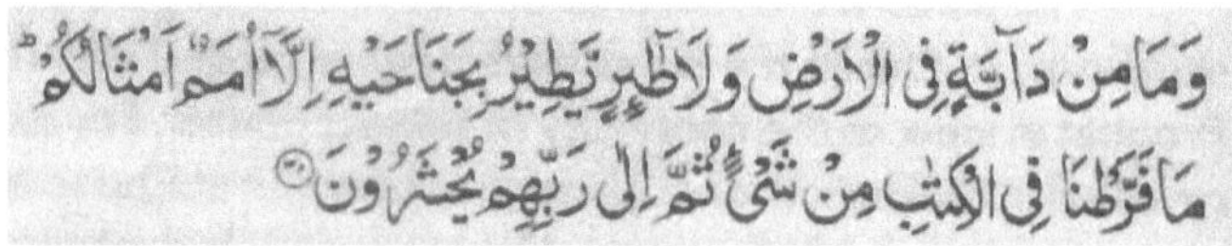

Tr- "There is not an animal (that lives) on the earth, not a being that flies on its wings but (forms part of communities like you. Nothing We have omitted from the Book, and they all) shall be gathered to their Lord in the end."

Sura-e-Anbiyaa-21:106:

إِنَّ فِى هٰذَا لَبَلَاغًا لِّقَوْمٍ عٰبِدِينَ

Tr:- "Verily in the (Quran) is a message for people who would (truly) worship Allah."

Islam is not merely a religion of worship but a complete code of conduct for man. Quran has summarized the philosophy of the noblest life.

The word 'Quran' literally means 'A Book to be read'. It is derived from the word 'Iqra'which means 'read' Quran claims to be the complete, absolute and unaltered communication from the single Supreme Power (Allah)and which has been incorporated with brief information's about the universe. The Holy Quran claims that its contents are scientifically valid. Some 1425 years back, people could not understand the importance of Quranic verses which led to several of knowledge, the scope of science proved to be valid consistent to several controversies. With the march of time, advance of civilization and promotion doe the scientists were induced to extract data from Ouran do research and explore science in universe. With the advance of science, the Quranic Verses are being be valid one by one. In the future still more verses will be found to be scientifically Consistent.

Quran is a Book of warnings and admonitions and a Book of guidance. When Allah has Provided man with every guidance, it is the man's duty to ponder over the Eternal Truth, tread of righteousness and must be most mindful about the everlasting spiritual life in the light of Quranic Warnings. Quran is a Book of Truth revealed with the purpose of perishing and dispelling falsehood from the world society.

Surah Bani Isra'il-17:81:

Tr. And say "Truth has now arrived and Falshood perished; for Falsehood is (by its nature) bound to perish."

THE AMANUENSES OF REVELATIONS (KATIBEEN-E-WAHI). Prophet Muhammad (PBUH) received Divine revelations from God for 22 years and 3 months since he attained prophethood in 610 A.D. i.e. twelve years before Hijrat. Our Prophet was quite unlettered. Whoever was available among his companions obliged him by recording the revelations. There were several companions who were the scribes of the Holy Quran. Among them about 25 were great contributors. Among those twenty-five companions, some were most prominent and they were as follows:

1. Hazrat Abu Bakr Siddiq.
2. Hazrat Umar Bin Al-Khattah
3. Hazrat Usman Bin Affaan.
4. Hazrat Ali Bin Abi Talib.
5. Hazrat Khalid Bin Thabit.
6. Hazrat Khalid Bin Waleed.
7. Hazrat Ma'awia Bin Abu Sufyan.
8. Hazrat Khalid Bin Sayeed Bin Abi Al-Aus.
9. Hazrat Amr Bin Al-Aus.
10. Hazrat Ubai Bin Kaab.

(The few names of the Katibeen enumerated above were extracted from Maja-uz-Zawa).

It is said that Hazrat Khalid Bin Sayeed was the fortunate companion of our Prophet who scribed the first revelation with 'Bismillah'. He was the 5th man to embrace Islam. The last

Wahi revealed to our Prophet was recorded by Hazrat Ubai Bin Kaab.

Quranic verses have been revealed in the poetic style so that people might be attracted by its Qir'at, the musical recitation of Quran. Before embracing Islam, the idolators of Makkah rejected the truth of the Divine revelations by saying that Quran was authored by literate persons and its verses were composed by eminent poets. At this situation the following Verso was revealed with the Divine challenge to the idolators to write a like sura.

Sura-e-Baqara-2:23-

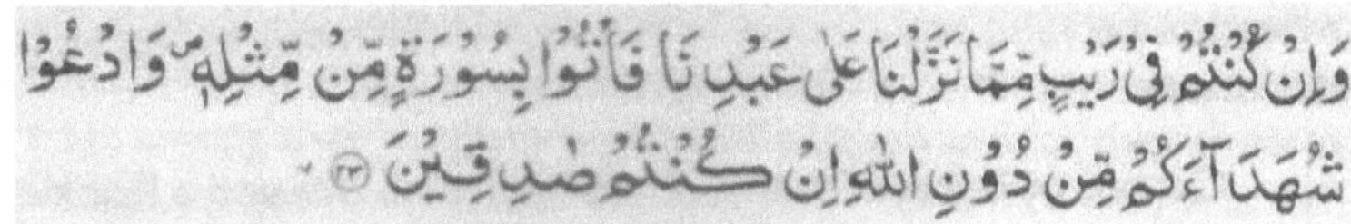

Tr:- "And if ye are in doubt as to what we have revealed from time to time to Our servant, then produce a sura like thereunto, and call your witnesses or helpers (if there are any) besides Allah, if your (doubts) are true."

In Sura Huud-11:13. Allah instructs our Prophet to throw such challenge to them. Every time the idolators were defeated in the challenge.

The idolators of Makkah rediculed our Prophet for his illiteracy and said "Oh Muhammad. ask your Allah to reveal a sura in which the Arabic alphabet 'Meem' should not be used." Allah accepted their challenge and revealed Sura-e-Kausar (Sura No: 108). According to Divine inspiration Prophet Muhammad wrote the first line of the sura on the wall of the Ka'abathullah and threw his challenge to them to compose a line suitable to its import. After failing to do so. inspite of great attempts, the Makkains sent for the most efficient scholar and greatest poet of Arabian Peninsula, who could not meet the challenge. He got convinced that it was the true revelation from Allah. He wrote below the line "Ma Haaza Qowlul Bashar" meaning that it was not the word of human being. It is very interesting to observe that the poet's reply started with the letter "Meem". It was a great defeat to the Makkains who felt extremely ashamed. One can observe that out of the 114 suras of Quran, Sura-e-Kausar is the only one in which the alphabet "Meem" has not been used.

Inspite of being an illiterate Apostle, Our Prophet learnt the Quran by heart. It was after the completion of the revelations and perfection of our religion Angel Jibra'il recited Quran twice to our Prophet in the present serial order of the suras.

After the expiry of our Prophet and during the Caliphate of Hazrat Abu Bakr, the Muslims incurred a heavy loss of life in the Battle of Yamamah. Among the martyres most of them were those who had the manuscripts of different Verses of Quran in their custody and who remembered the Verses by heart. At this serious situation, Hazrat Umar pointed out the urgency and emergency of compiling the Quran in the form of a book, the Verses of which were scattered here and there. Khalifa Abu Bakr assigned this noble duty to Hazrat Zaid Bin Haris. With absolute carefulness, he started the hectic task of compiling Quran with the help of the companions of the Apostle who had contributed in scribing the revelations.

During the reign of Hazrat Umar, he conquered many countries and the Islamic empire became very Vast. During the Caliphate of Hazrat Usman, he had numerous copies of Quran calligraphed and sent them to different countries. As a result, thousands of Hafizes (persons who learnt Quran by heart) emerged in Islamic Empire. There was also a large number of Women Hafizes, among whom Bi Bi A'aisha, the daughter of Hazrat Abu Bakr and third wife of our Prophet, was one. Even small children were able to easily memorise Quran. In India Princess Zaibunnisa, the daughter of the mighty Mughal Emperor Aurangazeb, memorised Quran at the age of six years. Was it not miraculous?

Some of the miracles of Quran are as follows.

a. The contents of Quran and pronunciation of its words are still unaltered, unadulterated and uncorrupted. According to Allah's promise, they will continue to be so till the Day of the Doom.

b. The greatest scholars and poets of Arabia were defeated in the challenges thrown to them by Almighty Allah and His Apostle.

c. The challenge thrown by the idolators of Makkah was won by Allah who revealed Sura-e-Kausar without the letter "Meem"

d. Quran is being easily memorised even by small children if attempted.

Quran has been given the name Al-Furqaan because this word means, the Scripture which enables us to discriminate between the scales of values, pointing out which, acts are good, better and best and which ones are bad, worse and worst, and the Virtues and Vices which are great, greater and greatest. All these qualities of Quran explain that it opens its doors to all the human beings who can choose their own conduct and way of life.

Quran is the last scripture revealed for the last religion Islam through our last Apostle Muhammad (PBUH). It has succeeded in guiding the whole human race in all aspects of life, social, religious, economic, political, educational, cultural, judicial, legislative etc. In Sura-eMaa'ida Allah has said that He has completed His message to humanity and perfected the religion for the Muslims. Hence Quran is the last Testament of Allah.

This Last Testament is incorporated with the stories of the past prophets, their sufferings and miracles, and the Divine Laws (Shari'at) regarding all aspects of life.

While explaining the wisdom contained in Quran, Daleel Sahib says that the religion without wisdom and which is based on superstitions is nothing but insanity. The true religion is that which is the result of Divine inspiration.

Superstition is troublesome for human life. It is the excessive reverence and fear for imaginary factors based on ignorance. It is the excessive exaction in religious opinions or practices It is an irrational and ignorant belief in natural agencies and omens. It is the divination of creations based on morbid belief.

When a cat passes across the way the superstitious people take it for granted that it is a bad omen which makes them stop and waste their time. In case, a snake passes across the way from right to left, it is a bad omen in their opinion; and if it passes from left to right, it is a good omen for them. These people think that particular times are auspicious for solemnizing ceremonies and some particular times are inauspicious which will entail calamities. Inspite of other conveniences, they abstain from holding functions at these times. These people forget that destiny is controlled by one Supreme Power, God, and destiny can never be altered by the particular times and the movements of the animals.

The Pantheists and Politheists worship the nature and several dieties. They believe that different Gods have different and specific powers. They even personify some of their dieties as females. According to their belief, Weddings took place among their Gods and Goddesses and they procreated. If they married and procreated, what is the difference between the Creator and His Creations and the Worshipped and the Worshippers? In the following, some Quranic Verses have been quoted regarding such superstitions:

Sura An-Najm-53:19, 20, 21, 22:

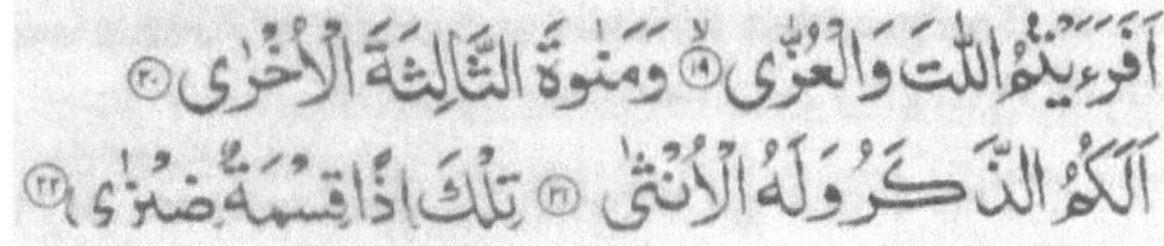

Tr:- "Have ye seen Laat and Uzza (names of gods). And another the third (goddess) Manaat? What! For you the male sex and for him. the female? Behold, such would be indeed a division, most unfair."

These are all false notions and superstitions which make the religion corrupted and adulterated. That is why Daleel Sahib has said that religion based on superstitions and false notions, is nothing but insanity.

What is inspiration? Inspiration is the Divine instruction and superior influence infused into the minds of human being. It is the Divine influence by which the sacred writers of scriptures were instructed. It is the superior, elevating and exciting influence from Divinity by which true religions were descended conveying the same messages. In Quranic Stanza 4:163 (already quoted) inspiration has been referred to. In the Stanza 4:163 Allah has named eleven of his prophets to whom He sent inspiration and has said that He gifted the inspired Book Psalms (Zaboor) to Prophet David (PBUH).About Quran Allah says:

Sura An-Najm-53:4:

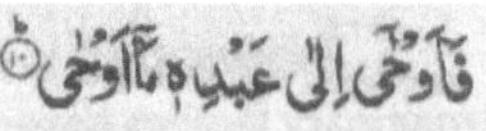

Tr:- "It (revelation of Quran) is no-less than inspiration, sent down to him (Prophet Muhammad)"

Sura An-Najm-53:10:

فَاَوْحٰٓى اِلٰى عَبْدِهٖ مَآ اَوْحٰى ۞

Tr:-"So did (Allah) convey the inspiration to His Servant - (conveyed) what He (meant) to convey".

Now it is clear that Holy Quran is an inspired Book revealed to Prophet Muhammad free from superstition and incorporated by true religion Islam.

Taking into account the contents the purposes, qualities, and miracles of our Scripture, all Muslims will justify in calling it a Book of Wisdom which means Quran-e-Hakim. (Quranic concept of inspiration and superstition).

CHAPTER - XIII

BELIEF IN UNITY OF GOD

Stanza:-30

13 /توحید

30۔ یہ زمیں مہر و مہ انجم ہیں جو گرم سفر

سرعت رفتار سے ہے جنکی حیرت میں بشر

زیر فرماں ایک ہستی کے نہوں گا اگر

محفل کون و مکاں ہو اُن میں زیر و زبر

انکی گردش میں ہویدا نغم توحید ہے

نعرہ تکبیر ہے تہلیل ہے تحمید ہے

Tr. The speed of revolution of the sun, the moon and the stars causes a great surprise In case they do not revolve in response to the command of One Supreme Power, he whole universe will be upset and it will be a great mess. The organized and ordered ion of the planets speaks about the Unity, greatness and Glory of God.

Stanza.31

31۔ بادہ توحید سے جو ہر زماں رہتے ہن مست

ساز فطرت ہے سراپا جنکا گلبانگ الست

غیب کی قوت سے دیتے ہیں وہ دنیا کو شکست

کچھ نہیں انکی نگاہوں میں جہان بود و ہست

مرد مومن پر کسی رعب چھا سکتا نہیں

سر کٹا سکتا ہے لیکن سے جھکا سکتا نہیں

(The last line of the Stanza has recently appeared in some film. But Daleel Sahib had composed it some 55 years back.)

Tr:-The nature of those people is itself a musical and pleasant note (glorification of God). who are engrossed in devotion and fascinated and obliterated by the Unity of God. They defeat the world by mysterious and Divine help. This present world which is transitory, has no value at all in their estimation. A true believer can rather agree to be beheahed but can never agree to be prevailed over by the terrifying influence or dominating infulence of others.

Stanza: 32

32ہر بت وہم ہوس ہو کعبہ دل کا مکیں

جلوہ حق سے اگر ہوجائے خالی وہ کہیں

زندگی جسکی خدا کے در سے وابستہ نہیں

وہ گھسے ہے آستاں پر نامراد اپنی جبیں

دولت عشق الٰہی سے جو دل ہیں سرفراز

ناز بردار جہاں ہوتا نہیں انکا نیاز

Tr:- If every superstition and worldly desire reside in the mausoleum of the heart; if the heart is vacant from the Beauty of Truth (God) and whose life is not connected with the Holy Abode of God, he will go on begging to every threshold but in vain. Those people whose hearts are benefited with and full of love for God will never entertain or try to satisfy their needs in the coquetry ways.

Stanza: 33

33- آزمائش جب تلک منصوبہ یزداں نہو

مرتکب جب تک گناہوں کہ دلِ انسان نہ ہو

وہ کبھی گھائل کسی طاقت سے اے ناداں نہو

قلب مومن میں کبھی انسان سے عدواں نہو

اہل دل کی ہے سدا ہر حال میں حق پر نظر

آفتوں میں وہ عمل کی اپنے لیتے ہیں خبر

Tr:-Until the test or trial of man is not the consequence of Divine discretion and as long as a person is sinless and his heart is pure, he cannot be offended by outer force. The heart the believer must be free from enmity for others. Those who have got pure hearts ever see the truth. At the times of adversities, they ponder over their own faults.

Stanza: 34

34 ۔ حادثاتِ دہر سے رفعت اگر پیدا نہو

خون تیرا گر سراپا سوز استغنا نہو

گر کمال بے کسی امید کا دریا نہو

ہیچ آنکھوں میں اگر ہر قوت دنیا نہو

تو ابھی توحید کے اسرار سے ہے بے خبر

ہے فریب ما سوا میں مبتلا تیری نظر

Tr:- If spiritual elevation is not obtained through misfortunes and calamities; if you are not desireless: if you do not have hopes at the time of absolute desperation; if you take into account any worldly force; it means that you are not aware of the Unity of God and have become the Victim of deceit and deception.

Stanza: 35

35-دل اگر توحید کی تنویر سے پرنور ہو

وہ مئے درد خلائق سے سدا مخمور ہو

معرفت کے نور سے فکر و نظر معمور ہو

ظلمت اوہام ساری خود بخود کافور ہو

جلوہ توحید میں کل نیکوں کا نور ہے

اس تجلی سے آندھرا ہر بدی کا دور ہے

نوٹ : فی الحقیقت وہ (جادوگر) کسی انسان کو نقصان پہنچا بھی سکتے تھے ۔ الا یہ کہ خدا کے حکم سے کسی انسان کو نقصان پہنچنے والا ہو اور پہنچ جائے (البقرہ ۲- ۱-۲)

Tr:- If the mind is enlightened by the light of the Unity of God; it will be intoxicated, inebriated and will be full of feelings for humanity. If our intellect is rich with Divine knowledge. the darkness of superstitions will automatically vanish. The beauty of piety is incorporated in the beauty of the belief in Unity of God. The darkness of evil is expelled by the refulgence of the Unity of God.

Stanza: 36

36 ۔ ہے وہی سر چشمہ ہر فوت و فضل و عطا

کون ہو سکتا ہے کس کا جب نہ ہو اس کی رضا

اہل عرفان کھا نہیں سکتے فریب ما سوا

ہو اسی کے در سے وابستہ ترا ہر مُدّعا

ہے عبادت میں اسی کی رفعت عرش بریں

ہے عنایت میں اسی کی دولت دنیا و دیں

نوٹ : پھر کیا تم نہیں جانتے کہ اللہ ہی کے لیے آسمان و زمین کی سلطانی ہے اور اس کے سوا کوئی چیز نہیں جو تمہارا دوست و مددگار ہو ۔(البقرہ -2 -107)

Tr:- Almighty Allah is the only source of strength, excellent grace, bounties and bestowals. As He is the Sovereign of all the worlds, nothing can be had without His Pleasure or Will. The man who is possessed of Divine knowledge seeks God's grace and bounties, he can never be attracted or allured by factors other than God's pleasure. The benefits of both the worlds and spiritual perfection can be obtained only through the worship to Allah.

C:- Wahdat' means Oneness or Unity of God. The 13th chapter of Kayinath is entitled Tauheed which means to believe in the Unity of God. In the first Stanza of the Holy Quran, Allah declares His Unity by calling Himself "Rubbul A'alameen" which means Cherisher of the worlds. In its turn, it means that He is the Sovereign for all the worlds He has created. His claim is evident in Sura No:112 i.e. Sura-e-Ikhlas, which means Purity of Faith which demands belief in the Unity of God. Sometimes this Sura is also called Sura-e-Tauheed because it lays emphasis on the Unity of God. It starts with the word 'Ahad' which means One and ends with the same word 'Ahad'.

S. Ikhlaas - 112:1-4

قُلْ هُوَ اللّٰهُ اَحَدٌ ۚ اَللّٰهُ الصَّمَدُ ۚ لَمْ يَلِدْ ۙ وَلَمْ يُوْلَدْ ۙ وَلَمْ يَكُنْ لَّهٗ كُفُوًا اَحَدٌ

(1) Say, He is Allah, the One and Only.

(2) Allah is Eternal. Absolute.

(3) He begeteth not, nor is He begotten.

(4) And there is none comparable to Him."

In the last line of the 30th Stanza of Kayinath Daleel Sahib has used three words "Takbeer", "Tahleel" and "Tahmeed".

Takbeer means declaration of the greatness of God. It amounts to uttering "Allahu Akbar". The words Eternal and Absolute in the 2nd Stanza imply Allah's splendour of Unity.

Tahleel is the declaration of the Unity of God i.e. to say "La llaha Illallahu. "The first and fourth Stanza of Sura-e-Ikhlaas declare the glory of Unity of God.

Tahmeed means to praise God. The third verse of the Sura extols the glory of God by confirming that Allah neither begets nor is He begotten.

It is interesting to note that a single line composed by Daleel Sahib is incorporated with the whole essence of Sura-e-Ikhlaas.

A few Quranic Stanza have been quoted in the following as the evidences of Allah's claim to be the single Creator and, the accuracy of the peculiar arrangement of His Creations, unparalleled administration in natural phenomena and wonderful equilibrium in the atmosphere.

S. Anbiyaa-21:33 (already quoted in the 2nd and 9th chapter of Kayinath:

Tr:- "It is He Who created the day and the night; and the sun and the moon' all (the celestial bodies) swim along, each in its rounded course".

S. Anbiyaa-21:22:

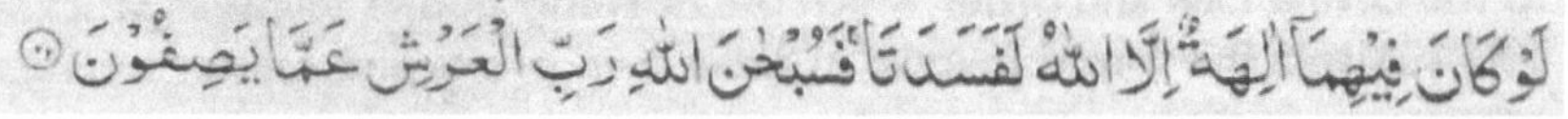

Tr:- "If there were in the heavens and the earth, other Gods besides Allah, there would have been confusion in both! But, glory to Allah, the Lord of the Throne, (High is He) above what they (Mushrikeen) attribute to Him!"

S Ghaashia-88:18-20:-

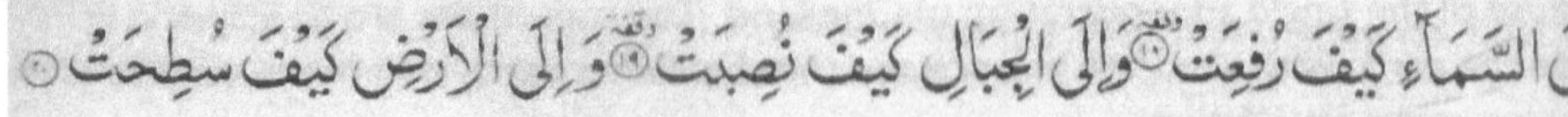

Tr:- "And at the sky, how it is raised high? And at the mountains how they are fixed firm? And at the earth, how it is spread out?"

S. Nabaa-78:6-7

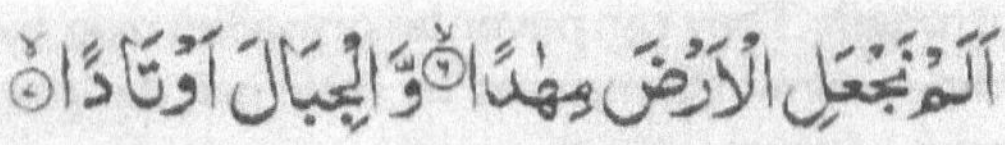

Tr:- "Have We not made the earth a wide expanse? and the mountains as pegs?"

overlap the day, and the day overlap the night. He has subjected the sun and the moon (to His Law). Each one follows a course for a time appointed. Is not He the Exalted in Power- He who forgives again and again?"

Hadith:- (A part of it) "The best deed is to believe in Allah" (Bukhari).

Hadith:- "Three states which in any person ensure the forgiveness of everything else (that is to whom Allah may wish) are: a person who dies having associated no partners with Allah, and having been no magician or who does not practice what magicians do and having harbored no grudges against his brother" (Al Bukhari).

The above mentioned Hadith lays emphasis on the Unity of God.

C:- The Law of gravitational pull of the innumerable heavenly bodies in the universe is accurate and suitable for them in their own atmospheres. They are moving across the space with tremendous speeds without clashing with each other or causing any catastrophe in the nature, due to the excellence of the administration of One God. Had there been more than one God their administrations will entail great disasters and life will become impossible. Hence it is our duty to bow down before the Divine administration of One Supreme Power, Allah, and accept His valid claims.

The Quranic Verses repeatedly refer to the earth, sky, sun, moon, stars as the manifestations of Allah because they are easily and clearly visible to us. These verses also refer to the Divine Law and order which the heavenly bodies follow in strict obedience to Divinity. The sun and the moon revolve in their own orbits and cannot interact. The day and night cannot occur at the same time because they are determined by the rotation of earth. Every creation of God is perfect, proper and in the correct proportion.

The sun has been emitting its rays since the creation of the universe and its energy is being consumed by other creations since billions of years. The proportion of the vital gases in the atmosphere and the equilibrium in the nature which are vital for the life, remain steady because of the single administration of One God. The mountains are deeply and firmly rooted inside the earth with accurate balance and the ship floats partly below the surface of the water in hydro-static equilibrium.

Those who are enticed by their belief in the Unity of God are never attracted by worldly pleasures. They prevent and defeat the evil fancies in the world by mysterious and Divine strength. They can never be prevailed over by the display of pomp or dignity of others, nor can they submit themselves to their evil designs. They can rather agree to be beheaded for the sake of preserving the truth.

In his 32nd Stanza of Kayinath, the poet has referred to the man who is the victim of superstitions and Worldly desires, whose heart is empty of love for God and whose life is not connected with Holy Abode of Allah. Such man will go on begging from door to door in vain. The poet has also referred to the person whose heart is full of love for God. Such man will ever be desireless and never try to satisfy his need in the coquetry ways. The poet means to explain that the person who is not enlightened with the Truth, will not strive for his survival but will depend on the favours of others to satisfy their unlawful desires by bowing at the thresholds of others, forgetting God and His bestowals for hard working and sincere people. The lovers of God realise that Allah is the only source and Ultimate source of bounties. The following Quranic Verse will explain the impact of the above argument.

S. Al-Baqara-2: 107:- (already quoted in the 8th chapter)

Tr:-"Knowest thou not, that Allah belongeth the dominion of the heavens and the earth? And besides Him ye have neither partner nor helper."

It is not at all desirable for a human being to be idle and dependent on others. He must strive hard according to Divine injunction.

When God wishes to test the firmness of faith of His devotee, He sends great disasters and turbulent difficulties on him. A believer should not blame others and should not harbour any enmity against another man. He must know that man can never offend a sinless man without Allah's permission. In this connection the poet has quoted a Quranic Verse and explained that even sorcerer cannot harm a man without the permission of God.

Sorcery or witch craft is the evil deed persuaded to perform by the devil. Those who resort to this unlawful practice lose their faith and will be deprived of Allah's bounties in the life hereafter.

Allah wanted to test the faith of the believers and sent two angels by name Haruut and Maruut to Babylon to teach them sorcery during the reign of Prophet (King) Solomon (Sulaiman Alaihis Salaam). The two angels informed and warned the believers of Babylon that they would lose the faith if they learn and practise black magic prohibited by the religion. Some true believers refused to learn, and some people learnt it and practised it in order to cause afflictions on their enemies. Consequently, Sulaiman Alahis Salaam became the victim of infamy and false allegations that Prophet Solomon had the power in sorcery and he himself practised it. In fact, when the Prophet heard about this illicit practice, he got enraged and tried his best to stop it. The following verse confirms the event and proves the innocence of Sulaiman Alaihis Salaam.

S. Al-Baqara-2:102:- (Part of the verse),

وَاتَّبَعُوا مَا تَتْلُوا الشَّيَاطِينُ عَلَى مُلْكِ سُلَيْمَنَ وَمَا كَفَرَ سُلَيْمَنُ وَلَكِنَّ الشَّيَاطِينَ كَفَرُوا يُعَلِّمُونَ النَّاسَ السِّحْرَ وَمَا أُنْزِلَ عَلَى الْمَلَكَيْنِ بِبَابِلَ هَارُوتَ وَمَارُوتَ وَمَا يُعَلِّمَانِ مِنْ أَحَدٍ حَتَّى يَقُولَا إِنَّمَا نَحْنُ فِتْنَةٌ فَلَا تَكْفُرْ فَيَتَعَلَّمُونَ مِنْهُمَا مَا يُفَرِّقُونَ بِهِ بَيْنَ الْمَرْءِ وَزَوْجِهِ وَمَا هُمْ بِضَارِّينَ بِهِ مِنْ أَحَدٍ إِلَّا بِإِذْنِ اللَّهِ وَيَتَعَلَّمُونَ مَا يَضُرُّهُمْ

Tr:- "They followed what the evil ones gave out (falsely) against the power of Solomon the blasphemers were, not Solomon, but the evil ones teaching men magic, and such things as came down at Babylon to the angels Haruut and Maruut.

But neither of these taught anyone (such things without saying Who are only for trial so do not blaspheme! They learned from them the means to sow discord between man and wife. But they could not thus harm anyone except by Allah's permission. And they learnt what harmed them".

It is quite convincing while the poet says that nobody can be harmed by others including sorcerers, without the Will of God.

It is known to all that Quran provides clues and data for all physical sciences, promotion of spiritual powers, researches, discoveries and invention. More developed Sorcery is still being continued and practiced by traditions. In the practice of black magic, the sorcerer is far from his object, the person to be afflicted. In my opinion, this practice is the clue for the discovery of remote control.

The enlightened minds always see the Truth. All the times of trials and tribulations, they ponder over their own faults and consider the hazards of their life as the test or punishment from God. They never bother about the outer forces which can cause afflictions because they believe in the Power of One God.

In the 34th Stanza of Kayinath the poet says, that if a man is unaware of the secrets of the Unity of God, he becomes the victim of deceit and deception of worldly factors which may entice him. There are some qualities which make the faith stronger. It is already said that when God likes to test the degree of firmness of faith of his devotee, he sends turbulent difficulties in his life. If absolute confidence is reposed on

Almighty Allah, the Divine dispensation clears off the hurdles and dispels the misfortunes. The total submission to Allah and the devotional fervor of the devotee enables him to overcome the insuperableobstacles and provides Divine protection. Such man can never be attracted by worldly desires and can never be harmed by forces except with the permission of God.

The poet says that by the misfortunes of life a believer must develop his own self which will result in spiritual elevation. He must be desireless of material benefits or satisfaction. At the of extreme desperation, he must have an ocean of hopes. He must not bother about forces but always look forward for Divine help.

There is an excellent example in Islamic history for the interpretation of matchless absolute confidence, ocean of hopes and the Splendour of Unity of God. It is the of Trench which is also called the battle of Ahzaab which means confederates. The ich of Makkah marched against the Muslims of Madinah along with their Jewish confederates in 5A.H.

Due to the treachery and deceptions of the Jews and the hypocrites the Islamic army numerically very weak. A handful of Muslims had to confront with 24 thousand strong non-Muslims.

By this time Hazrat Salmaan Farsi who was previously a Zoroastrian had come from Madinah and had embraced Islam. In those days the Romans and the Persians were at War. Hazrat Salman Farsi was, highly merited in war strategy, which the Muslims are not aware of. According to his instructions, a broad trench was dug around Madinah to vent the enemies from entering Madinah. The hostile army pitched its tents near the trench and stayed there for a few months. Prophet

Muhammad (PBUH) started this tough task of diging the trench like an ordinary labourer, followed by the help of all the Muslims. Due to the prolonged internment, the provision got exhausted. The pangs of hunger was unbearable for the Muslims. The Muslims including our Prophet tied stones on their stomachs in order to decrease the sufferings of hunger. Even at this critical situation, they did not lose confidence in God. Their faith in the Unity of God neither degenerated nor dwindled. They succeeded in the Divine test with flying colours and waited patiently for the Divine help with ocean of hopes. The general battle was not actually fought except a few duels in the pit. When the Muslims were at the collapsing state, a wonderful miracle took place which brought them a great victory and a handsome amount of booty

S. Ahzaab-33:9:

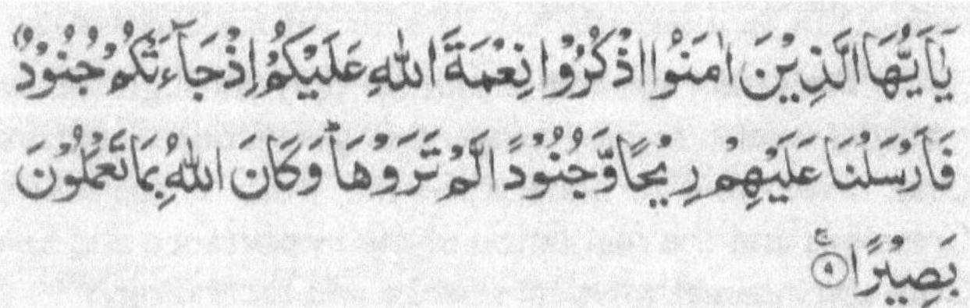

Tr:- "Oye who believe! Remember the grace of Allah (bestowed) on you, when there came down on you hosts (to over whelm you). But We sent against them a hurricane and force that ye saw not. But Allah sees (clearly) all that ye do".

Allah sent a violent storm which blew with all its force and scattered the tents and the hostile army. Some of them died and some fled, leaving behind them their provisions armors, weapons and wealth which came in the possession of the Muslims.

The Muslims of Madinah were at one side of the trench and their enemies were close to them and stationed at the other side of the trench. The hurricane which destructed the Mushrikeen did not harm a single Muslim. They were quite safe and unaffected. The not feel a single puff of wind which was blowing violently close to them. The several gods and goddesses of the Mushrikeen could not save them while the single Sovereign Ruler (Allah saved the Muslims from the terrible havoc of nature. After witnessing this miracle. a greatnumber of people embraced Islam and believed in the unimaginable grandeur of Unity of God Is this not a proper example for the ocean of hopes at the time of extreme desperation?

In the 35th stanza of Kayinaat the poet says that the effulgence contained in the light of the Unity of God, the heart which is full of feelings for other creations, and the effulgence of Divine knowledge will automatically dispel the darkness of superstitions. All sorts of piety are incorporated in the belief in the Unity of God by the refulgence of which the darkness of evil Vanishes.

Emphasis has been laid by Islam on compassion towards other creations.

S. Anbiyaa-21:107 (Already quoted in the 12th chapter)

Tr:- "We sent thee (Muhammad) not but as a Mercy for all creatures."

Hadith:- "Say salaam (Wishing Well) to your brother Muslim whenever you meet him."

Hadith:- "When a truthful believer visits a sick believing bonds man he is so to speak, in garden of paradise until he returns (Muslim).

The worst type of superstition is the belief in plurality of gods. This superstition of the man will automatically vanish once he is blessed with the Divine knowledge.

As Allah is the only source of strength, grace and bestowals, man should seek his objectives and requirements through supplications to God.

We attain spiritual elevation only through the worship of Allah. We are blessed with material wealth as well as spiritual perfection only through the favours of Allah who is only One. If we want to understand the Truth, it requires self-realization, realization of Unity of Creations and the realisation of the importance and Splendour of the Unity of God. (Unity of God, spiritualism, physical science and technology).

CHAPTER . XIV

LIFE AND ACTION

Stanza: 37

14 /حیات اور حرکت

37۔ حرکت ازلی پہ قائم ہے نظام کائنات

زخمہ سوز عمل ہے نغمہ ساز حیات

انہماک جاوداں ہے زندگانی کا ثبات

ہے سکوں سامان جو بھی موت ہے اس کی برات   (اسلامی عقیدہ)

نوع انساں کو خدا کی دین جو اسلام ہے

حسن ایماں و عمل کا سرمدی پیغام ہے

Tr:-"The administration of the universe depends upon the eternal activity (of God) the ne of which is not known. The prospects of life depend on the plectrum of pleasure in endeavor. The continuous effects and perseverance are evidences for constancy and stability of life. The inactivity of anything amounts to its death. The eternal and standing message of the beauty of faith and strife is a grand gift for human race from Islam, our religion.

Stanza: 38

38۔ ہے مشیت کی ادا حرکت کی صورت جلوہ گر

ہے اسی حرکت میں پوشیدہ زمانے کا سفر

ہے یہی حرکت شعور زندگی سے بہرہ ور

عشق کی ہے قوت تخلیق اس میں سر بسر

ہیں اسی حرکت سے گردش میں زمین و آسماں

ہے مشیت ہی کا ایک جلوہ وجود کن فکاں

Tr:- The pleasure of God is manifested in the form of activity. The march of time is dependent upon this activity. The activity of man benefited by the wisdom and God's creative sewer is totally due to his love for His creations. The universe exists and heavens and earth revolve because God's pleasure is active.

Stanza: 39

39- ہے ازل سے ہر صفت اللہ کی سر گرم کار

ہے اسی کا ایک جلوہ گردش لیل و نہار

ہے سفر میں زندگی گرم سفر ہے روزگار

دست انسان میں ہے اسکی زندگانی کی بہار

سب ہیں مجبور سفر ذرے ہوں شمس و قمر

ہے وہی انسان جسکا جانب حق ہے سفر

Tr:- The overlapping of night and day takes place because all the attributes of Allah are active from the beginning. With march of time, life advances, and the way of life is determined by the discretion of man.All things whether they are atoms or sun or moon, are bound to travel, But man can be called a human being only when his journey is towards God.

Stanza: 40

40- جس قدر ہوگا بلند انساں کا مقصود حیات

اسقدر ہونگے بلند اخلاق و کردار و صفات

جنکا ہو مطلوب خود پروردگار کائنات

انکی آنکھوں میں جچتے کیونکر جہاں ہے ثبات

عرش اعظم پر جو ڈالے ہوئے اپنی کمند

اسکی عظمت کو بلندی کونسی آئی پسند

Tr:- The degree of purity of character, deeds and traits of a human being will be according to the height and greatness of his ambition to achieve the goal of his life. This transitory world will never allure or attract the person whose goal is God Himself. The height of the highest thing of this world will not entice the person whose ambition is merge with God in His Holy Abode Arsh.

Stanza: 41

41۔ وہ مجاہد کا مسرت خیز ہے پایاں سفر

خود سفر منزل نما ہے خود خدا ہے راہبر

ہر قدم پر ہے نئی شان حقیقت جلوہ گر

زندہ تر ہے ہر زماں سوز جگر ذوق نظر

عرش کی جانب نہو پرواز پیہم گر حیات

قلب انساں میں ہو سوز جاوداں کیونکر حیات

Tr - The endless and pleasant journey of a person who crusades with or endeavors his life, itself leads him in the right path. At every advancing step of man, a new splendour truth is manifest as his desire for hard strife and interest for investigation are always more and more active and lively. If a man's life is devoid of continuous flight (spiritual elevation) towards its goal (God) he cannot have any eternal interest in life.

Stanza: 42

42۔ اہل ایمان و عمل مردان بے یاس و خطر

بادہ تسلیم کی مستی سے جب ہیں بہر ور

روح افزا ان میں ہوتا ہے حوادث کا اثر

اور ہوجاتے ہیں سوئے حق وہ سرگرم سفر

انکی رفعت ہے بلندی نوع انساں کیلئے

وہ ہے داروئے شفا ہر درد پنہان کے لیے

Tr - Those believers who are hardworking, confident , valorous and fearless are fortunate enough to get engrossed in total submission to God. Their misfortunes result in their spiritual elevation which take them towards God with more speed. The spiritual elevation is gifted only for human race which is more than enough to overcome difficulties.

Stanza:-43

43 ۔ جب رضائے حق سے جاتی ہے بدل انکی رضا

قوت رب اُن میں ہوتی ہے سکوں نا آشنا

پیکر حسن عمل ہوتے ہیں یوں اہل وفا

سے نگوں ہے اُن کے آگے قوت ارض و سما

عاشقان حق یہی ہوتے ہیں سالار جہان

سوئے منزل خلق کا چلتا ہے ان سے کارواں

نعت:

Tr - Divine strength is always active without any break in those people whose pleasure changes according to the Divine pleasure. Those people who are sincere in the struggle of their life become the personification of the beauty of endeavor and the earth bow down. These are the people who are lovers of God, and leaders of the world. They lead others to the desired destination.

Stanza: 44

44۔ صاحب معراج کی زندگی پیش نظر

زندگی کے راز کھل جائیں گے سارے سر بسر

اس کی عظمت تصور کیا کرے فہم بشر

ثبت ہیں نقش قدم جس کے فراز عرش پر

چاہیے آگے ثریّا سے ہو امت کا مقام

اسکے ہے کردار کی منزل ہو حیرت کا مقام

Tr:- If we have in view the life of Prophet Muhammad (PBUH) who ascended to the height of Allah's throne, the secrets of life will be disclosed. The greatness of our Prophet is beyond human imagination and intellect as his foot prints are permanently impressed at the height of Arsh, the Holy Abode of Allah. The station of the followers of the Prophet must be above the exalted place and status of ordinary folk and their virtuous deeds must be surprising.

C:-In the 14th chapter, the poet has dealt with the topics life and action, Islamic of strife, eternal message for endeavor and perseverance. God's will regarding moment of activities, wisdom and action, creative power and love, creation of universe d's pleasure, activities of God's attributes in every creation, advance of time, human life I discretion, difference between the activities of other things and man's highest ambition towards God, goal of human being, highest ambition, continuous spiritual flight, changing total submission, Divine Strength and co-operation, preceptors, ascension (Mei'raj) bet Muhammad (PBUH) to God's Holy Abode Arsh Spiritual height etc.

It is already said that Allah's Attributes and the faculties of man are identical because be rational creation of Allah. As Allah's attributes are ever active in discharging His duties, man also exploit his faculties to receive benefactions from Allah. Life depends upon Hence Allah's existence is eternal as His activities are never ending for the benefit of His creations.

S. Al-Baqara- 2:255 (Part of it):

اللَّهُ لَا إِلَٰهَ إِلَّا هُوَ الْحَيُّ الْقَيُّومُ لَا تَأْخُذُهُ سِنَةٌ وَلَا نَوْمٌ لَهُ مَا فِي السَّمَاوَاتِ وَمَا فِي الْأَرْضِ مَنْ ذَا الَّذِي يَشْفَعُ عِنْدَهُ إِلَّا بِإِذْنِهِ يَعْلَمُ مَا بَيْنَ أَيْدِيهِمْ وَمَا خَلْفَهُمْ وَلَا يُحِيطُونَ بِشَيْءٍ مِنْ عِلْمِهِ إِلَّا بِمَا شَاءَ وَسِعَ كُرْسِيُّهُ السَّمَاوَاتِ وَالْأَرْضَ وَلَا يَئُودُهُ حِفْظُهُمَا وَهُوَ الْعَلِيُّ الْعَظِيمُ

Tr- "Allah! There is no God but He the living, the self-subsisting, eternal. No slumber man sieze him nor sleep. His are all things in the heavens and on the earth".

Islam emphasizes both faith and action (Amal) to lead a noble life. In Islam action is the test of faith. Faith must be coupled or backed by action. All Muslims are bound to progress and promote goodness and dispel evil for the uplift of a good society.

Labour is one of the factors of production which is necessary for the sustenance of life Progress and prosperity of all the countries and communities depend solely on the labour and production. Due recognition of sincere labour and honest earning have brought material prosperity, better standards of life of the people and social and spiritual harmony in this world . where there is due appreciation for the dignity of labour there is notable difference in the course of societies.

The concept of dignity of labour has been given the weightage and recognition since the advent of Adam Alaihis Salaam, the father of humanity who ploughed the fields and undertook all sorts of laborious tasks for the survival of himself and his large family. Other prophets still more dignified labour by adopting and exercising labour-based professions and occupation. Hazrat Nuh took up carpentry. Hazrat Idris used to stitch clothes. Prophet Muhammad (PBUH) himself used to graze the sheep and persuaded his contemporaries to give full respects to all the labours. The good relationship between the employer and the employee optimizes good terms and maintains collective prosperity through more output of the products. Personal efforts coupled with reliance on the blessings of Allah will surely fetch prosperity in the life sooner or later.

In the 37th of his Stanza, the poet has explained the Islamic concept of action and life. The action involving the whole administration of the universe depends upon the eternal Divine activities. The prospects of and the interest evinced in the life are nothing but the plectrum of pleasure in endeavor: The vital requisites for the constancy and stability of real life are continuous efforts and perseverance. Anything which ceases its activity has no more life it is rather dead. The whole human race has been offered the grand and eternal gift from Islam namely the beauty of faith and endeavour. Our religion, Islam with these gifts ware sent through propher Muhammad (PBUH) for the whole humanity.

S: Sabaa-34:28:

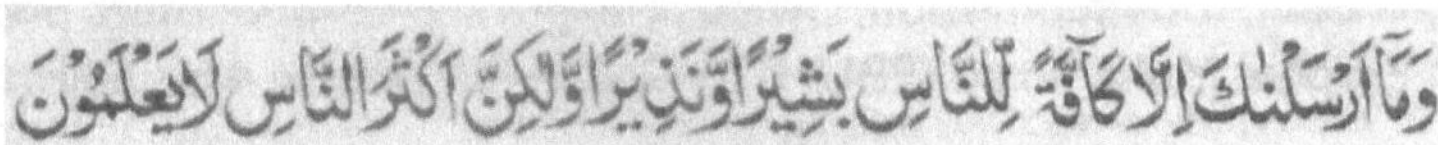

Tr.- 'We have sent thee as a universal (Messenger) to men giving them glad tidings and warning them (against sin) but most men understand not".

Islam urges the believers to translate the philosophical theory to practical ethics.

The subject matter of the 38th Stanza of Kayinat explains that Divine discretion is the ultimate source of all sorts of activities in the universe on which the march of time depends in fact the time is ever passing and does not stop for a single second. The poet means to say that not even a single second passes without activity in the universe. Life advances with the advance of time. This activity is the result of Divine bestowal of wisdom and life, because the creative power of Allah is based on His love for His creations. The creation of the universe and the revolutions of the heavens and earth have their foundation in the ever-active attributes Allah such as his creative power and pleasure.

H:- Islam initiated as something strange and it would revert to its old position of being strange, so good tidings for the strangers (Muslim).

This Hadith implies that although the teachings of Islam are so akin to the nature of man yet when these were preached, the people shunned them as strange and unfamiliar things. Islamic teachings are natural.

S: Naml -27:60 (Part of the Stanza):

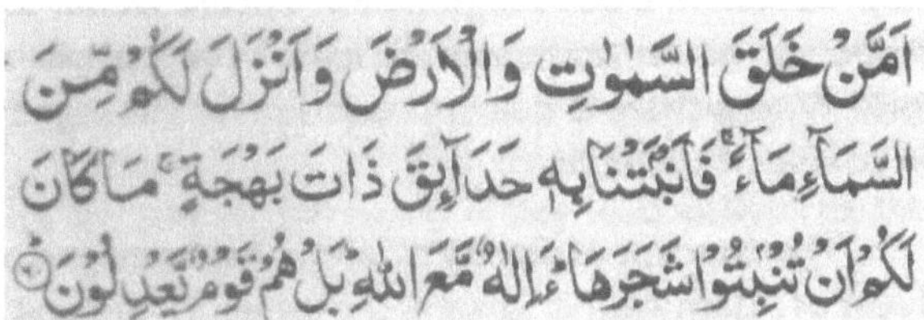

Tr:- "Or Who has created the heavens and the earth and who sends you down rain from the sky ? Yes, with it We, cause to grow well planted orchards full of beauty and delight".

The above Quranic verse implies that Attributes of Allah are always active everyday for the welfare of His creations.

The main ideas, interpreted in the 39th stanza of the text are the position of man in Islam, his power of discretion and spiritual perfection through his thoughts words and deeds.

For the convenient and comfortable life of man, the eternal activities of Allah's different attributes cause the night. The revolution of the earth which causes day to appear is meant for the man to toil and exert his efforts for his survival and the occurrence of night is necessary for him to take rest which will enable him to work for the course of next day. Man is Allah's highest whom He has bestowed with the power of discretion God's Providence is not sufficient noble life. The thought words and deeds, he adopts, determine his way of life. Of course the atoms, sun and moon are bound to revolve. But that man only can be called a who tries to scale the spiritual height and merge with God which is called the stage of human who tries to scale the spiritual perfection.

Islam aims at cultivation of civilization and culture of entire human race through the sincere attempts of people. Islam is a kind of culture, prescribed by Allah for the promotion being of entire humanity and to attain a definite and avowed Goal i.e. God and HIS If we ponder about the spiritual truth the corporeal life and death are not the whole man's sojourn. When we are alive in this world, we may be dead in the spiritual world; and our bodily death may open broader way to spiritual world and take us nearest to God the true spiritualism lies both in the toil and devotion to God, through which we can attain eternal peace in the spiritual life.

The 40th Stanza of this book, the poet has discussed, the status of man, his purity of character his refined traits, his ambitions, target, sublimity of his purpose, exaltation of his de the value of human life, magnanimity and magnificence of man's Goal.

The purity of character and exaltation of man's deeds will be according to the sublimity of the purpose of his life. Allah has created him in the best form and has granted him the status of vicegerent of the World.

S. Al-Baqara-2:30 (Part of the Verse already quoted in the 12th chapter)

Tr: "Behold, thy Lord said to the angels 'I will create a Vicegerent (Adam) on the earth."

Of all the creations on earth, human being is the only rational animal whom Allah has granted such an exalted status. It is man's duty to exploit the faculty of rationality in order to realize the value of human life and attain the magnificent Goal, God. The Vicegerency of man on earth is established by the great value, Islam gives to human life, his role on earth, the position he occupies in the system of existence, the standard that determines his value, and his bond of covenant made with Allah. The greatness of man is evident by the Divine announcement that the angels were commanded by Allah to prostrate before Adam Alaihis Salam, the father of humanity.

The most valuable and most beautiful object of this transitory world can never succeed to allure or attract the person whose ambitions and sublime purpose and exalted destination is the Arsh, the Holy Abode of Allah.

The 41st Stanza of the text consists of the discussion about righteous strife, perseverant endeavor, Divine guidance, Divine cooperation and new splendour of truth, discovered due to hard labour.

The endeavourer who crusades with struggles in life finds pleasure in his endless journey in this world and hereafter. His hard work brings to light discoveries of new splendour of truth. His interest in investigation arouses his desire for righteous strife. At the same time, he must be equally interested in the continuous spiritual elevation. Otherwise, human being will be devoid of eternal peace and heavenly bliss.

Allah promises success in this world and hereafter to those people who adhere to Divine principles one of which is hard strife. The trait of perseverance can be achieved only by inherent human faculties and power of reasoning. Islam does not persuade people to remain in the existing condition and lead an idle life. But it persuades them to go on striving for progress and improvement. Regarding His promise Allah says in Quran, "Nay, whosoever surrenders his purpose to Allah, (while doing good to others), surely his reward is with his Lord and there shall be no fear come upon them, neither shall they suffer grief".

The message of Islam to the World is peace, love, progress as well as spiritual advancement through righteous and noble deeds. Man is the crown of all creatures, because he is endowed with thinking faculty. He can decide issues rationally and can understand spiritual values. His thoughts, Words and deeds must be identical. With the status of vicegerent of earth, he should not be a hypocrite.

In the 42nd Stanza of the text, total submission to God, faith and fearlessness, misfortunes, spiritual heights and remedy for calamities have been discussed.

Those people who are completely resigned to the Will of God and whose faith is firm and unshakable are fearless and valorous to confront with the misfortunes of life. They see in their misfortunes some Divine advisability which strengthens their faith, elevates their soul and take them nearer to God. This spiritual height of human beings is the remedy for all calamities.

H:- "He realized the fervour of faith (Iman) who became pleased with Allah as Lord, with Iman as the code of life and Muhammad as the Messenger of Allah. (Muslim).

Total submission to Allah does not mean that people should not supplicate to Allah for relief in the duration of adversities. Allah gets pleased with the supplications of the believers for success after toiling hard. In Quran Allah says:

"If my servants ask you about Me, I am indeed near them. I answer the prayer of the supplicant when he calls to Me and believe in Me so that they may be wise".

The 43rd Stanza of the text describes Divine strength, Divine Cooperation and good leadership.

Intolerance in professed Muslims can come only from ignorance of Islamic principles. The height of intolerance indicates the depth of ignorance. Inspite of sincere and hard endeavours, some people suffer thundering failures in their life. But these failures cannot have any adverse or disappointing influence on the minds of true believers because they get reconciled with the pleasure and decision of God. In such situations they feel that the Divine strength is ever active in their own selves. This is nothing but Divine cooperation with the sincere devotees.

These are the sincere people who are the real personifications of beauty of endeavour and before whom the pomp and splendour of all the heavens and earth are subdued. The virtuous lovers of God possessed of such noble qualities become the accomplished leaders of the world who guide humanity to desired and right destination.

Any noble venture is bound to face hurdles. Wisdom lies in trying to surmount these impediments and complete the task instead of losing the heart. We can expect Divine strength vine cooperation only after hard strife and resignation to the Will of God.

Islam has ennobled labour. Its founder Prophet Muhammad himself was a worker and instructed his companions to be hard-working. Regarding labour, they never minded the dignity the construction of Masjid-e-Nabvi, Prophet Muhammad laboured like the mason. while digging the trench around Madinah as a war stratagem, his whole body was covered in mud, Islam does not recognize any social barrier between master and servant. Prophet Muhammad (PBUH) used to milk the cattle like a slave did. In order to lay more emphasis on sincere work and earning by honest means, Islam enjoins on us to have special regard for the labour.

H:- "Pay the labourer before his sweat dries".

Divine grace does not take into account the highness of man's birth. God confers special boons on those who work hard and await Divine grace which is another name for Divine cooperation. God probes into the purity of their hearts, their sincerity and their steadfast attitudes. Even a man of extraordinary scholastic merits and high birth, blessed with affluence. cannot claim Divine cooperation if he is bereft of faith. A humble and pious man of low birth who displays abundant faith in God, is entitled to material benefactions, spiritual benefactions as well as Divine cooperation.

For every human being the leaders or preceptors are either prophets or saints or noble people of selfless attitude. The guidance is the Divine Law (Shari'ah) of Quran and the Goal is

Allah. As a child a human being is born entirely innocent and ignorant of principles of life. In order to lead a noble and disciplined life, Divine guidance and religious tenets are absolutely essential which were revealed through chosen ones. According to the Islamic concept of leadership, a leader must have some refined traits such as belief in the Unity of God, the basic strength of morality, patience, piety, hard work, sincere efforts for the well-being of the public, selflessness, capacity to maintain law and order, administrative power, hatred for unlawful desires and desire for scaling spiritual heights. The perfect and powerful leader must feel himself completely powerless before the Omni-Potent Allah. This sense of humility must make him the most humble servant of the people and devotee of God. Prophet Muhammad was the best leader ever born in the world and the best exemplar because he practised what all he preached. The Quranic Verses prove the validity of the above statements.

S:Ahzaab-33:21:

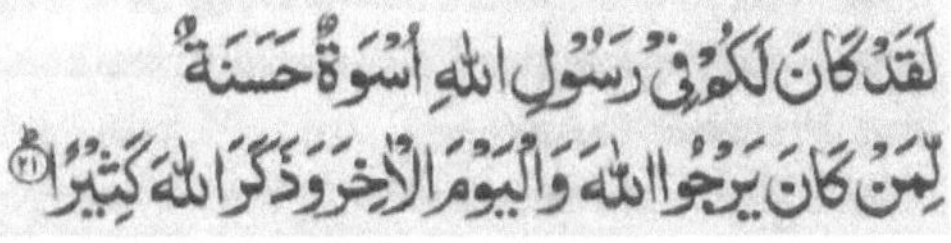

Tr:- "Ye have indeed in the Apostle of Allah, a beautiful pattern of (conduct) for any one whose hope is in Allah and the Final Day, and who engages much in the praise of Allah."

S:Ahzaab-33:46:

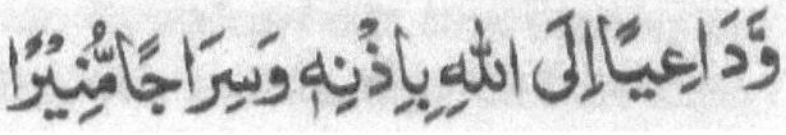

Tr:- "And as one who invites to Allah's (grace) by His leave, and as a Lamp spreading Light."

While instructing the leaders of different territories our Prophet advised them as fallow:-

H:- "Let your subjects be always happy. Your behavior should not allow them, any hatred against you. You must make their life pleasant and easy. Do not involve difficulties (Bukhari, Muslim)

S. 33:45:

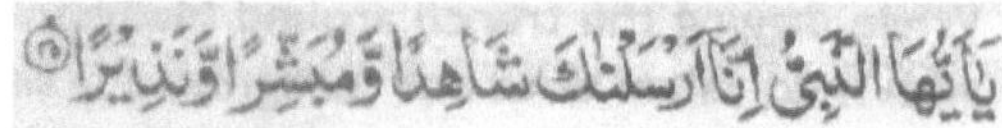

Tr:- "O Prophet, We have sent thee as a witness, a bearer of glad tidings and a warner"

H- "Let your subjects be always happy. Your behaviour should not allow them to harbour any hatred against you. You must make their life pleasant and easy. Do not involve them in difficulties." (Bukhari, Musiim)

H:- "Among the rulers (leaders), the best ones are those whom you love and who love you, and for whom you pray and who pray for you. The worst rulers are those with whom you have grudge and who have grudge against you and to whom you curse or reproach and who curse you." (Muslim).

In the 44th Stanza of the text, the poet has praised Prophet Muhammad (PBUH). described his greatness and his ascension to Arsh which is called the Mei'raj-e-Nabvi.

Quranic Verses are full of praise for Prophet Muhammad (PBUH) some of which I have already quoted. He has set examples of ways of life by following which, the secrets of life will be revealed.

Mei'raj-e-Nabvi is the glorious event in Islamic history of the journey of our Prophet to Arsh, the Holy Abode of Allah, far above the seven heavens described in Quran, and the event of his direct audience, he had with Allah. This was one of the special and grand prestige's, granted by Allah to our last Prophet which was not granted to the past prophets.

Isra and Mei'raj are among the most magnificent aspects of Islam which took place on the 27th night of Rajab, the 7th month of the lunar calendar in the late 619 A.D. It was before the introduction of Islamic Era which commenced from the third and final Hijrat, from Makkah to Madinah and after his return from Taif which is called the second Hijrat in Islamic history. The first Hijrat was the fleeing of a Muslim delegation to Abbisinia, (now called Etheopia seeking refuge in the Christian empire of King Negus who embraced Islam later, without meeting our Prophet (SAW).

The amazing, yet historic event of Mei'raj-e-Nabi remains both as inspiration and a challenge to human intellect. Some people thought that, it was a Vision and spiritual transportation, but it was proved to be a physical ascent through a number of interrogations of the people and the replies of our Prophet for the explanation of which several pages are required. His replies were about the description of Jerusalem where he had never been in his life and the returning of the Caravan of the merchants of Makkah from Syria from the particular route and the date of their arrival according to his approximation. The Quranic verses from 18 of Sura-e-Najm (no. 5. to every Muslim. Allah chose to universe where even angles -Najm (no. 53) are full of confirmations and descriptions of Mei'raj. The miraculous real and historic audience that our Prophet had with Allah is of infinite importance Muslim. Allah chose to invite his chosen

Messenger to Him to the highest place of the where even angles are not allowed to reach. Allah invited him for some purposes which two were important ones namely to elevate the position of man over all other and to inform him of his command of Namaz (Prayer) to the devotees of Allah which brings them ten-fold rewards.

According to Moulana Yusuf Ali, the mystic story of Mei'raj is a fitting prelude to the human soul in its spiritual growth in life.

Both Al-Isra' and Al-Mei'raj are commonly known as Al-Mei'rajun-Nabi. The following a describes the night journey of our Holy Prophet from the sacred Mosque (Masjid AlHaraam) in Makkah to the Majid-Al-Aqsa in Jerusalem.

S.Bani Isra'il-17:1:

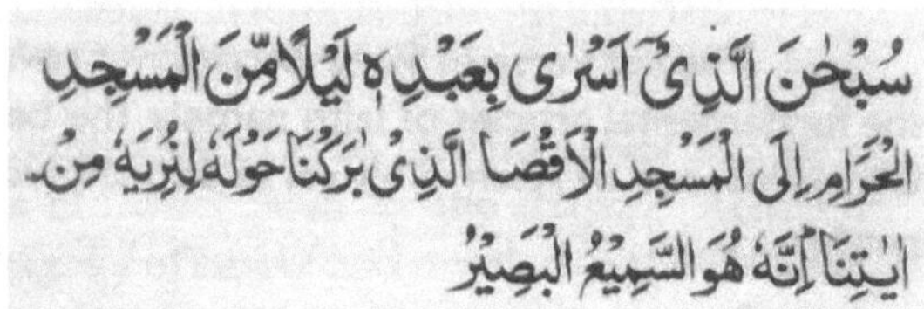

Tr- Glory to Allah who did take His Servant (Prophet Muhammad) for a journey by nicht from the Sacred Mosque to the Farthest Mosque whose precints We did bless-in order that We might show him some of Our signs for He is the one who heareth and seeth all things".

Al-Mei'raj means Prophet's physical ascension to the Arsh from the Mosque of Aqsa in Jerusalem, his personal audience with Allah and the survey of paradise and hell with his Lord's permission.

The detailed account of Mei'raj requires scores of pages. In this commentary only a brief outline is presented. On the 27th night of Rajab our Prophet slept in the house of his cousin after offering prayers with the inmates. Arch Angel Jibra'il took him unawares to Hateem, a part of the Masjid Al-Haraam. Jibra'il (A.S) woke him up and informed him of Allah's invitation for which Allah had sent a white, beautiful and fantastic steed called Buraaq, which was faster than the lightening in its fight. It sped like an arrow and reached Jerusalem in a single wink of the eye with our Prophet on its back. His night journey to Masjid-e-Aqsa is called Isra. He led a congregational prayer with the past prophets and angels. Al-Isra is the first stage of Prophet's ascension. The second stage of ascension to Arsh is called Mei'raj. This miracle has been mentioned in the books of Ahadis including Sahih Bukhari and Muslim. The word Mei'raj was derived from the Arabic word 'Uruuj' which mean's progress to a higher level. From Masjid-eAqsa, the Buraaq took him again on his back and reached the 7th heaven. Our prophet had the privilege of meeting the past prophets in every firmament of heavens.

In the 7th heaven, he saw a proto type of Kabathullah around which angels use to circumambulate. He saw Prophet Ibrahim (A.S) leaning against the wall of Kabathullah. He greeted him calling him "My Son". At last our Prophet reached Arsh through a glorious ladder, Sidratul-Muntaha (a heavenly nicht tree) and another heavenly conveyance called Rufruf.

Our Prophet felt engulfed with the refulgence of Allah and he prostrated barn Allah informed him of some of Divine secrets, showed him His Signs which not When he was engulfed with Divine splendour(Tajalli and Noor-e-Ilahi), he and his Lord the distance of two bow lengths or nearer (Quran).

After receiving the necessary instructions and wisdom from God, he descended 7th heaven from the same route where Jibrail(A.Sand the Buraaq were waiting for his Buraag accompanied by Jibra'iVAS brought our Prophet to his cousin's house at early before the time for morning prayers. The distance of travelling to Arsh and his stay at seemed to be long enough for the discussions and audience with Allah. How miracle that all these happenings took place in a short duration of the auspicious 27th night of Rajab.

Among all other prestiges and privileges of Mei'raj-e-Nabi, its three main gifts are follows:

1. The last verse of Sur-e-Baqara was revealed during Mei'raj. This revelation emphasizes the fundamental articles of faith namely, the belief in the Unity, Sovereignty, Benevolence and Omni-Potence of Allah. This verse also shows the way as to how to seek Allah's refuge and pardon.

2. The five daily prayers were made obligatory for every adult believer. Hence Salaat is called 'Al-Mei'rajul-Mumineen' which means union of the believers with Allah.

3. Allah promised Prophet Muhammad, His last Messenger, that He will pardon every member of his Ummat and admit the believers into paradise after the punishment or pardoni of his sins in case, he does not commit shirk i.e if he does not associate anybody or anything in the Divine Worship.

Religion is a way of realization of God's existence which seeks to raise the excellence of the whole humanity. Mysticism aims at raising the level of individuals above the level of common people. Islam is not merely a religion nor is it a mere mysticism. The mystic event of Mei'rai has proved that Islam is a combination of both religion and mysticism. Islam seeks to save the whole humanity as well as raise the individuals to different degrees of spiritual progress. The mystic event of Mei'raj raised Prophet Muhammad to the highest position and facilitated his union with God. While praising him, the poet has called him Sahib-e-Mei'raj. While praising him Allah says in Quran that Prophet Muhammad had the character which was at the pinacle of moral excellence.

For this chapter it will be fitting to present some more Ahadis-e-Nabvi, pertaining to total surrender, faith Jihaad values of life and action

. H:- "To have faith in Allah and to fight for His cause are best deeds." (Bukhari, Muslim, Ahmed).

H:- "That man is virtuous who is contented with what Allah has granted to him. He is unfortunate who stops supplicating to Allah. Hence, it is also his misfortune if he is dissatisfied with his destiny." (Ahmed, Tirmizi)

H:-"if the hour of Doom is highly imminent and any one of you has a young date sapling and he can manage to plant it before the hour strikes, then he should do it." in his hand, and he can (Bukhari).

H:- "When a young human being dies, all his actions come to an end except in ways of He act of charity (continuous benefactions of his charity), or a useful contribution to knowledge or leaving a dutiful child who prays for him."

H-Strive hard in this transitory world thinking that you will live for ever. Perform vous deeds for the hereafter as if you are going to die tomorrow itself." (Al-Madinah, Al Islam)

H:- "The man who endeavours will definitely get the fruits. He will always be receiving something or other for endeavours". (Al-Madinah, Al-Islam).

H- "To earn an honest living is a duty next to principal duties of Islam." (Baihaqi).

The above mentioned Ahadis explain the significance of action for life. They also serve as evidences for the apt and beautiful discussions of Daleel Sahib for the chapter "Action of Life." (Religious philosophy, logic, human dignity, dignity of labour and mystic event of Mei'raj).

CHAPTER – XV

CREATIONS OF WORLD AND HUMAN BEING

—◦।◦~ ◆ ~◦।◦—

Stanza:45.

15 /عالم ایجاد اور انسان

45۔ کیا خبر کہ سے سے چلا ہے سلسلہ ایجاد کا

ہے زمانہ کا تعلق دہر سے حیرت فزا

ازلیت کا رنگ ہر ذرے سے ہے جلوہ نما

جیب میں کہریا ہے جو سمجھا بھی تو ہے چیز کیا

ایک قبرستان ہے کیا کہیے کتنے ہیں مزار

اس میں ہے مدفون لاکھوں سال کے کرمک ہے شمار

Tr:- Everybody is at loss to know the time of starting point for the continuous and consecutive creations. The connection and relation of time and world are wondrous and perplexing. The evidence of permanent existence of matter is present in every atom difficult to understand the original matter contained in the chalk piece. No person can estimate the number of tiny insects buried in the earth since the creation of the universe

Stanza: 46.

46۔ کون جانے کب مشیّت سے ہوئے ذرے عیاں

کب ہوئے مہر و مہ انجم بہار آسمان

ملتہب سورج سے کٹ کر کب زمین آئی یہاں

کب ہوئی آراستہ یہ محفل کون و مکاں

کب بنی گہوارہ نشو ونما روئے زمیں
زندگی کا کب ہوا ایجاد تخم اولین

Tr:- Human beings are ignorant about the time when these atoms came into existence when the sun, the moon and the stars beautified the sky; when our earth which was a splinter of flaming fire came here after separating from the sun; when this universe was arranged in the proper order; when this world became the cradle for progress and evolution and when the first protoplasm which is the basic substance of life was created.

Stanza: 47

47۔ ہے ابھی پردے میں حیوانوں کی تاریخ حیات
کون بتلائے ہوئی کب رونما انسان کی ذات
ہے وجود آدمی میں جوہر کل کائنات
ارتقاء کا ہے تقاضا روح انساں کا ثبات
خلقت آدم کی خاطر حکمت پروردگار
کیا بلا مقصود تھی لاکھوں قرن مصروف کار

Tr:- The origin and history of animal life in this world is undiscovered. Nobody can tell the time as to when the human race appeared on the earth. The sterling value and the quintessence of the whole universe are imbibed in the existence of man. The importunity and the vexatious issues are those of the eternity and constancy of man's soul. Wisdom was active since ancient times for the sake of the children of Adam.

Stanza: 48

48۔ آہ خالق کی مشیّت سے وہ انساں کا سفر
قالبوں اور عالموں سے کتنے گزرا ہے بشر

عالم ارواح ارواح کی منزل ہے اب پیش نظر

اور کتنی منزلیں آگے ہیں اس کا کیا خبر

کس لئے انسان کو ہے یہ شان فضیلت عطا

روح کیا ہے اور حاصل ہے اسے کیونکر بقا

نوٹ :

عالم کے معنی ہیں (1)حالت (2) کیفیت(3۳) قیام کر نیکی جگہ۔ انسان کی زندگی میں اس کی حالت بھی بدلتی رہتی ہے اور مقام بھی بدلتا رہتا ہے ، سوائے انسان کے اس دنیا کی کسی مخلوق کو روح عطا نہیں ہوئی ، انسان کے لیے روح خدا تعالیٰ کی خاص دین ہے اور جوہر لطیف ہے ۔

انسان دنیا میں پیدا ہونے سے پہلے اور ازل سے اس کی روح عالم ارواح میں رہتی ہے۔ یہ عالم کبھی عالم امر بھی کہلاتا ہے ۔ انسان کی زندگی کے سفر میں یہ سب سے پہلا عالم ہے ۔ ماں کے پیٹ سے جب بچہ پیدا ہوتا ہے تو وہ اس اسباب میں یعنی اس دنیا میں داخل ہوتا ہے کبھی دنیا کبھی عالم ناسوت بھی کہلاتی ہے کیونکہ ایک دن فنا ہونے والی ہے عالم اسباب۔ کا سفر ختم ہونے کے بعد انسان مر جاتا ہے ۔ انسان کے مرتے ہی اس کی روح عالم برزخ میں داخل ہوتی ہے۔ یہ وہ عالم ہے جہاں موت اور یوم الحساب کے درمیان روحیں قیام کرتی ہیں۔ عالم برزخ میں دو مقامات ہیں جو علیین اور سیجین کہلاتی ہیں۔ علیین ایک راحت و آرام کا مقام ہے ۔ جس میں نیک روحیں قیامت یعنی یوم الحساب تک ٹھہرائی جائں گی۔ سیجین ایک تکلیف اور مصیبت کا مقام ہے جہاں پر خبیث روحیں یوم الحساب تک ٹھہرائی جاتی ہیں۔ یوم الحساب میں عالم برزخ کی قیام کی مدت ختم ہو جائے گی۔ اس کے بعد انسان حساب و کتاب لینے کی خاطر پروردگار اپنی لاجواب قدرت سے تمام مردوں کو دوبارہ زندہ اٹھائے گا تمام لوگ میدان محشر میں داخل کئے جائں گے۔حساب کتاب ختم ہونے کے بعد جو لوگ جنت کے مستحق ہونگے اُنھیں جنت میں داخل کر دیا جائے گا اور جو لوگ دوزخ کے مستحق ہونگے اُنھیں دوزخ میں داخل کر دیا جائے گا۔ انسان کی زندگی کے سفر میں جنت یا دوزخ آخری عالم ہوگا ۔ اب اسلامی عقائد ہیں ۔ اب صاف ظاہر ہے کی انسان کی حالت کس طرح بدلتی رہتی ہے۔ اور اس کو اپنے زندگی کے سفر میں کتنے عالموں سے گزرنا پڑتا ہے اور کتنے مقام پر قیام کرنا پڑتا ہے ۔

قالب کے معنی ہیں جسم اور قّالبوں کے معنی ہیں جسموں۔ سب سے پہلے باپ کے جسم میں نطفہ رہتا ہے اس کے بعد وہ نطفہ ماں کے پیٹ میں علق بنتا ہے جسمیں خدائے تعالیٰ اپنی روح کا ایک چھوٹا سا حصہ پھونک کر جان بھرتا ہے اور رفتہ رفتہ اسکو انسانی جسم کی صورت بخشتا ہے۔ روح کو اپنے جسم کے اندر لیکر بچہ پیدا ہوتا ہے۔ جب آدمی مر جاتا ہے تو اس کی روح جسم خاکی کو چھوڑ کر جسم مثالی میں داخل ہوتی ہے۔ یوم الحساب یعنی قیامت کے دن پروردگار تمام لوگوں کو دوبارہ زندہ اٹھائے گا حساب کتاب کے بعد جنت یا دوزخ بھیج دیگا۔ لہٰذا شاعر نے اپنے کلام میں لفظ قالبوں کا استعمال کیا ہے ۔

ہندو مذہب کا عقیدہ جو تناسخ کہلاتا ہے اس کے مطابق انسان اس دنیا میں یعنی عالم اسباب میں اپنی ماں کے پیٹ سے کئی مرتبہ پیدا ہوتا ہے اور کئی مرتبہ مرتا ہے اور اس کی روح مختلف جسموں میں داخل ہوتی ہے۔ یہ اسلامی عقیدہ کے خلاف ہے ۔ خود حضرت دلیل مرحوم نے بھی اس نظم کے ایک باب تناسخ میں لکھا ہے کہ یہ عقیدہ خام خیالی ہے۔ اس عقیدہ کے خلاف شاعر نے اپنے کلام میں امکان بھر بحث بھی کی ہے۔

میں نے حضرت دلیل مرحوم کے دو مصرعوں کی تشریح اس لیے کی اور نوٹس اس لیے لکھے ہیں کہ ان کے الفاظ "قالبوں" اور "عالموں" کو پڑھ کر ناظرین کو تناسخ کا شبہ پیدا نہ ہو جائے۔ جی زید رضیہ بیگم

Tr-It is the pleasure of the many bodies and station know the number of stages over other creatures has soul by Allah are the pleasure of the Creator that the voyage of life of man has to pass through stations of many worlds. The world of soul is now in view. Man does not know of stages he has to go through in the future. Why the pride of excellence res has been bestowed on human being and why eternity has been gifted to Allah are the issues of mystery for man.

Stanza: 49

49۔ رحم مادر علق بنتا ہے نطفہ جس زماں

روح اپنی پھونکتا ہے اس میں خلاق جہاں

روح انسانی کا ہوتا ہے وہیں جلوہ عیاں

تا بشر سے ہو عیاں شان خدائی انس و جان

اختیار و عقل کا انساں محل کیونکر نہ ہو

دوزخ و جنت سے وابستہ عمل کیونکر نہ ہو

نوٹ :

خدائے تعالیٰ محسوسات اور غیر محسوسات کا جاننے والا عزیز اور حکیم ہے جس نے جو چیز بھی بنائی حسن اور خوبی کے ساتھ بنائی۔ چنانچہ یہ اس کی قدرت و حکمت ہے کہ انسان کی پیدائش مٹی سے شروع کی، پھر اس کے توالد و تناسل کا سلسلہ (خون کے) خلاصہ سے پانی کا ایک حقیر قطرہ ہوتا ہے قائم کے دیا۔ پھر اس کے تمام قوتوں کی درستگی کی اور اپنی روح(روح کا ایک چھوٹا سا حصہ) پھونک

دی اور اس کے لیے سننے،دیکھنے،اور فکر کرنے کی قوتیں پیدا کر دیں۔۔۔۔۔۔
دلیل(السجدہ -32 -6-7-8-9)

Tr:-When the sperm, contained in the seminal fluid of man fertilizes an ovum, and it congealed clot of blood, Almighty Allah blows into it a minute fraction of His spirit. de of blood with soul inside it, develops into a human form, the splendour of Allah's love and affection for human being gets manifested. Man is bestowed with wisdom and power because he contains a little amount of Divine spirit in his own self. As he has been e power of reasoning his evil deeds are sure to lead him to the hell and his noble deeds are sure to lead him to the heaven.

Stanza: 50.

50۔ دو ہواؤں کے توصل سے وجود آب ہے
آب میں جو بات ہے اجزاء میں و نایاب ہیں
رحم سے نطفہ کا ملنا روح کا اک باب ہے
آہ کیا امر خداوندی کی آب و تاب ہے
ہو نہیں سکتی مثالوں سے حقیقت جلوہ گر
کچھ حقیقت کی طرف البتہ جاتی ہے نظر

نوٹ:
دو ہوا یعنی آکسیجن اور ہائڈر وجن

Tr.- Water is formed by the two gases namely oxygen and hydrogen. Water cannot be made by one of its constituents. The fertilization of the ovum by the semen in the mother's womb provides scope for the soul to enter into the human feotus which is nothing but the bewildering command of God and the amazing splendour of Divinity. Though man has acquired a little knowledge, it is beyond his capacity to understand or explain the whole truth by illustrating examples

Stanza: 51.

51۔ خاک کے ذروں سے انسان تک نمود اختیار

فہم انسانی پہ ہے رد عمل سے آشکار

خیر و شر سے ہے بشر ہی کو جو ربط استوار

ارتقاء جاوداں ہے روح انساں کی بہار

اختیار ابن آدم میں ہے یہ حسن و جمال

شیوہ تسلیم میں ہے اس کی معراج کمال

(اختیار بشر میں اختیار الہی کی شان پیدا ہو جاتی ہے)

Tr:- The power of man to decide the issues starts from the particles of earth. The avoidance of endeavour is due to his wrong and undesirable attitude. Human life is strongly and steadily connected with his good and evil deeds. The beauty lies in spiritual evolution through noble deeds. The power of discretion of man is a beautiful gift of God. This beauty can be utilized for exercising total surrender to God which is the perfection of spiritual height.

Stanza: 52.

52۔ عالم اسباب میں مجبور ہے انسان بھی

ہے مگر و ہے بہا حکمت کے جوہر سے غنی

ہے صفت اس قادر مطلق کے جو اس میں بسی

اسکو مجبوری میں ہے قدرت بھی حاصل ہو گئی

حکمت انسان نے کیسے گل کھلائے ہیں یہاں

اس کی قدرت میں ہے تسخیر زمین و آسماں

Tr:- Though man is helpless by birth Allah has blessed him with rich sterling invaluable wisdom. Inspite of his helplessness, man has obtained a little amount because of his faculty contains the attributes of God. The scientific research and devicec have resulted in grand achievements. He has got the power to conquer the earth and heavens.

Stanza: 53

53۔ آدمی سے دفتر ہستی ہے بامعنی کتاب

ہے اسی کے عقل سے اسرار قدرت بے نقاب

اختیار اس کا ہے گو نا گوں جہاں میں انقلاب

اسکے قابو میں ہے آتش برق بادو خاک و آب

ہیں ابھی انسان سے اسرار جو لاکھوں نہاں

اسکی حکمت کے لئے ہیں ارتقائے بے

Tr:- The record of life in this material world became meaningful, only because of man's existence in it. A few Divine secrets were revealed only due to his wisdom and endeavour. His Down doing research, has yielded and exhibited the different types of revolutions in the fields of physical sciences, geography, electronics, electricity, atmosphere, geology and all other branches of studies.

To a little extent, the earth, water, gases, fire and electricity have come under the of man, Still lakhs of secrets are undisclosed, for some of which the endless evolution of win provides scope for research for the benefit of man.

C:- It has already been said that Allah has preserved a lot of knowledge for Himself has imparted a very little knowledge to man through his prophets and scriptures which necessary for man's survival as well as spiritual bliss and prosperity, and the limited know which provides scope for researches in all branches of studies.

In this 15th chapter of the text the poet expresses the ignorance of man about antiquity and ancientness of matter, the time of creation of matter, the origin of life in world, the time of the advent of Adam and Hawwa (Eve), the parents of human race, on ear In this connection, he has discussed some topics, some theories and the law of natural phenomena, most of which have already been discussed in the previous chapters. Deep study will show that the repetation of topics is connected with different aspects in the different chapters.

In this context, it is necessary to explain our little knowledge (imparted by Allah) about the creation of the universe, eternity of matter, beautification of sky by heavenly bodies formation of earth, development of matter, the law of changes, origin and history of animal life, appearance of human beings, eternity of soul, purpose of creation, seven stages of devotion fertilization of foetus, infusion of Divine spirit into the foetus, reward and punishment, interdependence of matter, need for the union of opposite elements or forces, discretion of man, avoidance of endeavour, eternal spiritual evolution, beauty of total surrender, grand achievements of scientific research, the limitation of man's power and control over natural elements, revolution in the scientific field, scope for research in the field of technology and different sciences such as physical, chemical, biological, geological, etc.

In the 45th Stanza of the text it is said that no person can find out the time since when the chain of consecutive creations of Allah, started. The connection between this world and its time of creation is really bewildering. The eternity of matter can be observed in every matter by the Pleasure of God, natural forces, and the industry, diligence Chalk piece was manufactured by man by using the required materials w the origin of matter, contained in it. The ancientness of the world is unknown. This world is the grave of unimaginable number of insects through the ages unknown.

No scientist can discover the correct time of the creation the universe nor can he calculate the correct time of the destruction of the present universe nor can he calculate the age of the matter by which it was created. Quran has given us some information about the verse in some Stanzas, two of which have been quoted below.

Anbiya'a-21:30- (Already quoted in the 9th chapter)

"Do not the unbelievers see that the heavens and the earth were joined together (as creation) before We clove them as under? We made from water every living thing. Will they not then believe?"

S.Haa Miim-41:11 (Already quoted in chapter 5)

Tr.Moreover, He comprehended in His design the sky and it had been (A.S.) smoke. He said to it (sky) and to the earth, 'Come ye together willingly or unwillingly'. They said, 'We do come together in willing obedience."

Now the modern scientists agree with the contents of the above mentioned Quranic stanza. From the research in Cosmology, matter and space were compressed into a single unit. I state then exploded to form the heavens and earth. Quran reveals the basic truth about the past and future of the universe. The creation of universe includes earth, stars, galaxies, stem etc. According to several scientists, the whole matter was in the form of a big very hot smoke before the creation of the universe. With the command of Allah, this mass of smoke exploded with a thundering sound which the scientists call 'Big Bang Explosion.'

This explosion scattered the matter into minute fragments in the space and thus the Universe was formed. The Big Bang theory is quite relevant to Quranic Stanzas. Our earth was one of the fragments.

In these lines the poet has expressed his surprise about the formation of this world. It must be remembered that the whole mass of hot matter was joined together. According to the scientists the Big Bang Explosion created the whole universe including the earth and all the heavenly bodies. Consequently, different atmospheres were formed for different planets. The fragment of hot smoke which formed this earth cooled down due to the influence of the temperature of its own atmosphere. The cooling effect converted the smoke (gas) into water. With passage of time certain proportion of water got condensed and formed the earth crust.

In the 46th and 47th Stanzas of the poem, the poet has pointed out the human ignorance about the ancientness of atoms, time of beautification of sky by sun, moon and stars, the time of parting of the fragments of flaming fire from the sun, the time of beautiful arrangement and proper order of the universe, the time when this world became the cradle of evolution, the time of the creation of the first life-giving seed, protoplasm, the history of animal life in thisworld, and the time of advent of human being in this world.

A few Quranic Verses have already been quoted about the creation of the universe with the support of 'Big Bang

Explosion' theory of the scientists. According to the Big B Explosion, the big mass of smoke burst out, its fragments spread all over the space formed the earth and the different heavenly bodies. The bright light of the sun and the twinkling stars beautified the sky.

It must be remembered that the whole hot mass of the universe was a single unit upon a time and that our earth is an integral part of it. In our solar system, we receive best from the sun. That is why the poet has described our earth as a piece of flaming fire (Multahib) which separated from the sun.

The poet has expressed surprise about the time of origin and creation of the first life giving seed which is called protoplasm. It is the first life-giving matter. It can be defined as the homogeneous structureless substance, forming the physical basis of life. It consists of chemical compositions which are necessary for life. The Quranic verses say that Allah started creating living beings in the water.

S. Anbiyaa'-21:30:-(part of the verse)

Tr:- "We made from water every living being."

The modern data given by the scientists are referred to here.

After The Big Bang Explosion, the part of the gas which constituted the earth got converted into hot water by the influence of the atmosphere. This hot water was not fit for habitation. This hot water gradually cooled down and the first protoplasm was created in the water. The living cells in the water jointed together in different numbers and the animals assumed different shapes. When the water got condensed and formed the earth crust, some part of it including the mountains came above the water level which brought some animals with them. Both the animals which came above the water and the animals which remained in the water procreated. The modern data provides the information that the oldest life must have belonged to the vegetable kingdom and that the algae has been found from the Precambrian period i.e. the time of the oldest known land organisms, belonging to the animal kingdom.

All lives require water for biological activities and need this compound for propagation and survival. hence the early life appears to have its origin from water. Furthermore, the flora. fauna and the fossils found in the excavated rocks provide data for the scientists to infer that life started from the water, and thus the process of evolution started in this world.

In the 48th Stanza of the text, the poet has expressed his ignorance about the reason as to why Allah has bestowed human being with the pride of excellence over other creations and why He has granted eternity to soul, the unique gift for man. He has also hinted regarding the developments and stages, the man has to get through during the voyage of his life.

A'alamthe world, or condition or state. Changes in condition takes place in rations also go on changing. Except man, no other creature on earth has with soul, the invaluable and beautiful gift with its sterling and intrinsic value.

Before the birth of man, his spirit existed in the specific world (station), the world of the time unknown. The world of the spirits is called the "A alam-e-Arwah" as Amr". The stay in A alam-e-Arwah is the first stage of man's sojourn of life. he is the second world for the fertilized foetus. The material world in which we The A'alam-e-Asbaab as well as "A'alam-e-Nasoot". When child is born, it enters od After his death, his soul enters into "A alam-e-Barzakh". The word "Barzakh duration between the death of the man and the Day of Judgement. There are in this world called "liyeen" and Sajjayeen". Illiyeen is a place of peace and comforts of sipless people while Sajjayeen is a place of torment and torture for the souls of The duration of the period of Barzakh will come to an end on the Day of Reckoning. by the astounding power of Allah, all the dead people will be resurrected. All the awarded with punishment or reward according to their deeds during their life in Those who deserve punishment will be sent to the hell; and those who deserve all be sent to the heaven. These are their last and final worlds. This is my own reward will be sent to explanation.

According to Moulana Khaja Kamaaluddin, the first A'alam is A alam-e-Arwah: the second the mother's womb, the third a'alam is the stage of childhood, the fourth a'alam is the stage of youth and the final one is the stage of old age.

Qalib means body (Jism). The soul travels through many bodies. This assertion means the stage of development of the foetus in the mother's womb. Every development changes shape of the foetus. Every change in the structure of embryo is considered to be a different body (Qalib). According to some scholars, body in the childhood, body in the youth and body in the old age are different bodies.

First, the spirit is blown into the material or corporeal body (Jism-e-Khaki) and after the man's death, the soul enters the immaterial or astral body (ism-e-Misali) in the hereafter.

Just as the corporeal body (Jism-e-Khaki) has several stages in this world, the astral body (Jism-e-Misali) has its own spiritual stages. The mention of seven firmaments of heaven in Quran connotes the seven stages of spiritual evolution.

This Stanza deals with embryology, birth of man, his resurrection which explain the stages of life and different conditions. In order to support the statements of the poet, the following Quranic Stanzas have been quoted.

S.Mu'minuun-23:12-14

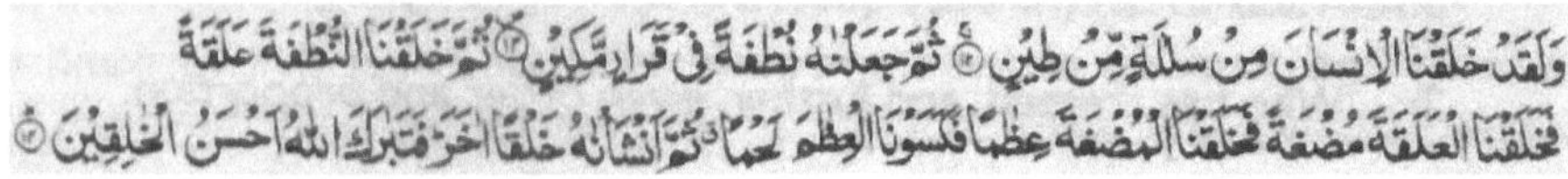

Tr:- "Man, We did create from quintessence of (clay). Then We placed him as a (drop of) Sperm in a place of rest firmly fixed. Then We made the sperm into a congealed clot of blood of that clot. We made a (foetus) lump, and bones and closed the bones with flesh, then we developedout of it another creature. So, blessed be Allah, the Best to Create."

S:Hajj-22:5- "O Mankind! If ye have a doubt about the Resurrection, consider) that we created you out of dust, then out of sperm, then out of a leech like clot, then out of a more of flesh, partly formed and partly unformed, in order that We may manifest (our power you and We cause whom we will to rest in the womb for an appointed term. Then you We bring you out as babies; then foster you, that you may reach your age of full strength: a some are sent back to their feeblest old age, so that they know nothing after having known (much), and further thou seest the earth barren and lifeless. But when we pour down rain it, it is stirred (to life), it swells and puts forth every beautiful growth in pairs."

The above-mentioned verses have explained the development of foetus, stages of lie in this world and the Day of Resurrection. These Stanzas provide data for the research in embryology also.

In his poem Kayinath, the poet has said that the soul passes through many worlds and several bodies. This statement arouses the doubt about the notion of Rebirth which explain that the cycle of rebirth of man in this world with the same soul, goes on. Islam is dead agains the concept of incarnation. According to Islamic concept, the soul enters into the corpore body only once and the man will never be reborn in this world from another mother's womb. I have presented this explanation in order to prevent and expel the doubts of the readers regarding the usage of plural words as worlds and bodies in the poem.

The 49th Stanza of the poem has dealt with fertilization of ovum by the sperm, infusion of Divine spirit in the human foetus and the cause of retribution in the hereafter.

In these lines, a brief description is presented about the process of creating man by Allah which He does out of His love and affection for human race. When the sperm fertilizes the ovum in the mother's womb, it becomes a small lump of congealed blood.

At this stage, Almighty Allah infuses a minuted fraction of His spirit in the human foetus in order to display human excellence over other creatures on earth. Then the foetus begins to develop with proportions prescribed by Allah till it assumes the human form. Many Quranic Stanzas including the above mentioned Stanzas and the following two Stanzas provide data for the research in genetic engineering and embryology.

S.Alaq-96:2:

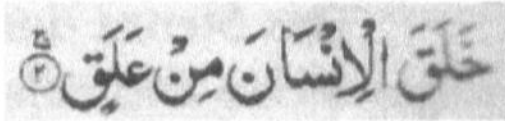

Tr:- "Created man out of a (mere) clot of congealed blood."

S.Al-A'alaa-87:2:- (Already quoted in the 12th chapter)

Tr:- "Who has created, and further, given order and proportion."

This presence of Divine spirit in human being, facilitates him to acquire wisdom and power of discretion. As he is at liberty to choose his way of life, he is bound by Divine Law to

taste the bitter fruits for his evil and good deeds respectively. Every action of Allah manifest His greatness splendour. The issue of "Retribution will be dealt with detail in the 18th chapter of the text. The following three Stanzas explain the process of creation of Adam Alaihis Salam with clay, in the paradise and his progeny on this earth witha fully developed body with faculties of vision, audition feeling and comprehension.

S. Sajda-32:7-9.

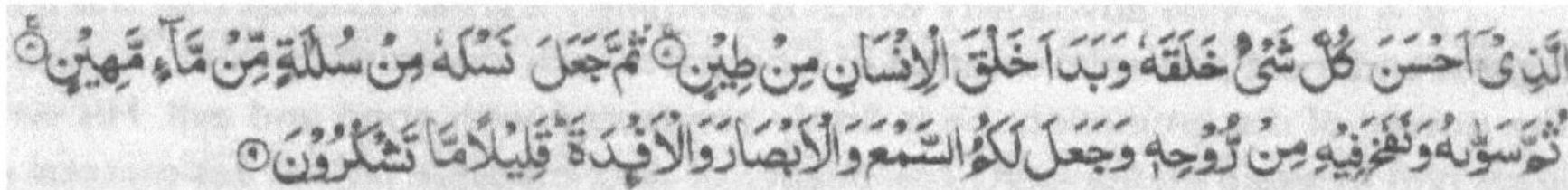

Tr - "He Who has made eve creation of man with nothing more the nature of a fluid despised. But something of his spirit. And He has made everything which He has created, most good: He began the othing more than clay. And made his progeny from a quintessence of coised. But He fashioned him in due proportion, and breathed into him of his spritsomething And

He gave you the faculties of) hearing and sight and feeling and understanding). Little thanks do ye give."

The subject matter of the 49th Stanza of the text can be clearly understood by the careful scrutiny of the commentary.

The 50th Stanza of the text expounds the sexual and asexual reproduction by the combination union of two opposite forces. The duality of the constituents of any matter will be dealt with in detail in Chapter No.25.

In the first reference to the notion of pair'in the kingdoms of all spheres,has been made in Quran,most vividly in Sura-e-Yaseen. It may be observed in Quranic Stanzas that the word expressed in the same way for the plant, animal and human reproduction. With the advance of the Science, the Quranic exhortations of creation in pairs have been well understood and have been found to be accurate. Every person has the knowledge of the fact are a male and a female are absolutely necessary for the birth of a new individual. Jual production, there are also asexual production through multiplication of cells. opposite forces and also certain things can be formed by the union of two opposite its. Deeper scientific research discloses the amazing presence of pairs and beauty of Allah's creations.

The poet has explained the formation of air by two constituents, namely Oxygen and Hydrogen, the two gases having the opposite faculties. Oxygen is a hot gas while hydrogen is a cool gas. Heat and coldness are required to form the air. Hence the opposite constituents are interdependent to form the air, we respire.

Now the poet proceeds to explain the sexual reproduction of human being and expresses his amazement at the incomprehensible Divine command and the splendour of Divinity. The fertilization takes place when the semen is deposited in the mother's womb and when the sperm unites with the ovum. Man and woman possess opposite sexes. The sperm is the male factor and the ovum is the female factor for reproduction. By the astounding command of God, a scope is created for the soul to enter the human foetus. The stages of development of the foetus also have been described in Quran. Only this much is known to man through Quranic Stanzas and scientific discoveries have promoted a little more knowledge. Though man has acquired a little knowledge about the truth, the whole truth can never be explained by any number of examples. Only Allah is All knowing.

The 51st Stanza of the text deals with the most powerful creation of God, man's wrong discretion, avoidance of endeavour and total surrender to Allah.

It is the Divine advisability which is seemingly a great contrast that the life of man, the highest and most powerful creation of God starts with lowest thing mud. As human being has the power of discrimination, he is firmly connected with good and evil. His wrong attitude leads him to avoid endeavour. The beauty of discriminative power lies on total surrender to God which is the height of spiritual perfection.

Total surrender does not mean to be inactive or to stop supplicating to God. We must be completely resigned to the will of God after exerting maximum efforts and due endeavours. Supplication is equally important which pleases God.

No human being is immune to grief and there is no human being in the world who has not suffered the pangs of failures in life. Many people may think that God has been unkind to them. But those who repose confidence in God and are aware that it is impossible to escape the consequence of their misdeeds, will bear the catastrophe with equanimity. While caught in the whirlpool of calamities, one can overcome the grief by submission to God. The hallmark of steadfast devotion is the trait of remaining absolutely calm in the midst of disasters. True devotees submit to Divine dictates. They will not feel frustrated or disturbed inspite of offensives from outside. The devotee will cling to God in times of adversities. If so, God will grant His devotee sufficient courage to face the ordeals. Though Allah is supreme, He is accessible to those who are devoted to Him. Faith in the Supreme Being and surrender evoke and ensure Divine grace.

H:- "Our Lord! grant us the good in this world and the good in the hereafter and save us from hell". (Muslim)

H:- "It is a virtue of man to be satisfied with what Allah has granted to him. It is a sin if he is not satisfied. It is undesirable if he stops supplicating to Allah". (Ahmed, Tirmizi)

H:-"The heart of man is a branch in the jungle. He is always worried about his problems. The man who reposes confidence in Allah and leaves his problems to be solved by Allah, He sets right his problems (Ibn-e-Maja).

To sum up, endeavour, supplication and surrender to Divine dictates are sure to lead to spiritual perfection.

The 52nd Stanza of the text explains about the grand achievements through scientific researches and modern technology.

When compared to the unlimited knowledge of All-Knowing Allah, man's knowledge is nothing. Inspite of this great limitation, Allah has blessed him with rich sterling quality of invaluable wisdom. It is by God's Pleasure that man's faculties have in them Allah's attributes. Man's capacity to invent modern devices and to promote knowledge by doing research have brought him grand achievements. To some extent he has acquired a little power to conquer the earth and heavens. The exploitation of his power is quite beneficial to him. By the conquest of earth ,the poet means to say that man extracts, minerals, metals, coal, gas and oil from the conquest of heaven, he means to say that man can fly above our atmosphere into the atmospheres of other planets. Men landed on the Moon. They have taken photographs of other higher planets. Several man-made satellites and space shuttles are revolving in the space.

A few discoveries through analytical devices have been presented below for which Ouran has provided data. :

S.Nahl-16:66

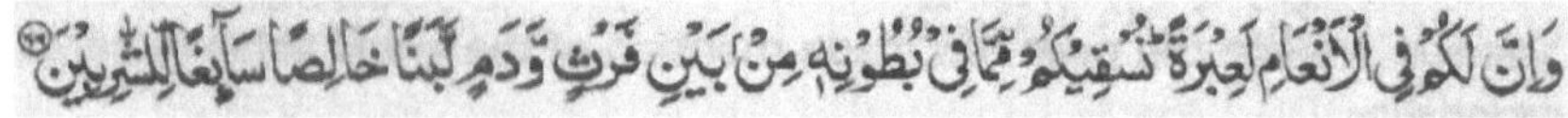

Tr:-And verily in cattle (too) will ye find an instructive signs. From what is within their bodies between excretions and blood, We produce for you drink, milk pure and agreeable those who drink it".

Through analytical devices, scientists have come to know about the components of milk are vital and essential to maintain health and physical strength.

S.Nahl-16:69:

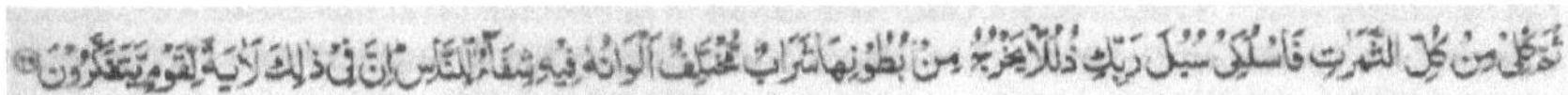

Tr:-"Then to eat of all the produce (of the earth) and find with skill the spacious paths of there issues from the bodies, a drink of varying colours, wherein is healing for men. Verily in this is a sign for those who give thoughts."

The above-mentioned Quranic verse speaks about the advantages and usefulness of Different tasty drinks are prepared out of honey Quran says that honey has healing effects Having benefited by the data furnished by Quran the doctors started the analysis of honey and discovered the healing effects in it. Experiments proved that stomach ulcers were cured by oral intake of honey, and the skin ulcers are being healed.

S. Al-Baqara-2:233:- (Part of the verse

Tr:- "The mothers shall give suck to their offspring for two whole years".

Quran has recommended breast feeding. Doctors also say that mother's milk is the best food for the babies. Modern research findings have disclosed that avoidance of breast feeding is one of the greatest causes for the blindness and defective vision of the children.

S.Zumar-39:42:

اللّٰهُ يَتَوَفَّى الْأَنْفُسَ حِيْنَ مَوْتِهَا وَالَّتِىْ لَمْ تَمُتْ فِىْ مَنَامِهَا ۚ فَيُمْسِكُ الَّتِىْ قَضٰى عَلَيْهَا الْمَوْتَ وَيُرْسِلُ الْأُخْرٰى إِلٰى أَجَلٍ مُّسَمًّى ۚ إِنَّ فِىْ ذٰلِكَ لَآيٰتٍ لِّقَوْمٍ يَّتَفَكَّرُوْنَ ۞

Tr:- "It is Allah that takes the souls (of men) at death, and those that die not. (He takes) during their sleep' those on whom He has passed the decree of death, He keeps back (from returning to life). But the rest He sends (to their bodies) for a time appointed. Verily in this are Signs for those who reflect.

Sleep and death are said to be the twin sisters. In the case of death, the soul separated from the body forever and all the physical systems cease to function. Quran that Allah takes out the soul temporarily from the body of man during his sleep and sends the soul to his body when he wakes up. But, even during his sleep, all the cells of his body. alive and active. Hence, sleep is sometimes called half death. Quran clearly says that takes out the soul during sleep. The scientists who do research in the spirits put man to for experiments. They have expressed their amazement after observing something on out of the body of the sleeping man. Such mysteries are being discovered with the advanc Science. Hence the poet has made mention of the grand achievements of man owing to his rationality.

In the 53rd Stanza of the text the poet has pointed out the importance of human life in this world, his rationality, his wisdom and potentiality which have brought about revolutions all walks of life.

The realization of God's existence is most essential aspect of life. The absence of this aspect makes the creation of the world meaningless. Except man, no other creature on earth has rationality which is required for God-Realization. The records of human existence constitute a book, full of sense and wisdom. His power and capability has brought about revolution in all aspects of life which other creatures cannot do. Though he cannot obtain control over the nature, his limited power has brought, the fire, the electricity, air, earth and water under his control to some extent. For example, man can produce electricity and can utilize it in different ways at times of need. Man has acquired powers to compress a lot of gas into a small container Water can be stored in the reservoirs by constructing dams, to be used at the times of necessity There is ample scope for the endless evolution of wisdom of man as lakhs and lakhs of secrets are being undisclosed.

The above explanation proves that man is the most meaningful creation of God. (Geography, genetic engineering, embryology, mine, space technology, history of origin of animals, chemistry, cosmology, biology and mystic worlds).

CHAPTER - XVI

CHANGE, DEATH, DAY OF DOOM RADIATION, GALAXIES AND EVOLUTION

———⊙⊙↭ ♦ ↭⊙⊙———

16۔ تغیر , موت , قیامت , ریڈیاشن
محفل انجم اور ارتقا۔

Stanza: 54

54۔ ہے جہاں اس حی قیوم کی جلوہ گری
کیوں نہ ہو ہر چیزمیں شان حیات سرمدی جوبھی ہے
موجودہ معدوم ہو کیوں نہ کرکبھی
ہم نہیں سمجھے عدم کیا ہے فنا کیا ہے ابھی
دہر میں لیکن تغیر ہے ازل سے ہر زماں
وہ نہیں مٹتے نگاہوں سے جو ہوتے ہیں نہاں

Tr:- All the creations in this world are the manifestations of Allah. As everything is imbibed Allah's effulgence, it is possessed of the splendor of eternal life. The matter created by God can never be annihilated. We cannot understand the meaning of the destruction of matter but the change in shape or form is going on in the matter from the beginning. Those things which get concealed from our Vision do surely exist in another form

Stanza: 55

55، شمع روشن ختم ہوجاتی ہے جو بن کر دھواں

اور صورت میں وہ ہوتی ہے فضاؤں میں نہاں

آب ہوتا ہے فنا پیش نظر جو ہر زماں

ہے وہے چلکر بخار و ابر زیر آسماں

اس تغیر میں بقاۓ زندگی مستور ہے

نقل منزل ہی فنا کے نام سے مشہور ہے

Tr:-The Candle-stick of wax converts into smoke after burning. This smoke gets absorbedin and mixes with the atmosphere in another new form. The vapour and cloud below the sky the water which vanishes from our sight. The stage of shifting and changing is destruction. In fact, the eternity of matter is concealed in this change.

Stanza: 56

56۔ ہے تغیر باغ ہستی کی بہار ہے خزاں

داستان زندگی ہے انقلابوں میں نہاں

بے تغیر زندگی ہوجائے مرگ جاوداں

کیا قیامت ہو جو محروم تغیر ہو جہاں

یہ تغیر جس کا جلوہ دمبدم دن رات ہے

زندگی اور حسن کی تجدید ہے اثبات ہے

Tr - The factor of change is the result of even blooming beauty of life. The history of life depends upon these revolutions of changes. The absence of change in the matter amounts to eternal death. There would have been greatest disaster in the world, had there been no changes in the matter. The changes in the matter take place continuously night and day. This process is the evidence for the renewal and revival of beauty of existence.

Stanza: 57

57۔گر نہ ہوتی موت کب جینے کے قابل ہو

موت مؤمن کے لئے ہے باب فردوس بریں

موت کا دن ہے تعین اور اٹل بالیقین

موت کا ڈر پھر بھی ہے اہل ہوس میں جا گزیں

چاہئے انساں کو ہر دم گناہوں سے حزر

ہے خدا کی راہ مرنا سعادت سر بسر

Tr:- In case no person dies, this earth will become inhabitable. Death opens the door for the believers to enter into the high paradise. One day the people will surely and certainly pass away from this world. Inspite of this certainty, the people who have worldly desire have fear for death which has killing effect. Every human being must abstain from ills and evil. That person is fortunate and auspicious who dies for the sake of God.

Stanza:58

58۔گو صفات رب میں گوناگوں تغیر ہے عیاں

دست حکمت میں ہے رہوار تغیر کی عناں

مصلحت زیر فرماں ہے عمل پیرا جہاں

اسکی بآئیں روش ہوتی ہے معیار زماں

ہے عدم نا آشنا شآن الہی کا ظہور

ہے زمانے کے تغیر میں نہاں روز نشور

Tr:- Though all sorts of changes are seemingly present in the attributes of Allah reign of change is under the control of human wisdom. The world is active under the common of the expediency of God. The regulated activities of the world determine the standard of life The splendour of the manifestations of God can never be extinct. The day of Resurrection will be the result of the march of time and the charges it brings about.

Stanza: 59

59۔ ہے نتائج سے عمل اپنے ہمیشہ ہم بغل

عرشئہ محشر میں ہے برزخ ہو یا دارالعمل

سب یہاں ملتے نہیں اعمال انسانی کے پھل

گر نہ ہو روز جزا ظالم ہو رب لم یزل

امتیاز نیکوبد و خیروشر مفقود ہو

زندگی گمراہ ہو بے معنی و مقصودہو

Tr.- Whether they are on the Day of Reckoning or the period of Barzakh (period between death and the Day of Resurrection) or in this world of activities, the effects on life are concerned with the deeds of man. The man does not obtain all the fruits for his noble deeds. If Allah does not resurrect man and grant him his due rewards. He will be regarded as an oppressor and unjust. In case, God does not resurrect man, his life will be obscure, meaningless and purposeless and there will be no more distinction between good and evil and between vices and virtues.

Stanza: 60

60۔ کائنات دہر ہو اور اقوام ہوں

بے خبر دست قضا سے کس طرح آزاد ہوں

بے مقدر دوسرے انکی جگہ آباد ہوں

یک نئی دنیا نئے آئین پھر ایجاد ہوں

بے کلام پاک سے انکی حقیقت گو عیاں

اہل حکمت سے بھی سن لے کچھ قیامت کا بیاں

قرآن پاک کے بیان کو سائنس سے ثابت کیا گیا ہے

Tr:- Whether they are individuals or nations or Universe they are bound to be destructed one day, but some people are unaware of this. They are destined to occupy another place for their evolution. They find a new world with the newly formulated laws. Both the Quranic verses and scientific assessments ascertain the approaching event of the Day of the Doom.

Stanza: 61

61۔ آسماں کے یہ مہ و انجم یہ مہر ضوفشاں

سربسر تاریک ہوجائیں گے یک دن بے گماں

گردش املاک میں بھی ہے تغیر ہر زماں

چور ہوسکتے ہیں ٹکرا کر زمین آسماں

پہلے اس دن سے کہ جب برہم ہو بزم کائنات

گل جہاں میں ہو چکی ہوگی ہر ایک شمع حیات

Tr- All the heavenly bodies viz, the stars, moon and sun which strew their light to illumine, the world will definitely lose their lustre and become dark one day. There is continuous change even in the revolution of heavenly bodies. The heavens and earth can clash with each other and be destructed. Before the occurrence of this phenomenon namely the destruction of the Universe, every life in this world would have gone out of existence.

Stanza: 62

62۔ ہیں رواں بھی یہ زمین و ماہ سوئے آفتاب

مہر کے پہلو میں یک دن ہو نہ کیونکر ماہتاب

ہے بپا پیہم زمین و آسماں میں انقلاب

زلزلوں سے کانپتا ہے یہ جہاں خاک و آب

کوہ خود اسباب طبعی سے سرک آتے بھی ہیں

آتش خود سے پگھل کر دھات بنجاتے بھی ہیں

Tr-This earth and Moon are coming closer and closer towards the Sun. The Moon may clash with the Sun one day. Continuous changes are going on in the revolutions of heavens and earth. This world of mud and water is trembling owing to the earthquakes. The mountains themselves change their positions due to their natural, physical or innate causes. mountains melt with their own inner heat and become metal such as bronze, aluminium etc.

Stanza:63

63 ۔ یک تجلی دہر میں ہوتی ہے گو قوت فزاں

گو زمانے میں ہے جاری سلسلہ تخلیق کا

ہو رہی ہے قوتیں اشیاً سے جدا

زندگی خاص گوشوں میں فقط ہے ارتقآ

عالم قدرت کوحاصل ہو چکا شاید کمال

ہے نمایاں اسکے ہرحصے میں آثار زوال

Tr-Though the refulgence of Allah is capable of granting strength and the succession of God's creation is evident, some energies are separating from some creations and find their specific places for their evolution. Perhaps some creations have obtained perfection. Inspite of this, the signs of declining and waning are present in every part of the creations.

C:-The main subject matter of this chapter is "The Law of changes" which have already been discussed in the previous chapters, but in connection with different factors. Now the factors Death, Day of Doom, Galaxies, Radiation, Evolution, standard of life, Expansion of Universe, Destruction of Universe, Recreation of Universe, Retribution etc., all of which are bound by the Law of changes have been elucidated.

The developments and changes are considered to be revolutions. Changes can be brought about by the intention of man, industry of man, nature of deeds of man, shifting of places, advance of time and natural forces. But the first and ultimate cause is the pleasure of Allah.

In the 54th Stanza of the text the poet asserts that it is but natural that every creation has in it the splendour of eternity because, it is only the manifestation of God who is an Eternal Being. The extinction of the present matter can never be imagined. Right from the origin of the world Law of changes is continuously active. Though the matter goes out of our vision, it is present in the nature in another form. Matter does not get destroyed or destructed.

For further explanation, the poet has presented the examples of candlestick (made of wax) and water in his 55th Stanza:

The bright candle-stick gets extinguished after melting and burning completely. Though it is invisible, it is in the form of smoke in the atmosphere. The water, present before always evaporating and converts itself as vapour or cloud under the sky. The shifting or stage of a matter is understood as its destruction. The poet says that eternity will continue only after losing the previous forms.

In the 56th Stanza of the text the poet says that the eternal beauty of existence depends on changes. The history of life is full of revolutions of changes. If there is no change in the life, it will mean the eternal death, which is impossible. In case of absence of change in the matter, the calamities and distress will be beyond human imagination. The law of Changes which is active night and day is the proof or evidence for the beauty of renewal or revival of life. Let us take an example of a seed. When a seed is sown and watered, it bursts and gives up shoot after losing its original form. This shoot grows as a great tree which begins to flower. This flower loses its form and becomes a fruit.

In his 57th Stanza, the poet says that the earth will become uninhabitable if things do not die and provide scope for the renewal of life of the matter in the different form. This death is essential for everything and it opens the door of the high paradise for the believers. Death is certain. Even then, people having worldly desires have horrible fears for death. Abstention from crimes and vices are necessary for human beings because they have to reap the fruits of their deeds in the hereafter. It is definitely our fortune if we die for the sake of God.

A true believer abstains from evil deeds, and worldly desires, fights with his carnal emotions and fears God every moment. Hence this world is considered to be a prison for the believer where he has to fight with all sorts of evils. It is very tough for the believer to lead a noble life in this world. Death is a blessing for him which relieves him from all hazards of life and transfers him to the High Paradise, abode of endless comforts, luxuries and pleasantness.

Inspite of the knowledge of the certainty of death, the people of worldly desires and lust, wish to live longer and longer in order to enjoy the revellings of this world. They always have horrible fear for death. Unlike the believers, they do not realise the fact that to die in the way of God is quite auspicious.

Though the Attributes of Allah are of changing colours, the rein of change is in the hand of wisdom. The world is active under the advisable command of God. The regulated activity of the world determines the standard of life. Though the involvement of man's industry contributes much in the law of changes, the ultimate controller is Allah. The amount of man's contribution and intensity of grace of Allah determine the standard of life. The continuous manifestations of God in the changed condition are responsible for the Day of Resurrection from life to death and from death to Resurrection.

In the 59th Stanza, the purpose of Allah and the necessity of the Day of the Doom has been explained.

The results and effects are always connected with the nature of man's actions,whether the are in the duration of the span of life in this world, or Burzakh (the period of station Resurrection) or in the period of Day of Reckoning. The Reckoning. The purpose and that Allah wishes to give ample rewards to the virtuous people rewards in this world. If He ignores the virtues of the people and does not grant deserving rewards He will be considered an oppressor and an unjust Sovereign. Allah is Most Merciful rewards to the virtuous. The second necessity of the Day of the Doom is to preserve the distinction between good and evil. In the absence of the concept of Day of Doom this distinction will vanish.

The third necessity explains that there is no certainty of the Day of Doom, the human life will become obscure, meaninglessand purposeless. Its certainty may lead the virtuous believers to tread on the path of righteousnesstry to attain spiritual perfection and achieve their goal, God.

In the 60th Stanza of the text it is said that whether they be nations or individual or the Universe, nothing can escape from destruction.They are destined to evolve in another place after their destruction from their previous forms.A new world will be created for them and formulated. The Quranic verses and the scientific discoveries confirm the Day of Doom.

The 61st Stanza of the text deals with the description of the event. One day the shining moon, the twinkling stars and the light strewing sun will lose their luster and become completely dark. There is possibility for the earth to clash with the heavenly bodies as there are continuous changes in their revolutions.Before this jumbled disorder In the Universe all sorts of have life become extinct.Here is a point to be carefully noted.Almighty Allah's providence is astonishing. Allah created the living beings in this world after providing them with other creations which are essential for life.

Life depends on the services of Allah's creations especially the sun and vegetations. Vegetations also depend on the light and heat of the Sun. It is the astounding scheme of Divinity that it causes the heavenly bodies lose their lustre after extinguishing life from the world

The 62nd Stanza describes the continuous occurrences of revolutions in the heavens and the earth due to physical reasons.

Scientists have observed that the earth and moon are travelling closer to the Sun and one day the Moon may clash with the sun. The trembling of the earth due to earthquakes, the changing of positions of the mountains due to innate or natural reasons and melting of the mountains due to their inner heat bring about great changes on the surface of the earth. Here is the hint about about the volcanos and the thrown out and cooled lava full of metallic substances like bronze, alumimium etc.

The 63rd Stanza deals with the change in the physical phenomenon of Radio evolution of the radiated rays of the heavenly bodies on earth.

Though the refulgence of God is strength giving and though the succession of is continuous, the energies of rays are being emitted by the heavenly bodies. These rays evolve in their own particular spheres on earth. Their light and heat help for the of man. beast, birds and vegetations. They give different colours to the different things there been no change in the emitted rays, life on earth would have come to an end. Du perfection of Divinity, the signs of declining are present in every part of the creations.

Quranic verse Ahadis-e-Nabvi and scientific discoveries confirm the occurrence Day of the Doom. The scientific explanation has been given in commentary later. Some Quarnic verses and some Ahadis have been presented in the following - which describe the very Day of the Doom and the description of the signs of the nearness of that event.

S:Infitaar:82:| -3

Tr:- "When the sky is cleft as sunder: When the stars are scattered; when the oceans suffered to burst forth."

S. Takweer-81:6:

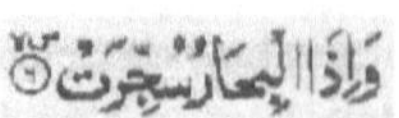

Tr:- "When the oceans boil over with a swell."

S. Takweer-81:11:

وَإِذَا السَّمَاءُ كُشِطَتْ ۝

Tr:- "When the World on High is unveiled."

S. Takweer-8|:| -3

إِذَا الشَّمْسُ كُوِّرَتْ ۝ وَإِذَا النُّجُومُ انْكَدَرَتْ ۝ وَإِذَا الْجِبَالُ سُيِّرَتْ ۝

Tr:- "When the sun (With its spacious light) is folded up, when the stars fall losing their lustre, when the mountains vanish (like a mirage)."

S.Aaraaf:7:187 (Part of the Sura)

يَسْأَلُونَكَ عَنِ السَّاعَةِ أَيَّانَ مُرْسَاهَا قُلْ إِنَّمَا عِلْمُهَا عِنْدَ رَبِّي لَا يُجَلِّيهَا لِوَقْتِهَا إِلَّا هُوَ ثَقُلَتْ فِي السَّمَاوَاتِ وَالْأَرْضِ لَا تَأْتِيكُمْ إِلَّا بَغْتَةً يَسْأَلُونَكَ كَأَنَّكَ حَفِيٌّ عَنْهَا قُلْ إِنَّمَا عِلْمُهَا عِنْدَ اللَّهِ وَلَٰكِنَّ أَكْثَرَ النَّاسِ لَا يَعْلَمُونَ

Tr:- "They ask thee about the final hour - When will be its appointed time? Say, 'The knowledge thereof is with my Lord alone."

S.Ahqaaf: 46:3:

مَا خَلَقْنَا السَّمَاوَاتِ وَالْأَرْضَ وَمَا بَيْنَهُمَا إِلَّا بِالْحَقِّ وَأَجَلٍ مُّسَمًّى وَالَّذِينَ كَفَرُوا عَمَّا أُنْذِرُوا مُعْرِضُونَ

Tr-We created not the heavens and the earth and all between them, but for just ends, and for a time appointed. But those who reject Faith, turn away from that, whereof they are warned.

S Maaarif-70:89.

يَوْمَ تَكُونُ السَّمَاءُ كَالْمُهْلِ ۞ وَتَكُونُ الْجِبَالُ كَالْعِهْنِ ۞

Tr-"The Day that the sky will be like molten brass and mountains will be like wool."

SMursalaat-77:8-11:

فَإِذَا النُّجُومُ طُمِسَتْ ۞ وَإِذَا السَّمَاءُ فُرِجَتْ ۞ وَإِذَا الْجِبَالُ نُسِفَتْ ۞ وَإِذَا الرُّسُلُ أُقِّتَتْ ۞

Tr- "Then when the stars become dim, when the heaven is cleft asunder, when the mountains are scattered (to the winds) as the dust and when the Apostles are (all) appointed a time (to collect)."

S.Yaaseen-36:38:

وَالشَّمْسُ تَجْرِي لِمُسْتَقَرٍّ لَهَا ذَلِكَ تَقْدِيرُ الْعَزِيزِ الْعَلِيمِ ۞

Tr-"And the sun runs his course for a period determined for him; that is the decree of (Him). The Exalted in Might, He is All-Knowing."

S.Inshiqaaq:84:3-4:

وَإِذَا الْأَرْضُ مُدَّتْ ۞ وَأَلْقَتْ مَا فِيهَا وَتَخَلَّتْ ۞

Tr- "And when the earth is flattened out and caste forth what is within it and becomes (clean) empty."

Arabic 5. Zumar-39:68:

وَنُفِخَ فِي الصُّورِ فَصَعِقَ مَنْ فِي السَّمَاوَاتِ وَمَنْ فِي الْأَرْضِ إِلَّا مَنْ شَاءَ اللَّهُ ثُمَّ نُفِخَ فِيهِ أُخْرَى فَإِذَا هُمْ قِيَامٌ يَنْظُرُونَ

Tr:- "The Trumpet will (just) be sounded, when all that are in the heavens and on earth will swoon. Except, such as it will please Allah (to exempt). Then will a second one be sounded when, behold they will be standing and looking on."

S.Hajj-22:2:

يَوْمَ تَرَوْنَهَا تَذْهَلُ كُلُّ مُرْضِعَةٍ عَمَّا أَرْضَعَتْ وَتَضَعُ كُلُّ ذَاتِ حَمْلٍ حَمْلَهَا وَتَرَى النَّاسَ سُكَارَى وَمَا هُمْ بِسُكَارَى وَلَكِنَّ عَذَابَ اللَّهِ شَدِيدٌ ۝

Tr. "The day, ye shall see it, every mother giving her suck will forget her suckling baby and every pregnant female shall drop her load (unformed). Thou shalt see mankind as in a drunken riot, yet not drunk, but dreadful will be the Wrath of God."

In the following are a few Ahadis about the signs of the nearness of the impending Day of the Doom.

H:-"This is also one of the signs of the Last Day that the low people will build big houses and lofty mansions and will be proud of them'. (Bukhari)

H:- "When the Day of the Doom approaches, the war booties will be considered as own belongings, cheatings will become common, knowledge will be acquis not for spiritual benefit but it will be acquired only for the material and worldly benefits. Zakaat will be considered as the penalty. Man will carry out the commands of the woman. People like the company of friends and desert their fathers. There will be riots, chaos and commotion in the mosques. Leadership will be transferred to the hands of undesirable people (Tirmizi)H.- "By Allah, the Day of Doom will not occur till the time when you do not murder your ruler will not fight among yourselves with swords and undesirable people will inherit the worldly powers! (Bukhari)

H:-" The event of the Last Day will not occur till the time when the wealth does not begin to flood in all directions, till the time when the land of Arabia will not become fertile and will not have canals". (Mishkat)

Hi-"When the murders and massacres become common, imagine that the Doom of Day is nearing" (Mishkat).

H. "It is doubtless that when the Day of Doom approaches, the Divine knowledge will be vanished from the world society, adulterations will increase and the men population will be more". (Bukhari)

H- The Day of Doom will occur when honesty would have disappeared, adhere Divine Law would be finished and power would have been transferred to evil-natured rulers at this situation, you can wait for the Last Day". (Bukhari)

H:- "When the worship of True God diminishes and idolatory increases, you that the Last Day is approaching" (Mishkaat)

H:- "When the Last Day approaches people will reach the far off countries very soon and they will seem to be very near. There will be music in every house". (Tirmizi)

H:-"When the Day of Doom approaches, the Muslims will fight with the Jews and cause the unbearable afflictions to that extent that they will run away and hide themselves behind the rocks. (Muslim)

The above quoted Quranic verses and the prevailing conditions of the society and Ahadis-e-Nabvi have confirmed the certainty of Death and the occurrence of the Day of the Doom.

The belief in the unity of God and belief in the Last Day and Resurrection are very essential. Those people irrespective of their religions who believe in those two concepts will have no grief or difficulty on the Day of Reckoning.

S.Al Baqara:-2:62:

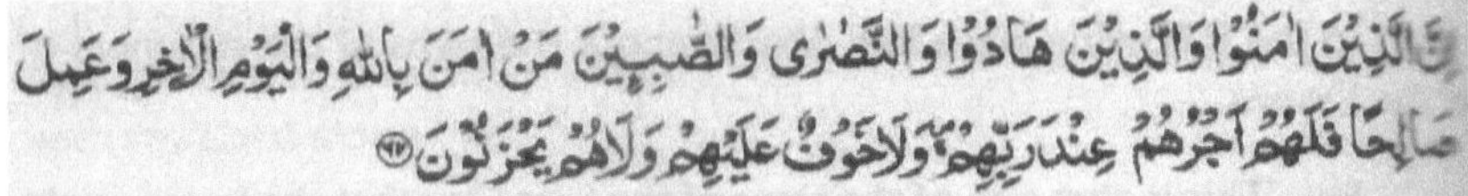

Tr:- "Those who believe in (the Quran), and those who follow Jewish (scriptures) and the Christians and the Sabians, and who believe in Allah and the Last Day and Work righteousness with their Lord; on them shall be no fear nor shall they grieve."

Even for sinners, redemption requires belief in the unity of God and Hashr, the Day of Reckoning. Allah has promised to reward those who believe in these two aspects irrespective of caste and religion.

The standard of life of people in this world and in the hereafter depends upon the nature of deeds viz., good and evil. The necessity of the Day of the Doom and Resurrection to do certain acts which will cause his ruin. If he is not conscious of his weakness but continues arises for the sake of Retribution. The accomplishments of a person through years and discipline can be destroyed in a moment's carelessness. Not knowing his limitations, man may venture his mistakes, his life will end in misery in this world and hereafter as well.

S.Muddassir-74:38:

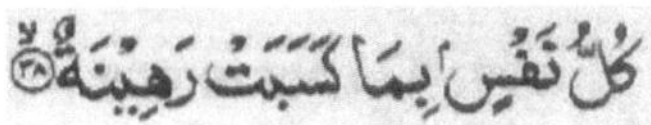

Tr-Every soul will be held in pledge for its deeds."

H:- "Itikaaf restrains a person from sin". (Itikaaf is considered to be a source of spiritual enjoyment and the highest order and standard of life)

H:- Those people who cause torture to people in this world Allah will cause them torment in the hereafter (Retribution) (Muslim)

S.Waaqia-56:88-94:

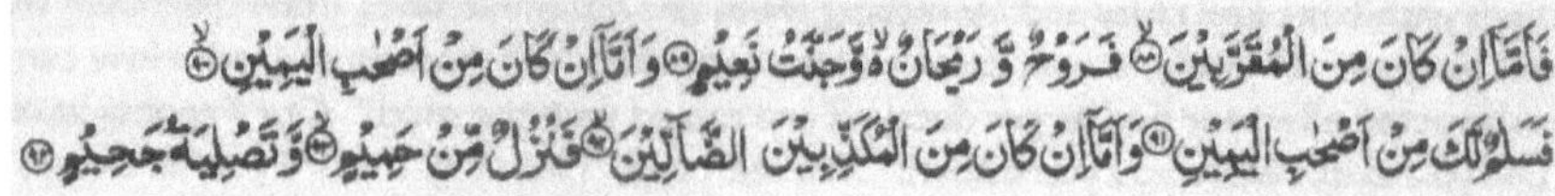

Tr-"Thus, then if he be of those who are nearest to Allah, (There is for him rest and satisfaction and a garden of Delights. And if he be of the Companions of the Right Hand, (for him is the salutation) 'Peace be unto you" from the companions of the Right Hand. And if he be of those who treat (Truth) as falsehood, who go wrong, for him is entertainment with boiling water and burning in hell-fire". (Retribution)

The significance of the Last Day is well understood. Next comes the confirmation of Resurrection. After passing through the stage of Burzakh and the event of the last Day, the whole humanity will be resurrected.

S.Hajj-22:7:

Tr:-"And verily the hour will come; there can be no doubt about it or about the (fact) that Allah will raise up all who are in the graves."

S.Qiyaamah-75:1:

لَا أُقْسِمُ بِيَوْمِ الْقِيَامَةِ

Tr:- I do call to witness the Resurrection Day."

S.Qiyaamah-75:3-4:

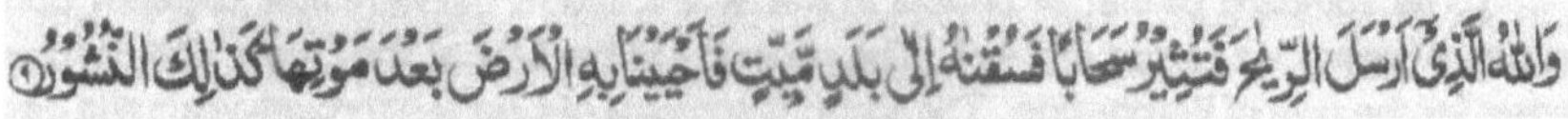

Tr:- "Does man think that We cannot assemble his bones? Nay. We are able to puttogether in perfect order, the very tips of his fingers."

S.Faatir:-35:9:

وَاللَّهُ الَّذِي أَرْسَلَ الرِّيَاحَ فَتُثِيرُ سَحَابًا فَسُقْنَاهُ إِلَى بَلَدٍ مَيِّتٍ فَأَحْيَيْنَا بِهِ الْأَرْضَ بَعْدَ مَوْتِهَا كَذَلِكَ النُّشُورُ

Tr:- "It is Allah who sends forth the winds, so that they raise up the clouds and Wed them to a land that is dead. And We revive the earth therewith after its death; even so (will the Resurrection."

H:-"Do not wrong anyone. You will be resurrected in the light (not in darkness) on the Day of Resurrection".

H:- "The Day of Resurrection will come when the murders will become abundant"

During the life time of Prophet Muhammad (PBUH), people used to come to him having their doubts cleared. In simple words and in an easy manner he would clear off their doubts.

Sometimes he used the Socratic method for interpreting the issues ie., by interrogating them with hints and clues and by making them draw the inference from their own thoughts and tongues. One day, a man came to him and asked "Oh Apostle of God! How can we be resurrected after our bodies get decayed and mixed with the mud?" Our Prophet asked him "Did you exist before you were born?" The man said, "Not at all". Our Prophet asked, "Then how did you come into existence?" The man said, "I came into existence by the Divine power Our Prophet asked him "Can't this same peerless Divine power and Omni-Potence of Allah resurrect you?" The man said, Certainly it can. Now, I am convinced about resurrection"

At all times and in every nation Prophets were sent with the message of unity of God and some specific mission.

After the period of Jesus Christ, Jerusalem was conquered and totally destructed by a Zoroastrain Persian King. The scribe, priest and reformer by name Azeez was sent by the Persian King to reconstruct Jerusalem and reform its people. In Quran his name is referred to as Uzair and the Jews call him Ezra. The Judes, a sect of the Jews believe him to be the son of God. Hence Judaism dates from the period of Uzair. He passed through a ruined, hamlet of Jerusalem and expressed grief that God could not bring that land to life. Allah wanted to display his astounding Divine Powers. When Uzair was riding on his ass with a hot meal to be consumed later, Allah put him to sleep for hundred years. When he woke up, he saw the bones of his donkey, dead long ago and found his meals still hot. When he was perplexed Allah spoke to him and asked, "How long did you sleep?" He said, " Perhaps less than a day". God said, "No, you slept for hundred years. See the bones of your donkey, which died decades back, but your meal is still hot". Then Allah resurrected the donkey which stood up. After witnessing the resurrection of the donkey, he believed in the Omni-Potence of one God and believed in resurrection. He became a believer and boldly started his mission of reconstructing Jerusalem after being convinced that the completely annihilated land can be revived.

Uzair was a Prophet and Allah spoke to him thoughs the Angel. This story has been 259:- This incident took place after the period of Jesus Christ and before advent of Islam. Jesus Christ was the last Prophet in the lineage of Prophets. Who were the descendant of Ishaq (AS), the younger son of Ibrahim Alaihis Salaam. Our last Prophet Muhammad was the descendant of Isma'il Allaihis Salaam, the elder son of Ibrahim Alaihis Salaam Uzair was not the descendant of Prophet Abraham but he hailed from someother Persian tribe.

The following versespeak about the request of Prophet Abraham to display his peerless power of Divinity for his Own Satisfaction.

S.Bagnra-2.260 -2:260:- Behold! Abraham said "My Lord! Show me how thou gives life to the dead He said, "Dost thou not then believe?".Yea, but to satisfy my own understanding He said' take four Birds tame them to turn thee. Put a portion of them on every hill and call to them. They will come to thee flying with speed.Then know that Allah is Exalted in Power Wise". Prophet Abraham did according to Allah's instructions. The slain birds came flying from the hills in response to Abraham's command.

On the day of Reckoning, the good and evil deeds, vices and virtues of man and spiritual evolution will be taken into account. Hence it is necessary to examine the issues of good and will be evil and spiritual evolution.This also is an important change in the sojourn of man's life.

Maa'ida-5:35:

مِنْ اَجْلِ ذٰلِكَ كَتَبْنَا عَلٰى بَنِيْ اِسْرَآءِيْلَ اَنَّهٗ مَنْ قَتَلَ نَفْسًا بِغَيْرِ نَفْسٍ اَوْ فَسَادٍ فِى الْاَرْضِ فَكَاَنَّمَا قَتَلَ النَّاسَ جَمِيْعًا ۖ وَمَنْ اَحْيَاهَا فَكَاَنَّمَا اَحْيَا النَّاسَ جَمِيْعًا ۚ وَلَقَدْ جَآءَتْهُمْ رُسُلُنَا بِالْبَيِّنٰتِ ثُمَّ اِنَّ كَثِيْرًا مِّنْهُمْ بَعْدَ ذٰلِكَ فِى الْاَرْضِ لَمُسْرِفُوْنَ

Tri:-"On that account, We ordained for the children of Isra'il that if anyone slew a person spreading mischief in the land-it would be as if, he slew the whole wed the life, it would be as if, he saved the life of the whole people." unless it be for Good and Evil).

H:-Observe truthfulness as a duty and always speak the truth for truthfulness puts you and path of virtue leads you to heaven, and a person tells truth as a rule and makes truthfulness a way of life he attains the place of sincerity and truthfulness, and withGod, his name is written among the sincere. Stay strictly away from falsehood as it puts you on the path of immorality and leads you to hell: and when a man takes to lying, the sequel is that, his name his written God among the faithless and the insincere" (Good and Evil) Bukhari Muslim).

Spiritual evolution: Religious Muslim scholars have postulated three states of the development human souls.

Ammarah (Nafs-e-Ammarah). In this state, the soul is prone to evil. It is neither checked nor controlled. This state will lead the soul to perdition or total destruction. .

b.Lawwama:- In this state of soul, the man is conscious of his evil deed.

He resists it and regrets over his sin. He tries to mend his ways. After true and sincere repo seeks God's grace and pardon and hopes to attain salvation.

Mutama'inna:. In this state of soul the man is sinless. This is the highest soul. He is blessed with rest and complete satisfaction.

The two states of soul viz, Lawwama and Mutamainna will enable it to elevate cross through the seven stages (seven firmaments of heaven) and reach the stage of perfection.

Our bodily life and death are not the whole story of human existence. Human comprised of both bodily development and spiritual evolution. The corporeal body die a short stay in this world. But the soul never dies and has to taste the fruits of vices and virtues. We must try to avoid the bitter fruits.

In our life of probation on this earth, our faith is tested by God, by causing calamities adversities, prosperity and temptations. In order to pass our probation with success, we prove our true mettle, prove the values of human life and at all situations we must be patient and thankful to God. We must attach the greatest value to our spiritual life which is eternal.

In the foot notes the poet has commented against the wrong notions of some philosophers. He says, "Some philosophers who accept the theory of the controlling authority of evolution, imagine that the manifestations of God are meant for His evolution. They believe that God changes Himself and manifests in His creations for His Evolution, reinforcement stability and pleasure in the struggle of life. Hence, He is engaged in the struggle from the beginning. This is anti-Islamic : notion. The creations do not know where they have to go and where their destination is. But Allah knows everything. They adopt any new condition, they come across and accept the new habitats and begin their activities. This wrong and anti-Islamic theory makes God imperfect, defective, unsound, worthless and incapable of attaining perfection. This wrong concept makes our faith invalid and our wisdom perverted every way Allah doesn't need any evolution as He is infinite, perfect and All-Pervading"

Day of Reckoning:- Resurrecting is as easy for Allah as He wakes us from our sleep. Resurrection of the whole humanity is meant for Reckoning the deeds of people and awarding retribution. i.e. good for good and bad for bad.

In the first Chapter of Quran (Sura-e-Fatiha) itself Allah has claimed Himself to be the Lord on the Day of Judgement.

S. Hajj-22:1:

يَٰٓأَيُّهَا ٱلنَّاسُ ٱتَّقُوا۟ رَبَّكُمْ ۚ إِنَّ زَلْزَلَةَ ٱلسَّاعَةِ شَىْءٌ عَظِيمٌ

Tr:- "O mankind! Fear your Lord! For the convulsion of the Hour (of Judgement) will be a thing, terrible."

S. Nisaa-4:30:

وَمَن يَفْعَلْ ذَٰلِكَ عُدْوَٰنًا وَظُلْمًا فَسَوْفَ نُصْلِيهِ نَارًا ۚ وَكَانَ ذَٰلِكَ عَلَى ٱللَّهِ يَسِيرًا

Tr:- "If any do that in rancour and injustice-soon shall We cast them into the Fire; and easy it is for Allah."

S.Naaziat-79:14:

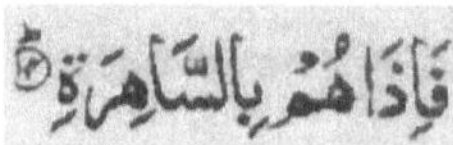

فَإِذَا هُم بِٱلسَّاهِرَةِ

Tr- "When, behold, they will be in the (full) awakening (to Judgement),"

H-Do not invoke Allah's curse against one another nor invoke Allah's wrath nor invoke the curse of the fire (of hell). (Bukhari Ahmed, Dawood, Tirmizi).

H-A poor man among the people is he who will bring on the resurrection, Prayer, fasting, Zakaat, but will come having reviled a man, aspersed another, devoured the property of another, shed the blood of some and beaten others. Then the people, he harmed will be given some of his good deeds. If taken and cast upon him and he will be cast into the hell" (Muslim)

H:- By inflicting harm on others, a person harms himself. When he restrains himself from doing that, he spares himself of Allah's displeasure. That is a net gain". (Punishment for inflictions and reward for goodness.)

The above-mentioned Ahadis and Quranic verses reveal that the Day of Judgement will be established soon after the Resurrection and people will be awarded punishment and reward. They will be finally sent to the places they deserve .ex. hell or paradise. This is the greatest change in the spiritual life of man.

The Day of Reckoning (Mahshar) will be extremely dreadful but less dreadful than the wrath of Allah which will be at its peak. It is best for us to believe in the Day of Reckoning and make preparations for the hour so that we may be blessed with the mercy of Allah. We have finished discussing about the changes in man's sojourn in this world and in the hereafter.

Stanza: 64

64 ۔ محفل انجم کی سرگرم سفر ہے ہر زماں

فاصلہ ہر دم فزوں ہوتا ان کے درمیاں

ہیں زوال آمادہ اجزائے زمیں و آسماں

یک نئی دنیا سے جائیگا بدل سارا جہاں

ہند کہتا ہے جہاں سیلاب سے ہوگا تباہ

ہر کتاب آسمانی ہے قیامت کی ہوا

Tr- The galaxies are revolving night and day. The distance between them goes on increasing. All the parts of heavens and earth show the signs of their indulgence in declining or waning. Once an Indian scientist said that this world will be destructed by submerging in the water: Every scripture has revealed the certainty of the event of the Day of Doom.

Stanza: 65

65- عام ہے یوں تو زمانے میں قیامت کا یقیں

آشنا ہے اس حقیقت سے نگاہ نکتہ چیں

منتشر ہونگے بدل جائیں گے افلاک و زمیں

اصلیت ان کی مگر معدوم ہو سکتی نہیں

یک نئے سانچے ڈھالی جائیگی بزم حیات

یک نئے انداز میں ہوگا نظام کائنات

Tr:- The concept of the certainty of the Day of Doom has been accepted by all. People blessed with high intellect and good comprehension are fully aware of the impending event of the Day of Doom. The heavens and the earth will be scattered and changed. But, the original essence and basic substances which have constituted the Universe can never be destructed. Life will be moulded in the different form in the recreated universe and its administration willbe of a novel type.

Stanza:66

66- ارتقاء کے گر نہ سانچے میں نہ ڈھلا ہوتا جہاں

گر سکوں ہوتا خمیر محفل کون و مکاں

گر نہ یہ نشونماں ہوتی بہار جاوداں

کیا زمانہ حکمت کامل کی ہوتا داستان

عین خلقت ہے صفات رب کا گونا گوں ظہور

ارتقائے ذات اسکو کسطرح سمجھے شعور

66/باب ۔ ارتقا

نوٹ :

بعض مفکرین جو کائنات میں اصول ارتقاء کی کار فرمائی کو تسلیم کرتے ہیں ، ظہور صفات کو ارتقاء ذات سمجھتے ہیں ، اُن کا یہ عقیدہ ہے کہ ذات باری (کائنات کی خودی) اپنی خودی کی تکمیل نشو ونما استحکام اور لذت پیکار کے لئے غیر خود (جو اپنی مخلوق ہے) سے بدلتی ہے اور ازل سے مصروف جہاد ہے لیکن یہ نہیں جانتی کہ اس کی منزل کہاں ہے اور اس کو کہاں ہیں جانا ہے ، جو۔ نئے حالات پیش آتے ہیں اُن کے سانچے میں خود کو ڈھال کر مصروف جہاد ہو جاتی ہے ، نہ وہ اپنے انجام سے واقف نہ اس کو کوئی منزل مقصود ہوتی ہے ، اس غیر اسلامی نظریہ سے خداوند کریم کی ذاتناقص ناقابل تکمیل ثابت ہوتی ہے نیز ایمان مجروح اور عقل سلیم گو نا گوں ہو جاتی ہے اس لئے مناسب معلوم ہوتا ہے کہ اس خطرناک نظریہ کچھ اشارہ کر دیا جائے تفصیلی بحث اور تنقید کے لئے اس مختصر نظم میں گنجائش نہیں ہے ۔۔۔۔۔۔ دلیل

Tri-If the world is not prone to evolve; if the quintessence of the matter contained the Universe is inactive, if the development in the eternal beauty is absent, how can art and Divinity be realized by people? It is true that there are different manifestations of God It is a wrong notion to assume that these manifestations are meant for the Evolution of God.

Stanza:67

67- مقصد ہستی ہے تخلیق حیات و آگہی
منزلیں طے کر کے آئی ہے بشر کی زندگی
ارتقاء ہے بستہ تکمیل روح آدمی
ہے عطا پھر کس لئے اس کو حیات سرمدی
ارتقاء یک حرف بے معنی ہے انسان کے بغیر
اور ہے انسان ہی کیا عقل و ایماں کے بغیر

Tr:- The purpose of life is the creation of life with awareness and insight of man. The life of man has finished crossing several stages. The soul of man is bound to reach the stage of perfection. For this purpose, it has been bestowed upon him the eternal life. In the absence of human life in this world, the idea of evolution is meaningless . A man cannot be calleda human without wisdom and faith.

Stanza:68

68- ارتقاء ہے ذات باری میں تو وہ ناقص ہوا

اس پہ جو قربان ہی وہ عقل کیا ایمان کیا

وہ کبھی کامل نہ ہو اب تک جو ناقص ہی رہا

ارتقاء کا ذوق ہی کیسا یہ عالم جب نہ تھا

لازمی ہے ذات بے پایاں و ازلی میں کمال

آپ ہی ناقص نہو داخل کہاں سے ہو زوال

غیر اس کی ذات سے ہو کس طرح جلوہ نما.

Tr:- The concept of evolution of God, makes Him imperfect and defective. Those who believe in the evolution of God, their wisdom is perverted and their faith is unsound and worthless. If God is still imperfect, He will remain imperfect forever. How could He have desire to evolve before the creation of this Universe? God, the Eternal and Shoreless Ocean is certain to be perfect. Divinity which is essentially perfect can never decline.

Stanza:69

69- خلق کے کس راز سے خالق رہے نا آشنا

عالم مجبور سے یہ لذت پیکار کیا

ہے اُسے جانا کہاں رہ رو نہیں یہ جانتا

ہے مراد ارتقاء انسان میں تکمیل شعور

کونسی کمزوریاں اللہ کی ہوتی ہیں دور

Tr:- How can the whole of Divinity be present in God's creation? Which is the secret of the people which is concealed from God?

In this world of helpless condition, how can God taste the pleasure of struggle? The traveler does not know his destination. The purport of evolution in human being is nothing but the achievement of the perfection of wisdom. By the evolution of God, which of His weaknesses are being eradicated?

Stanza: 70

70۔ ہے اُسے یکساں صفت اسکی عیاں ہو یا نہاں

ہے اسی میں ہے اسی سے یہ زماں ہو یا مکاں

چشم بینا ہے وہی وہ وحدت ہے عیاں

جس میں گم ہے آب تغیر اور کثرت کے نشاں

حاجت تکمیل کیا ہو ذات کامل کے لئے

بحر بے پایاں نہیں بیتاب ساحل کے لیے

Tr:- Whether it is manifested or concealed, the Attribute of God is the same. The time and place depend upon the activity of His Attribute. The vision which sees the Truth realizes the unity of God. The changes and signs of diversities are merged with the unity of creation god is neither anxious nor desirous of evolution or to achieve perfection, Who is already perfect from the beginning.

Stanza:71

71۔ پا نہیں سکتی خدا کی ذات کو چشم بشر

پا رہا ہے وہ زمانے کی نگاہوں کو مگر

اس کے جلوہ دیکھنے کو چاہیے اس کی نظر

اس تجلی گاہ میں جبریل کے جلتے ہیں پر

عاشقان خاص محبوب خدائے کار ساز

ہو بھی جاتے ہیں کبھی اسکی نظر سے سرفراز

God but He can resembles Divine visare blessed we cannot see werful a vision which resembles Divine vision. God overs of God who are also the beloved of God are blessed with

Tr:- The human eye cannot see God but He can see everything in this world.In order to see God, the man needs so powerful a vision which resembles Divine vision. Sometimes, some special and sincere lovers of God who are also the beloved of God are blessed with a little amount of Divine vision.

C:- In some of the above mentioned verses of the text, the poet has attempted to wrong notion of the evolution of God by presenting his own arguments and interrogations.

The Eternity of Allah is itself an evidence that Allah is perfect.

S. Furqaan-25:58

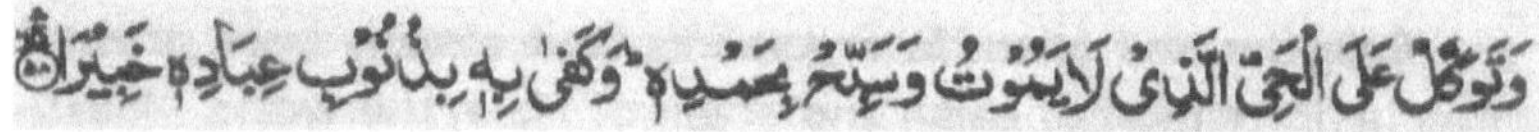

Tr- "And put thy trust in, Who lives and dies not; and celebrate His praise; and enough is He to be acquainted.

An eternal Being cannot be imperfect. The origin of Allah can never be known to anybody. To know it is beyond human intellect. By Quranic verses, we have come to know that Divine power existed before the creation of the Universe. Those people who say that God manifests in His creation for the sake of evolution, should know as to how could He have desire for evolution before the creation of the Universe. The whole of Divinity cannot be manifested in the creations. The creations exist in this world in the helpless condition. They of act on their own accord but they have to carry out the command of God.

How can the Supreme Commander wish to have the pleasure of struggle of life in the world which is helpless under His domination? Evolution is meant for the perfection of human wisdom and certainly no weaknesses , weaknesses to be eradicated from Divinity. God is never anxious to evolve as it is not at all required.

God can see everything but human eye cannot see Him. The poet says that some devotees with this prestige. At the times of concentrated devotion, the devotees feel the refulgence of God in their hearts and minds. At the persist Moosa Alaihis salaam. Allah showed him a minute fraction of his refulgence swooned. The vision of Prophet Mohammad (PBUH) was strong and capable enough to see the entire refulgence of God on the night of Me'iraj because he was His most Beloved Apostle. The conversation between Allah and Prophet Moses through the clouds is a clue for the Invention of satellite transmission.

The poet centrated persistent request of fulgence by which he pable enough nost clue for the invention

For providing scientific explanation for my commentary, I collected points pertaining to space Exploration and other phenomena of nature from the articles of several scientist Zakir Naik of Bombay and Zahir M.Ahmed of California to whom I am highly grateful and indebted.

Galaxy - The luminous band or the splendid assemblage of stars, comets, satellites and planets is called a galaxy. These heavenly bodies contained in the galaxy circle around the and constitute the solar system. Allah has said in the Holy Quran that He has created suns and many moons. Our solar system is called The Milky way of galaxy. It revolves the sun which gives us light and heat. According to the astrologers our solar system is extremely small fraction of other galaxies in the universe. This small galaxy the Milky way estimated by the scientists to have 400 billion stars in it.

Right from the childhood, human beings observe some striking and mysterious phenomena in the nature such as rising and setting of sun, the changing phases of the moon appearance and disappearance of comets and occurrences of solar eclipses, lunar eclipses etc. Before the advancement of Science, it was a total mystery for man.

In this 16th Chapter of the text "The Expansion of Universe" and The Recreation of the Universe remain to be discussed.

Religious and scientific arguments have already been presented about the creation of Universe, formation of earth and origin of life in the world. Next, we have to examine the change in the development of the universe, namely "The Expansion of the Universe". The Quranic information and observations of the scientists regarding the Expansion of the Universe tally with each other.

S. Zaariyaat-51:48:

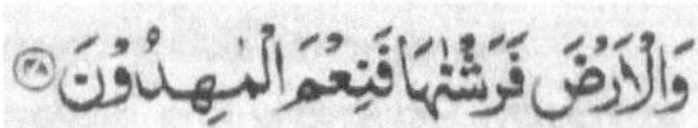

Tr.- "And we have spread out the (spacious) earth. How excellently we do spread it."

In the above quoted verse, Allah says, "We do spread it out". It means he is still spreading and expanding the Universe. The following paragraph has been extracted from the article written by astrologer Zahir Ahmed of California.

"It is only during 1900's that a famous scientist Edwin Hubble (1889-1953 A.D.) discovered through observations and experiments that all galaxies are receding from one another and expansion of Universe can be illustrated by a simple mode. Consider a rubber balloon with ink-dots (representing galaxies) marked on its surface. As the balloon is being inflated, the

distance between increases and they appear to move away from one another. In the way if we imagine the Universe to be expanding, there will be a recession of all the Hubble's "Law of Recession of galaxies" forms the basis of moderncosmology and is taken as the evidence of an expanding Universe which also confirms the initial explosion (Big Bang) at the beginning of creation. The force of the explosion is still active and pushing the heavenly bodies away."

What will happen when a balloon is inflated beyond limit? It will explode. In the same way if the Universe goes on expanding it will explode one day and bring about its destruction way, This is what is confirmed and described in the Quran and Ahadis as the Day of the Doom.

Some observations of other scientists regarding space Science, are worth mentioning here.They say that theTime limit has been mentioned (in Quran also) for the lives of the sun, the moon and the Stars. In modern cosmology, each star has a life time. The sun is a star. Stars live and die in the universe and this is a continues process. Our sun is five billion years old and it is predicted by the scientists that this star will also die.The sun runs its course in a settled placeThe observations in the space Science, today reveal that the sun is movinga nearly roundedpath about the nucleus of the Milky Way galaxy at a speed of 12 miles per second.With it the whole solar system Is moving in the direction of constellation Cyguns and it will settledown there and die.This place is also called"The ApexSun's way".

Before the death of the sun, each and every life would have been extinguished. The scientific observation about the time of death of the sun are all approximation. Allah only knows the facts. The scientists say that the sun has its own axial rotation as does the moon, and both bodies exhibit orbital revaluations as well. In the case of the sun, it revolves around the center of our Milky Way galaxy and would require about 250 million years to complete one revolution. The fact that sun rotates, was not discovered until the invention of telescope in the 17th century.

Recreation of the Universe:- How can the Eternal Being God can be idle when he has send message of continues strife and endeavor to man who leads a temporary life in this world? Allah does not want to keep us in total darkness. In Quran, He has given us information as to what will happen after the distraction of the universe, what will happen to the law of nature and what will happen after the termination of the present Universe. Some Quranic verses have been quoted in the following confirming the recreation of the Universe.

S.Ankabut-29:20:-

قُلْ سِيرُوْا فِى الْأَرْضِ فَانْظُرُوْا كَيْفَ بَدَاَ الْخَلْقَ ثُمَّ اللهُ يُنْشِئُ النَّشْأَةَ الْآخِرَةَ اِنَّ اللهَ عَلٰى كُلِّ شَئٍ قَدِيْرٌ

Tr: - "Say, Travel through the earth and see how Allah did originate creation; so will Allah produce a later creation, for Allah has power over all things."

S.Anbiyaa-21:104:

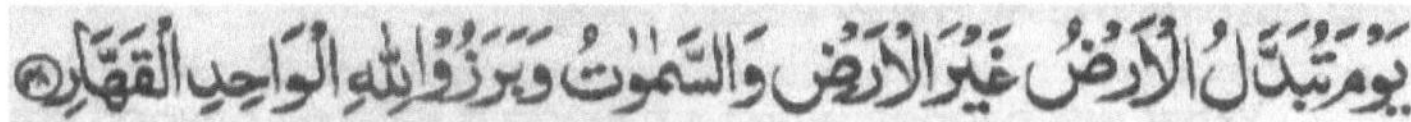

Tr:-"The day that We roll up the heavens like a scroll, rolled up for books (completed). even as We produced the first creation, so shall We produce a new one; a promise We have undertaken' truly We shall fulfil it."

S.Ibrahim-14:48:

Tr:- "One day, the earth will change to a different earth, and so will be the heavens, and men will be marshalled forth before Allah, the One, the Irresistible."

From the above quoted verses, it is very clear that the recreation of the Universe has been promised by Allah. He will repeat the creation based in memory of the first creation and in order to continue His functions and administrations. It is understood from 21:104 that the new universe will be created soon after the destruction of the present Universe. Quranic verse 14:48 explains that the new heavens and earth will be different from that of the present ones. The words "The earth and heavens will be changed to different ones" mean that the originally created matter of the destructed universe will be reused by Allah in creating the new Universe. Allah wants to give eternity to the matter originally created by Him. All the above-mentioned points have been mentioned in the Poem Kayinath. Allah has given us only this much of information about the recreation of the Universe. Allah has preserved the remaining knowledge for Himself. The transformation of the present universe into a new type of universe is a mysterious link in the chain of "Law of Changes". Allah is Omni-Potent and Omni-Scient (Perfection of God, Law of Changes, Geography: Physics, Chemistry, Technology, Space Science, Re-creation of Universe).

CHAPTER - XVII

STRUGGLE OF LIFE-JIHAD ARABIC

Stanza: 72

17۔ پیکار حیات

72۔ درس تسخیر و تکامل ہے نظام کائنات

داستان رزم ہے دنیا میں رو داد حیات

ناتوانی ہے شکست و قید و ادبار و قما ت

صرف طاقت ہے حیات و فتح و اقبال و نجات

قوت ایماں و حکمت طاقت مال و ہنر

زور بازو عزم فولادی جہاد بے خطر

Tr:- The Divine administrationthe universe itself is a lesson for the conquest and perfection. The account of life in this world is the historywar-like fights in all aspects of life. Weakness entails defeat, imprisonment,downfall and death.Only strength can fetch real life,victory prosperity and relief for the conquest of Power and achievement of perfection, some factors are required, namelystrength of faith and wisdom,financial capacity, dexterity of art physicalpotentiality strong determination and fearless fight.

Stanza: 73

73۔ بندہ محتاج کا ہے دین کیا دنیا ہے کیا

مرد مومن کے لیے دولت بھی ہے فضل خدا

تندرستی جب ہوئی غارت تو باقی کیا رہا

بستہ ادراک ہے روح بشر کا ارتقاء

یوں شگفتہ ہوں قوی حسن تناسب سے تمام

رفعت دل سے عیاں ہوں وصل باری کے مقام

چاہیے مردان حق کی کامیابی پر نظر

Tr:-This world and religion are meaningless for those people who are indulged in or like begging.For a true believer financial prosperity is a grace of God.Nothing can be said about the man who is sick. But spiritual is under the control of human wisdom.The Powers of man must become fresh by means of the beauty of proportion.The place of meeting God be known from the people of high spirit.

Stanza: 74

74 ۔ دہر میں افضل ترین قوت ہے اخلاق بشر

روح کی خیر و مسرت اس کی تکمیل و ظفر

بالیقیں ہے اُلفت و ایثار و ایما ں کا ثمر

یک نحوست ہے زمانے کے لئے مرد بخیل

بو الہوس ہوتا ہے یک حیوان و خونخوار و ذلیل

Tr:- A true Muslim must always aim at success. In this world the most important factor in the purity of character. The spiritual bliss, perfection and Victory are the fruit of love and sacrifice for other fellow beings. A stingy person causes evil influence in the society and a lustful person is contemptible and like a beast.

Stanza.75

75۔ مالک ارض سماں ہے اس کی ذات لا یزال

ملکیت اس کی ہے مومن کا متاع جان و مال

کام لے محنت سے دل کی موت ہے دست سوال

ہے ضیاء دل حیات جان و تن نان حلال

غیر کی محنت کا جو کھاتا ہے وہ انسان ہے کیا

جو تہی ہو آتش غیرت سے وہ ایماں ہے کیا

Tr:- The Eternal Being God is the Lord of heavens and earth. Life and material prosperity of a believer belong to Allah.Earn with hard strife,because begging amounts to the death of the heart. Those who have enlightened minds have got the real life and who earn their bread by honest means and earnest strife. The man who consumes the bread earned by others cannot be considered as a human being. The faith which is devoid of sense of honour, can never be called the real faith.

Stanza.76

76۔ عمر بھر رہنا پڑے گو آفت و غم کا شکار

صبر و استقلال اور ہمت سے رہ سرگرم کار

ہے اگر مرنا تو مر ہنستے ہوئے مردانہ وار

رائیگاں کرتا نہیں محنت کبھی پروردگار

زندگی کا سلسلہ ہے انتہا ہے بالیقین

اہل دل ناکام دنیا سے کبھی جاتے نہیں

Tr:- Though one becomes victim of calamities and grief, he should go on striving with patience, constancy and courage. Even when he has to face death, he must die with pleasure and manly courage. Allah never wastes the labour and endeavours of the people. It is certain that life is eternal. The enlightened man of courage does not leave this world without success.

Stanza.77

77۔ ہے جہاد زندگی سرمستی جام طہور

حادثات دہر میں ہے زندگی سوز و سرور

انتہائے عیش کا ہوتا ہے خطروں میں ظہور

اس حقیقت کو مگر سمجھے نہ بزدل کا شعور

پوچھ لطف زندگی کیا ہے دل بے باک سے

زندگانی کا سبق لے صاحب لو لاک سے

Tr:- The struggles of life have an intoxicating effect of a cup of pure wine which makes one engrossed in love for God. The mishappenings of this world disclose the real worth and values of life. The coward man cannot understand the fact that excessive reveling will entail dangers in life. Ask a fearless man about the real pleasure of life, learn moral lessons from the life of Prophet Muhammad (PBUH) and follow his example.

Stanza:78

78۔ اہل ایمان اس کی توفیق و رضا سے ہیں مگن

وہ صفات زندگی میں بے خطر ہیں گامزن

ہو نہیں سکتی کوئی طاقت کبھی ہمت شکن

ابتلا وں میں بھی ہے امید اُن کی خندہ زن

کامیابی دہر میں مخصوص ہے اُن کے لئے

مشکلیں آسان ہیں دنیا میں مومن کے لیے

Tr:- The believers are overjoyed and satisfied with the Divine guidance and Divine pleasure. At all situations of life, they are stepping forward fearlessly. They are never discouraged by the adversities. They always have confidence in God and their hope smiles. Hardships and hazards are easily overcome by the believers to whom success is certain

Stanza.79

79۔ ہے خلائق کے لیے کیا خوب رحمت کا نظام

ہے فلاح روح و تن پر منحصر عیش دوام

تاکہ ہوں کامل قوائے ظاہر و باطن تمام

روح سے غافل ہے انساں نفس دوں کا ہے غلام
اس ادھوری زندگی سے زندگی برباد ہے
نعمہ عشرت میں پنہاں نالہ و فریاد ہے

Tr:-The Divine administration is splendid for Allah's creations. The eternal bliss depends upon the purity of body and soul, so that the physical potentiality and spiritual potentiality may become perfect. But the lustful man is careless about the soul. The lust of man spoils his life and this sort of life entails sorrows.

Stanza: 80

80۔ زندگانی کے حقائق پر نہیں جس کی نظر
قدر و قیمت سے رہے ہے چیز کی وہ بے خبر
منحصر ہوتے ہیں اندازوں پہ اخلاق بشر
فقر کی عظمت کو کیا سمجھے غلام سیم و زر
خلق پہ کوئی کرے قربان اپنی جان و مال
خون بھائی کا روا رکھے کوئی بہر منال

Tr:- The person who cannot realize the aspects of life is unaware of the value of each and everything. The character of man depends upon the estimations. The slave of material desires cannot understand the glory and greatness of desire lessness. Certain man sacrifices his own life and wealth for others while another man murders his own brother for the sake of wealth.

Stanza: 81

81۔ مشعلیں راہ عمل کی ہیں برائے آدمی
نور و وجدان و حواس و عقل و ایمان و وحی
عقل ہوتی ہے جو تنویر ہدایت سے تہی

فی الحقیقت ہے زمانے کے لئے آفت بڑی

صاحب عقل و ہنر یہ شہ گردوں نشین

نیک جو انسان نہیں وہ در حقیقت کچھ نہیں

Tr:- The guiding lights for all performances, gift of knowledge, consciousness, wisdom, faith and divine revelations have been procured by God for the sake of man. In fact, the wisdom, devoid of guidance is a great misfortune and disaster of the world. Whether a man is wise or expert in art or a king seated on the highest position, is nothing in case he is bereft of piety.

Stanza: 82

82۔ عقل انسانی کی عظمت نہیں ہم بے خبر

اے کہ بحر فلسفہ میں غرق تھا شام و سحر

کون سا نایاب ہاتھ آیا حقیقت کا گہر

ہیں بہت اسرار حق بیرون ادراک بشر

ہائے وہ حکمت کہ جس میں سوز و ساز دل نہ ہو

رحمت و عدل و ربوبیت پہ جو مائل نہ ہو

Tr: We are not unaware of the greatness of human wisdom. It is true that man has been submerged night and day in the ocean of philosophy in order to acquire knowledge. But he could not bring the real pearl of ultimate truth because it is beyond human wisdom to know all the Divine secrets. That wisdom is pitiable which is bereft of divine enlightenment and which s not attracted by Divine bounties, justice and providence.

Stanza: 83

83۔ دین سے ہو کر جدا یوں عقل ہوتی ہے خراب

حلت و حرمت کا ہوتا ہے غلط اس میں حساب

اسکی گمراہی کرے ثابت گناہوں کو ثواب

ہو روا فحش و قمار و دزدی و سود و شراب

وہ ہوس کے ہاتھ میں یک خنجر خونخوار ہے

اسکی زہریلی ہوا سے زندگی بیمار ہے

Tr:-Wisdom gets perverted by discarding religious tenets and it miscalculates the dignity and legality. This perverted wisdom proves the unlawful factors such as foul language, gambling, theft, usury and wine, to be lawful. This sort of wisdom is a bloody dagger in the hand of a lustful person and its poisonous influence in the society fetches ills of life.

Stanza:84

84 ۔ کس قدر ہر ذرہ دنیا میں قوت ہے نہاں

جوہری بم اور آبی بم کی آفت الامان

ہے بہت تحصیل قوت میں جو انساں کامراں

ہو بہار جاوداں گلزار ہستی کی خزاں

عقل و قدرت لاکھ ہو تکمیل اخلاق بشر

ہو سدا پابندی احکام رب پر منحصر

The atom bomb and hydrogen bomb. To very great extent, man has been successful in achieving ability. This capacity must be utilized in converting the autumn of life to the eternal beauty of the garden of existence. Wisdom and power will be meaningless without the perfection of character which depends on carrying out the commands of God.

Stanza: 85

85- ہے وہ نیکی جس سے حاصل ہو کمال زندگی

وہ بدی ہے جس میں پنہاں ہے زوال زندگی

خیر سے ہے قوت و عیش و جلال زندگی

شر سے ہے ضعف دل و حزن و بال زندگی

ہے نکوی قدرت و ایمان و حکمت کی دلیل

ہے بدی کمزوری و کفر و حماقت کی دلیل

Tr:- It is piety which can make the life perfect while the decline and destruction are brought out by viciousness. Strength, happiness and splendour of life depend upon the goodness while the weakness of heart and sorrows of life are the results of evil deeds. Piety is the proof for strength, faith and wisdom while evil is the proof for the weakness, infidelity, flaw and folly.

C:- The title of this 17th chapter is "struggle of Life". Of course life is a struggle for survival, pleasure, progress prosperity and spiritual attainments. There are some injunctions and some prohibitions in Islamic law. The poet exhorts the readers to adhere to the Divine laws and exercise restraints against the prohibitions and carry out Divine commands.

In this chapter some sorts of fights, physical, moral and spiritual which man has to confront with have been elucidated. The lawful fight is called Jihad. The general concept of Jihad is participating in the Holy War (Only defensive war) for the sake of Islam. Of course, it is a great Jihad. But according to Islamic concept, any activity with noble and pure intention is called Jihad, no matter it is a smallest strife. The noble fights such as achieving spiritual perfection, acquiring knowledge earning by honest means, avoiding begging, controlling carnal emotions. preserving chastity, making sacrifices for others, rendering service to humanity, giving charity safeguarding one's own self, taking pleasure in noble fights (Jihad) all sorts of worships leading virtuous life etc are some kinds of Jihad. Some definitions of Jihad may elucidate its meaning. According to Islamic concept, the word 'Jihad' implies the noble efforts, exerted in order to make the Islamic injunctions supreme. Every noble activity whether small or big is called Jihad. The main aim of Jihad is to convert the wrong, unjust, un-Islamic activities and falsehood to be good, just, true and Islamic. Any amount of activities without any noble intentions can never be called Jihad. Every effort of man should be coupled with noble intentions which accounts much in this world and in the hereafter.

Jihad means sacrifice, service to humanity, strife to earn by honest means, maintain discipline, adherence to divine Law and lead righteous and Islamic way of life.

The history of life is the history of wars and struggles. It is evident that idleness entails defeat, difficulty and deathunprevented wisdom, dexterity of talents,physical strength strong determination and fearless fight result in meaningful life,victory, wealth and relief.The Divine administration of the universe and the divine talents teach us the best lesson to beautif your life and to succeed in achieving perfection.Examine the beauty of Divine administration in the following Stanzas.

Al-Aalaa-87:2-5(Already quoted in the 12th chapter)

Tr-'Who hath created and further given order and proportion,who had ordained laws granted guidance, and who bringeth out the (green and lustrous) pasture, and then dothmake it (But) swarthy stubble and granted".

S. Furqaan-25:53

وَهُوَ الَّذِى مَرَجَ الْبَحْرَيْنِ هٰذَا عَذْبٌ فُرَاتٌ وَهٰذَا مِلْحٌ أُجَاجٌ وَجَعَلَ بَيْنَهُمَا بَرْزَخًا وَحِجْرًا مَحْجُورًا

Tr. It is He Who has let free the two bodies of flowing water: one palatable and sweet, and the other salt and bitter; yet has made a barrier between them; a partition that is for bidden to be passed".

The above mentioned Stanzas explain how much the providence of God is active for the comforts, conveniences and well-being of His creations and for their own material and spiritual pleasure in the activities for their survival. When God displays this much of interest and concern for the welfare of His creations,it is the duty of human beings to take pleasure, in performing all sorts of noble deeds called Jihad.

Inspite of the mishappening in the life,noble struggles afford pleasure, satisfaction and above all spiritual ecstasy.The unwise and cowardly people do not understand that too much of indulgence in worldly pleasures are extremely dangerous.They eventually lead to destruction and perditions.

Hadith-e-Qudsi is that revelation which Prophet Muhammad (PBUH)received in his dream.One of such revelations his received in his dream was "But for thee, I would not have created the universe".

In the above revelation, God has expressed His love for his Apostle. Here it is meant so that our Prophet could see the whole of it with his own material eyes. By the permission of Allah,Prophet he saw the entire universe on the 27th night of Rajab during the mystic event of Mei'raj.Hence our Prophet was given the title "Sahib-e-Lawlaak" of the universe.The revelations which our Prophet received in his dream (Hadis-e-Qudsi) have not been included in Quran. Whatever, he preached, he practiced to the fullest extent. His life and teachings are best examples for us to lead a righteous life.

S. Ahzaab: 33:21 (Already quoted in chapter 14)

Tr. You have indeed in Apostle of Allah a beautiful pattern of (conduct) for any one whose hope is in Allah and the last day; and who engages much in the praise of Allah".

All the teachings of our Prophet cannot be elaborated in this book. The messages of Islam and his teachings have been briefly summarized in his sermon delivered on the occasion of his last pilgrimage (Hajjatul-Wida'a), Zilhaj 10 A.H. in the plain of Arafat. That sermon has been presented in the following.

Before starting his sermon, he extolled the glory of God, expressed his faith in the unity and Omni-Potence of God, sought Allah's refuge for the Muslims from evil and supplicated to Allah to lead all the Muslims on the right path.

"Behold ummah, listen to the message of Islam I am going to convey, for I do not know whether after this year, I shall ever be among you here again. (A hint of his approaching death after three months) O people! Your blood, your property and your honour is as sacred and inviolable and significant as this day and this month is sacred for all until you appear before your Cherisher. Without fail you will meet your Creator and you will be held answerable for your deeds, you performed in this world. He who has any rig in trust with him, should restore it to the person who deposited it with him. Beware of such crimes. Neither is the son responsible for the crimes of his father, nor the father responsible for the crimes of his son. Each Muslim is the brother of the other and form one brotherhood. Nothing of his brother is lawful for a Muslim except what his brother himself willingly offers. Do not oppress one another. All the practices of paganism and the attitude of blood-revenges which was in vogue in Age of Ignorance have been abolished by me. Do not take interest for the money you have lent. You are entitled to recover the Capital you have invested. Do not deviate from the Divine law, otherwise you will be punished by Allah. Fear Allah regarding the treatment you give to your women. You have taken them on the security of Allah and have made their persons lawful to you by the words of Allah. You have got certain rights over your women and your women have got certain rights over you. It is incumbent upon the women to honour their marital rights and not to commit acts of impropriety. If they do so, you have got authority to chastise them, yet not severely. If they repent and refrain from sinful acts, maintain them suitably and treat them kindly. Listen and obey your Amir even though he is an Abyssinian slave in case he executes the commandments of Quran. Allah has allotted a share of inheritance to every man. Every child belongs to the marriage-bed. The adulterer should be stoned. He who attributes his ancestry to other than his father and claims his service to other than his master, the curse of people, angels and Allah will be upon him. No Prophet will come after me, and no new faith will be born. Your lives, your property and your honour must be as sacred to one another as this sacred day in this sacred month in this sacred town. Stick to the religion of Islam. Those who are caught in the trap of shaitaan. Allah will not accept their repentance and righteousness. Hence beware of Shaitaan and safeguard your religion. Feed your slaves with such food as you eat yourselves and clothe them with the clothes that you yourselves wear. If they commit fault which you are not inclined to forgive then part with them for they are the servants of Allah. They should not be chastised. Worship your Rubb (God) and offer prayers five times a day, observe fast in the month of Ramzan, undertake pilgrimage (Hajj), pay the poor-due Zakaat according to your wealth saved; and obey me whatever I command you, so that you can enter paradise. Your Lord is one and your father is one. All of you belong to one ancestry of Adam and Adam was created out of clay. There is no superiority for an Arab over a non-Arab and for a non-Arab over an Arab; nor for white over the black nor for the black over the white, except in piety. Verily, the noblest among you is he expect them to be more mindful of them than the present audience".

After concluding his sermon, he addressed Allah and asked Him whether he had delivered all the Divine messages to the people and accomplished the duty entrusted to him.The large assembly of Muslims who were clustered around him declared loudly that he had discharged his duties.

Finally Prophet said," O! Rubb, I beseech you to bear witness to it".

Now it is vivid that the Law enunciated in Quran, exemplified by the life and teachings of our Prophet, is supreme in all cases.The Divine Law applies equally to the highest and the lowest, prince and the pauper, ruler and the ruled, richest and poorest, master and the slave,in short the entire humanity hence adhering to the Divine Law, following the examples of the life of Sahib-e-Lawlaak and practicing his preaching are great fights of life called Jihad..

So far, we have been discussing the Islamic concepts of Jihad in general. Let us now examine the individual factors in particular. It must be remembered that all noble activities with good intentions (Jihad) are inter-related.

I. Jihad: Holy War:- In fact Islam is a peace loving religion. Islam should not be spread propagate Islam not by force but by all humility and humble preaching's. Many of the expeditions by the use of sword but by conveying the message of Islam. Muslims were enjoined upon to were meant only for the propagation of Islam. Offensives and invasions are absolutely prohibited in Islam. When the Muslim army was attacked or any individuals were wronged, defensive war was permissible. Even in the battle field, the Muslims waited till the enemy threw the challenge for the duel, and waited till the hostile army started the war. Of course, they can start their expedition for defensive war when there was any danger or threat from the foes. For example, the Muslim army undertook Tabuk expedition in the scorching heat of the sun as there was a great threat from the Byzantine empire of the Roman Emperor Heraclius. While the Mushrikeen of Makkah were fleeing after their defeat in Battle of Uhad in 3 A.H. they threw challenge to meet the Muslim army in plain of Badr next year itself and to defeat the Muslims. As it is permissible to accept the challenge, it became lawful to get ready for the war and proceed towards the plain of Badr in 4 A.H. This is called the 2nd Battle of Badr in Islamic history, but has no significance as it was not actually fought. When the Mushrikeen of Makkah saw the higher spirit of the Muslims and a little promotion in the numerical strength in the Muslim army, they got frightened and fled. The Muslim army did not chase them, as taking the first step in war is prohibited in Islam.

The Muslims of Madinah started for the 1st Battle of Badr in 2 A.H. only after Prophet Muhammad received revelation from God, commanding him to fight with the Mushrikeen as the Muslims had been wronged by the Mushrikeen. The Muslims should accept the offer of treaty from the hostile camp. In case the enemies put down their weapons, the Muslims should stop the war. Islamic war ethics should be observed strictly. The following Quranic Stanzas and Ahadis will prove the above-mentioned facts and principles. Our Prophet himself participated in several wars including Battle of Uhad in 3 A.H. when he was more dead than alive as he received more than eighty wounds.

S.Hajj-22:39.

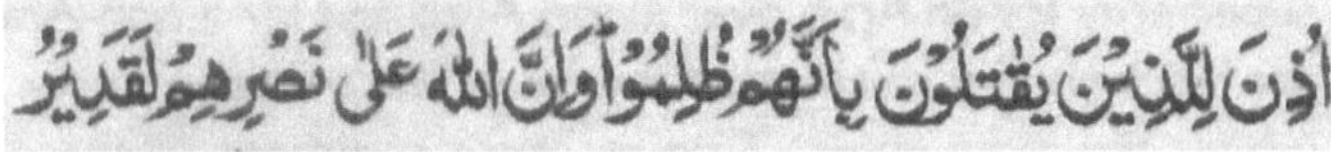

Tr:-"To those against whom war is made, permission is given to fight because the wronged, and verily Allah is most powerful for their aid."

S.Nisaa-4:74:-

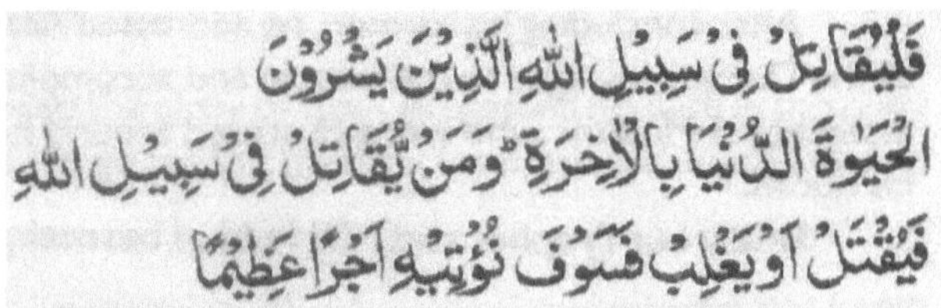

Tr. "Let those fight in the cause of Allah who sell the life of this world for the hereafter. To him who fighteth in the cause of Allah whether he is slain or gets victory - Soon shall give him a reward of great.

S.Baqara- 2:244:-

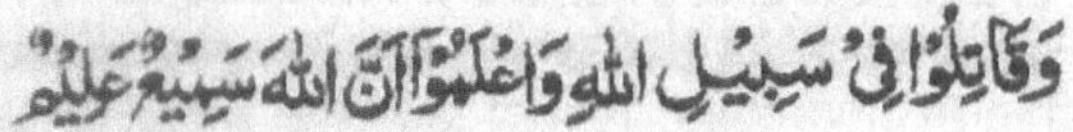

Tr:-"Then fight in the cause of Allah and know that Allah heareth and knoweth all things"

S. Tawbah-9:14:

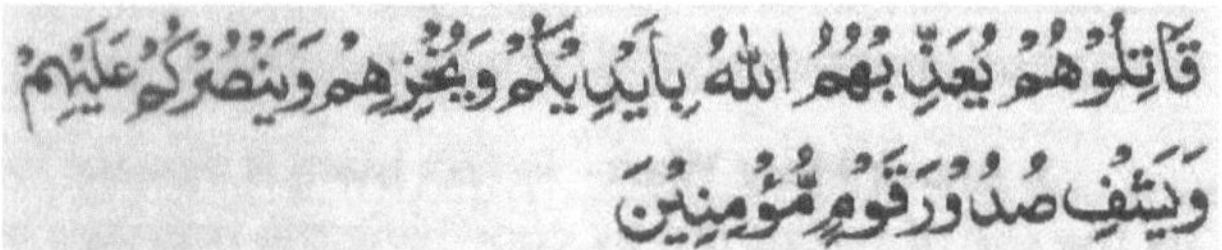

Tr:- "Fight them and Allah will punish them by your hands. Cover them with shame he you to (Victory) over them, heal the breasts of the Believers."

S.Nisaa-4:90

Tr:- "Except those who join the group between whom and you, there is a treaty (of peace) or of those who approach you with hearts restraining them from fighting you, as well fighting their own people. If Allah had pleased, he could have given them power over you and they would have fought you. Therefore, if they withdraw from you but fight you not and instead send you guarantees of peace; then Allah hath opened no way for you (to war against them)."

H:- Strengthen yourselves as much as possible to fight with the enemies of Islam. Archery is a great strength". (Muslim)

H:- "For he who fights for Allah's cause, God's word Islam, should be superior". (Bukhari)

H: "That believer is better who fights for the cause of Allah with his wealth and life". (Bukhari)

H:- "By Allah, I wish to fight for the cause of Allah repeatedly and attain martyrdom repeatedly ". (Nasayi, Muslim, Bukhari).

H:- (War ethics) "During the war, you must have fear of God. You must have good intentions regarding your companions. Defend yourself from those who reject to accept Allah, Do not seek pretext to attack on them.Refrain from mutilating others by cutting their noses and ears.Refrain from killing women and children.Desist from cheating regarding the war booty, if the women and children become your captives, treat them politely". (Bukhari).

H:- "In the course of war, do not kill the sick, weak and old people. Do not beat the women and children. Do not cheat regarding the booty. Maintain peace among yourselves, because Allah loves the pious people. (Abu Dawood)

The above-mentioned Quranic Stanzas and Ahadis explain that only defensive war is permissible, and explain the amount of considerations Islam advocates for the enemies. According to Islamic war ethics, the Islamic army should neither destruct the cities, nor vegetables nor any property of the foes.

II. Jihad: Islamic Socialism: - Different economists have given different definitions for socialism. The great economist Gedes has defined socialism as the protest against capitalism. Regarding socialism, there are more than fifty isms with slightly different policies in different countries such as Marxism, Fabianism, syndicalism, communism etc. In general, socialism deals with the distribution of wealth among the natives. Among all the isms, Russian communism is abolished. Every policy has its own merit and demerits. In the case of communism, the strictest one under which private enterprises and owning private property (capitalism) are demerits overweigh the merits. What happened to Russian economy? What is being happened in other communist countries which are facing economic crisis? When all the enterprises get nationalized, people lose incentive and interest in striving hard. How can such nations progress economically and succeed in maintaining the natives by equally distributing the wealth, all of which belongs to the government?

The system of Islamic socialism is quite different from other forms of socialism. In all aspects of life Islam teaches moderation which is most beneficial, and prevents extremities which entail difficulties. Under the system of Islamic socialism, private enterprises and private ownership of property (capitalism) are permissible. At the same time, Islam is against amassing too much of wealth. Communism aims at equal distribution of wealth. While Islamic socialism aims at better distribution of wealth through selfless services, sacrifices, obligatory charity (Zakat) and voluntary charity (Sadaqa). Though Islamic governments undertake their own projects to help the needy people in different ways, Islam urges to Muslims to be charitable, generous and compassionate towards the down-trodden and spend in charity from their own pockets. This system of capitalism in which factors of socialism are involved is called mixed economy. This mixed economy is the essence of Islamic socialism which is now being prevailed in several countries.

In Pre-Islamic period, this system was unknown. The down trodden people suffered a lot under the merciless capitalists of high birth. Besides charity, Islamic socialism involves many more factors which are beneficial to the economy of the Islamic society. It prohibits some factors such as drinking, gambling, stealing, cheating, and taking interest on loan which harmful for and have very bad influence on the economy of the society. In order to bring about reforms in the Islamic society Islamic banking has been introduced in which capital is invested in the industries and loss or profits are shared in equal percentage according to the amount of investment. This system Is operating wonderfully and most successfully in some Islamic countries.

consider to bring about capital is to the some Islamic remost concept

ISLAMIC SOCIALISM:

1. Everything Belongs to Allah: - In Islamic socialism, the first and foremost concept to be realized is that Allah is the owner of our life, body, soul, wealth and all other things in universe and that Allah is the ultimate source of bounties for His creations. This greatest capitalist distributes wealth among His creations. This is mixed economy of Allah. Our religion is natural and its laws are also natural. Even Allah does not distribute his bounties equally among his creations regarding all aspects. He distributes some bounties equally and so unequally. For example, He has provided equal facility to inhabit on the earth and offers equal opportunity to breathe the air but He does not distribute comforts and wealth equally. The one who suffer in this world will have everlasting comforts in the hereafter. There can be no injustice in the realm of God. This is the unique socialism of Allah. He is more generous and compassionate towards the down-trodden and the poor community.

We belong to nothing but Allah. Allah has enjoined on us to share His bounties with others Otherwise, we will lose our own single belonging namely Allah and His Pleasure.

S. Baqara-2:107:- (Already quoted in the 8th and 13th chapters)

Tr:- "Knowest though not that to Allah belongeth the dominions of the heavens and the earth? And besides Him, ye have neither patron nor helper".

S.An'am:- 6:13:

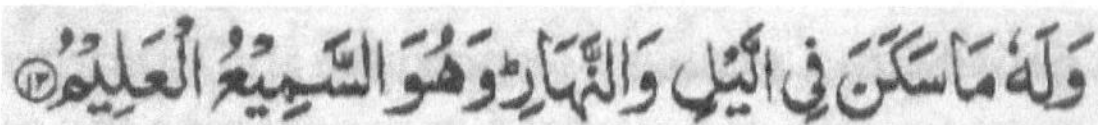

Tr:- "To Him belongeth all that dweleth (or lurketh) in the day and the night for He it is the One Who heareth and knoweth all things."

When our lives belong to Allah, He has got the right to take back this wealth any time. Hence Islam has enjoined on us not to mourn the demise of our dear ones for more than three days.

A great saint Hazrat Gouse-e-A'azam Abdul Qadir Jeelani, the descendent of Hazrat Ali and Bibi Fatima expired in the period of Abbasi dynasty and is laid to rest in Baghdad. He was a great spiritualist and trader by profession. A certain person brought a sorrowful news that the saint's ship full of merchandise was caught in the whirlpool and got wrecked in the sea. But Mahboob-e-Subhani (a title of the saint) never expressed his sorrow at all, but instead he said, "Alhamdu Lillah" which means "praise be to Allah". After some days, the same person brought the news that the ship had been driven by the winds out of the way and was coming back safely. On hearing this he repeated the same words, "Alhamdu Lillah". The messenger got curious and asked him, "Why did you say Alhamdu Lillah at the receipt of the sorrowful news of the ship-wreck?" The saint replied, "Everything belongs to Allah. He has got powers to shower His bounties on us whenever He likes. He has got rights to take back His belongings whenever He likes.

Now it is clear that our ownership of wealth is only temporary.

2. Charity: - As Allah is generous, He expects us to be generous. He has enjoined on us to spend in charity to help the needy (voluntary charity) irrespective of caste, creed and race. dishonest means by removing the dirt of dishonesty. The greater the sincerity and the intensity There are several advantages of charity one of which is that, it purifies the wealth earned by of the compassion with which one spends for the sake of Allah, the greater will be Allah's reward. Allah has promised to multiply the reward for our virtuous deeds of charity.

S. Baqara-2:261:

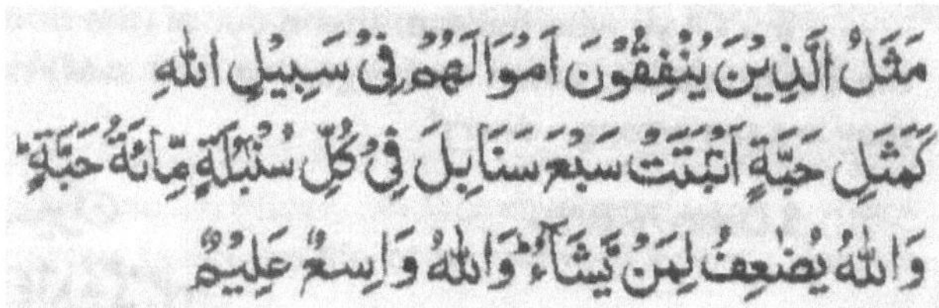

Tr:-"The parable of those who spend their substance in the way of Allah is that of a grain of corn. It groweth seven years and each year has a hundred grains. Allah giveth manifold increase to whom he pleaseth; and Allah careth for all and knows all things."

S. Al-Baqara-2:3:

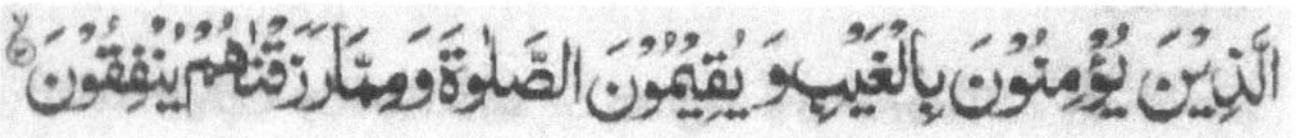

Tr:- Who believe in the unseen are steadfast in prayer; and spend out of what We have provided for them."

The above-mentioned Stanza 2:3 suggests that the believers should share with and give in charity whatever Allah has provided for them. On this basis the Muslim jurers have promulgated some laws and have legalized blood donation and organ transplantation but not at the risk of the life of the doner. In order to prevent organ trading Saudi Arabia has adopted a policy that only near relations may donate their organs in live transplantation. Without such policy, poverty may lead them to sell their organs for the sake of their families and even stake their own lives. Donation of organs after death is however permitted regardless of Kinship.

S.Baqara-2:219:- (Part of the Stanza)

Tr:-"They ask thee how much they are to spend Say, "What is beyond your needs."

S.Baqara-2:274:

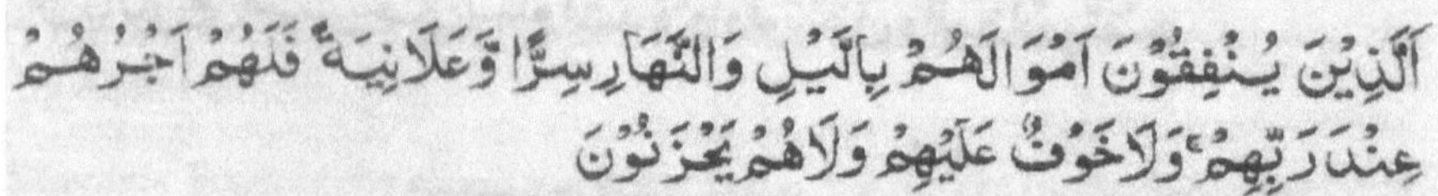

Tr-Those who in Charity spend of their goods by night and by day in secret and in have their reward with their Lord. On them shall be no fear nor shall they grieve."

S. Baqara 2:27

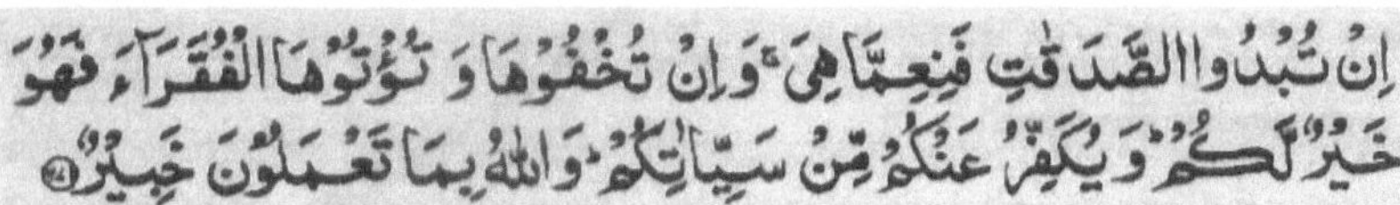

Tr:- "If ye disclose (acts of) charity, ever them reach those (really in need), that is best for (stains of) evil, and Allah is well acquinted with what ye do."

S.Al-Baqara-2:254:

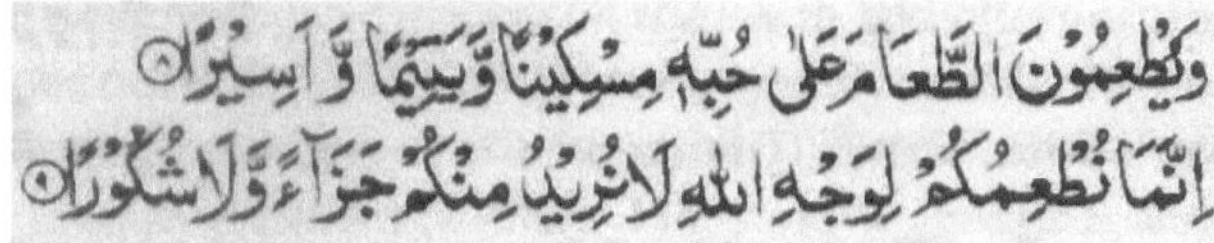

Tr:- O! ye who believe, spend out of the bounties), We have provided for you before the doom comes, when no bargaining (will avail) nor intercession. Those who reject faith they are the wrong-doers"

S.Dahr-76:8-9

Tr:- "And they feed for the love of Allah, the indigent, the orphans and the captives Saying "We feed you for the sake of Allah alone. No reward do we desire from you nor thanks."

H:- "There are rights of the needy other than Zakat also in the wealth of the rich (Tirmizi)

3. Earning Bread By Hard Strife and Honest Means:

The Divine munificence befalls on those who deal in business transactions honestly and true to their conscience.

The Midianites (the people of Madyan) who purchased Yusuf (A.S) and sold him in Egypt were indulged in dishonest business. They did not measure and weigh properly. As a refc-mer Allah sent Prophet Shuib (their own relative) to them who dissuaded them from this sinful acts. Except a few, those Midianites stuck to their own whims and fancies. Allah destructed the unbelievers through tremendous earth quake as a punishment for their dishonesty and disobedience.

S.An'am-6:152 (Part of the verse)

وَلَا تَقْرَبُوا مَالَ الْيَتِيمِ اِلَّا بِالَّتِي هِيَ اَحْسَنُ حَتّٰى يَبْلُغَ اَشُدَّهٗ وَاَوْفُوا الْكَيْلَ وَالْمِيْزَانَ بِالْقِسْطِ

Tr:- "Give measure and weight with full justice".

H:- "The best livelihood is the one which is earned through hard work and honest means".

H:- "The livelihood earned through the worker is most liked by God".

H:-"Be laborious. will always be getting for your strife". (Al-Madina, Al-Islam)

H:-The honest trader will be with the prophets, the truthful and the martyres". (Tirmizi).

H:-" To earn honest livingis a duty next to the principal duties of Iman". (Baihaqi).

H:- "The cleanest food is that which a man earns by his own hands".(Baihaqi).

H:- Those who obtain profits through legal ways, their faces will shine like the moon of the14th night on the day of Resurrection". (Mishkat)

5. Service and Sacrifice:

One who likes to attain the pleasure of Allah, shall sacrifice every dear to him. This is not only the test of charity but also the test sincerity towards Allah. Ibrahim (A.S) succeeded in the test of his faith by Ismail (A.S) (Prophet Ishaaq was born after this incident). As Allah does He saved Ismail (A.S) but accepted the sacrifice of Ibrahim (A.S).

It is a common proverb that service to humanity is service to God. Self-development only by selfless service and sacrifices. In fact the benefactor is more beneficiary. Certain person saved the life of his avowed enemy. Such a person is the real pride of humanity.

S. Aal-e-Imran 3:92

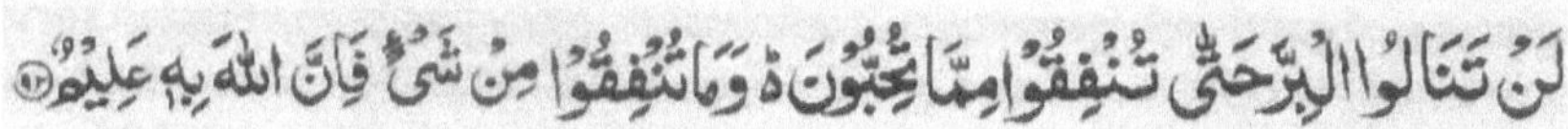

Tr:-By the means shall ye attain righteousness unless ye give (freely) of that which ye love, and whatever ye give; of a truth Allah knoweth well."

S. Ma'ida-5:35:- (part of the verse):

Tr - On that account for the children of Isra'il that if anyone slew a person-unless it be for murder or for spreading mischief in the land it would be as if, he slew the whole people. And if a person saved a life, it would be as if he saved the life of the whole people".

H:- "He who has an extra mount should give that to one who has no mount and who has surplus of provisions should give them to him who has no provision". (Muslim)

5.Waqf:- The concept of Waqf is a significant exposition of the Islamic doctrine for the benefit of the poor and needy. There is no Divine law (Shariat) as such. Neither Quranic verse as nor any Hadith have specified Wafq. But the repeated exhortations in Quran to spend the wealth on the needy motivated the service-minded and generous people to establish the Waqf organizations. The Institutions of Waqf are purely motivated ones and are being conducted satisfactorily. Every Muslim is enjoined upon to sacrifice his wealth in the way of Allah and the reward is assured by Allah Himself.

6. Freeing Slaves: - Freeing the slaves is a great piety. It involves humanitarian service, the matter of material sacrifices and relieving humanity from desperation. This voluntary charity will definitely fetch great rewards. This act of piety persuaded the freed slaves to render great services to Islam. The Abyssinian slave Bilal was severely persecuted by his master for having embraced Islam. Hazrat Abu Bakr Siddique purchased him and free Consequently Hazrat Bilal became the devoted companion of our Prophet. Hazrat Bill Hazrat Zaid accompanied our Prophet to Taif (the 2nd Hijrat in Islamic history) and all of went without food and drink for a whole month. This tolerance of thirst and hunger is example of patience. Hazrat Bilal had the prestige of being the first Muazzin of Masjid.e who called the Muslims for the congregational prayers. Our Prophet bought a slave by Zaid and adopted as his son and treated him with peerless affection. After this adon was called Zaid bin Muhammad. Our

Prophet received revelation that adopted son has no right of inheritance. This also meant that the name of the foster father should not be added with his name. Hence his father's name had to be associated with his name and he had called Zaid Bin Harisa. At last, he attained martyrdom in the war for the sake of Islam.

The above mentioned two incidents are enough to explain as to which extent the freed slaves were enticed by Islam. Some believers emancipated slaves in thousand some according to their financial capacity. Some masters relieved their own slaves from the bond of slavery. The emancipated slaves (believers) were very faithful to Islam till their last breath.

H:- "Visit sick persons, feed the hungry ones and emancipate the slaves and the bonded (Bukhari).

7. Lending And Borrowing: - Advancing a loan to a needy person without interest is a gesture of good-will, generosity, compassion, piety and humanitarian service which contribute to promote brotherhood and good relationship. Islam has prescribed the principles of right and obligations of the borrowers and the lenders. It is an enjoinment on the rich to lend money to the poor brethren at times of need. It is the duty of the borrowers to clear their loans as early as possible. Those who do not care to repay the loans are warned of the dire consequences on the Day of Reckoning. Out of his appreciable piety and generosity, the lender forgives the borrower who is not able to repay, Allah will give him manifold rewards.

H:- "The reward for lending is greater even than that of charity".

H:- "The recompense on charity is ten-fold while on giving a loan is eighteen-fold". (Tabari)

H:- If a man is killed in the path of Allah, all the sins are forgiven (by virtue of martyrdom) except a loan". (Muslim)

H:- "Good among the servants of Allah is he who is best in paying off the debts. (Muslim).

8. Earthly Life is Lawful: - Islam does not preach the worthlessness of earthly life. We are living in this world which has been created for us. Allah has showered His bounties to satisfy our physical needs, material needs and has permitted Aesthetic satisfaction. At the same time, He sent Prophets and preceptors and revealed scriptures for our spiritual development. This world is only the ground on which we sow the seeds of eternal life and hoard up stocks for eternal bliss. In case our life in this world is only for worldly goals and revellings and material pursuits, our life becomes worthless and yields nothing but eternal misery and perditions. Money or time should not be extravagantly and unlawfully spent. It is permissible in Islam to make merriment and enjoy the bounties of Allah in a decent, lawful and moderate way

9. Moderation and simple life: - In every aspect of life Islam preaches us moderation because extremities have several disadvantages. For example if some people become too rich poverty increases in the poor community. When a few people enjoy too much of luxuries, the comforts of the common people decrease. Moderation and simple life of advantageous to the society,

S.Hadid-57.25:- (part of the verse)

لَقَدْ أَرْسَلْنَا رُسُلَنَا بِالْبَيِّنَاتِ وَأَنزَلْنَا مَعَهُمُ الْكِتَبَ وَالْمِيزَانَ لِيَقُومَ النَّاسُ بِالْقِسْطِ

Tr:- "We sent aforetime our apostles with clear signs and sent down with them Book and Balance"

S.Furquaan.25:67:-

وَالَّذِينَ إِذَا أَنفَقُوا لَمْ يُسْرِفُوا وَلَمْ يَقْتُرُوا وَكَانَ بَيْنَ ذَلِكَ قَوَامًا

Tr:- "Those who when they spend are not extravagant and nor niggardly, but hold a just (balance) between those (extremes)"

S.Bani Isra'il-17.29:-

وَلَا تَجْعَلْ يَدَكَ مَغْلُولَةً إِلَى عُنُقِكَ وَلَا تَبْسُطْهَا كُلَّ الْبَسْطِ فَتَقْعُدَ مَلُومًا مَحْسُورًا

Tr:- "Make not thy hand tied (like a niggard) to thy neck: nor stretch it forth to the utmost reach; so thou become blameworthy and destitute."

H:- "Leading a simple life as an article of faith."

H:- "Don't you hear that simplicity is the essence of faith? (Abu Dawood)

Islam exhorts the muslims to lead a simple life observing moderation and thus facilitate the proper circulation of money which is quite necessary for the good economy of the society.

10. Interest on Loans:- In the early period after Hijrat, financing etc. lending money and charging interest on the loans was in vogue in Madinah even in the muslim society. Of course it was a profitable business for the lenders at the cost of human rights of the poor community. Money lenders devoured the money received by way of interest leaving the poor people hungry. How can the perfect religion tolerate this? Our prophet received revelation to stop this inhuman practice. Quron exhorts the muslim money lenders to desist from charging interest and devour them. If the believers disobey this commandment it is meant nothing but declaring war with Allah and His Aposcle. The money lender is permitted to take backe the money he had already lent. Quran has prescribed severe punishment for those who continue the condemned practice. Ban on interest has motivated some muslim countries to introduce Islamic banking as a social reform.

S.Aal-e-Imran-3: 130:

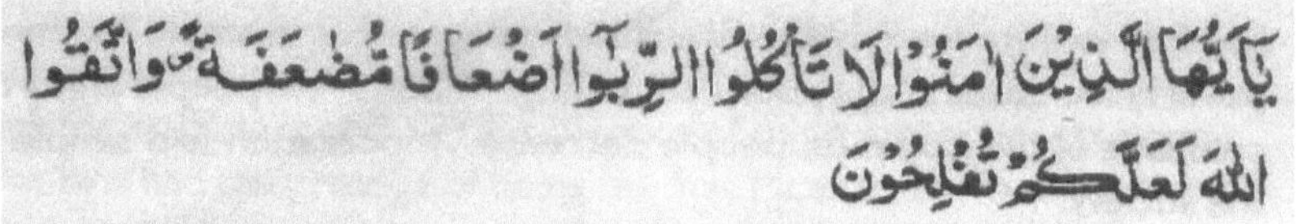

Tr:- "Oye who believe, devour not usury, doubled and multiplied; but fear Allah that ye may (really) prosper".

S.Nisaa-4: 161:-

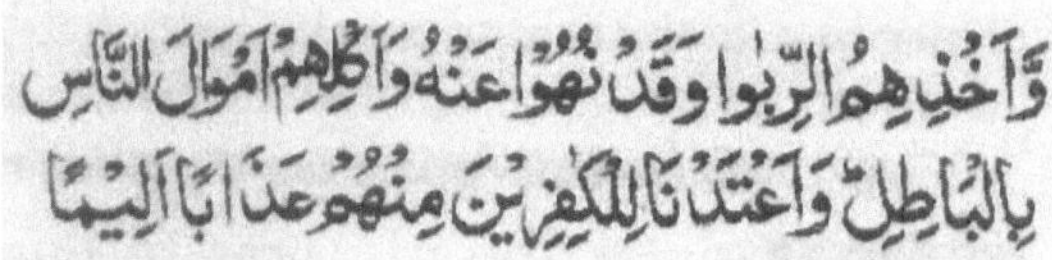

Tr:- "That they took usury though they were forbidden and that they devoured men's substance wrongfully - We have prepared for those among them who reject faith, agrievous punishment".

S.Baqara-2274 275,276,278,279 280:

S.Baqara-2:274,275,276,278,279,280:- اَلَّذِيْنَ يُنْفِقُوْنَ اَمْوَالَهُمْ
بِالَّيْلِ وَالنَّهَارِ سِرًّا وَّعَلَانِيَةً فَلَهُمْ اَجْرُهُمْ عِنْدَ رَبِّهِمْ وَلَا خَوْفٌ عَلَيْهِمْ وَلَا هُمْ يَحْزَنُوْنَ
اَلَّذِيْنَ يَاْكُلُوْنَ الرِّبٰوا لَا يَقُوْمُوْنَ اِلَّا كَمَا يَقُوْمُ الَّذِيْ يَتَخَبَّطُهُ الشَّيْطٰنُ مِنَ الْمَسِّ ذٰلِكَ بِاَنَّهُمْ قَالُوْا اِنَّمَا الْبَيْعُ
مِثْلُ الرِّبٰوا وَاَحَلَّ اللّٰهُ الْبَيْعَ وَحَرَّمَ الرِّبٰوا فَمَنْ جَآءَهٗ مَوْعِظَةٌ مِّنْ رَّبِّهٖ فَانْتَهٰى فَلَهٗ مَا سَلَفَ وَاَمْرُهٗ اِلَى اللّٰهِ
وَمَنْ عَادَ فَاُولٰٓئِكَ اَصْحٰبُ النَّارِ هُمْ فِيْهَا خٰلِدُوْنَ ۝ يَمْحَقُ اللّٰهُ الرِّبٰوا وَيُرْبِي الصَّدَقٰتِ وَاللّٰهُ لَا يُحِبُّ كُلَّ
كَفَّارٍ اَثِيْمٍ ۝ اِنَّ الَّذِيْنَ اٰمَنُوْا وَعَمِلُوا الصّٰلِحٰتِ وَاَقَامُوا الصَّلٰوةَ وَاٰتَوُا الزَّكٰوةَ لَهُمْ اَجْرُهُمْ عِنْدَ رَبِّهِمْ وَلَا
خَوْفٌ عَلَيْهِمْ وَلَا هُمْ يَحْزَنُوْنَ ۝ يٰٓاَيُّهَا الَّذِيْنَ اٰمَنُوا اتَّقُوا اللّٰهَ وَذَرُوْا مَا بَقِيَ مِنَ الرِّبٰوا اِنْ كُنْتُمْ مُّؤْمِنِيْنَ ۝ فَاِنْ
لَّمْ تَفْعَلُوْا فَاْذَنُوْا بِحَرْبٍ مِّنَ اللّٰهِ وَرَسُوْلِهٖ وَاِنْ تُبْتُمْ فَلَكُمْ رُءُوْسُ اَمْوَالِكُمْ لَا تَظْلِمُوْنَ وَلَا تُظْلَمُوْنَ ۝ وَاِنْ
كَانَ ذُوْ عُسْرَةٍ فَنَظِرَةٌ اِلٰى مَيْسَرَةٍ وَاَنْ تَصَدَّقُوْا خَيْرٌ لَّكُمْ اِنْ كُنْتُمْ تَعْلَمُوْنَ

Tr:- "Those who devour usury will not stand except as stand one whom evil one by his touch, driven to madness that is because they say, 'Trade is like usury'. But Allah had permitted trade and forbidden usury. Those who after receiving direction from their Lord, desist, shall be pardoned for the past, their case is for Allah (to judge). But those who repeat (the offense) are companions of the fire, they will abide therein (forever)".

"Allah will deprive usury of all blessings, but will give increase for deeds of charity; for He loveth not creatures ungrateful and wicked"

"O! ye who believe! Fear Allah and give up what remains of your demand for usury, if ye are indeed believers".

“if yedo not take notice of war from Allah and His Apostleif ye take back, you shall your capitalsum:deal not unjustly and ye shall not be dealt with unjustly” war from cum: ye shall not be dealt with have your capital d

"If the debtor is in difficulty, grant him time till it is easy for him to repay. But if ye remitit by way of charity,that is best for you if ye only know.

It is evident through the above-mentioned Stanzas that to which extent the usury is condemned and to which lending charity are advocated by the policy of Islamic socialism.

11. Hoarding Commodity And Piling:

Wealth: A Merchant who withholds his commodity when the price is low and sells it when the prices rise up in the hope of realizing enormous profit, is called a hoarder.Piling of wealth and hoarding commodities are great sins as they obstruct the legitimate circulation of wealth.İslam likes the welfare and bounties of Allah to be distributed among the people unhindered.The acts which disturb the distribution system basically rob the welfare of the society.Islam does not tolerate such injustice.The illegitimate desires for hoarding commodities and amassing wealth lead to all sorts of sins such as rivalry,niggardliness, bribery, and greed, and worldly gains distract humanity.

S. Takaasur-102:1-2:

أَلْهَىٰكُمُ التَّكَاثُرُ ۙ حَتَّىٰ زُرْتُمُ الْمَقَابِرَ ۚ

T. "The mutual rivalry for piling up the good things of the world) diverts you (from the more serious things)

"Humazaa-104:2-4:

وَيْلٌ لِّكُلِّ هُمَزَةٍ لُّمَزَةٍ ۙ الَّذِى جَمَعَ مَالًا وَّعَدَّدَهُ

Tri- "Who pileth up wealth and layeth it by, thinking that the wealth will make him last forever, by no means! He will be sure to be thrown into that which breaks to pieces".

S.Hashr-59:7:

مَاۤ اَفَآءَ اللّٰهُ عَلٰى رَسُوۡلِهٖ مِنۡ اَهۡلِ الۡقُرٰى فَلِلّٰهِ وَلِلرَّسُوۡلِ وَلِذِى الۡقُرۡبٰى وَالۡيَتٰمٰى وَالۡمَسٰكِيۡنِ وَابۡنِ السَّبِيۡلِ ۙ كَىۡ لَا يَكُوۡنَ دُوۡلَةًۢ بَيۡنَ الۡاَغۡنِيَآءِ مِنۡكُمۡ ؕ وَمَاۤ اٰتٰىكُمُ الرَّسُوۡلُ فَخُذُوۡهُ ۚ وَمَا نَهٰىكُمۡ عَنۡهُ فَانۡتَهُوۡا ۚ وَاتَّقُوا اللّٰهَ ؕ اِنَّ اللّٰهَ شَدِيۡدُ الۡعِقَابِ ۘ

Tr:- "What Allah has bestowed on the Apostle and (taken away) from the people of thetownshipbelongs toAllah- to His Apostle and to kindred and orphans the needy and thewayfarer in order that it may not(merely) make a circuit between the wealth among you.So,take what the Apostle assigns to you;and deny yourselves that which he withholds from. And fear Allah for. Allah is strict in punishment".

H:- "He who makes hoarding is a sinner". (Al-Muntaqa)

The worst type of person is a hoarder. When Allah brings down the price down and when Allah makes it soar high, he is rejoiced.

12. Wine And Gambling: - Islam being perfect religion evolved gradually people became conscious and convinced of the good and evil in the society adhere to the already received revelations, our Prophet received other revelation and eradicated the evils of the society one by one. He received revelations for twenty-two years and three months. For a few years after Hijrat Muslims were allowed to take the liquor. After they stopped lending on interest, the prohibition of gambling and wine was revealed, on wine was revealed in three phases. Firstly, praying, while under the influence of was prohibited. Secondly, taking liquor was prohibited. Even after the second prohibition, Muslims were allowed to do trading in wine. Thirdly and finally trading prohibited. As soon as this revelation was received, the Muslim wine traders spilth quantity of wine and emptied their casks. They incurred heavy loss but our Prophet consoled them by explaining that they would receive manifold rewards and recompense for their loss and sacrifices.

In the case of drunkard, the intoxication takes away his senses. He resorts to absurdactivities and utter vulgar words.For the sake of this illegitimate pleasure, his family suffers a lot and sometimes goes without food. In the case of gambling, one gains and the other loses. This is not agreeable to Islam.

S. Baqara-2:219:- (Part of the Stanza):

Tr:- "They ask about the wine, gambling, say "In them is great sin and some profit for men. But, the sin is greater than the profit".

S. Ma'ida-5:93:

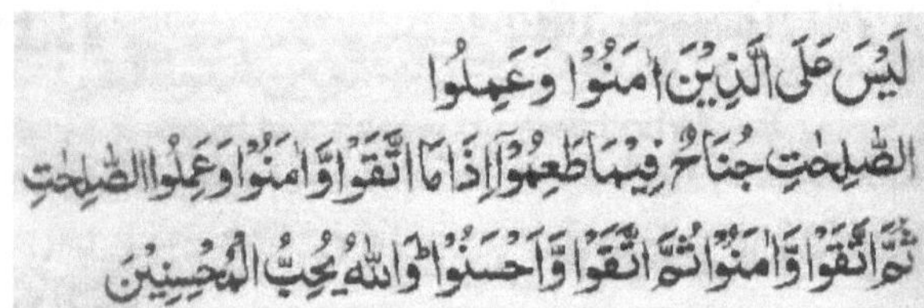

Tr:- "Oye who believe! intoxication and gambling, (dedication of) stones, and (Divination) by arrows are an abomination of Satan handwork. Eschew such (abomination) that ye may progress".

S. Ma'ida-5:94:

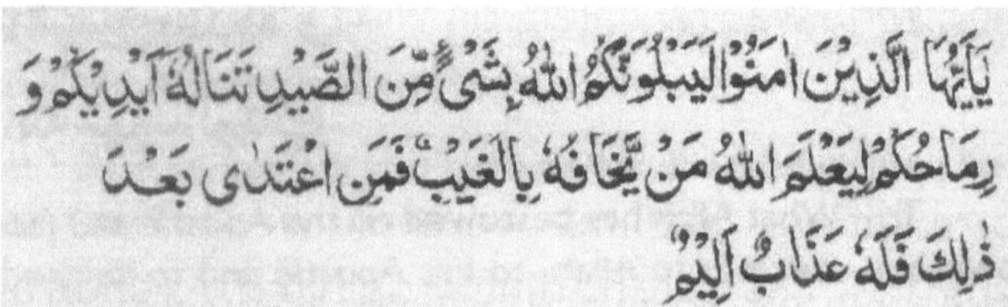

Tr:- "Satan's plan is (but) to excite enmity and hatred between you with intoxicants and gambling; and hinder you from the remembrance of Allah and from prayers. Will ye not abstain?"

13. Begging - Begging is not allowed to persons who are young and physically strong enough to work Stretching hands before others is ridiculous, disgraceful, disrespectful and below human dignity. Human beings have been and are being created by God with some amount of wisdom and power of discretion. They are expected to have will-power to work hard and earn their breadby honest means. Spending time in labour will keep them away from evil and may lead tospiritual perfection. Laborious people are highly appreciated in Islam. It is idleness which leads them to begging, absurd temptations and unlawful acts like theft cheating and murders for their own unworthy survival.

Yunus- 10:106:

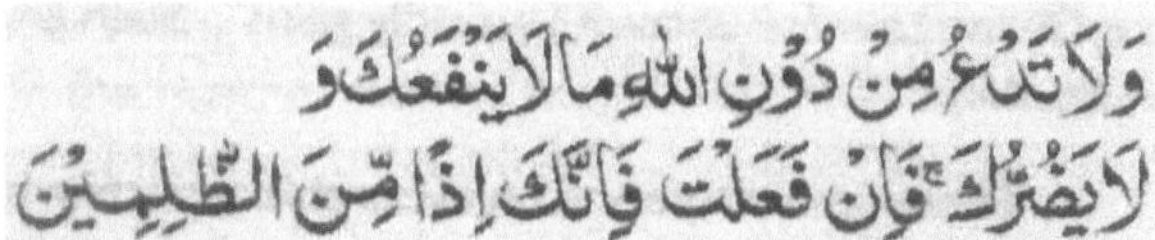

Tr:- "Nor call on any other than Allah- Such will neither profit thee nor heart thee, if you dost-Behold! Thou shall certainly be of those who do wrong.

S Anlam-6:152:- (Already quoted):

وَلَا تَقْرَبُوا مَالَ الْيَتِيمِ إِلَّا بِالَّتِي هِيَ أَحْسَنُ حَتَّى يَبْلُغَ أَشُدَّهُ ۚ وَأَوْفُوا الْكَيْلَ وَالْمِيزَانَ بِالْقِسْطِ ۖ لَا نُكَلِّفُ نَفْسًا إِلَّا وُسْعَهَا ۖ وَإِذَا قُلْتُمْ فَاعْدِلُوا وَلَوْ كَانَ ذَا قُرْبَىٰ ۖ وَبِعَهْدِ اللَّهِ أَوْفُوا ۚ ذَٰلِكُمْ وَصَّاكُم بِهِ لَعَلَّكُمْ تَذَكَّرُونَ

Tr:- "And come not nigh to the orphan property, except to improve it, until he attains the age of full strength, give measureand weight with (full) justice. No burden do we place on any soul, but that which can bear.Whatever you speak, speak justly.Even if a near relative is concerned and fulfil the covenant.Thus doth He command you that ye may remember.

H:-If someone is in need and seeks it from the people,he will not be permanently relieved of his trouble.But if he seeks God's help,. he will be soon relieved or he will meet his death if the appointed time is near at handor God will give him prosperity later". (Dawood: But if he or Tirmizi)

H.- "He who wrongly took a span of land of others, Allah shall make him carry around his neck seven earths on the Day of Resurrection"

In spite of warnings against begging, Islam is very lenient with the disabled and indigent people. At the time of desperation and indigence, the old, sick and weak people are allowed to beg. Wealth in the possession of generous people is a great blessing of Allah for the benefit of the needy ones.

14. Undue Advantage:-Anti Islamic:- A rich Jew in Baghdad was leading a most luxurious life. He was living in a palacial house beautifully decorated and spread with costly carpets. The wind of his fortune blew in the wrong direction and he became very poor. He had to sell his belongings one by one in order to maintain his family. He lost everything except a big carpet. He could not find any customer who could afford to purchase such a costly carpet. Though, he went on diminishing the price of the carpet, it was too much for others. At last, he approached the merchant, the same saint Hazrat Abdul Qudir Jeelani, Mahboob-eJudhani. He requested him to purchase the carpet for a very low price. Mahboob-e-Subhani assessed the worth of the carpet and noticed the intensity of the distress and desperation, evident in the Jew's face. Our saint, the beloved of Allah went on asking him raise up the price of the carpet and the Jew went on increasing the cost accordingly. At a certain point he stopped asking to increase its price and offered a handsome amount for the carpet. The Jew was greatly surprised at the new experience unheard and very humbly asked the reason. Hazrat Abdul Qadir said, "I assessed the worth of the carpet understood the cause for the low price for which you were prepared to sell it. It is against the principle of Islam to take undue advantage of the helplessness and indigence of others. At the same time, as a merchant,I should have some profit in the transaction.If I sell this carpet to another it will fetch a little profit for me.That little profit is enough for me.I never like to transgress the Divine Law for unlawful worldly gains".Such an example would be very rare in the of mankind.

These favourable and unfavourable aspects which influence on the economy of the are the concepts of Islamic socialism.

III. Jihad:Worship:- Real worship means desisting from violating the Divine Law pursued from the fear of and love for God. Worship establishes a direct relationship between man and God without anybody's interference or mediation. Muslims are enjoined up obligatory worships called the five pillars of Islam which are as follows:

1. Declaration of Faith: - It is the first and foremost duty of a Muslim to declare and bear witness that there is no diety other than Allah (Shahaadat) and that Muhammad (SAW) is His messenger to entire humanity till the Day of Judgement.

2. Salaat or Namaz: - Offering prayers five times a day is the second obligatory worship to God. There are several advantages of Namaz. It inspires man to a higher morality, purifies heart and keeps the man away from evil deeds. Performing Namaz is a daily training for self-discipline. Namaz is the right of Allah for having created us and for having showered His bounties upon us. Namaz is a physical exercise for the nerves, muscles and joints of bones. This exercise prevents as well as cures diseases. It is a prelude and preface for the invention of the devices of Physio-Therapy. It enables us to remember Allah in standing, bowing, sitting and prostrating postures. There are Quranic Stanzas and Ahadis regarding punctuality, purpose of Namaz, specified times of Namaz and virtues of Namaz.

The main purpose of Namaz is to cultivate discipline and punctuality in praying five times a day. Five-times prayer was commanded by Allah during Prophet Muhammad's audience in the Holy Abode (Arsh) of Allah on the night of Mei'raj-e-Nabii.e., on the 27th night of Rajab two years before Hijrat.

The commandments and times of prayers have been mentioned in Ahadis and Quranic Stanzas such as 4:103. 11:114, 17:78, 20:130,30:17-18 etc.. moves up and encounters the calamities and continue to do so till the Day of Judgement".

H:-"Never get tired of praying; never forget to pray for him who prays,so that he may prosper".

H:- To offer the prayers at their early stated fixed time is the best deed". (Bukhari)

S. Baqara:-2:239.

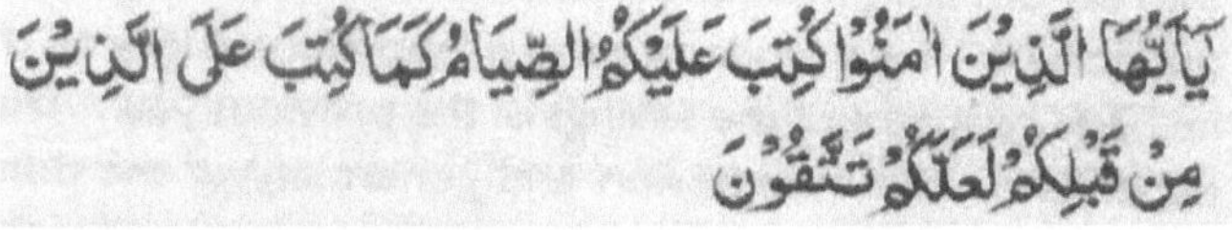

Tr:- "If ye fear an enemy), pray on foot or riding (as may be more convenient), but when ye are in security celebrate Allah'spraises in the manner He has taught you, which ye knewnot (before)"

The above-mentionedStanza explains the special privilege that praying on foot will ward off dangerous situations.

Sawm or Fasting: - Fasting is the third pillar of Islam.In fact, fasting is moral, physical and spiritual exerciseas well as spiritual discipline"

All other fasting are voluntary while the fasting during the whole month of Ramazan are obligatory. The fasting during the month of Ramazan transforms the entire Muslim society into one single family and thus weaves the wreath of Islam which presents a unique picture social conflux.It is the duty of every Muslim to strengthen this conflux more and more".

Baqara:- 2:183:

يَا أَيُّهَا الَّذِينَ اٰمَنُوْا كُتِبَ عَلَيْكُمُ الصِّيَامُ كَمَا كُتِبَ عَلَى الَّذِيْنَ مِنْ قَبْلِكُمْ لَعَلَّكُمْ تَتَّقُوْنَ

Tr.- "Oye who believe, fasting is prescribed to you: as it was prescribed to those beforeyou; so that ye may (learn) self-restraint".

S. Baqara-2:185 (Already quoted in 12th chapter)

also dear (signs) for guidance and judgement

Tr:-Ramazan is the month in which, we sent down the Quran as a guide to mankind. Also, clear (signs) for guidance and judgement (between right and wrong). So, every one of you. who is present at his home during that month should spend it in fasting. But if anyone is ill or on a journey the prescribe period should be made up by days later. Allah intends every facility for you. He does not want to put you into difficulties. (He wants you to complete the prescribed period and to glorify Him. In that He has guided you, and perchance, ye should be grateful".

Total abstention from eating and drinking and completely refraining from physical pleasures from dawn to dusk during Ramazan is sure to benefit both body and soul. While fasting, our entire attention is focused in worshipping Allah and thus it elevates our spiritual heights. It gives us strength to restrain from all sorts of emotions and to reject the selfish call of mundane pleasures. During Ramazan, we get trained to refrain from evil for the rest of the year and life. Fasting makes the digestive system stronger, prevents gastric trouble cures diabetes, reduces obesity, and strengthens Iman. Fasting is a servitude to Allah, a hidden worship. long practice of obedience, shield for protection from sins and a valuable reward hereafter

H:-"Fasting will extinguish the fire of hell"

H:- "There is a gate in paradise through which only those people will enter paradise on the Day of Resurrection who observe fasts".

H:- "Whoever observed fast imbibed with faith and with expectations of reward from Allah. all his past sins are forgiven"

H:- 'Whoever in Ramazan provides a person who is keeping fast for iftar (evening meals for breaking fast), this act will become a source of forgiveness for his sins and safety from hell fire and he will get as much reward as will the keeper of fast, without any reduction in the recompense Of the latter".

The main purpose of fasting is to make our own selves more conscious about Allah and more obedient to Him.

4. Zakaat: Obligatory Charity: - Zakaat literally means purification.

It is one of the five pillars of Islam. Zakaat promotes and purifies the economy of Islamic society and thus facilitates better distribution of wealth. It is called poor due which interprets. the religious obligation, social justice. social security, generosity, material purification and spiritual purification. It is a moderate and proportionate levy on the Muslims who have surplus savings.i.e., 2 1/2 percent of the savings of the previous year. The amount of other voluntary charities depends on the compassion and generosity of the doner. Zakaat is the right Of the poor Muslims while all other voluntary charities are meant for the entire poor community irrespective of caste and creed. Zakaat must be paid with absolute pleasure, which reduces selfishness and contributes in promoting the sense of solidarity of Islamic brotherhood. The most significant aspect is that Allah increases His blessing on charitable people. Poverty leades to moral and ethical degradations like cheating, murdering and stealing. To some extent Zakaat saves the Muslim community from the plight of poverty and ethical degradation.

There are Ahadis and Quranic Stanzas about the advantages of Zakaat and disadvantages of the negligence of

Zakaat, A research scholar says that significance of Zakaat is mentioned in Quran at eighty places.

S.Tauba:-9: 105:- (Part of the Verse):-

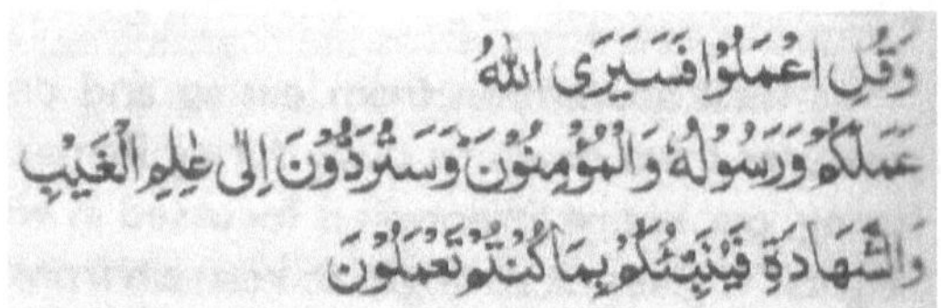

Tr:- " And establish regular prayers, practice regular charity; then open the way for them for Allah is Oft-Forgiving, Most Merciful".

S.Aal-e-Imran-3:180:-

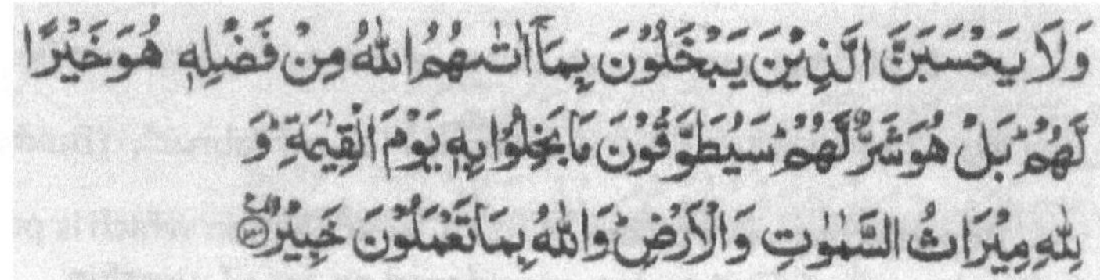

Tr:-And let not those who covetously with hold of the gifts Which Allah has given them of His grace think it is good for them: nay. it Will' be worse for them 'Ven them covetously with hold be tied to their necks soon collar, on the Day of Judgement. To Allah belongs the heritage of the heavens and the earth; and Allahwith all that ye do"

H:- "I have been commanded to fight against people till they testify that there is no God but and establish prayer and pay Zakaat. If they do it. the blood and property are guaranteed protection on my behalf and their affairs rest With Allah'. (Muslim)

H:-Alms given in secret and good treatments to relatives Will pacify the wrath of Allah"

Zakaat in combination with prayers and fasting is considered to be the foundation stone of practical faith.

5. Hajj:- Kabathullah is the center and fountain head of Islam right from the advent of Adam(A.S), The journey to Makkah and the rituals performed during Hajj can be considered a huge international gathering in order to promote Inter-national Islamic brotherhood and Sacrifice.

Hajj and its rituals are performed in commemoration of Ibrahim Alajhis Salamis sacrifice to Allah. Muslims come from every corner of the world. refresh their communion God at Baithullah (House of Allah) once a year. The congregation at Makkah is a grand sacrifice. equality. brotherhood and devotion. Hajj pilgrimage is a focal point for the entire humanity to frame and practice a better social order based on Piety.Equality peace and justice. Hajj removes the barrier and distinction between rich and poor. fair and black, and low. and high. It levels the Muslim brethren, the consciousness of. which strengthens and inspires universal fraternity among the Muslims.

S. Hajj-22.27:-

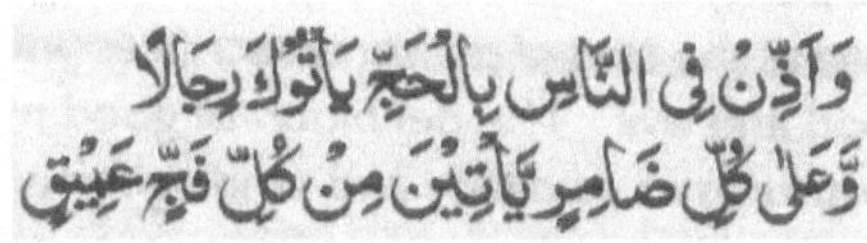

Tr • 'And proclaim the pilgrimage among men; they will come to thee on foot and on every kind of Camel; lean on account of journeys through deep and distant highways".

8 • O' people. Hajj IS prescribed for you, so you should perform it. (Muslim)

H:- "The best deed is to believe in Allah and His Prophet. Next to it is to participate in Jihad in the cause of Allah. Next to it is to perform Hajj". (Bukhari)

H:-Both Hajj and Umrah absolve sins as furnace purifies iron.

H:-The best Jihad for women is Hajj-e-Mabrur". (Bukhari)

Besides these five pillars of Islam, every action which is performed in the awareness that it fulfills the will of God is also considered an act of worship.

IV . Jihad:- Morality, Modesty, Piety, Goodness, And Virtue:

Human beings can be classified on several bases. According to some broad classifications they can be moral or immoral: modest or immodest; good or bad: vicious are virtuous action of man depends upon the interplay of some of their traits in different circumstances Misconduct good or evil is determined by the manner in which he utilizes his faculties.Piety, purity, morality, modesty, virtue and intelligence make him remain calm, pure, chase contented, while immorality, immodesty, lust and evil thoughts lure him to unlawful world pleasures and perdition. Man's tendencies may change with his new experiences in his life. The virtuous tendencies to worship, to love God more and more and to serve humanity enable him to get detached from material benefit, undesirable physical urges carnal emotion and all evil temptations. Instead, his virtuous tendencies will lead him to the path of righteousness and to adhere to codes of ethics. The food habits and daily discipline have considerable amount of influence over morality. In every aspect of life Islam advocates moderation which results in self-restraint. A person of morality and modesty must be true and pure in his thoughts, word and deeds, in other words they must be identical and should never be at variance with another. Morality, piety, and modesty are all tenets of Islam. The Quranic laws have broad been classified into injunctions (good) and prohibitions (evil). Trust in Allah's revelations is sure defense against evil temptations.

It is not enough to be moral and modest. The higher level of morality lies in the realization of its potentiality, feeling of moral responsibility, making a man's own self, a key to good and a barrier, against evil, spreading good into the world and preventing and eradicating social evils from the society. Such are the higher levels of morality advocated by Islam.

The moral excellence lies in practical ethics such as wrapping the body fully, maintaining the purity of mind and body, and raising the human dignity. The people who uphold moral law even at the cost of personal sacrifices will be able to discriminate between right and wrong and good and evil. The definition of good must include sanctity of all human life. After revealing scriptures as guidance and sending Prophets as preceptors, Allah unmistakably and fully places the burden of making the choice between good and evil, on the shoulders of man. The good and evil deeds will be judged on the Day of Reckoning. A spiritualist has said, True freedom is not in your way, but in yielding to God's way".

S.Nur-24:31:- (Part of the verse):

Tr:- "And say to the believing women that they should lower the gaze and guard their modesty, that should not display their beauty and ornaments except what (must ordinarily) appear there of; that they should draw their veils over their bosoms and not display their (women's) beauty except to their husbands, their fathers, their husbands fathers, their sons and their husband's sons, their brothers or their brothers' sons".

S.Araaf:-7:33:

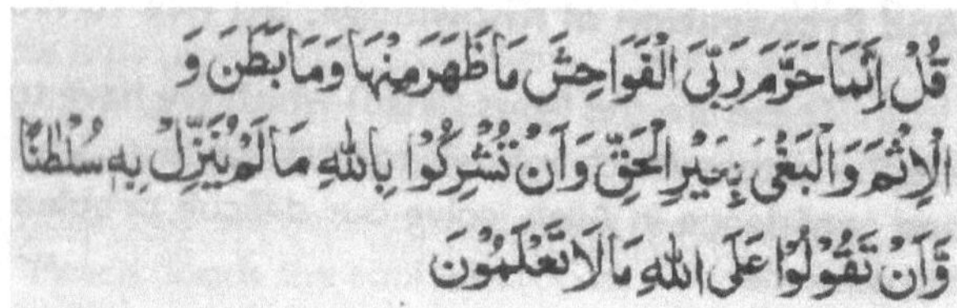

Tr:-"Say, that my Lord has indeed forbidden shameful deeds, whether open or secret sins and trespasses against truth or reasons; assigning of partners to Allah for which He hath authority; and saying things about Allah of which ye have no knowledge".

S. Hajj-22:49:

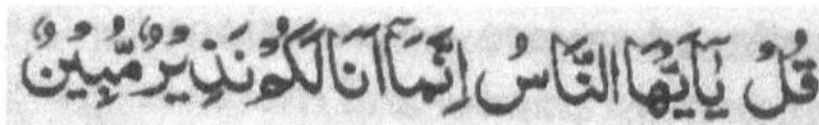

Tr:-"Say O men! I am (sent) to you only to give a clear warning".

H: "To control ourselves from illicit and carnal emotions is one of the greatest Jihads"

H:- "Improve your character, your faith will be perfected".

H:- "Protect your private parts (from their forbidden use) so that you may not be disgraced before mankind"

H:- "Undoubtedly, this world is a sweet and fresh to look at and certainly, God has made you succeed in it the people of the past to see how you act herein. So be on your guard against the (guiles) of the world and the (guiles) of women". (Muslim)

H:-Every religion has a distinctive quality and the distinctive quality of Islam is modesty (Bahagi, Ibn-e-Maja)

H:- "Modesty is a part of faith and the believer will enter the paradise. Immodesty is an evil and immodest man will be sent to hell'. (Masnad, Imam Ahmed)

H:- "It is a unique splendour of a believer that all his actions are imbibed with piety. At the times of prosperity and happiness, he thanks God, and at the times of adversity he exercises patience which is a great piety". (Muslim)

H:-"That believer is very bad who is blinded and lured by carnal emotions. The worldly attraction becomes the cause of his infamy". (Tirmizi).

H:- "Piety is another name of the beauty of character. Sin is that factor which pricks your conscience and that which you conceal from others". (Tirmizi)

H:-The best among you are those whose appearance reminds you of Allah'. (Bukhari, Baihaqi)

The people of Sodom and Gomorrah resorted to sexual sins especially homo-sexual activities. Their contemporary and nephew of Ibrahim (A.S), Prophet Lut (Lot) was sent to them by Allah to warn them. Except a very few, those people did not listen to him and continued their illicit activities. Allah's wrath destructed them through two angels by showering brim stones on them.

Jihad: Patience, Perseverance, Justice, Bravery, Reconciliation, Acquisition And Propagation of Knowledge, Service to Humanity:

This perseverance These are the fights (Jihad) which we have to practice in the true spirit of Islam. These are the factors which are sure to fetch success. Stepping forward with maximum perseverance and confidence in Allah, solve our difficult problems very easily and consequently make hopes smile.

Patience is firmly rooted in the unity of God and advocated by Islam during turbulence and trying circumstance. This act of piety strengthens our faith in Tawheed and Islam newly converted Muslims of Makkah exhibited the best examples of patience. The early converts suffered severe persecutions by the Mushrikeen of Makkah and many attained martyrdoms after most painful and merciless persecutions. But their faith in Islam never dwindled and they upheld the unity of God till their last breath.

The early converts er dwindled and they suffered .

Islam enjoins on both men and women to acquire knowledge in all branches of studies to earn their livelihood. At the same time reading the scriptures and other sacred books strengthens the moral forces and drives away the tendencies which lead them to ruin and destruction. Such books are pregnant of comprehensive system of thoughts and practical ethics. It is the duty of every Muslim to carry out the Jihad of preserving and propagating Islam as well as the Islamic civilization. Our propagation of knowledge is nothing but the echoes of the messages of God and His prophets over the ages i.e., from the advent of Adam (A.S) on earth.

The act of reconciliation between two individuals or two hostile groups involve justice courage and sincerity of faith.

S. Luqman:-31:15 (part of the verse)

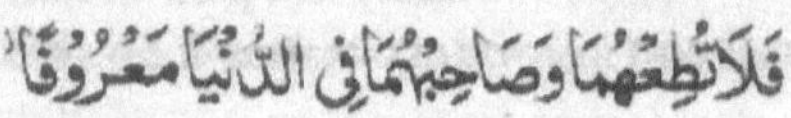

Tr:- "obey them (unbelievers) not; bear them company in this life with justice.

S.Ma'ida-5:8

يَٰٓأَيُّهَا ٱلَّذِينَ ءَامَنُوا۟ كُونُوا۟ قَوَّٰمِينَ لِلَّهِ شُهَدَآءَ بِٱلْقِسْطِ وَلَا يَجْرِمَنَّكُمْ شَنَ‍َٔانُ قَوْمٍ عَلَىٰٓ أَلَّا تَعْدِلُوا۟ ٱعْدِلُوا۟ هُوَ أَقْرَبُ لِلتَّقْوَىٰ وَٱتَّقُوا۟ ٱللَّهَ إِنَّ ٱللَّهَ خَبِيرٌۢ بِمَا تَعْمَلُونَ

Tr:- "O ye who believe! stand out firmly for Allah, for witnesses to fair dealing and let not the hatred of others make you to swerve to wrong and depart from justice. Be just; that is next to piety; and fear Allah for Allah is well-acquainted with all that ye do".

H:- "Restore peace between two contending persons, since a dispute between the two is destructive to both".(Abu Dawood, Tirmizi)

H:- "It is out of the greatest Jihad to speak the truth in front of a tyrant ruler". (Muslim)

Jihad: Spiritual Perfection: - Of course the above-mentioned struggles of life (Jihad) are extremely difficult. But surmounting the difficulties in the true Islamic spirit coupled with faith in the unity of God ensures spiritual perfection. In order to succeed in achieving this goal; believers should adhere to all Divine injunctions. For achieving this goal, the potentiality of body and soul should be realized. Without this success, our life will be grievous and unaccomplished. A spiritualist has stated, "Peace floods the soul when God rules the heart".

Those preceptors who practice austerities and profess their own preaching's can easilypromote spiritual enlightenment among the innocent and ignorant people. Trials and turbulence of life must make our life better but not bitter. By the hazards and hardships of life, we can self-purification which will definitely lead to spiritual perfection. Devotion and noble activities satisfy the doctrine of spiritualism. One who witnesses the manifestations of Allah by his physical eye testifies the mystic and unseen truth (God), treads the path of righteousness and can attain spiritual perfection.For such a man the apostles and divine revelations serve as spiritual eyes.Spiritual perfection means, merging with God, the greatest and final goal of the believer.Allah has promised the believer to send to paradise, who succeed in attaining this grand goal.

S. Talaaq-65:11:

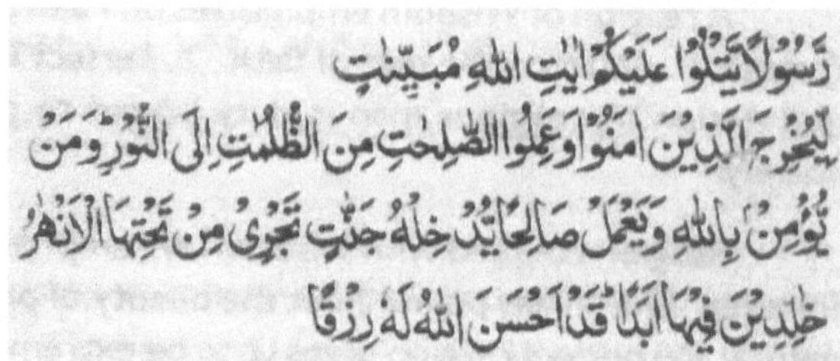

Tr:-"An Apostle who rehearses to you the signs of Allah, containing clear explanations. that he may lead forth those who believe and do righteous deeds from the depth of darkness into light. And those who believe in Allah and work righteousness, He will admit to gardens beneath which rivers flow, to dwell therein forever, Allah has indeed granted for them a most excellent provision".

Attainment of spiritual perfection is the greatest Jihad because it involves all sorts of noble activities called jihad.

Now, we have to examine the factor which is the hindrance and obstacle on the way of spiritual perfection and the undisputed requisite which leads to spiritual perfection.

2. Wisdom Without Religion: - The wisest man or the most powerful king in the a. world is worse than nothing and rather dangerous for the society if he is devoid of Faith. The man without religion who is called an atheist is steeped in ignorance. Every man has got his own problems and sufferings. Because of his wisdom without religious enlightenment, he stands baffled not knowing how to solve his problems. An atheist justifies vices which have ad Stanza influences on society. Atheists are always materialists. They are completely blind to spiritualism. They can never know the worth and splendour of the piety of desire lessness.

b. Religion and Wisdom: It is quite essential that a true religion should be based on wisdom and Divine inspirations. In the real sense, it is not a religion which is based on superstitions, absurdities and obscurity. The worth, virtues and values of a true religion can be assessed by some definitions and explanations.

Wisdom acquired through a true religion removes the hurdles, and hindrances along our spiritual sojourn, enables us to surmount the difficulties, wards off our adversities and solves the problems easily.

A believer having confidence in the munificence of God, should be firmly determined and steadfast in achieving spiritual success. This courage and constancy make up him live happily and die happily. He is attracted by the Divine gifts and uses his powers in a lawful way.

A true religion is akin to nature. It is very easy, feasible and practicable to follow a natural religion. True revelations purify our mind and give moral strength. They provide guidelines to cultivate devotion, rely on Divine dispensation and be happy and contented. They convert the bitterness of life into sweetness. They are guiding lights and gifts of knowledge. They trim the beauty in human character and eradicate all sorts of evils.

A religion of Wisdom emphasizes on Faith (spiritualism). Knowledge (Theory) and Action (practice). Action is the test of faith. A perfect faith must be in combination with knowledge and Action. A religious man is duty bound to promote goodness and sever evils from the society.

Religion coupled with wisdom lays emphasis on the beauty of proportion which can last forever. Quran has pointed out the beauty of proportion in Allah's creations. Islam being the natural and perfect religion urges us to be extremely careful about the proportion in everything. Anything disproportionate cannot last long. Disproportion creates defects which result in the extinction of the worth of the human faculties.

Al-Mulk-67:3 (Quoted in Chapter 8)

Tr:-"He who created seven heavens, one above another; no want of proportion will thou see in the creation of (Allah). Most gracious; so, turn thy vision again. Seest thou any flaw?"

S. Rum-30:30:

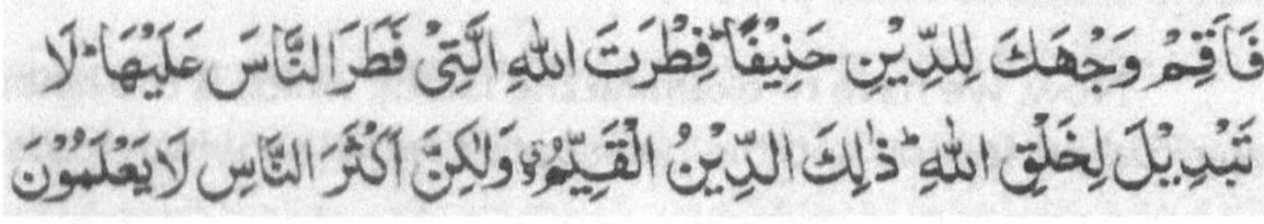

Tr- "So see thou thy face steadily and truly to the Faith; (Establish) Allah's handwork according to the pattern on which, he has made mankind. No change (let there be) in the work (wrought) by Allah, that is the standard Religion; But most among mankind understand not".

Islam being the perfect religion is blessed with final codes of ethics for entire humanity. Now, we can realize the significance and potentiality of the vehicles of religious knowledge and wisdom which take human beings to the desired destination, namely the stage of spiritual perfection, the greatest Jihad. (Jihad, Islamic socialism, economic science, physical potentiality and spiritual potentiality).

CHAPTER - XVIII

RETRIBUTION

Stanza: 86

18 /مکافات عمل

86- ہے سدا بیدار قانون مکافات عمل

جب حدود حکم رب سے کوئی جاتا ہے نکل

ڈالتا ہے ہم آہنگی خلقت میں خلل

اپنی بربادی سے ہوتا ہے وہ فورا ہم بغل

ہے مکافات عمل سے یہ حقیقت جلوہ گر

شاہد قدرت ہے اخلاق نکو سے بہر ور

Tr:-When any person transgresses the limits of Divine Command, the law of retribution Is always active or awake.When he creates any hindrance or disturbance in the harmony of people,he confronts with his own destruction.It is clear that Divine Law is the evidence for reaction for action.

Stanza: 87

87- زندگی تیری فقط کیا ہے گناہوں سے خراب

کیا نہیں اولاد تیری مورد رنج و عذاب

یہ غضب بھی تُجھ پہ ہے اللہ کا قہر عتاب

مصلحت کا ہے تقاضا پاک ہو تیرا حساب

گردش اولاد بھی کیا کم ہے سوہان حیات

تا رہے گرد گنہ سے دامان حیات

Tr:- Your sinful deeds not only influence on your life but also make your progeny the victims of grief and torment. It is advisable to keep your account clear and pure or to prevent indignation and wrath of God.The adversities and calamities of your children are more painful which cause vexation and grief. Hence let your life be clean from the dust of crimes.

Stanza.88

88۔ چشم ظاہر سے بہت اسرار وحدت ہیں نہاں

جب گرفتار الم ہے کوئی جان تواں

درد کی بجلی رگ ہستی میں ہوتی ہے رواں

در حقیقت عرش تک جاتا ہے آہوں دھواں

اہل قدرت جو نہیں لیتے غریبوں کی خبر

دیکھتے ہیں اُن پہ قدرت کا غضب اہل نظر

Tr:-The vision which sees only the outward things does not see the inner secrets of the unity of creations. When a weak and desperate person becomes the victim of grief, the thunderbolt of calamities runs through his very nerves. The wise people who see the truth, notice the wrath of Allah descending on those rich and powerful people who are unmindful of the sufferings of the poor community.

Stanza:89

89۔ جو ہوائے دہر کی منزل پہ جاتے ہیں گزر

اُلفت و ایثار کی دنیا میں کرتے ہیں سفر

حادثات دہر میں رہتے ہیں مست و بے خطر

آفت دنیا بھی رحمت جن کو آتی ہے نظر

جن کا جینا اور مرنا ہے خدا ہی کے لیے

ہر زماں حاصل حیات نو اُن کو غیب سے

Tr:- Those who voluntarily cross the stage of worldly desires, start to travel in of love and sacrifice. They remain calm, frenzied with love, careless and fearless at all sorts of situations in the life and consider the disasters of life as the blessings of God. Those who live for the pleasure of Allah,and die in the way of Allah,are blessed with a new life mysteriously at every stage

Stanza.90

90۔ کس لئے ہے فرض ہر انساں پر صوم و صلٰوۃ

کس لئے ہے صاحب قدرت پہ واجب ہے زکات

دیکھنا اُن میں نہیں کیا راز تکمیل حیات

اُن سے وابستہ زمانے کی نحوست سے نجات

عام ہو اُن سے زمانے میں نشاط زندگی

پاک ہو گرد کدورت سے بساط زندگی

Tr:- Prayers (Namaz) and fasting are obligatory worship for every Muslim and Zakat isobligatory only for the rich people who have got considerable amount of savings of the previous year.It must be noticed that perfection of life depends upon these pillars of Islam which are connected with the relief from misfortune.The happiness of life depends upon worship. Hence our life should be free from ill-will.

Stanza.91

91۔ سایہ گل داغ بن جاتا بھی ہے فولاد پر

صحبت بد سے بشر کو چاہیے کتنا حذر

نیک صحبت ہو ہمیشہ زینت قلب و نظر

بے حیا پر لعنتیں قدرت کی ہے شام و سحر

ذرہ ذرہ بزم ہستی کا امین راز ہے

بندہ مہر و وفا کا مونس و دمساز ہے

Tr - Even the shadow of flower leaves impression on the iron. Man should beware bad company and safeguard himself. Good company is the graceful beauty for heart and vision. Divine imprecations descend on the immodest man night and day. Every atom of life is the custodian of secrets and companion of faithful worshipper.

Stanza.92

92۔ فطرت انسان جب حیوانیت کافور ہو

جلوہ ایمان سے عقل بشر معمور ہو

جب ہوائے دہر کا دل سے اندھیرا دور ہو

جوہر انسانیت شرم و حیا کا نور ہو

جس چمن میں آہ افسردہ گل عصمت ہوا

قہر حق کی بجلیوں سے وہ چمن غارت ہوا

Tr:- When the beastly instincts get vanished from the nature of man, when human wisdom is full of the beauty of Faith; when the darkness of worldly desire gets dispelled, the quintessence of humanity becomes the effulgence of modesty and bashfulness. It is painful when the flower of character gets withered and the garden of morality gets destructed due to the Divine wrath.

Stanza:93

93۔ پاک ہو قلب و نظر پاک گفتار عمل

بے نہاں پاکیزگی میں جلوہ حسن ازل

تیرا ہر ذرہ رہے حسن صفائی کا محل

یہ تن خاکی بھی ہے عرش خدائے لم یزل

قلب انساں میں صفائی قوت بے باک ہے

شوکت روح و نظر ہے صیقل ادراک ہے

Tr: Our thought, visiondeeds must be pure because the Eternal Beauty is concealed in purity.Every action of yours must be the residence of beauty and purity because this corporeal body is nothing but the Abode of Eternal God. Purity in the human heartis the bold and daring strength.Spiritual and Visualmagnificence and dignity are the burnishersof human intellect.

Stanza.94

94۔ بہر غلبہ زندگی ہر وقت مصروف جنگ

ہو ادا عشق الٰہی کی تیرے دل کی امنگ

شیشہ دل پر   آفت خواہش بے جا رنگ

ہو تیرا حسن طبیعت فاطر ہستی کا رنگ

تیری ہستی ہو صفات رب سانچے میں ڈھلی

تیرے ہر کردار میں ہو شان خلق ایزدی

نوٹ : ہدایت اور نجات کی رہ کسی رسمی اصطباغ یعنی رنگ دینے کی محتاج نہیں جیسا کہ عیسائیوں کا شیوہ ہے۔ یہ اللہ کا رنگ دینا ہے اور بتلاؤ اللہ سے بہتر اور کس کا رنگ دینا ہو سکتا ہے ہم اس کی بندگی کرنے والے ہیں ۔۔۔۔۔۔۔ دلیل

Tr:-"In order to obtain mastery, You must be engaged in fights or struggles of life. Your earning ambition must be forthe love for Allah;The undesirable worldly desires will rust your heart. The beauty of your nature must consist of the qualities of the attributes of the creator of the universe.Your life should be moulded according to the moulds of the attributesof Allah. Every action of yours should Yours should be akin to Divine goodness and civility,

Stanza. 95

95۔دین بر حق ہے سے ہو تکمیل اخلاق بشر

بندہ ناچیز میں شان الٰہی جلوہ گر

ہیں اسی فاش اسرار حیات خیر و شر

ہو اگر دستور پر اس کے حقیقت ہیں نظر

اس کے بر حق اور بجا ہونے پہ از روز ازل

ہے گواہ قدرت کا قانون مکافات عمل

Tr:- The perfection of human character can be obtained only through a true religion. The worshipper who is nothing when compared to the worshipped, display a little of Divine Grandeur. The person who see the truth and sticks to the religion laws, can realise that the secrete can be disclosed only through a true religion. From the beginning, the law of retribution has been the clear evidence for Islam to be the True Religion.

Stanza.96

96۔ ماتحت مقصود کے ہوتے ہیں کردار بشر

دہریوں کا دین ہے دنیا پرستی سر بسر

معنی اخلاق سے ہے علم اُن کا بے خبر

درد انسانی سے کیونکر چاک ہو انکا جگر

دہریت دل کے لیے افیون زہر آلود ہے

بو الہوس کے واسطے آزادی مردود ہے

Tr:-Human activities are controlled by our Goal, God. The religion of lustful person is nothing but the worship of worldly desires. His knowledge is devoid of the impact of character. Such people cannot have painful feelings over the grief and misfortunes of others.

Stanza.97

97۔ عالم اسباب کے آئین سارے ہیں اٹل

ہے نتائج سے ہمیشہ اپنے وابستہ عمل

ہے برائی کا برا اور نیک ہے نیکی کا پھل
جبر کی حجت سے یہ جاتی نہیں سُنت بدل
قسمت انسان میں ہے ہر ایک محنت کی جزا
ہے کمال کامیابی کوششوں کی انتہا

Tr:-As the laws of this material world are certain and unchanged our activities are always liable to their consequences. The consequences for bad deeds will be adStanza and for now deeds pleasant and favorable. The religious law cannot be changed by forceful arguments coercion. Every human being is sure to reap the fruit for his endeavour and the perfection success depends upon the uttermost limit of attempts and perseverance.

Stanza.98

98۔ رحمت رب کی ہے یہ بھی ایک شان در گزر
جو سیہ کاری کا انساں میں ہے تدریجی اثر
ہو عمل اللہ کے قانون کافوری اگر
سر زمین مہر میں مشکل ہے جینا سر بسر
راہ پر اس دور مہلت میں نہ آئے جو کبھی
شامت اعمال سے بچتی نہیں وہ زندگی

Tr:- It is the magnanimity of the beautiful attribute of forgiveness of God that the vicious deeds of man have only gradual effect. If the Divine law allows our action to have immediate effect, this bountiful earth will become uninhabitable. If we do not get corrected in the permitted span of our life, it cannot escape misfortune and misery

Stanza.99

99 ۔ عدل و رحمت پر مکافات عمل کی ہے بناء

ایک ذرہ بھر عمل ہو ہے اٹل اس کی جزاء

سو گناہ ہوتا ہے کار خیر کا لیکن صلہ

ایک دانہ کہ عوض ہو سینکڑوں دینے عطا

رحمت رب سے نہ ہو مایوس عاصی زینہار

پھر چلے اس کی طرف خود مغفرت ہے بے قرار

نوٹ : دیکھو اپنا عہد پورا کرو میں بھی اپنا عہد کرونگا اور دیکھو میرے سوا کوئی

نہیں پس دوسروں سے نہیں صرف مجھ ہی سے ڈرو۔(قرآن)

اور نیک کردار انسانوں کے اعمال میں برکت دیتا ہے اور کے اجر میں فراوانی

ہوتی رہتی ہے۔ (قرآن)

Tr:- The law of retribution is based on justice and favour. Even a little amount of favour is sure to obtain its remuneration. The recompense of a good deed is hundred-fold just as a seed sown properly gets for us crores of grains. Oh, sinner, by no means, get frustrated and unhopeful of Divine Mercy, because, the salvation itself is anxious to get Divine pardon for the repentant.

Stanza:100

100۔ رحمت و عدل۔ و ربوبیت کا مظہر ہے جہاں

ہو تیرے لب پر سدا حمد خدائے کن فکاں

ہو جبیں شوق تیری اور اس کا آستاں

ہے وہی خلقت کا معبود معاون بے گماں

ہو تیرا ہر حال میں ہادی خداوند کریم

جادہ اعمال ہوں ترا صراط مستقیم

Tr:- You must always glorify Allah, because, this world is the manifestation of His Bounties, Justice and Providence. You must always be desirous to bow at the Holy Abode of Allah, because, undoubtedly, Allah is the only God and only abetter.

C:- Retribution means reaction or repercussion on an action. According to the Divine Law, one will obtain reward for his noble deeds and punishment for his evil deeds.

Just as all sciences and technical devices are inter-related: all social aspects are closely inter woven. In this chapter most of the aspects dealt with have been already dealt with in the previous chapter Struggles of Life" (Jihad). Allah has promised ample reward for noble deeds (Jihad), and warned of severe punishment for evil deeds (anticipated activities). The consequences of a man's deeds arethe quint essence of this chapter.Now, it is clear that retribution is there compense for the man's deeds according to their naturei.e., good for good and bad for bad.

Some of the fights (Jihad) are sacrificing life for the sake of service to humanity, having maintaining inner purity and outer purity, struggles for noble achievements,preserving and perfecting the status of humanity, worship earning to acquire Divine attributes,excellence of Divine Dignity,endeavor for the perfection of success,treading the path of righteousness, in short adherence to Divine law. These fights (Jihad) are remunerative in this world as well as in the hereafter Some of the anti-Jihad activities are indulgence in Atheism, creating disturbance in the harmony between two persons or two factions, inflicting pain on others spreading chaos and commotion in the society by all sorts of malicious deeds, laziness and lust which entail Divine displeasure and Divine wrath,

It is a notable point here poet has been very careful regarding the continuity subject matter and the arrangement of contend. He has presenting different ideas and different arguments, repeated the topics,but he has done it with reference to different contexts,presenting different ideas and different arguments,

S. Jaasiya:-45:15

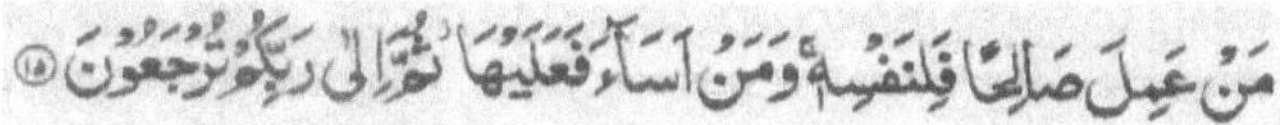

Tr:-Whosever doth right, it is for his soul; who doth wrong,it is against it. And afterward unto your Lord, ye will be brought back".

S. Nahl-16:11:

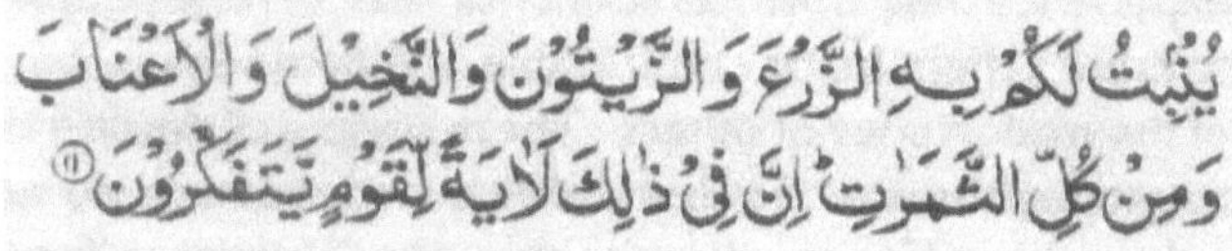

Tr:- Therewith. He causeth crops to grow for you and the olive and the date-palms and grapes and all kinds of fruits, Lo! Herein is indeed a portent, for people who reflect"

Tr:- "Do not be angry with anyone and you will be saved from Allah's wrath and His displeasure"

Tr:- Allah will surely punish those people who torture their fellowmen .

Tr:-Everyone of you is a shepherd and everyone of you is accountable for what is placed in your charge". (Bukhari, Muslim, Abu Dawood).

H:-When a truthful believer visits a sick believing bondsman, he is so to speak in the garden of paradise until he returns". (Muslim).

H:- "Allah defers punishment of all sins to the Day of Resurrection excepting disobedience of parents, for which Allah punishes the sinner in this life before hereafter". (AlHakin)

H:- Verily Allah recorded the good and evil and then made it clear that he who intended one good and did not do it. Allah recorded one complete good in his favour; but if he intented it and also did it, the glorious and great Allah recorded ten to seven hundred virtues and more to his credit. But if he intended evil and did not commit it. Allah wrote down full one good in his favour. But, if he intended that and also committed it. Allah made the entry one evil against him. (Muslim).

Man has to enjoy the fruits of his actions. A mistaken impression exists among people that God is responsible for their sufferings. Some prosperous people do not bother to worship Allah, but go on continuing their blind pleasures and raveling's.

But when they get entangled in difficulties, they blame Allah. Sometimes Allah teste Faith of the believers by causing calamities, who never blame Allah and go on worshipping Him Religion clearly lays down through the theory of cause and effect that both happiness and misery, calmness and commotion, fortunes and misfortunes are consequences of one's own deeds and God is impartial towards the human race.

Repercussion of Evil Deeds on the progeny: - Evil deeds and mischievous inflictions on others recoil on the perpetrators and their progeny. The acts of men with evil intention solely to harm others are bound to recoil. They may be under the mistaken impression that they are wiser than the unseen God. They carry on their evil schemes of harming and offending others according to their whims and fancies. Such powerful people enjoy the sufferings of others. While destroying others, they never realise the existence of the unseen Arbitrator Allah. These wicked people who violate the religious doctrines of pious conduct are sure to experience their downfall sooner or later. These people are selfish and heartless. They cannot tolerate others being comfortable and prosperous, but they are eager to prosper at the cost of the misfortunes of others. These people of devilish traits and demonish qualities are bound to get punishment. Their evil deeds are sure to cause sufferings to their children, and will have unbearable adStanza effect on their life. The sighs of sorrows of the afflicted people go high up to Arsh, the Holy abode of Allah where, even angles cannot reach. The sighs of the oppressed rebound with all force. The Divine wrath, indignation and fury descend on the perpetrators and their children which make them sigh more painfully with absolute vexation. This Divine Law of Retribution is ever active about which stupid people are careless.

The question arises as to how are the innocent children responsible for the criminal acts of their parents. Divine Law is never defective. The sorrows and sufferings of children are more painful and tormenting to the parents, than those of the sufferings of their own. In recompense for the sufferings and calamities, caused by Allah to the innocent children, Allah will give them peace and pleasure in the hereafter. There can never be any injustice in the realm of God.

New Life:- Those believers who have abandoned materialism and have crossed the stage of worldly desires begin to travel in the world of love, ever prepared to make sacrifices for other creations of Allah. As they realise the unity of God and unity of creations, they give due regards to other creations and do not attach undue value to their own enjoyments. This change of attitude is a milestone in the spiritual journey which offers them a new life. The mis happenings of the world do not cause them worries and vexations. They are intoxicated and frenzied by the love for God and His creations. They consider the calamities as the Divine

Blessings which are capable of purifying their selves.Those who live for Allah and die for Allah,obtain a new life at every advancing step in the spiritual sphere.Such selfless people will be amply rewarded by Allah.

Worship, Meant For Spiritual Perfection: -Out of His Love for His creations, Merciful Allah, desires to forgive the sins of His worshippers and ever yearns to award paradise.Allah has made Namaz, Fasting and Zakat obligatory worships for Muslims which can enable His worshippers,to attain spiritual ward evil influences and escape from ominousness andinauspicious events.May the happiness of life depend upon the noble activities of the worshippers and may this transitory and unreal life be free from ill-will, turbidness and muddiness. Pure life will facilitate obtaining spiritual perfection and grand remuneration.The commandments Allah are never meaningless or without any specific purpose.Through worship Allah wants to beautify the Law of Retribution.

Good Company: -in the 91st Stanza of the text, the poet has explained the significance of good company. By saying that a hard metal like iron gets the impression on it of the shadow of the delicate flower, he means to explain that weather it is good or bad, companionship has its great effect over other people. Hence it is advisable for man to abstainfrom evil and dangerous friendship. A good company should leave a graceful and beautiful impression on the heart and vision of the friend. Otherwise, Divine cause or imprecation will descent on the immodest people. Every atom of life is a custodian or guardian of the secrets of life. It is a mysterious consoler, sympathizer and cooperative friend for that person who has high regards for love, faithfulness and piety and who has to confront with great fights in order to maintain his nobility.

Saintly company curb evil influence. Those who consider life a burden, want to escape pernicious influences. Several methods have been prescribed in the sacred text to enjoy peace and maintain equanimity for which one of the steps is to cultivate association with stalwart with saintly qualities. They distinguish themselves of personal conduct and spiritual powers obtained through austerities and noble habits. The only misery of the saint is to turn people towards God and convince them about the truth.

Sometimes they may perform miracles. They are not intended to display their distinction but to bring relief to their disciples. Such dynamic personalities embody in themselves complexes of excellences of worship and devotion.

The tendency among many people is to support an evil doer when he takes delight doing despicable deeds so long as the consequences do not affect them. When their devilish acts result in serious difficulties or deadly impact on them, they will condemn the same. There may be rare occasions when the good takes predominance over the bad, even in a person, considered to be the incorrigible, when he will listen to the suggestions, tendered by a sane man.

Man's character and conduct can be judged by the company he keeps. It is repeatedly urged by spiritual scholars to be very careful about the natural inclination of the person we come across training the child starts from the with aht

Of course, it is a fact that the bringing up of and training the child starts before the wedding of the parents. The child must be born healthy and due status, because the bustards have no status in the society nor do they have right of inheritance.The plight is unaccountable.

The parents have some responsibilities regarding the up-bringing of the child and he has some rights over his parents. In order to produce a healthy child, the parents should preserve their chastity from the beginning of their life and they should be free from dangerous, malicious and contagious diseases, contacted due to immorality. As soon as a child is born into the contact of his parents and other family members. They must love the whether it is a boy or a girl. They must choose a good name for it. They must nourish educate him in accordance with their financial capacity and guide him on righteousness. The parents themselves must be good and advise him to have the good friend. They must give him best training possible so that, he becomes affectionate relative to his kith and kin, an obliging friend to his neighbors, a for a good citizen his nation and above all a sincere devotee of God. By the best guidance and the company of the parents, both the parties i.e., the parents and the grown-up child handsomely benefited by the Law of Retribution.

Morality And Modesty: -In the 92nd, 95th and 96th stanza of the text, the poet has discussed the Law of Retribution concerning morality and modesty.

First of all,the poet has mentioned some aspects which have their influence quintessence of humanity. When the beastly instincts and shamelessness vanish from the of nature his mind is filled with the beauty of Faith and when the darkness of worldly desires are dispelled from his heart, the sterling quality and excellence of humanity her the light of modesty. On the other hand, when the chastity is lost, the thunderbolts of Divine wrath will descend on the man.

Nothing else than a true religion can lead a person to the stage of perfection of character Spiritual perfection means merging with God. It is really wonderful that a man who is not when compared with God, has the pride and power of capability of merging with God. It is the true religion which discriminates between good and evil and discloses the secrets of life to those people who understand the value of true religion and see the truth. From the beginning the Divine Law of Retribution has been the clear evidence for Islam to be the real and true religion for which it is quite indispensable to attain the perfection of characteristics.

Though activities of man are controlled by divinity, Allah has given man the liberty to choose his ways of life. People of lustful passions worship only worldly desires. Their perverted knowledge does not consist of any impact or importance of good character. According to their point of view, morality is meaningless. Such perverted people who cannot safeguard their own morality, cannot have feelings over the sufferings of others which is mercilessness. They are not concerned with nobility. The above mentioned three stanzas explain the necessity for a true religion which can expound the worth of perfection of morality and its consequences.

Once a certain person went to our prophet and said, "Oh Apostle of Allah! Marriage is advocated by Islam but, I am ever poor and have no means to maintain the family. What can I

Do?" Our prophet replied, "You are exempted from this advocation. As a true Muslim Preserve you chastity. Allah will amply from reward you for this act of piety":

On another occasion, a man asked our prophet,"Ya Rasoolullah! I have too much of sexual passion,but my wives are not available now.What can I do at this situation?"Our prophet said,"Food habits have greatinfluence over the passions.Take less food or observe fast. Fasting will definitely diminish your passion.Thus, you can preserve your morality. You will get a grand reward for safeguarding your modesty and for fighting with your emotions".

Cleanliness and purity: Cleanliness is an article of faith and hallmark of piety. Islam lays emphasis on both inner purity and outer purity.Our thoughts, words and deeds must be identical in sincerity and purity completely free from hypocrisy, filth and vulgarities, because the Eternal Beauty of God. Is concealed in purity. Every tom of our body must contain beauty of purity because this corporeal body also is the manifestation of Eternal Divinity.Whose heart is pure,can never be influenced over by the outer forces.They ever remain strong, firm and fearless.The poet Daleel Sahib defines purity as the spiritual magnificence and dignity.He again defines it as the burnisher of human intellect which enlightens humanity.

S. Baqara:2:168:

يٰۤاَيُّهَا النَّاسُ كُلُوْا مِمَّا فِى الْاَرْضِ حَلٰلًا طَيِّبًا ۖ وَّلَا تَتَّبِعُوْا خُطُوٰتِ الشَّيْطٰنِ ۚ اِنَّهٗ لَكُمْ عَدُوٌّ مُّبِيْنٌ ۝

Tr: "O mankind ! Eat what is lawful and wholesome in the earth, and follow not the footsteps of the devil. Lo ! He is the open enemy for you."

H: "Remain clean (with ablution) always; you will be given abundance in livelihood".

H: "Itikaf restrains a person from sins. "(Being in Itikaf is considered a source of spiritual enjoyment of the highest order, which leads to purity)"

H: "Cleanliness is half the creed".

In short purity is highly remunerative.

In the 94th stanza of the text, the poet interprets the theory of salvation. In order to achieve this end, we must always be engaged in hard strife to obtain mastery, we have yearning for the love for God. Our hearts must be free from the rust of worldly desires, the beauty of human qualities must be in consonance with Divine attributes; our life must be moulded according to the of Divine attributes and the excellence of the activities must contain the splendour of Divine civility,pomp and glory. Salvation cannot be procured by the parents to the child by solemnizing ceremonies and observing rituals, such as Baptism.

Allah has given different colours to the people of different faith.The last message of Islam has established an all – embracinghuman unity free fromall grudges and fanaticism. giving no special status to any race colour.

Some people of different faiths consider' Baptism as a religious tenet observed to convert their child to their respective religions. How can the people give better colour counter Allah in giving the specific colour to the Faith. According to Islamic point of view ceremony can instil any particular belief in the minds of the child. In several cases, the people choose their own religion, abandon the religion of their parents who have Baptisedthem or sometimes become Atheists. Then what impact has Baptism? The parents consider it as a religious tenet, which is the means for guidance and salvation for their children. Allah is the Greatest Baptist who can give different colours to different people?

S. Baqara -2:138:-

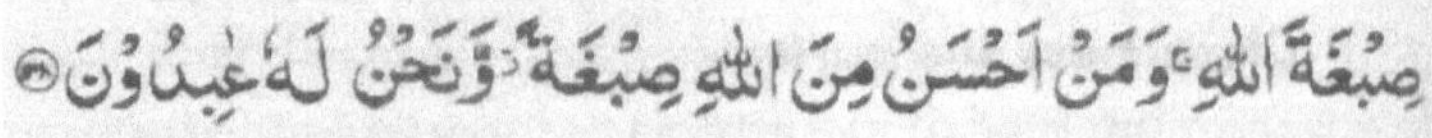

Tr:-" (Our religion is) Baptism of Allah and who can baptise better than Allah? And, it is He Whom we worship".

People are allowed to change the faith of others by preaching and propagation of Allah's messages, but the ultimate Baptist is Allah. Holding ceremonies of Baptism is meaningless.

Prophet Zakria (PBUH) was a believer Jew who hailed from one of the twelve tribes of Bani Israil and co-brother of Imran, the father of BiBi Maryam. Zakria Alaihis Salam prayed Allah for a noble son, who could continue his mission of propagating Allah's message. In his old age Allah blessed him with a son who was named Yehiya. Prophet Zakria was slain for preaching the unity of God and for claiming to be the prophet. Yehiya was the cousin of St. Mary and contemporary of Jesus Christ. Yehiya grew up and attained prophethood. With the permission of Allah, he spread the message, revealed to his father and Jesus Christ and converted many people to Christianity i.e he gave a new colour to their faith by means of preaching's and propagations and not by means of rituals invented by man. In Quran, Allah has given him a title and calls him," Yehiya, the Baptist", though Allah is the real and ultimate Baptist. In those days, Jerusalem was under the domination of Roman Emperor Herod. Yehiya was slain by the agent of Herod. Yehiya Alaihis Salam's contribution to Christianty left an indelible impression on the people and it spread fast in Rome in later days.

The child is born with the religion of the only God, the Creator of the child. As Allah has bestowed the power of discrimination the grown-up human being accepts his parent's religion or chooses his religion according to the environmental influence or his own fancy. By the reference of Baptism in this chapter, the poet means to explain that salvation can never be obtained by means of ceremonial Baptism but only through repentance, austerities and recompense for noble deeds.

Forgiveness and manifold remunerations: -

If we deeply ponder over the issue of the law of retribution, it is nothing but the law of cause and effect regarding the activities of human beings. The laws of this material world are stable and unchanged, as we see with our own eyes that no action goes without its reaction or consequence. Good for good, and bad for bad" is the basic principle of law of retribution. This religious code can never be changed by baseless arguments.

It is divine grace or dignity of Divine pardon that gives the sinner sufficient time to gethimself corrected, to repent and to get salvation.It is the Divine scheme which makes the effect of his sins.In case the sinners immediately become the victims of Divine wrath and punishment.life in this bountiful earth will become impossible.Allah patiently waits for the sinners to repent up to certain length of time.In case they continue their sinfuldeeds, Divine fury is sure to descend followed by his misfortune as the recompense for his misdeeds.

Even a small amount of endeavor does not go without its remuneration, because the aw of retribution is based on the Divine justice and grace.It is the wonderful beauty of Divinegrace that Allah does not multiply the vices of misdeeds of man but His generosity multiplies the virtues just as his providence procures crores of grains in exchange of a single grain.By nomeans the sinners may get frustrated or disappointed and become hopeless of salvation because Allah is most Merciful and Divine pardon is ever available for the repentant.

Quran - "Fulfil your promise and I shall also fulfil My promise. There is nobody to be afraid of except Me. Hence fear Me"

Quran: - "Good deeds of people increase their virtues and their remuneration becomes abundant"

S. Tauba -9:112

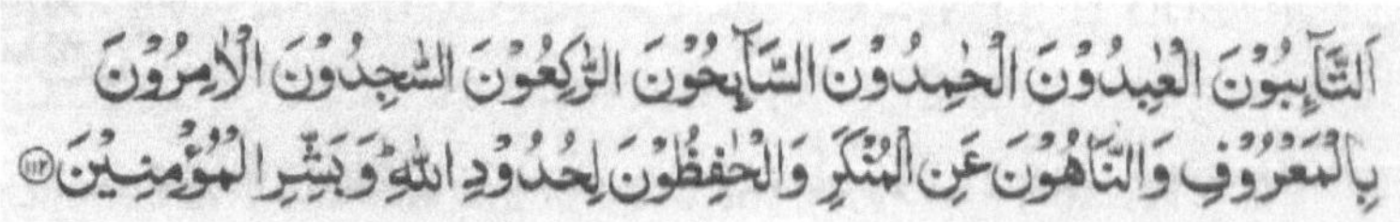

Tr:- "Triumphant are those who turn repentant (to Allah) those who serve Him, those who praise Him, those who fast, those who bow down those who fall prostrate in worship).

those who enjoin the right and who forbid the wrong, those who keep the limits (ordained) of Allah and give glad tiding to believers"

S. Nur-24:22:

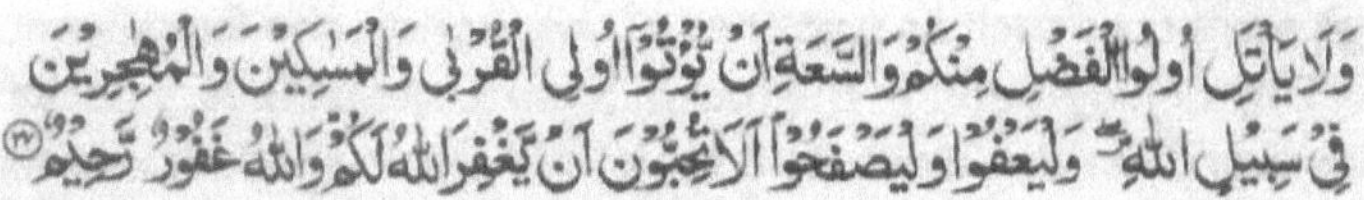

Tr:- And let not those who possess dignity and ease among you swear not to give to the near of kin and to the needy and to fugitive for the cause of Allah. Let them forgive and show indulgence. Yearn ye not that Allah may forgive you? Allah is forgiving Merciful)

H:- "Seek forgiveness of Allah, Your sins will be obliterated"

H- "You are my Lord and I am your servant. I have wronged myself and I do acknowledge my wrong action. My Lord forgive me" (Bukhari).

In this chapter the law of retribution has been interpreted regarding different aspects of life.

Sura-e-Fatiha - The concluding verse of this chapter consists of the subject matter sura-e-Fatiha with which the poet has connected the law of retribution.

This world is itself the manifestation of Allah's Providence, justice and grace. If Allah does not provide our necessities, or does not render justice or does not shower his grace on us. our life will become impossible. He is our Abetter and Whom do we worship. The unit God is the first and foremost factor to be realized in Islam. The poet urges the reader to be down his head with all sincerity on the threshold of God. The poet also urges the reader supplicate to Allah that at all situations Allah may guide him on the path of righteousness because the law of Retribution is ever active. Sura-e-Fatiha is the opening chapter of Quran consisting of seven small Stanzas.

S. Fatiha -1:1-7:

Tr:- "Praise be to Allah, the Lord of the worlds. The Beneficent, the Merciful owner of the Day of Judgment, Thee (alone) we worship; Thee (alone) we ask for help. Show us the straight path, the path of those whom Thou has favoured; not (the path) of those who earn Thine anger nor of those who go astray".)

In the first three Stanzas, the believers extol the glory of God by uttering some of his high attributes such as sustainer of the worlds, the Beneficent, the Merciful and the master of the Day of Judgment. In the fourth Stanza, the believers declare their Faith by announcing that they worship Allah alone and seek His help. In the fifth and sixth Stanzas they have requested Allah to guide them in the path of righteousness. In the seventh Stanza they have requested Allah to protect them from evil.

This opening chapter of Quran consists of three main aspects namely glorification Declaration and supplication. The Whole subject matter of Quran, including the injunctions and prohibitions come under the categories of aspects mentioned above. Hence Sura-e-Fatiha is called the essence of Quran. The 7th Stanza contains the subject matter of Sura-e-Naas, the 114th and the last Sura of Quran, in which the believers have requested Allah to guard them against evil. The beauty of the serial arrangement of Suras is that Quran starts with supplications and ends with supplications. The enticing beauty of the serial arrangement of Suras involves the beauty of continuity of subject matter of Quran. Sura-e-Fatiha is considered to be containing the best supplication as the believers have requested Allah both to guide them on the straight path and protect them against evil.

The significance of Sura-e- Fatiha can be assessed by the fact that it is oft repeated Sura in our daily life.In every unit of Namaz (Rak'at), it is compulsorily recited.Allah wants us to supplicate again and again and wants to answer our prayers.Divine pleasure lies in the supplications of the worshipers Allah's promise to do justice is firm and certain.

S. Zaariyaat-51:6

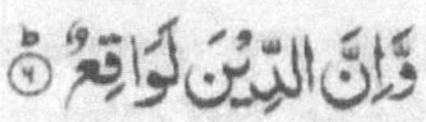

Tr:-Verily Judgment and Justice must indeed come to pass

Sooner or later, whether in this world or in the hereafter, we will have Divine Justice on which is based the Law of Retribution.(Retribution character, good company and spiritualism)

CHAPTER - XIX

HAPPINESS

Stanza: 101

19/مسرت

101۔ یہ خدا کی نعمتیں کیس لئے ہیں بے شمار

ہیں انہی کے دم سے کل ہنگامهاہائے روزگار

زندگی خود ہے تلاش عشرت و جوش و قرار

وہ سرور عیش کیا لیکن جو بن جائے خمار

دین کا مقصد جہاں میں عشرت جاوید ہے

وہ مسرت کیا ہے بربادی کی جو تمہید ہے

Tr. Allah's unlimited bounties are meant for the benefits of his creations. These bounties are the causes for hustle and bustle of daily life. The life itself is the quest for happiness, contentment and enthusiasm. But that happiness is not real happiness which intoxicates (or makes one lose his senses). The purpose of religion is the eternal happiness of humanity. But that sort of happiness which serves as the preamble for destruction is not permitted by religion.

Stanza:102

102۔ مقصد ہر آرزوئے جاں ہو گر جاں آفریں

اس جہاں کے پھول ہوں گلہائے فردوس بریں

کاسہ تلخاب ہو جام طہور و انگبیں

ہر مسرت ہو جمال و قوت و علم و یقیں

ہیں بہار بے خزاں سے بے خبر اہل ہوس

ہیں خزاں سے خوار تر ان کی بہار کم نفس

Tr:- Every desire of human being must be life - giving. The flowers of this world may resemble the flowers of high paradise. The cup of bitter water (difficulty of life) may be the cup of honey and the pure wine which cause frenzy of love for God (pleasure of life). Every happiness may be the beauty, strength, knowledge and certainty. The lustful people are unaware of unceasing beauty of happiness. Their short-lived and temporary beauty is worse than the autumn.

Stanza.103

103- اہل عرفاں کے لئے ہے موسم گل ہر زماں

عشرت فانی بھی ہے انکو سرور جاوداں

عشق بن جاتا ہے دنیا کا جوہر سود و زیاں

رنج و راحت میں ہے انکا دل برابر شادماں

آشنا راز حقیقت سے جو ہو جائے نظر

آگ میں گل بھی گلوں آگ بھی آئے نظر

Tr:- It is always the flowering season for those who possess the mystic knowledge of Allah. The temporary happiness of this transitory world is the eternal bliss for them. The people feel cheerfulness at all circumstances of pain and pleasure, whose material outlook changes into love for God. Those who are aware of truth see flowers in the flame and flame in the flowers.

Stanza.104

104- ہے حدوں میں دین کی آزادی کامل کا راز

ہر برائی اور خباثت سے یہاں ہے احتراز

شوق کی لذت سے ہر نعمت ہے از بس جانواز

عاشقان رب کی معراج مسرت ہے نماز

وہ سراب دہر میں خود کو ڈبو سکتے نہیں

جلوہ حاضر سے اپنے ہوش کھو سکتے نہیں

Tr: The secret of perfect freedom lies within the scope of religion, because every impurity is objected in it. Every Divine bounty becomes life - giving due to the pleasure of gratitude to Allah. The height of happiness is felt by the lovers of God on performing Namaz. Neither can they drown themselves in the worldly mirage nor can they lose their consciousness by the alluring beauty of the present unreal things.

Stanza.105

105۔ ہے اسی کے عشق کا جلوہ ظہور کن فکان

ایک حرف عشق میں ہے معنی کون و مکاں

عشق کی فطرت میں پنہاں ہے سرور جاوداں

کونسی نعمت زمانے کی نہیں اس میں نہاں

دولت عشق الٰہی سے جو دل آباد ہیں

خوف و غم یاس و ہوس کی زد سے وہ آزاد ہیں

نوٹ : نحو یوں کی اصطلاح میں لفظ حرف لفظ کے معنی میں استعمال کیا جا سکتا ہے۔

Tr:- Allah expresses his love for his creations through the manifestation of this world. The single word of Divine law carries the meaning of the whole universe. Every Divine bounty and eternal bliss are concealed in the word "LOVE" Those people whose hearts are full of love for God, escape from the stroke of grief, fear, despair and lust.

Stanza.106

106۔ ہے ضمیر پاک خود سر مستی جام طہور

وہ قرار قلب کا یاد الٰہی سے ظہور

بادہ الہام سے وہ روح انساں کا سرور

خود شناسی میں وہ لطف حق شناسی کا شعور

ہیں نصیب عاشقان دنیا میں جنت کے مزے

سارے قدرت کے ترنّم میں قیامت کے مزے

Tr:- The pure conscience without any prick of thorn is itself the intoxication of love for God. The spiritual bliss is the result of inspiration. Those who enjoy self-realization possess the wisdom of realization of God. The lovers of God are fortunate enough to enjoy heavenly bliss in this world as the melody of the song of whole nature are highly pleasant.

Stanza. 107

107۔ دین سے حاصل نہ ہوتا گر سرور جاوداں

دین کی ہم پر ضرورت ہی نہ کچھ ہوتی عیاں

یہ مسرت ہی علاج ہر ہوس ہے بے گماں

اس مسرت میں کمال خلق آدم ہے نہاں

جس قدر خلق خدا میں یہ مسرت عام ہو

اس قدر ہو دور آفت خیر برکت عام ہو

Tr. In case, the eternal bliss could not have been attained by means of religion, necessity of religion would not have been felt.There is no doubt that the happiness derived from religion is the remedy for every lust and greed and it is the perfect character of human being. May the comfort and abundance go on increasing in the society to that extent as this happiness becomes common among the lovers of God.

C. This chapter has been entitled "Happiness"- Islam aims at providing comforts and eternal bliss for humanity both in this world and in the hereafter.At the same time, it attempts to dispel despair and frustration from human minds.Allah has described his providence inSura-e-Rahman by mentioning some of His creations which are at our service and which fulfil our needs.There is nothing lacking in Allah's Providence. But the welfare and happiness of people depend upon the proper,moderate and lawful exploitation of His bounties.The stupid and unfortunate people misuse His bounties,adopt the wrong way of life and get wrecked.

In this poem the poet has discussed some factors which go on increasing the happiness are which spoil happiness and result in adStanza consequences. The favourable factor are noble activities, hard strife, love and feelings for God's other creations, service, generosity, valour, simplicity,satisfaction contentment, thankfulness to God, glorification God all sorts of prayers, utterances of hymns (Zikr) austerities, morality, remembrance of God firm faith confidence in Allah and above all total submission to Allah.

Some of the unfavorable factors are transgression of lawful rights, breach of Divine principles, immorality, discontentment, greed for worldly gains, bad habits, lack of confidence in and remembrance of God.

The poet has discussed his philosophy of true happiness. He says that the great tumults in engagements for the sake of livelihood are the consequences of availability of Allah's unlimited bounties, as life itself is the quest for happiness, comfort, contentment and zealous exuberance. It is the real happiness which is in consonance with the purpose of Islam. The illicit desire for too much of luxuries is nothing but a frenzy and it is short-lived. By means of happiness and contentment, the flowers of this world can be converted into the flowers of paradise, the bitter water can be converted into honey and heavenly wine, every happiness can be converted into strength, knowledge and certainty, and the temporary beauty of life can be converted into eternal beauty. For those people who are blessed with mystic knowledge of Divinity and its heir whole life is flowering season and their temporary happiness becomes the eternal bliss. Those who see the truth, see flame in the flowers and flowers in the flame.By this the poet to explain that a wise man can foresee the disasters in the unlawful merriments of and can foresee the pleasant consequences in the miseries of the patient devotees.

Ibrahim Alaihis-Salam was the native of Babylon in Iraq. The country was steeped in idolatry.

The then ruler of Iraq Namrood was a staunch idolater. Later, he himself chain Divinity in this dark part of the world, the Prophethood of Ibrahim Alaihis-Salam who courageously fought against idolatry and confronted with Namrood with absolute Ibrahim Alaihis Salam's father Tarooq alias Aazar was the sculptor and trader of idols also employed as light-bearer and guard of Namrood during nights. When Ibrahim Ald Salam opposed Namrood, Aazar supported the king for the fear of losing his job. The argu between Ibrahim Alaihis- Salam and Namrood were highly interesting. When Ibrahim (A.S) could not be overpowered, it was decided to kill him by throwing him into the fire by the command of the king his subjects amassed a huge mountain of fuel in a square and invented device to throw him in the fire from a distance. Though Ibrahim (A.S) was fully aware of scheme. He was calm and frenzied with devotion, unconcerned with the preparations for his execution. When the flame was raging high up to the sky, Ibrahim (A.S) was brought and thrown in the flame, by pulling the rope of the machine. The fun lies in the fact that his father Aazar himself participated in pulling the rope. The whole assembly of spectators was overtaken by surprise when an astounding Divine miracle took place. When Ibrahim (A.S) reached the center of the square, the raging flame immediately got extinguished and the square got converted into a beautiful garden with streams of cool water. He received the mysterious Divine help in recompense of his devotion and confidence in Allah.

Though Namrood was convinced of the Prophethood of Ibrahim (A.S), he was not prepared to lose his powerful position. He went on confronting with him. With utter despondence and frustration, he launched a great military attack on Ibrahim (A.S) and his followers. Another miracle took place on this occasion also. A great host of big mosquitoes gushed out from the hole of a rock and killed the whole army of Namrood. Namrood fled. suffered greatly of mosquito bites and died after six months. It is interesting to notice how the flame was converted into garden by the happiness, Ibrahim (A.S) felt in his devotion to God.

Islam has prescribed a certain limit for perfect liberty in order to prevent impurity, wickedness and depravity which exist beyond the limit. Those lovers of God who feel the height of their happiness in prayers, and fervour of gratitude to God can never lose their consciousness by attraction of worldly desires or by the alluring sight of the mirage of the world.

Out of love for His creations, Allah created the universe and showered His bounties. In the nature of love, happiness is concealed. The lovers of God can never become the victims of any stroke of sadness, despair or lust.

A pure conscience without a single prick of thorn is a pure frenzy. Remembrance of Allah fecilitates contentment while inspiration results in spiritual bliss. The person who is incapable of realising his own self cannot realise the existence of God. So the poet says that the enjoyment of God - realisation depends upon the self-realisation. The lovers of God are lucky to enjoy the melody of Divine music and heavenly bliss in this world.

In case we are not benefited by eternal bliss through religion it is not at all necessary for us. The happiness, derived from religion is the best remedy for all social evils and troublesome circumstances and this is the sort of happiness which brings about the abundance of prosperity in the whole society

God's commands are not meant to frustrate us but to optimize us.Gratitude must be acontinuous attitude,not an occasional incident. Prayer purifies the worshippers mind and enables him to him to rivet his thoughts to God which lead him to the realm of bliss.Contentment is apositive virtue and not negative suppression. It is a sublimating force which transforms the desire and greed for transitory objects into a wish to secure universal good and realize God. It gives one a detached outlook towards life and thereby the person develops peace within himself raising himself above selfish limitations and avarice.He gets moral strength and his energies will not be dissipated inexerting for petty ends and making himself restless for ordinarygains,aided byaided by jealousy and retaining within himself hatred towards those who are better placed Contentment is a powerful antidote for the poison of greed.

Infinite bliss is in perception of God. Contentment and happiness depend solely on the mind, on external object and circumstances. Both heaven and hell are created by the mind.

Religion teaches us how to live a calm life while living this world of diversities. Religion realizes it form thoughts and emotions and from dependance on worldly objects. It helps men to reach the state of eternal bliss and to tread the path that leads to elimination of ego.

people are in need of peace and tranquility which they feel have disappeared from the world. They embrace the physical comforts of the external world and hence the internal realm becomes a living hell for them. Intellect and reasoning now have no doubt, reached great heights, but people have lost faith in themselves in the heart and also its fragile feelings.

What one should realize is that the enjoyment obtained through ephemeral pleasures is only a minute's reflection of the infinite bliss which arises from themselves. That which gives happiness today can easily become a source of tomorrow's sorrow. Religion teaches us how to understand this simple fact that God alone can give us happiness.

The diverse and contradictory nature of life is a delightful play for one who is aware of its ever-changing nature. He should smilingly welcome both the negative and positive experiences with equal vision. Those who are not aware of this, will feel life miserable and a burden.

A special characteristic of a true servant and a sincere devotee of the Almighty is he who wants nothing from Him in return for the display of his dedication. Every soul should work out its moral life and thus prepare to receive God's grace and eternal bliss.

H:-. By God. I am not afraid of the Muslims, being forced with poverty and want, but am afraid that the doors of the pleasures of the world are opened for them and they begin to love them more and more vying with one another as their predecessors did, and God destroyed them as He destroyed their predecessors". (Bukhari, Muslim).

H- "Leading a simple life is an article of faith " Abu Dawood).

H:- "In this world. I am not interested in comfort and luxury I am such a type of traveler and a rider who halted under a tree for some time and then started to continue the journey (Tirmizi).

H.- Wealth is not in the riches, but in the contentment". (Bukhari),

S.-Ra ad - 13.28 Allah's remembrance:

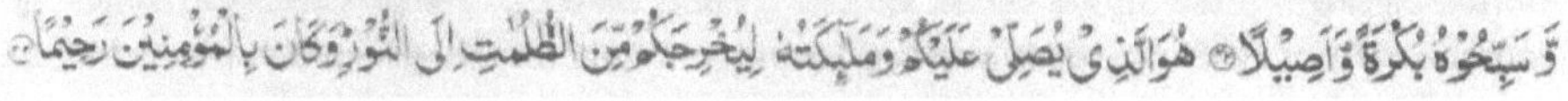

الَّذِينَ آمَنُوا وَتَطْمَئِنُّ قُلُوبُهُم بِذِكْرِ اللَّهِ أَلَا بِذِكْرِ اللَّهِ تَطْمَئِنُّ الْقُلُوبُ ۞

Tr. Those who believed and whose hearts have rest in Allah's remembrance: Verily in the remembrance of Allah do hearts find rest")

S. Ahzaab 33:42.43

وَسَبِّحُوهُ بُكْرَةً وَأَصِيلًا ۞ هُوَ الَّذِي يُصَلِّي عَلَيْكُمْ وَمَلَائِكَتُهُ لِيُخْرِجَكُم مِّنَ الظُّلُمَاتِ إِلَى النُّورِ وَكَانَ بِالْمُؤْمِنِينَ رَحِيمًا ۞

Tr. And glorify Him early and late. He, it is Who blessed you and His angels bless you that He may bring you forth from darkness to light and he is merciful to the believers

S. Hashr -59:19

وَلَا تَكُونُوا كَالَّذِينَ نَسُوا اللَّهَ فَأَنسَاهُمْ أَنفُسَهُمْ أُولَٰئِكَ هُمُ الْفَاسِقُونَ ۞

Tr:-And be not ye as those who forget Allah: therefore, He caused them to forget their souls. Such are the evil-doers".)

S. Munafiqun -63.9:

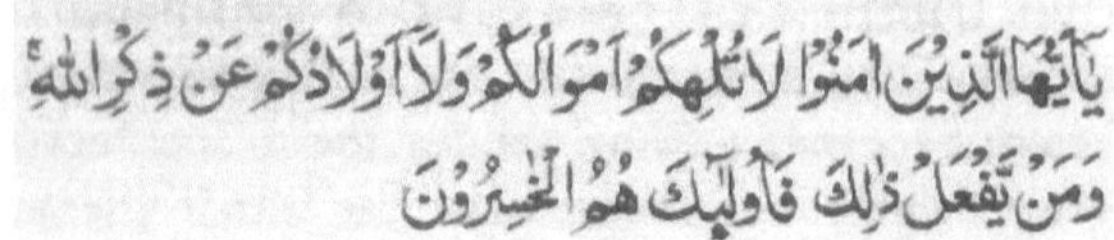

Tr:-O ye who believe! Let not your wealth nor your children distract you from remembrance for Allah. Those who do so, they are the losers".

In his book Nara-e-Darwesh. Daleel Sahib's poem has been published entitled "Eternal bliss (Ishrat-e-javeed)" the substance of which is stated below:

Once the beloved prophet of Allah, Ibrahim (A.S) who devoted his whole life in the cause of Allah, had a queer experience. On the occasion of hajj season, he was circumambulating the Kaabah along with a great congregation of pilgrims. All of a sudden, he felt a new light inside his heart when he saw a pious woman who was more beautiful than the moon and, in whose face, a unique effulgence of happiness was manifest. The cheerfulness on her face resembled the blooming freshness of blossoming flowers of paradise by which her enticing piety was being revealed. Ibrahim (A.S.) was highly pleased that he was fortunate enough to witness a perfect happiness. He said to himself." This is a garden which has never experienced an autumn, this is a garden which has developed in the state of never-ending spring season (flowering season)". He could not contain himself and spoke to her thus" Oh, you are enviable to the garden of paradise. What are the reasons for this amount of blessings of God, the cheerfulness, the freshness and the effulgence of your cheeks? In reply the pious woman dispersed the veil from her lips and explained the philosophy of the life with perfect happiness.

She said. "For my share in my life. I have been blessed with Islam. Of course, God has bestowed on me this eternal bliss. But your idea that my life is unbitten by sorrows and grief, is wrong. The heart which is not afflicted with grief will not be capable of realizing the value of happiness. Our happiness should be so, by the influence of which we should not bother about our adversity or prosperity. What is the worth of the happiness which spoils or destroys our life? It is the real happiness which can dispel our grief. The person who has not experienced any misery is unaware of the secrets of truth. How can person become courageous who has no opportunity to face woes and worries and to surmount the difficulties with bravery and happiness? Calamities only can enable him to cultivate the quality of total surrender and to have a real vision. His religion is valueness, the sterling qualities of his intellect is meaningless and he cannot be called human being in case his faith is defective and devoid of submission to God. I inform you as to what sort of disasters have engulfed me in the current week. My father who was the real personification of love and sacrifice, my three beloved sons, and my faithful and affectionate husband went to Allah one after another, leaving me alone, helpless and without any protection. It is only because of my perfect faith that the influence of these mishappening are not being revealed. There are some reasons for considering calamities as the pleasure giving factors. Allah has owned me and made me his humble supplicant. Whatever pleases Allah pleases me. I am frenzied with the unity of God because His love has gifted me with eternal bliss".

The pious Muslim women, intoxicated with lover of Allah, overlooked her calamities and derived eternal bliss from her religion, Islam.

True happiness does not depend on material wealth or achievements. If true happiness has to be attained, one should have contentment, peace of mind, patience, satisfaction and thankfulness to God for whatever He has provided. This is the theory beautifully brought to light by the poet. The essence of his poem" Gawala(cowherd)" published in his book.

"Once upon a time there was great king of great repute, ruling over his empire and was greatly respected by all his subjects. But he was not happy and always submerged in vexatious anxieties. With all sincerity he made an announced in his court and said, " My treasury overwhelms with weath, but I am bereft of happiness. I am not aware of mental contentment and my mind is full of anxieties. If anybody succeeds in making me happy, I shall benefit him with half of my kingdom".

The courtiers got stunned to hear his royal announcement. Many people went in quest of the object which could make the king happy. They sought the advice of a devotee of God. He advice to clothe the king with the shirt of happy man which might make him ever happy. In the empire, a cowherd (Gawala) was very famous for always being very happy and cheerful. They went to him informed him of the promise of the king and the advice of the devotee of God. They requested the cowherd to give his shirt. He replied, "it is true that I am always happy, but I do not have a single shirt".

But for the loincloth in his hip. The cowherd's body was naked. His contentment and gratefulness to God were the reasons for his eternal bliss. (Happiness, optimism, philosophy of life)

CHAPTER – XX

BEAUTY

—◦І○ ◆ ○І◦—

Stanza. 108

20 /حسن

108- ہے شعور حسن عرفان خداوند جمیل

عشرت جاوید کی ہے حسن نہر سلسبیل

حسن کے جلوے ہیں سب فیضان رحمت کی دلیل

حسن کی تنویر ہے وصل الٰہی کی سبیل

دیدہ حق بیں میں ہے دنیا کی ہر صورت حسین

حسن کے جلوے سے ہو انسان کی سیرت حسیں

نوٹ : وہی غلب رحم کرنے والا ہے جس نے ہے چیز پیدا کی

اس کو اچھا بنایا اور انسان کی پیدائش کو مٹی سے شروع ۔۔۔۔۔دلیل(قرآن)

Tr: "The beauty of Divine Knowledge is the beauty of knowledge and it is the heavenly stream of eternal happiness. The manifestations of beauty is the evidence for Divine beneficence because the light of the beauty of manifestations is the mediator for us to unite with God true vision, everything in this world is beautiful. The manifestation of Divine beauty makes a traits and character beautiful.

Stanza.109

109- حسن سے ہے ذرہ کون و مکاں معمور ہے

دہر کی ہر چیز میں ہر بات میں مستور ہے

چشم بینا میں شب ظلمت بھی کوہ طور ہے

حسن کا جلوہ حقیقت کا مبارک نور ہے

جو ہے تاروں میں چمک دل میں حرارت ہے وہی

حسن جو ظاہر میں ہے دل میں محبت ہے وہی

Tr:-Every atom in this universe is full of Divine beauty which is hidden in every creation For those who can see the truth, the dark night is Mount Senai and the manifestation of Divine Beauty in Mount Senai is the auspicious effulgence of truth. The heat in the heart is due to the diffusion of brightness from the stars and the love in the heart is due to the Divine beauty.

Stanza.110

110- ہے قیامت خیز دل پر حسن سیرت کا اثر

حسن ایثار و محبت سے فرشتے ہوں بشر

حسن ہوتا ہے جو تنویر حیا سے بہر ور

عالم بالا کی کی جانب عشق کرتا ہے سفر

حسن سے گر عفت قلب و نظر پیدا نہ ہو

حسن کے اسرار سے آگاہ تو اصلا نہ ہو

Tr:- The beauty of character has great influence on the people which, by human beings become angels. When the beauty is blessed with the luster of modesty, love for God finds elevation. If beauty does not create true vision, pure heart and Chasity, you can never come to know about the secrets of Divine Beauty.

Stanza.111

111 حسن کی تنویر سے جاتے ہیں جل اکثر حجاب

حسن بن جاتا بھی ہے روئے حقیقت پر نقاب

حسن کی آتش میں جلنے کا نرالا ہے حساب

بُو الہوس کے واسطے ہے اُلفت خانہ خراب

حسن کی زد سے کبھی جو دل نہ گھائل ہو سکا

حق شناسی کے کبھی قابل نہ وہ دل ہو سکا

Tr:- Sometimes the curtain on our vision is burnt by the luster of Beauty. Sometimes the beauty becomes a veil on the truth. The manner of being burnt due to the flame of Divine beauty is strange. The same beauty of God's manifestations in different material objects destructs the life of alustful person.The person who was not influenced by Divine Beauty could not be capable of realization of God.

Stanza.112

112۔ حسن عالم گیر ہے اُلفت بھی عالم گیر ہو

بے خبر تحدید انکی باعث تکفیر ہو

حسن کی ایک موج کیوں دل کے لیے زنجیر ہو

موجب آہ و فغاں کیوں نالہ دلگیر ہو

عاشق حسن ازل یک بندہ آزاد ہے

وہ جدھر جائے ادھر شور مبارک باد ہے

Tr:- Both Divine beauty and pure love are universal conquerors. To point out a limit for those aspects leads to infidelity. The attraction of a single wave of beauty should not be the cause for painful lamentationand an imprisonment of the heart. On the other hand the true lover of Eternal Beauty (God) is the free worshipper.Wherever,he goes, the uproar of

Stanza:-113

113۔ یہ سراسر ہے مذاق حسن ازل کا بے گماں

ہے منور جو ضیاء حسن سے سارا جہاں

حسن اظہار حقیقت کی ہے رنگیں داستان

یک ادائے خاص ہے اسکی تناسب سے عیاں

ہیچ ہے اپنی نظر وہ سخن ہو یا سرور

حسن کی تنویر سے خالی رہے جس کا وجود

Tr:- It is nothing but the taste for nice joke of the Eternal Beauty (God) that the whole universe is illuminated with the Divine Beauty. Beautyis the colourful account of the of truth depends upon the special and proportionate act of manifesting. According to our outlook, whether it is poetry or music,it is worse than nothing if it is devoid of the light of Eternal Beauty.

Stanza.114

114۔ عشق حسن جاودانی سے ہے درد لا زوال

ہے کمال حسن اُلفت کے لیے حسن کمال

عشق کی آتش کہ ہے پروردہ حسن و جمال

زندگی خود ہو تیری حسن و محبت کا جمال

اہل ایمان و نظر سے حسن کے اسرار پوچھ

معرفت کی دور منزل ہے بہت سو بار پوچھ

Tr. The eternal pain of love of God is caused by permanent Beauty of God. The perfection of beauty is the perfect beauty for love. The warmth of love is cherished by Beauty Your life should become the Beauty of love. Ask the believers about the secrets of Beauty Ask them hundred times because the stage of acquiring Divine knowledge about Beauty is very far off.

Stanza.115

115۔ حسن کا جادو بہت ہے بست ہ قلب و نظر

یوں تو روشن ہیں ضیاء حسن سے شمس و قمر

ہے کمال حسن کا انسان میں جلوہ مگر

ہے یہی وہ حسن جس سے چاک ہوتے ہیں جگر

حسن انسانی ہے جنت اہل ایماں کے لئے

ہے خدا کا خاص جلوہ چشم انسان کے لئے

Tr:- The effect of Beauty is under the control of heart, vision or mentality. Only because e Divine Beauty, the sun and the moon are bright and lustrous. The Beauty by which the love is felt, consists in human nature. For the believers, the human beauty is a paradise. The special Divine Beauty is meant for human eye.

C:- In this chapter, the poet has described and defined Beauty in several ways. He discussed both the Divine Beauty which is constructive and beneficial to human being way and the worldly beauty which allures, distracts and ruins human beings every way. The poet says that the Divine Beauty involves the beauty of creations, beauty of intention, beauty of action, beauty of behaviour beauty of love and sacrifice, beauty of adoration to God and beauty of Divine knowledge and spiritualism. Quranic verses about the proportions and beauty of fictions of Allah's creations have been quoted below:

S. Baqara - 2:29: -(Already quoted)

Tr: "It is He Who has created for you all things that are on earth. Moreover, His designs comprehended the heavens for He gave order and perfection to the seven firmaments and of all things"

S. Al-A'ala -87:2-5 (Already quoted)

Tr:- "Who hath created and further given order and proportion; Who hath ordained laws and granted guidance; and Who bringeth out the (green and lustrous) pasture and then doth make it (but) swarthy stubble".

S. Saffa-37:6:

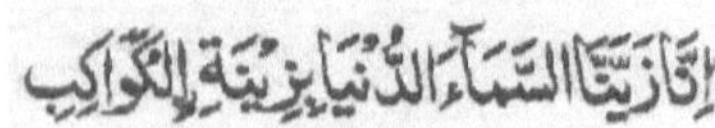

Tr: - "We have indeed decked the lower heaven with beauty in the stars)".

C.- The poet defines beauty as Divine knowledge, the heavenly stream of eternal bliss. the proof for bounties of Allah and a mediator for us to unite us with Allah. This Divine Beauty makes every creation beautiful and the good character of man is the result of Divine Beauty is concealed in every atom of the universe. It can convert the darkness of night into the Divine Refulgence revealed to prophet Moosa (PBUH) in Mount Senai (Koh-e-Toor). The light which appeared before Moosa Alaihis-Salam was the auspicious effulgence of God. Moosa (A.S.) used to spend days together in devotion to Allah In the Valley of Aemen in Mount Senai . Allah used to constanza with him through the clouds. This was the clue in Quran for the invention of satellite transmission. The title of Moosa (A.S.) is Kaleemullah which means one who converse with Allah. After speaking with Allah, his desire to see Him increased day by day. He requested Allah to appear before Him. But Allah refused to do so saying that his vision is not strong enough to see him. Like a darling child, Moosa (A.S.) insisted on seeing Him. In accordance with his request Allah revealed a minute fraction of the Refulgence in the form of lightning. As soon as Moosa (A.S.) saw this lightning, he swooned. After his recovery, he begged pardon of Allah for his stubbornness. The poet has compared the beauty with lightning, seen by prophet Moses in Mount Senai. The poet has also hinted about the unity of creations by saying that the luster in the stars, the heat in the heart, manifestations of beauty and love are one and the same thing.

By the perplexing effect of the beauty, character, love and sacrifice make the people angels. It has already been explained that human being is the supreme and highest creation of God and he is superior than the angels. There are some reasons for the mention about superiority of angles.

Angels are pure spirits and have no corporeal body. They have neither sex nor carnal emotions. Their responsibilities are to worship Allah and carry out His commands. They have no scope to commit any sin. They are completely sinless. That is why the poet says that by the virtue of beauty of character, people can become sinless as angels. When the beauty is blessed with the lustre of morality and modesty, the love for God evolves and approaches Him. In case beauty fails to cause chastity of heart and vision, one can never Succeed in acquring knowledge about the secrets of real beauty. The Divine Beauty removes the curtain from the vision of the devotee. The beauty which allures the lustful person creates the barrier for realising the truth. The manner in which a person burns himself due to love for Divine Beauty is strange and undescribable. For a lustful person, the manifestation of Divine beauty in material objects is destructive. The person who is not smitten by the Divine Beauty can never realise the Truth.

Both beauty and love are the universal conquerors and it is undesirable to point out a limit for them. There is no limit for the Divine beauty because Allah is All-Pervading. The love of devotee for Allah is unlimited because, He is his creator and cherisher who showers unlimited bounties on him. The beauty, spread and strewn all over the universe, should not be the cause for mournful sigh and lamentation due to its misuse. The true devotee of God does not like to become the slave of any vulgar passion or bad habits, but he wants to be the independent worshipper who receives appreciations and greetings from all directions.

Lighting the universe with All-Pervading Beauty and giving the proper proportions to the creations are the purposeful pleasantries of Allah which are interesting and colourful accounts. Poetry and music which are devoid of the lustre of Divine Beauty are totally insignificant. To some extent the secrets of the Divine knowledge can be acquired through believers who see the Truth. Repeated attempts should be made to acquire the mystic knowledge which is very difficult and its destination is beyond our reach. The human beauty is the paradise for the believers who feel the presence of special Beauty of God. The sun, the moon and other creations shine due to the Effulgence of Divine Beauty.

In the last stanza of this chapter the poet has attempted to explain that Allah is the ultimate source for all sorts of Beauties. (Definitions, philosophy of Divine Beauty and Sufism).

CHAPTER - XXI

FINE ARTS

Stanza. 116

21 /فنون لطیفہ

116۔ نغمہ رنگیں دل مجروح کا مرہم بھی ہے

مرد میدان کے لیے جوش و قرار و دم بھی ہے

بزم و خلوت میں سرور جان دوائے غم بھی ہے

کاکل شعر و سخن کو حسن پیچ و خم بھی ہے

جذبہ پنہاں کی ہے تصویر بھی اس کا جمال

ہے ریاض حسن و اُلفت کو بھی یہ بھی آب و زلال

Tr- A Pleasant song proves to be a medicine or ointment for an injured heart. For a noble and valorous man, it affords zeal, contentment and strength. In poetry, bends, curves and music are present which in the solitude gives us happiness and dispel our grief. Its elegancebe devotee who is engaged in is the picture of hidden emotions. It is a wholesome water for the devotee who is mystic experiences.

Stanza.117

117۔ ہے بپا چاروں طرف ہنگامہ رقص و سرود

آفتوں میں گھر نہ جائے عقل و ایمان کا وجود

ہیں سبھی انکی لپٹ میں کیا مسلماں کیا یہود

ہو نہ جائے راہزن جذبات اسفل کے جنود

منزل مقصود کی جانب ہو دل گرم سفر

ہوں ضیائے عشق سے پرنور اخلاق بشر

Tr. The existence of Faith and wisdom may not be engulfed by calamities because of the tumult of dance and music everywhere. Whether they are Muslims or Jews, they are indulged to much in music.They not become the victims of the dacoity of mean emotion by means of music, we may reach the desired destination of spiritual perfection. The luster of love may enlighten the mentality and purify the character of man.

Stanza.118

118۔ صاحب علم و عمل ہوتے ہیں کم اہل کمال

ٹھمریاں ٹپے ترانے دادر دھر پہ خیال

حسن معنی سے بہت محروم انکا جمال

اُن سے جذبات نکو کا ولولانہ ہے محال

شکر ہے جو مائل ندرت ہیں ارباب ہنر

قصہ خون جگر ہوتا ہے ہر باب ہنر

Tr. Very few people who possess knowledge and sense of endeavour, reach the stage of perfection because they are more inclined in music. They can never yearn for dignified or decent emotions because their elegance and grace are bereft of meaningful beauty. Every new chapter of art consists of an account of hard strife. Thanks to those artists who love novelty

Stanza. 119

119۔ ہند کی سنگت میں ایک خاص خوبی ہے نہاں

جانفزا ایک موج غم ہے اس کی رگ رگ میں رواں

ایک جذب خاص کی ہر راگنی ہے ترجماں

رقص دل ہے تال سے لے نان و سم سے عیاں

آدمی کی روح جذب خاک سے آزاد ہو

آسمانی فرحت و عشرت سے دل آباد ہو

Tr.- The Indian music has a special merit which runs through every nerve.It is life-giving and stops the wave of grief. Every tune is the interpreter of some special taste and the rhythmic beats make the hearts dance. May the spirit of man get released from the corporeal body and his heart be blessed with pleasantness and happiness through decent music especially devotional out-pourings.

Stanza. 120

120۔ اہل فن ہو پاک طینت راز دان زندگی

سر بسر اُن کے ہنر ہو ترجماں زندگی

عفت و حسن و سرور و جاوداں زندگی

پاک ہر گرد کدورت سے ہو دامان ہنر

زہر بن جاتا کبھی ہے آب حیوان ہنر

Tr - Artists must be good-natured and custodian of the secrets of life. Their arts must entirely be the interpreters of life. Their art must be life - giving and must be the cause for chastity, happiness, beauty.progress, noble passions and pomp and splendor of life. The artists mustbe careful to keep their attire free from the stain of muddy resentment, which may convert the water of immortality into poison

Stanza. 121

121۔ غیب کے پردوں میں ہیں روپوش وہ اہل ہنر

دیدہ مشتاق کو اپنے جو آتے ہیں نظر

آہ وہ نغمے کہ بام فکر میں ہیں جلوہ گر

دیکھیے اس بزم ہستی میں ہو کب انکا گزر

بے نیاز نغمہ مطرب ہے دل اب کیا کہیں

وہ مزے حاصل ہیں قرآن کی قرات سے ہمیں

Tr:- The real artists are hidden behind the mysterious curtains who are visible only to wishful people. get see as to when the songs which are inside the scope of philosophy, get released in the social life.Now enjoy from the musical recitation of Quran (Qirat).

Stanza. 122

122۔ قوت تخلیق ہے کل ساز و سامان ہنر

یک نئی دنیا نئے جلوے نیا ذوق سفر

وہ ہنر جس کا تصور ہو حقیقت سر بسر

جس کا ہو سوز نفس تہذیب تکمیل بشر

شاعری سوز حیات و ندرت و تخلیق ہے

فلسفہ فکر و نظر ہے بحث ہے تحقیق ہے

Tr:- The creative power of Allah, provides materials for developing art which result in invoke our interest for advancement. The person who is interested in promoting and in achieving the perfection of life, must be real from top to bottom. Philosophy is concerned only with discussion and research while the art of composing poetry is concerned the intensity of passion in life, novelty and inventing new styles of composition.

C. In this chapter, the poet has discussed the creative art of Allah, all sorts of fine and pleasant arts of human beings in general and the elegant and exquisite arts of music and poetry in particular. Whether music or poetry or any other arts which are free from indecency and within the limits prescribed by Islam, can heal the mental wounds, invoke enthusiasm and noble passions in the mind of pious and valorous man while both in solitude and in social gathering. He is enticed by the art of composing poetry, the beauty of which lies in the bends and curves. The poet expresses his fear that people may become the victims of mean emotions as they are exceedingly interested in dance and music and transgress the lawful limits.

Moderate and decent music especially the devotional song can purify the character of man and lead him to spiritual perfection. Inspite of their intellect, very few people progress in their art because they are excessively prone to merriments and are bereft of the knowledge of meaning of real beauty. It is impossible for such people to aspire for dignified emotion of beauty. It is appreciable and applaudable that some artists are lovers of uniqueness and novelty and invent new things by their unending endeavours. Indian music is especially meritorious as is relishing and is dispelling sorrows. Every tune of the Indian song is the interpreter of life and the rhythmic beats are delightful and amusing. Devotional songs such as hymns lead us to spiritual perfection. Artists must be good-natured and their disposition pure. The arts must be the interpreters of life which may benefit us with chastity, happiness, strength, high pomp and splendour. Wrong exploitation and application of art will produce poisonous effects. Our life and attire must not have any stains of sins. The poet says that the days are gone when he desired to enjoy the melodious songs of the entertainer because he derives the pleasantness in the musical recitation of Quran. Qir'at. Allah has provided us with materials for developing all sorts of arts. It is the duty of the man to have fervour to make walks of life such as educational, professional etc. History of mankind proves that practice depends on theory, and civilization depends on art, education and technology. Poetry the creative art has contributed much to human civilization as it is more effective than the prose because of its metrical recitation.

The poet concludes by saying that arts including music is lawful in Islam. Let us proceed to prove his contention to be valid by Quranic verses Ahadis and our own arguments.

S. Saba-34:10:-

وَلَقَدْ اٰتَيْنَا دَاوٗدَ مِنَّا فَضْلًا يٰجِبَالُ اَوِّبِيْ مَعَهٗ وَالطَّيْرَ وَاَلَنَّا لَهُ الْحَدِيْدَ

Tr: We bestowed grace afortime on David from Ourselves; O ye mountains back the praises of Allah with him and ye birds also and We made the iron soft for him.

S. Muzammil-73:2-4:

قُمِ الَّيْلَ إِلَّا قَلِيْلًا نِصْفَهٗ اَوِ انْقُصْ مِنْهُ قَلِيْلًا اَوْ زِدْ عَلَيْهِ وَرَتِّلِ الْقُرْاٰنَ تَرْتِيْلًا

Tr:- "Stand (to pray) by night, but not all night; half of it, or a little less, or a little more: and recite the Quran, in slow, measured rhythmic tones".

The above two verses explain that Prophet Dawood (PBUH) sang in praise of Allah and Allah commanded the hills and birds to sing with him in the style of echo. Quranic have been revealed in the form of poetic composition which produces musical notes. Allah has commanded us to recite Quran with musical metre, measure and rhythm. Rhythm can be defined as the regular timings of music or the musical beats with metrical accuracy. Hymns can be defined as singing in adoration or in praise of Allah. Allah has commanded the believe sing the hymns with rhythm; in other words, the musical recitation of Quran called Oir'at.

On a festival day two girls from the Ansars (who helped the Muslim refugees of Makkah who were not professional singers, were singing with the accompaniments of musical instruments in our Prophet's house, in praise of the warriors of the battle of Bu'at. The first Khalifa after our Prophet, Abu Bakr Siddiq entered the house of his daughter Bibi Aisha (The third wife of the Prophet) and expressed his surprise by describing the playing of musical instruments as Satanic deeds in the Prophet's house. On hearing this Prophet Muhammad (PBUH) said, "Abu Bakr, every people have a festival and it is our festival. So, let them play on" (Muslim).

By the above Hadith it is evident that decent songs and playing musical instruments are permitted in Islam. Lauding the valorous and saintly people is not at all prohibited. Of course, the indecent and obscene songs which arouse the baser self in man is strictly forbidden. In the highly balanced system of Islam, there is room for merriments and sports also because it is a natural yearning of the human soul. The enjoyments must be free from sins.

H:- "The good of it (poetry or music) is good, and the bad of it is bad".

On the occasion of a wedding, Prophet Muhammad allowed the girls of Madina to sing lauding the martyres of Battle of Badr, in order to please him.He actually enjoyed those songs which moved him,remember them with great reverence.Music attracts every person without any exception. The second Khalifa Hazrat Umar Farooq, previously a staunch idolater.The second Khalifa Hazrat Umar Farooq, previously a staunch idolater attracted by the Qir'at of Sura-Taha and embraced Islam.Devotional lyrics containing to the masses,make a direct appeal to the masses. This was what happened in the case of Saint Moinuddin Chishti who is laid to rest in Ajmir, India.He succeeded in Propagating Islam by the media of his melodious hymns with the accompaniment of Sitar, a string musical instrument invented by a Sufi Urdu poet Ameer Khusru.There are several ways and virtues thrown open to the devotees to reach the realm of God.Adoring Allah's attributes is an incomparable medium in merging with Allah. Music transports the listeners to Allah's presence. It minishes the agony of the sick people.

In all literature, poetry is more meritorious than prose, regarding two main factors effectiveness and metrical effectiveness and metricalinfirst factor,a fund of idea contained in a few words which creates effect;and indelible impression is left in the minds of the readers.Secondly while reciting, the metrical accuracy and rhythmical lines of the poetry produce musical notes which attract the lovers of literature.They are also enticed by the musical rendering poise and dignity.If we peep into the history of literature, in most of them especially Urdu and Arabic, we find their origin in poetry.prose writing was started only after a certain stage of evolution of poetry.Ameer Khusru was the first Urdu Peot of India. Though the Arabs were quite backward in civilization before the of adventIslam, they were advanced in Arabic literature.Most of the Arabs were poets.

The dignified art of music shall consist of impeccable purity, immaculating, clear and delightful freshness in presentation.A clear understanding, correct teachings and alluring features are some of the requisites of musical and poetical endowments. Devotional pourings the enthuse the listeners to the maximum extent, and kindle the thoughts of the people with proper guidance and moral strength and make them pious.

The creative power of Allah is the greatest art. Allah is the greatest Artist. The design of the artist points to the Master Designer, God. How can the greatest Artist discourage art? The mysticism about Heaven says that it will be full of music. A spiritualist has said, "God's chanting is compassionate and never cruel. A heart in tune with God will sing His praise". There is nothing in Islam which prohibits one from becoming an artist, but indulging in immoral activities in the name of art is a sin. All fine arts free from sins and indecencies are permitted by Islam. Our Prophet himself highly appreciated the art of the non-Muslim sculptor who immediately embraced Islam to notice the appreciating quality of our Prophet.

It is now clear that Islam is in favour of pure and decent poetry dignified music and all other Fine Arts. (Quran and Fine Arts, Poetry, Music, Qira't)

CHAPTER – XXII

FEAR OF GOD

Stanza: 123

22/ہیبت حق

123۔ ہیبت حق سے ہمیشہ جن کے سینہ چاک ہیں

دامن دل اُنکے گرد معصیت سے پاک ہیں

وہ مبارک ہستیاں ہیں صاحب ادراک ہیں

کارزار زندگی میں اُنکے دل بے باک ہیں

اُن کی شوکت سے زمانہ گو بہت مرعوب ہو

ہر ادا اُن کی نگاہ خلق میں محبوب ہو

Tr:- Those whose heart is full of fear of God and those whose attire is free from the muddy stains of sins, are the lucky and noble ones, possessed of intellect. May their grand personalities prevail all over the world, and may their activity be appreciated by all.

Stanza.124

124ایک بزرگ با صفا کا قول ہے یہ بے بہا

ہیبت حق ہے شعور آدمی کی ابتدا

انتہا بھی ہے فراست کی یہی خوف خدا

ہے مصاف خیر و شر میں یک رفیق و رہنما

ہیبت حق کی جو ہوتی خلق کو دولت نصیب

یہ نہ ہوتی شامت اعمال کی آفت نصیب

Tr:- It is a valuable assertion of a great religious preceptor that fear of God is the beginning of wisdom. The same fear of God is the utmost limit of discernment and perspicacity. In the conflict of good and evil, it is the friendly guide which leads us on the path of righteousness. Those who possess the factor of fear of God are really fortunate people. Those who do not possess this quality are unfortunate as they will be awarded punishment for their evil deeds.

Stanza.125

125۔ دیکھتے ہیں جو یہاں اعمال انساں کا ثمر

ماتحت حق کی مشیت کے زمانے کا سفر

یک اشارے سے جہاں خلق کو زیرو زبر

رحمت باری پہ اپنی ہر سعادت منحصر

مورد بیم و رجا اُن کا سدا ایمان ہے

انتہائے فہم انسانی کی اُن میں شان ہے

Tr:- Those who witness the fruit of the deeds of people, understand that the sojourn of human life is controlled by the pleasure of God. The auspiciousness of every person depends upon the bounty of God. As with a single and simple sign, God can upset the whole world. In the life of a man of firm faith, occasions of pessimism and optimism occur, but his magnificence lies in the extreme understanding of truth

Stanza.126

126۔ ہے خدا کا خوف جن کے خون میں سوز حیات

عشق ہے اُن کا زمانے کی خباثت سے نجات

اُن کا دل خلوت میں خود ہوتا ہے روح کائنات

تازہ تر ہوتے ہیں ہر دم انکی رنگین واردات

خلق میں انکا تصور ہے نگاہ حق نگر

اُن کا دل خود اُن کو دیتا ہے حقیقت کی خبر

T: Those who enjoy fear of God in their life, their love for God relieves them from the filth and keeps them away from wickedness. In private devotion their hearts become the soul of the whole universe and every second their colorful account of life,becomes more and more fresh. People have high regards for them for having true vision.Their pure heart themselves give them information about the truth.

C- In this chapter, the poet has laid emphasis on the significance of 'Fear of God and'Primacy of Knowledge'.

Of course, Knowledge (Theory) and art and technology (Practical) are necessary for our survival, progress, prosperity promotion of culture and civilization. The sort of knowledge,the poet has associated with 'Fear of God' is Divine and mystic knowledge which is essential for attaining spiritual perfection.A scientist or artist or literary scholar may have great worldly knowledge, but may not have faith in any religion or hereafter.Atheist and Heathens neither believe in the existence of God nor have fear of Him.They may go on committing all sorts of sins.They are incapable of discriminating between good and evil.They attain grand successes in their life but these successes cannot lead them to spiritual bliss. Without spiritual achievements, their life is worse than nothing.In fact, they earn spiritual torment. That is why, the poet has combined Fear of God with mystic knowledge about the existence of God and the mystic knowledge, revealed to the Holy Prophets through angels,since the advent of Adam (A.S.) on the earth. In order to inculcate fear of God in the minds of the people, it is essential for them to believe in the mystic knowledge of Eternity and certainty of the existence of God through His messages and secrets of the universe revealed to the Holy prophets, angels (the messengers from God) such as Divine warnings, the Day of the Doom. torment during Barzakh (the transition period between death and resurrection). Day of Reckoning mystic and immaterial worlds of hell and heaven, the torment of hell for the unbelievers and evil doers, Almighty Allah's astounding deeds like creation of the universe. His mystic time, the mystic event of Me'raj, etc., came to be known to man. Now we understand, how much indispensable is Divine knowledge (M'arifat) for invoking fear of God.

The people who have fear of God, never fear for the most dangerous things. They are brave to the extent that they are fearless even when they are under the sword. They stick to Truth and never accept falsehood. They never commit sin intentionally, never mind the hardships of life. They are always completely resigned to the will of God, and try to acquire the pleasure of God through their noble deeds. Their magnificence prevail over the world and their magnanimous activities are highly applauded by people.

In the 124th stanza of the text, the poet has cited the quotations of Sulaiman (A.S.) and the great and famous Greek philosopher Socretes. Sulaiman (A.S.) has said, fear of God is the commencing point of acquiring knowledge and wisdom". He argues that a man without fear of not a real learned one. His real mystic and religious knowledge finds its primal origin in me fear of God. Socrates says that fear of God is the highest summit of knowledge and me explains, that among all sorts of knowledge and intellect. Fear of God is the highest and uttermost one. Though these two quotations seem to be contradictory, both the arguments of Socretes and Sulaiman

(A.S.) are quite convincing. Hence, the poet drawn the that fear of God is the beginning point of knowledge, sagacity and wisdom, as well as the highest summit of knowledge, shrewdness and discernment. The poet has described fear of God as sincere friend excellent guide and the greatest wealth, the absence of which will entail terrible hazards and worst misfortune both in this world and in the hereafter.

The poet has explained the wrath of Almighty Allah which destructed many a nation in second which rejected the messages of the Holy prophets, and did not adhere to advices. For example, the kinsmen of Nooh (A.S.) did not listen to the message of God denied his prophethood and went on committing crimes. In no time they were swallowed by the historical Deluge (flood) which persisted for six months. The family of Nooh (A.S) and few believers were saved who embarked the boat, constructed by Nooh (A.S.) Among his family members, his son, Saam was one who was the ancestor of Ibrahim (A.S.).

The people of Midyanite tribe, who bought yusuf Alaihis salam from his step brother got indulged in cheating in their business and improper weighing's Prophet Shuibe(A.S) war them against their fraudulent activities without fearing God. They did not give up their fraudulent transactions. Allah destructed them through a tremendous earth quake.

The people of Sodom and Gomorrah got intensely interested in committing home sexual sins. Prophet Lut (A.S.) the nephew of Ibrahim(A.S.) was sent to them by Allah who dissuaded them to abstain from the sins and abominations. But they never cared his exhortations. As instructed by two angels, Prophet Lut (A.S.) escaped with his family (except one wife who refused to accompany him), and a group of believers at midnight. As commanded by God, the two angels showered brim-stones on them and destructed them completely.

At the period of prophet Moosa (A.S.), the Pharaoh of Egypt confronted with him and chased his followers. The water of River Nile got divided apart and made a dry path for Moosa (A.S) and his followers to flee through and reach the other side of the river. But when the Pharaoh and his army entered the path, the water from two sides closed the path and overlapped the whole army due to the wrath of God. Thus, the whole army was drowned along with the Pharaoh.

When Namrood, the ruler of Iraq along with his great army was chasing Ibrahim (A.S.). and his followers, a mountain came on their way and they had to helplessly stop fleeing. All of a sudden, a host of lakhs of big mosquitoes appeared on the scene and killed the whole army of Namrood. Namrood was an idolater and later claimed Divinity.

Our Holy Quran is full of such parables and I have cited only five of them in order to fill the minds of the readers with fear of God. Those who are free from depravity and malignity their life becomes a colorful and memorable history for the people who have the knowledge about God and Fear of God.

The beautiful nature stires the mind of man to fear Allah and remember Him throughout his life. But when they are surrounded by attractive charms of the material world, their affluence makes them blind - folded, arrogant and proud. Their ephemeral prosperity makes them forget the ultimate reality, God and takes them out of His realm of love.

Islam lays great emphasis on speaking the truth. It tolerates no ambiguity or equivocal expression as they give rise to misunderstanding. The first trait of a true believer is the constant Fear of Almighty Allah which keeps him sinless and acts as a motivating force to strictly abideby his everlasting lurking for fear of God.

Islam has placed knowledge (Ilm- theory) in the highest level of endeavour. Quran repeatedly urges the acquisition of all branches of knowledge (Ilm) in general and Divine knowledge (M'arifat) in particular. The noble and lawful application of knowledge in the strife Amal (practice). The first call of Almighty Allah gave the first importance for reading, writing is called "Amal". Every piety, nobility, culture and civilization are the results of ilm (theory) and to Prophet Muhammad (PBUH) in the cave of Hira was "Read in the name of Allah! "Quran and acquisition of knowledge. The first message of Holy Quran, conveyed through Jibrail (A.S.) provides data for all branches of studies and scope for research. Several Stanzas of Quran end with the words, "Allah is all- knowing ". Quran contains injunctions to acquire knowledge in many places.

To lead a religious life, the significant necessities are to acquire Divine knowledge and have Fear of God, because knowledge is closely connected with fear of God. There are four aspects of Divine knowledge which include both theories and practice. They are Haqiqat, Marifat, Shariat and Tariqat.

1.Haqiqat (Theory): - Haqiqat means truth and truth means God. Haqiqat deals with the realization of the certainty of God's existence. His existence can be realized by his creations which are nothing but his manifestations and his All - Pervading effulgence. When there are creations, there must be their Creator.

2. Marifat (Theory): - M'arifat means Divine knowledge. It deals with the recognition and mystic knowledge about the existence of God, knowledge about His attributes through His messages, knowledge about the Divine laws (shariat) and the religious tenets advocated by Him the mystic knowledge about His mysterious administration and the knowledge, pertaintion to the secrets of the universe revealed in His scriptures.

3.Shariat (Theory): - Shariat means Divine law. As Islam has left scope for the promotion of knowledge and research, it has left scope for legislation also, because Islam should not be incapable of solving new problems, never faced before in the history of Islam. This legislation is called the Islamic Jurisprudence. Shariat consists of elaborate, convincing, and valid codes of ethics, religious duties, acts of worship, business transactions, penalties and solves all the present problems by the already accepted shariat and can solve the new future problems by means of Qiyas and Ijma'a. It is believed that the newly promulgated laws also are the results of Divine inspirations and prophetic traditions. Shariat shows the best way of life. There are four sources for shariat:-

(a). Quranic exhortations.

(b). Sunnat and Ahadis of Prophet Muhammad (PBUH)

(C). Qiyas which means analytical reasoning or legislation by analytical cases in the Divine law. There had been several ulamas (religious scholars) and Jurors who undertook the tough and tedious task of legislation through the help of analytical tenets in Quran in different contexts and analytical Ahadis in different situations and analytical case in the history of Islam during the We of prophet Muhammad (SAW).

Among all the Jurors (Faqeeh) four of them were highly renowned, namely, Hazrath Imam Numan Bin Abu Hanifa, Hazrath Imam Shafi, Hazrath Imam Malik and Hazrath Imam Hanbal. It is a wrong notion that their four schools of thought are different. But, in fact, it is not so. In all the four schools of thought the fundamental Divine Laws are identical, the Islamic tenets and codes of ethics are same, the obligatory (Farz) worships are same and their Faith in their religion is same. They differ In only minor points such as the procedure of ablution, the mode of giving bath to the dead bodies ect. Imam Numan attached more importance to sunnat-e-Muakkadah which our prophet (SAW) did not omit, while Imam Shafi attached less importance.

Imam Malik and Imam Hanbal were contemporaries while Imam Numan and Imam Shafi were contemporaries during the period of Abbasi Dynasty in Islamic history. Those Jurors (Faqeeh) used to consult with each other with uttermost humility and mutual reverence. They discussed the issues not displaying their difference of opinion, but in the manner as if they sought their suggestions.

The laws, promulgated by Hazrat Imam Numan are regarded as most authentic in the field of Islamic Jurisprudence (Fiqah) and are included in the books of Muslim law which are being followed even today.

Hazrath Imam Numan was extremely pious and tried to be in purity with ablution as much as possible. He never uttered the name of Muhammad (SAW) or explained any Hadith when he was not in the purity of ablution. He had great fear of God.

According to Islamic law two witnesses are required to pronounce the verdict of the judge. In the absence of witnesses or in the case of false witnesses, there are chances for pronouncing wrong or unjust verdict inspite of the honesty and sincerity of the judges. On the basis of piety and honesty, of Hazrath Imam Numan, he was appointed as judge (Qazi), the honorable and highest post in the judiciary, by an Abbasi Khalifa. But Hazrath Numan rejected the appointment for the fear that he might pronounce wrong verdict. The Khalifa sent the appointment order repeatedly and Hazrath Numan rejected the order every time. The Khalifa took it as a great insult, became his enemy and imprisoned him. He tolerated the severe hardships of the prison with absolute pleasure over the prospect that the scope was closed for him to pronounce unjust verdict. At last, he died in the prison after suffering a lot. May his soul rest in peace.

(d). Ijma'a :- Ijma'a means concensus among the ulamas (religious scholars). This is also a sort of joint legislation by a large assembly of Ulamas from different places, on the grounds of some indirect hints given in Holy Quran. For example, Almighty Allah has said in Quran several times that everything in the heavens and earth belongs to him and has commanded the people to share his bounties with the needy people. On the basis of such Quranic verses the Ulamas have drawn inferences that blood donation and organ transplantations are lawful. Such laws are the results of Islamic Jurisprudence (Fiqah).

4. Tariqat (Practice): - Tariqat can be defined as the practical applications of the theoretical knowledge about Haqiqat, M'arifat and Shariat. It is the procedure of observances of Divine principles and Divine Laws, mode of leading religious life and methods of worship. Without the theoretical knowledge, practice is impossible. When theory is not put into practice, it becomes quite useless. For all aspects of life both theory and practice are necessary. Hence Tariqat (Practice) is linked with Haqiqat Marifat and shariat (Theories).

To tread on the path of righteousness and to be sinless, maximum amount of fear of God is required. Fear of God leads us to adhere to all religious tenets and laws. Adherence to Islamic principles is called Taqwa. The practice of Taqwa is called Tariqat.

In the following some Ahadis-e-Nabvi and Quranic verses have been quoted to support the above-mentioned statements about primacy of knowledge and fear of God.

S: Fatir-35:28:

وَمِنَ النَّاسِ وَالدَّوَآبِّ وَالْأَنْعَامِ مُخْتَلِفٌ اَلْوَانُهُ كَذٰلِكَ اِنَّمَا يَخْشَى اللّٰهَ مِنْ عِبَادِهِ الْعُلَمٰٓؤُا اِنَّ اللّٰهَ عَزِيزٌ غَفُوْرٌ

Tr:-"And so among men and crawling creatures and cattle, are they of various colors. Those who truely fear Allah amongst His Servants, who have knowledge, for Allah is Exalted in might, often Forgiving"

S: 23:57-60:

اِنَّ الَّذِيْنَ هُمْ مِنْ خَشْيَةِ رَبِّهِمْ مُشْفِقُوْنَ وَالَّذِيْنَ هُمْ بِاٰيٰتِ رَبِّهِمْ يُؤْمِنُوْنَ وَالَّذِيْنَ هُمْ بِرَبِّهِمْ لَا يُشْرِكُوْنَ وَالَّذِيْنَ يُؤْتُوْنَ مَآ اٰتَوْا وَّ قُلُوْبُهُمْ وَجِلَةٌ اَنَّهُمْ اِلٰى رَبِّهِمْ رٰجِعُوْنَ

Tr:- "Verily, those who live in awe for fear of their Lord, those who believe in the singns of their Lord, those who join not (in worship) partners with their Lord, and those who dispense in their charity with their hearts full of fear, because, they will return to their Lord".

S: Hujuraat 49:13 (Part of the verse)

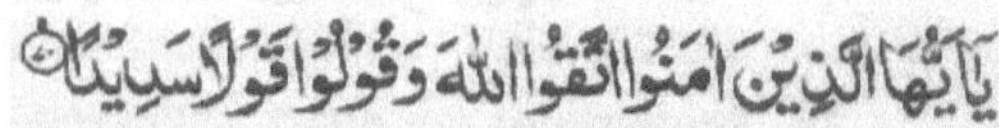

Tr: "The most honoured of you to the sight of Allah is (he who is) most righteous of you and Allah has full knowledge and is well acquainted (with all things)."

S. Ahzaab -33:70:

Tr.- "O ye who believe! Fear Allah, and (always) say a word decreed to the right)."

H:-"Muslim men and Muslim women have equal right to acquire knowledge"

H:-"The wonders of Quran will never cease to be unfolded"

H:- "I leave with you two things. If you hold fast both the things, you will never be misguided the book of Allah and the sunnat of the prophet"

H: "The ink of the pen of the scholar is holier than the blood of the martyre' Acquire knowledge as it enables us to distinguish between lawful and unlawful things. It shows the path of paradise.

It inculcates love among people. It is a companion in loneliness. It is a guide both at the situations of affluence and financial stress. It is the best weapon against the enemies and invaluable companion in the circle of friends.It makes the noble People leader in the society. People follow their example and repose confidence in their opinions.

Fear of God needs mystic knowledge about the certainty of the existence Mysticisim involves Mystery. We believe in the unseen things as they are interpreted by all the Holy Prophets and Holy scriptures, revealed by God. Hence, we can conclude that fear of God is inter-woven with knowledge,sagacity and intellect. Likewise,mysticism and woven. For leading a religious life, the foremost necessities are Divine knowledge (M'arifat) and fear of God. (Taqwa and primacy of knowledge).

CHAPTER-XXIII

FAITH IN ANGELS

Stanza.127

23/فرشتوں پر ایمان لانا

127۔ حادثاتِ دہر میں پابند اسباب و علل

اتفاق و بخت کا کیونکر زمانہ ہو محل

جسم کی کرتوت سے ہو روح میں کیونکر خلل

ہو میسر کس طرح انسان کو نیت کا پھل

ظاہری اسباب میں اسرار پنہائی بھی ہیں

حادثاتِ دہر کے اسبابِ روحانی بھی ہیں

Tr:- Though the incidents of the world are bound to have some causes for pretense and though we experience coincidences and good fortune, there are some mysterious causes which involve these factors. Without any mysterious source, soul cannot be degraded by our evil deeds, nor can we reap our fruits of our good intentions. Besides evident and clear outward reasons, there are mystic factors, influencing the incident of the world and spiritual change.

Stanza.128

128۔ کیا کبھی الہام سے ہوتا نہیں دل بار یاب

کیا کبھی کے جرم کا ہوتا نہیں نازل عذاب

کیا بچا لیتی نہیں طاقت کبھی کوئی شتاب

غیب کی تائید سے ہوتے نہیں کیا کامیاب

گو نگاہ عام ہو اُن کی نگاہ سے بے خبر

عارفوں کی صاف گرتی ہے فرشتوں پر نظر

Tr:- Sometimes our heart is blessed with inspiration. Sometimes torment descends on account of our crimes, sometimes an unknown strength saves us from immediate punishment and sometimes we succeed through mysterious help. Common vision is unaware of the fact, but those who have mystic knowledge about Divine administration, realise the mysterious interference of the angels as commanded by God.

Stanza.129

129- روشنی سے صورت اشیاء ہے آنکھوں پر عیاں

ہے صداؤں کا سفر دوش ہوا ہر زماں

برق کی رو سے چلے آتے ہیں اخبار جہان

چاہیے ایتھر کے ہو چشم تجلی کارواں

کاروبار غیب کا بھی ہے وسائل پر مدار

یہ وسائل ہی فرشتے ہے خدا کے بیشمار

Tr:- Light is a medium through which the shape of things are visible. Air is the medium of sound which carries it to the ears. Electricity is the medium which conveys the news of the world far and wide. The clear air, Ether is the medium which spreads the refulgence.Likewise,the innumerable angels are the mediators between God and the Divine administration in this world.

Stanza. 130.

130- کیا جہاں کیا اس کے اسبابِ و عمل کے کاروبار

اُن فرشتوں سے چلاتا ہے انہیں پروردگار

راز الہام و وحی کا ہے انہیں سے آشکار

ان کا منکر کیوں نہ ہو کفر و جہالت کا شکار

منکشف کیا خاک ہونگے اُن پہ راز کائنات

منکشف کیا خاک ہونگے اُن پہ اسرار حیات

Tr:- Whether it is universe of the creations or activities and affairs, Almighty Allah administers through the mediation of the angels. The secrets of inspirations and mystic knowledge by Divine revelation are disclosed through the angels. Those who do not believe in the mystic existence of angels become the victims of infidelity and ignorance. Without the mediation of the angels no secrets of the universe can be disclosed.

C. In this chapter, the poet has attempted to explain the Islamic concept of angels to convince the readers about their existence and some of their important duties which they have to carry out in response to the commands of Almight Allah.

The poet says that every, affair of the world whether it is fortune or misfortune is bound and controlled by Divine themes and Divine administrations through the angels. Those who are aware of the inner secrets of Divine knowledge only can realise the existence of angels, through the natural phenomena, worldy affairs of human life and spiritual upgradation and degradation. In order to interpret the exsitence of the angels the poet has mentioned some sources of communications. The light is the agent to display the creations; air is the conveyance of sound; electricity is the quick medium of conducting the news throughout the world; the damp and clear upper air called Ether having the qualities of great mobility and high power of refraction and a subtile medium to fill all the space. severs as a fountain of refulgence. Likewise, the Angels are the means of communications and resources for Divine administrations. The secrets of the universe, secrets of inspirations and the Divine knowledge. so far acquired by man, were revealed by the angels in the Holy scriptures and to the Holy Prophets. These were propagated by the pious theologians to the common people. This chapter speaks out also the significance of the relation between religion and mysticism.

Iman means declaration of faith. There are some articles of belief in this declaration which are as follows.

1. The Existence of Allah, the ultimate Sovereign and the Supreme Cherisher of the world's

2. Belief in the unity of God and His other Attributes.

3. Belief in the Holy Prophets of different ages.

4. Belief in the Holy scriptures, revealed through the Angels to the Holy prophets.

5. Belief in the existence of Angels

6. Belief in the destiny or measure (Taqdir)

7. Belief in the day of the Doom

8. Belief in the Hereafter.

9. Belief in life after death i.e- Resurrection.

10. Belief in the Day of Reckoning, etc.,

In Iman-e-Mufassil (Detailed Faith), the word "Angels has been mentioned name of God. Iman-e-mufassil is enough evidence to explain the impact significance in the belief of the existence of Angels. This article of Faith is very important because we have come to know about the Divinity, Divine laws, codes of ethics and of the universe only through the agency of the angels. Angels are the sure and only in revealing the Holy scriptures and informing us about the future happenings after short all other articles of Faith depend upon the contribution of the angels.

We have acquired some amount of knowledge through Holy Quran and Ahadis.

All Prophets are considered to be the guiding lamps on earth for the entire huma while the angels are the celestial or terrestrial lamps, created by Almighty Allah for kindling the earthly lamps.

We rise from the material world and reach the spiritual world after a due course of time ordained. This spiritual world is called by some scholars " The Realm supernal or celestial". (Aalam-e-Bala). This Realm supernal contains high lofty and light substances, called angels. They carry out the commands of Allah and effuse their light wherever and whenever required. While receiving commands from God they hear His voice from the Arsh, the Throne of Allah, situated on the unimaginable height. This is a clue for the invention of wireless (Technology).

Every believer must know about the nature of the Angels through Ahadis and Quran. Quran says that human beings are made from clay, Jinns were made of smokeless fire and angels are created by light. Angels are neither male nor female. In other words, they have no gender. They do not have any free will or independent will of their own. That is why their nature is said to be single - dimensional. They carry out all the commands of Almighty Allah without any question of negligence or opposition. Like all other creations in the universe, they are praising and glorifying God night and day and they never feel tired. They carry out their functions honestly and efficiently with absolute responsibility, never guilty of shirking work. The number of angels is not known to the greatest theologion. Some of them have been named having specific assignments. Four of them are very important namely, Jibrail, Mikail Israfil and Izrail.

Jibra'il (Gabra'il) conveyed divine revelations and Divine messages to holy prophets.

Allah has commanded angel Israfil to blow the trumpet on the Day of the Doom and she Day of Resurrection.

Mikail makes arrangements for the rainfall and supply of provisions to the creations of Allah.

Angel Izrail takes away the soul of the people and separates them from their bodies at the time of death.

Angels, Munkar and Nakir are sent to the grave to question the person soon after the dead body is buried.

Karamun and kathibun are two angels who are appointed to register both good and evil deeds of the people. They keep the hundred percent correct records.

Angel by names Harut and Marut were sent to Babylon to test the faith of the people and teach sorcery to the unbelievers during the period of prophethood and reign of Sulaiman Alaihis Salam.

The existence of the angels is quite different from human life.They were created by light.They have neither parents nor progeny.They neither eat, nor drink, nor excrete, nor have motions,which inculcate passions.They are devoid of biological urges or instincts.They are quite sinless.They can be defined as the messengers or instruments of Divine pleasure or Divine Laws.Quran mentions that angels were sent to the prophets in the form of human beings and Hadis mention that Arch Angel Jibra'il talked to them in the form of human beings.

Our me be angels is quite different from human life. Their existence is quite sinless. In laws and Hadis

Angel Jibrail was sent to the Virgin, Bi Bi Maryam with the shocking news of the birth of Isa Alahis Salam. Though no woman was chosen by Allah as the prophet Bi Bi Maryam and BiBi Sara, first wife of Ibrahim (A.S)saw and spoke to the angels.Two angels visited Ibrahim (A.S) and his wifeBi Bi Sara in the form of human beings and they gave them the glad tidings of the birth of Ishaq (A.S.) to Bi Bi Sara when she was ninety years old and Ibrahim (A.S.) was hundred years old. They also informed them of the birth of Yaqoob (A.S.) to Ishaq (A.S.). They and them on their way to Sodom and Gomorrah where Lut (A.S.) was sent by God to dissuade the people from committing sins. Those angels visited Lut Alaihis Salam and stayed in his home When the people of Sodom and Gomorrah heard about the two guests of Lut (AS)they raided his house with the intention of abomination and mal-practices. In order to protect his guests, Lut (A.S.) offered to give them his daughters in marriage. But they rejected his offer and demanded only those men. Some how, they were resisted and driven away. At the instruction of the angles, Lut (A.S.) fled with his family and some believers before day-break but his wife lagged behind. All the sinners were buried under the brim-stones rained heavily by the angels at the command of Almighty Allah.

Angels have few or numerous errands entrusted to them. For example, they helped the believers by fighting with them during the wars and defeating the enemies. The co-operation of the angels in the Battle of Badr (2.A.H) have specifically mentioned in the Holy Quran. In Battle of Badr only 313 Muslims had to confront with 1000 Mushrikeen of Makkah. But the Muslims emerged victorious after giving them a crushing Islam. That triumphant victory was only due to the deputation the Battle of Hunain, fought with the people of Taif after the bloodless conquest of Makkah, the Islamic army was numerically very weak during the life of a after his demise, but the Muslims won great battles by the grace of God, assistance of the angels and the zeal and enthusiasm of the Muslims.A very few Quranic verses have been quoted in the following for confirming the existence of the Angel and their service to humanity.

S.Al-Imran:- 3:45-47

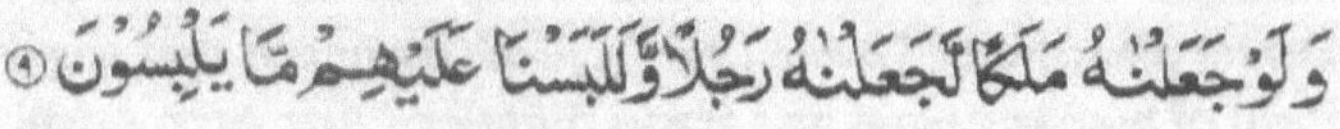

Tr: "Behold! The angels said. "O Mary! Allah has three glad tidings of a Him. His name will be Jesus Christ the son of Mary, held in honour in this world hereafter (and of the company of those nearest to Allah. He shall speak to people in childhood and maturity. And he shall be (of the company) of the righteous." She said, "O my lord how shall I have a son when no man has touched me?" He said, "Even so Allah created what he Willet. When He hath decreed a plan, He, but saith to it 'Be' and it is."

S. Anaam -: 6:9

Tr: - "If We had made it an angel, We should have sent him as a man, and We should certainly cause them confusion in a matter which is already to them obscure and confused

S. Aal -e- Imran - 3:23 - 125 :

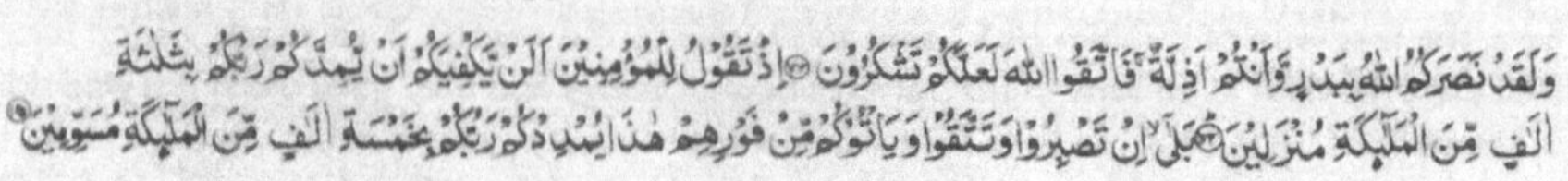

Tr:- "Allah had helped you in Badr, when ye were a contemptible little force. Then fear Allah. Thus, may ye show your gratitude. Remember thou said to the faithful 'Is not enough for you that Allah should help you with three thousand angels (Specially sent down? "Yea, if you remain firm and act right, even if the enemy should rush here on you in hot haste, your Lord will help you with five thousand angels making a terrific onslaught".

S.Aal -e- Imran - 3:46:

Tr:- " How many of the prophets (fought) in Allah's way and with them fought large bands of Godly men? But they never lost heart if they met with disaster in Allah's way, nor did they weaken in will nor give in. And Allah loves those who are firm and steadfast".

In most of his chapters, the poet has linked mysticism with religion. In this chapter also,he asserts that Faith in the mystic existence of the angels and their mysterious services to humanity is very important. All true religions without any exception were descended from Almighty Allah through the angels. (Faith in angels and their assignments).

CHAPTER - XXIV

LOVE FOR GOD AND SERVICE TO HUMANITY

Stanza. 131

24/عشق الٰہی اور خدمت خلق

131۔ دین حق کا مدعا ہے خدمت اہل جہاں

عزو شان انبیا ہے خدمت اہل جہاں

رفعت اہل وفا ہے خدمت اہل جہاں

رحمت رب کی رضاہے خدمت اہل جہاں

درد انسانی کی دولت سے جو دل ہیں بے نصیب

خیریت رک جاتی ہے جاتے ہوئے انکے قریب

Tr:- The objective of true religion is service to humanity. The honour and splendour of Holy prophets are service to humanity. The exaltation of faithful people is service to humanity. The pleasure of God is service to humanity by other fellow beings. Those unfortunate people who do not have feelings for others are bereft of welfare".

Stanza. 132

132۔ وقت شاید ہے بہت گھاٹے میں رہتے بشر

ما سوا ان اہل ایمان کے جو بے خوف و خطر

آپ ہوکر دولت حسن عمل سے بہرہ ور

کرتے ہیں تلقین حق و صبر کی شام و سحر

مرد مومن کی عبادت خدمت ایثار ہے

درد انسانی نہ ہو تو ہر عمل بے کار ہے

نوٹ : تم لوگوں کونیکی کا حکم دیتے ہیں مگر خود اپنی خبر نہیں لیتے کہ تمہارے
اعمال کا کیا حال ہے۔ حالانکہ خدا کی کتاب تمہارے پاس ہے ۔اور ہمیشہ تلاوت کرتے
رہو۔

Tr:- Some people are at loss that still there is time for doing work or worship. Inspite of the presence of the faithful people they are fearless. Those who are blessed with the wealth of beauty of good deeds, persuade them night and day to be patient and righteous. The worship of the believer is sacrifice and service to God. Every action of the person is useless who has no feelings for others.

Stanza:133

133-ہے عروج نفس ایثار و محبت کا اثر
انکا وہ ممنون ہو خدمت کرے جنکی بشر
انکی ک خدمت اصل میں اسکی ہے خدمت سر بسر
طاعت حق بھی یہی ہے پیش ارباب نظر
اہل دل کو اس لئے محبوب ہیں اہل جہاں
ہے انہیں محبوب خلاق زمین و آسماں

Tr:-Love and sacrifice is the consequence of self-development. The person should be grateful to the person, who renders service to him. In fact, service to humanity is service to God. Prudent people regard worship as service to God. Pious people love their fellow beings because the Creator of the earth and heavens, is Dear and Near to them.

Stanza. 134

134 ۔ کائنات خلق کی وحدت سے جو واقف ہیں ہم
کیا بلا یہ غیر ہے سمجھے نہ ہم تیری قسم
غیر ہے کوئی تو کب ممکن رہے وصل بہم

یہ کشش یہ وشق یہ نشوونما یہ عیش و غم
عالم کثرت کی وحدت پر جو ہو تیری نظر
ہو اخوت اور خدمت کی حقیقت جلوہ گر

Tr:- As we realise the unity in diversity, by God, we could not understand the meaning lien, the word 'Alien. In case, anything is considered to be alien, how is it possible to have connection, love, affinity, development and concern for other's pleasure and sorrow? If you realise the unity in the universe of diversities, the truth of service and brotherhood can be realised.

Stanza.135

135۔ اگر اغیار ابنائے زمانہ بے خبر ہوں
خام ہوجاتی ہیں ہر بنیاد اخلاق بشر
حرف بے معنی ہو ایثار و محبت سر بسر
چاک درد غیر سے ہرگز نہ ہو کوئی جگر
زندگانی کی حقیقت کے ہیں وہی رازداں
پھونکتا ہے جنکو مظلوموں کی آہوں کا دھواں

Tr:- The foundation of character of man is imperfect, if he has regards the for strangers, if his heart is not broken to pieces at the afflictions of others, the words Lou 'Sacrifice' become meaningless. Those who are afflicted with sighs of the oppressed custodians of the secrets of the truth of life.

Stanza.136

136۔ چشم حق میں میں نہیں ہوتی نگاہ امتیاز
جذب و الفت میں نہاں ہے وصل ویکرنگی کا راز
دل اگر خلق خدا کے عشق سے ہو سرفراز
ساری خلقت کا تعاون اس میں ہوجلوہ طراز

راز عشق وصل و وحدت سے رہے جو ہے خبر
خوبی خدمت سے بیگانہ رہے وہ سربسر

Tr:- Those who view correctly, do not distinguish between one and the other. The secret of unity and uniformity lies in the emotional love. The mutual co-operation of the people is adorned when the people are blessed with sincere love for others. Those people who are unaware of the secret of love, union and the unity of creations are entirely uninformed with advantages of service to humanity.

Stanza.137

137۔ یہ مجاز وغریب ظل و عدم عرض جمہور
ہیں سبھی اوہام انساں کے نہیں انکا وجود
ہے یہاں ہر شئی حقیقت ہی کی یک شان نمود
جلوہ کثرت سے ہے ہنگامہ بزم شہود
اے مسافر وحدت ہستی پہ ہو تیری نظر
غیرت یک وہم ہے ان اختلافوں سے گزر

Tr:- The factors such as unreal notions, strangeness, protection, nothingness, width, inertness do not exist, but they are all superstitions. Everything is the show of splendour of God. The disturbances in the diverse things is due to the Omni Presence of God. One should see the glory of unity in all creations. Nothing is different. Strangeness is nothing but superstition.

Stanza. 138

138۔ اہل ایماں ونظر کی ہے طریقت ہی خدا
خدمت و ایثار ہے وصل الہی کی بنا
ہے ولا ئے خلق حب خالق ارض و سماں

سوز ہمدردی ہے اسکی ذات میں ہونا فنا

کسطرح ہو پارہ فولاد آتش سر بسر

ہو بشر میں شان حق جب ہو فنا حق میں بشر

Tr:- The way of mysitc life of those who have faith and correct view, is quite different of people is identical with the love for the Creator of heavens and earth. The intensity of from those of others .Service and sacrifice are the basis for merging with God. The friendship and becomes fire when burnt, the man obtains the glory of God's attributes when he gets lost feelings for others is same as perishing and joining with God. Just as a piece of iron disappears in remembrance of God during the period of deep devotion.

Stanza. 139

۱۳۹۔ معرفت کی راہ میں ہر گام پر ہے یک فنا

ہرفنا میں وصل کی حالت جدا عشرت جدا

ہے بقدر وصل انساں میں تکا مل کی ضیا

ہے ترقی مرد مومن کے لئے بے انتہا

بیکراں وسعت سا قطرہ ہو نہیں سکتا کبھی

ذات لا محدود بندہ ہو نہیں سکتا کبھی

Tr:- At every step of mystic belief and religious way of life, there is some amount of squandering one's own self. In every such squander, there is a change in the condition of joy due to the union with God. There is some amount of light in the spiritual perfection of man due to his devotion and there is unlimited scope for the believer in the spiritual promotion. Just as a drop of water cannot become a vast expanse of and shoreless ocean, the power of worshipper of God cannot be compared with the unlimited power of God.

Stanza. 140

140 ۔ کفر سے اعمال ہیں وابستہ تن سر بسر

جلوہ ایماں سے روشن ہوں جو کردار بشر

روح قالب میں صفات رب سے جاتی ہے سنور

وصل عرفاں کی حقیقت ہے اسی سے جلوہ گر

وصل حق تکمیل نفس وانتہا ئے ہوش ہے

بیخودی اس ہوشکا یک جلوہ خاموش ہے

Tr:- The bad deeds of the infidel have Adverse connections with the body. The characterization of man is enlightened by the beauty of faith. The soul gets beautified by the attributes of our Cherisher by which the truth about the union of God and Divine knowledge is brought into light. The union with God benefits us with self-perfection and uttermost awareness. The senselessness or unawareness is actually the silent beauty of the awareness.

Stanza:141

141 ۔ راز و ایثارو محبت سے ہیں دہری بے خبر

جامسہ انسانیت مینں لاکھ ہوں وہ جلوہ گر

صاحب ایثار بھی آئیں اگر ان میں نظر

وہ حقیقت میں ہیں دنیا کے پجاری سر بسر

کفر کو انسانیت سے نام کو نسبت نہیں

دہریت کوروح انساں سے کوئی ملت نہیں

Tr:-Those who have material desires have no knowledge about the secrets of sacrifice and love, to whatever extend they appear in the guise of collective traits of humanity. Such people who do sacrifices for show, are in fact aspirants of worldly reputations. Even for name sake, there is no connection for infidelity with humanity nor has soul any connection with material aspiration.

Stanza.142

142۔ شعلہ ہائے عشق کا سوز تمام والتہات

پھونک ہی دیتا ہے سارے دیدہ و دل کا حساب

خود بخود ہوتی ہے تصویر حقیقت بے نقاب

جلوہ گاہ ناز میں ہوتا ہے عاشق بازیاب

عشق محروم صداقت ہے جو لب ہر ہوں فغاں

آتش فرقت میں بھی ہے وصل کا جلوہ عیاں

Tr:- The perfect passion and blazing affection of the intensity of love burn away the sight and snatch away the senses. When grace and benefits descend from the Beauty God on His lover, the picture of truth reveals automatically. That sort of love which bereft sincerity is nothing but lamentations and plaints on the lips.The sincere lover of God enjoys the beauty of union with God inspite of painful and intense feeling of separation from God.

C - Love is fondness, affection, affiliation, noble attraction and sincere devotion to Almighty Allah and His creations. These love and devotion persuade man to worship God and render service to humanity.

In this chapter, the poet has tried to bring to light the essence of the generalized accepted proverb " Service to Humanity is Service to God". He has also presented arguments related to this maxim. This chapter solely deals with the advantages of utilizing time and disadvantages of wasting time. The poet has explained the significance of pure love with people which is one of the causes for love for God. Service to people and other creations is the consequences of love of God. The meaning of these factors is same, because love of God leads to service to humanity.

The purpose and intention of Allah in sending in true inspired religion, the dignity and exaltation of the Holy prophets, the eminence and nobility of the faithful people, and the depth of feeling over the affections and adversities of others are all meant for service to humanity. Those people who are fearless and careless about the march of time are always guided by the learned people. Those who realise the unity of creations will never say that other creations are aliens and strangers to them, because everything is the manifestation of the Effulgence of God. Such people realise the true value of brotherhood and sincere service, because self-development can be achieved only by sacrifice and selflessness. As we are rational as well as social animals no person can enjoy life or make merriments when he is alone. In case, creations are alien to one another, the factors of love, attraction, evolution, civilization, enjoyment of gay life and feeling of sorrow are not at all possible. We are attracted both by beautiful and ugly insects, ferocious and poisonous animals, the movements of the crawling animals etc. We go to zoo and are attracted by the appearance and pranks of the ugliest animals like the ape. These factors explain the truth of unity of creations. Through the effulgence of God, imbibed in every creation, the relationship among the creations is established, sure, settled unfailing and certain.

Those people who consider others as unrelated and aliens, their foundation of character, love and sacrifice is entirely meaningless, defective and imperfect. The painful sighs of the aggrieved and victims of oppression, burn those people who are compassionate and those people who are the custodians of truth. Those people who believe in materialism, make some amount of sacrifices with the intention and aspiration of show of piety and for their own material benefits. Materialists have nothing to do with spiritualism. Those who love God are blessed with undefective views appreciate equality, uniformity sincerity and pleasantness of unity. The above-mentioned factors are the adorners of mutual help and mutual love in the society.The factors such as strangeness,nothingness, inertness, length and breadth actually do not exist.These are all metaphorical language, outward appearance, unreal, figurative and superstitious, because according to the Islamic concept of unity in diversity, all aspects and all things are grouped as one whole.Discrimination and distinction of colour race and status are entirely against the policy of Islam.

Unity, friendship, sacrifice,service to the needy community and intense Compassion lay the foundation stone for merging with God.which is in other words spiritual perfection.When compared to a human being who is mortal, having a little amount of power, Almighty Allah is shoreless ocean, unique expansion, unimaginable dimension of breadth and amplitude and above all Eternal.All human beings are sure to reap the consequences of their good and evildeeds because our bodies are prettily adorned with the soul which facilitate to attain spiritual perfection.same soul which makes us engrossed in devotion.It is the same soul which afford us the power of comprehension and appreciable amount of sense. It is the same soul makes us blind and unaware about the surrounding happening. This sort of silence is the pleasantness and liveliness of full sense. In silent devotion and blazing flame of love, the depth of passion and the power of mysterious vision and comprehension automatically reveals the truth. Though the sincere devotee is separate from God, he is blessed with enjoyment of union with God due to the intensity of love for Almighty Allah.

A believer has got some rights over other believer even after his demise. A deceased person is duly honoured, given bath and shrouded most respectfully, the Namaz of the bier (Janaza) is performed and prayers offered for him after burial before the people return home. People pray for the peace of his soul whenever possible. In the last two parts of Namaz namely Darood-e-Ibrahim and Dua-e-Maasoora, we pray for Ibrahim (A.S), Prophet Muhammad (SAW), their descendants, our parents our teachers and preceptors, all believing men and believing women also give charity in their names which is called Isaal-e-sawaab. (Transferring virtue in the name of the deceased)

Once a Muslim was engaged in Jihad (Holy war) and was out of station for a long time. Before his return, his mother whom he loved dearly, died. He was dismayed and very sad that he could not serve his mother in her last days. With the permission of our Prophet (PBUH). he gifted an orchard, for the peace of the soul of his mother, to the state Treasury (Bait-ul-Maal), most of the fund of which was utilized for the welfare of the poor and needy community. This Isaal-e-Sawaab affords some amount of comfort during the period of Barzakh (The transition period between Death and Resurrection). Thus, the lovers of God,can love, pray for and render service even to the expired believers. Of course, the soul of the deceased believer can be benefited by our prayers and worship.

The real devotion to God must be coupled with the motto of sacrifice and service to humanity. This has been prescribed by Islam to enable man to steer through the voyage of his life safely. Both love for God and love to humanity constitute the real God and love to humanity constitute the real Iman (Faith). True faith of hypocrisy is the sure refuge for man in this world and in the hereafter.

Allah has not created the universe for idle sport and play. He has a serious purpose towards Allah. He has granted to us a strong faculty to subdue the forces of nature. Some behind it. Each creature is given the opportunity for physical development and proceed persons have many facilities, abilities and Divine bounties while others are less blessed, less privileged and down-trodden. It is the duty of the strong people with great affluence, to love, to care for and show kindness towards them. One of the basic postulates of the doctrine of surrender,prescribed in the scriptural philosophy is that, a person who aspires to stay permanently in God's protection should declare his determination to serve others so long as he is in this world. As per the doctrine, he should do only those acts which will please God, and refrain from acts which will not be linked by the Almighty to plead that there is none to protect him other than God. In order to approach God, there are two main requisites namely sincere love cum worship to God and love cum service to humanity.

Q.S-Aal-e-Imran-3:148:

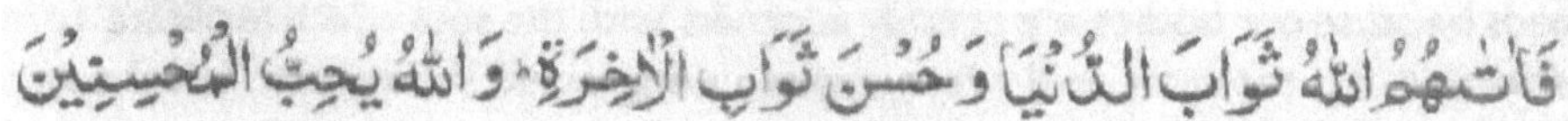

Tr:- "So Allah gave them the excellent reward of the world and the good reward of the hereafter, for Allah loveth those whose deeds are good"..).

Q: "We have not sent Prophet Muhammad but as mercy to mankind".

Q.S.Anbiya -21:16:

وَمَا خَلَقْنَا السَّمَاءَ وَالْأَرْضَ وَمَا بَيْنَهُمَا لَاعِبِينَ ۝

Tr:- "Not for idle sport did we create the heavens and the earth and all that is in between"

S. Anbiya -21:14:

قَالُوا يَا وَيْلَنَا إِنَّا كُنَّا ظَالِمِينَ ۝

Tr:- "Lo! I, even I, am Allah. There is no God save Me and establish worship for my remembrance".

H:- "Have respect for Allah's commandments and love his creations". (Baihaqi).

S.Bani Israel-17:26

وَآتِ ذَا الْقُرْبَى حَقَّهُ وَالْمِسْكِينَ وَابْنَ السَّبِيلِ وَلَا تُبَذِّرْ تَبْذِيرًا ۝

Tr:-"And render to the due rights and also to those in want and to the wayfarer, but squander not (your wrath) in the manner."

S. Nisa-4:36

وَاعْبُدُوا اللَّهَ وَلَا تُشْرِكُوا بِهِ شَيْئًا وَبِالْوَالِدَيْنِ إِحْسَانًا وَبِذِي الْقُرْبَى وَالْيَتَامَى وَالْمَسَاكِينِ وَالْجَارِ ذِي الْقُرْبَى وَالْجَارِ الْجُنُبِ وَالصَّاحِبِ بِالْجَنْبِ وَابْنِ السَّبِيلِ وَمَا مَلَكَتْ أَيْمَانُكُمْ إِنَّ اللَّهَ لَا يُحِبُّ مَنْ كَانَ مُخْتَالًا فَخُورًا ۝

Tr:- "Serve Allah and join not any partner with Him and do good to partents, kinsfolk, orphans, those in need, neighbors who are near, neighbors who are strangers, the companion your side, the wayfarer you meet and what your right hand possesses. For Allah loveth not the arrogant, the vain-glorious".

H: "Let your tongue beconstantly occupied with Allah's Zikr"

H:" The best among you is he who does good to mankind".

H: " Like for others what you like for yourself"

FRIENDSHIP

Friendship rules over our hearts when we realizethe relationship of our fellowmen, the importance of happiness humanity and uplift of the world society.There are social organizations in the locality level, city level, district level, state level, national level, international level. The main objectives of all these social organization are fellowship service to humanity. Of course, dividually we do some services and give in charity little or more. But if we maintain sincere and applaudable friendship with our fellow beings in the society we can mobilize our joint efforts and channelise our enthusiasm through proper grounding to serve humanity in a larger scale and obtain more pleasure of Almighty Allah. In fact the benefactors are more benefited than the beneficiaries. If we want to be called worthy friends, we must appreciateand emulate the good traits of our friends, by holding dear to our hearts,the good causes and the spirit of service with the firm determination and yearning to extend substantial cooperation.Even after their expiry,we must try our level best to accomplish their ambitions.These factors will become the best sources which will be conducive for building up a better world society and for promoting friendship.We must have high regards esteem for our present friends as well as expired friends.In this context a quotation of an English Scholar will be interesting to go through which is as follows:

"For Friendship is a nobler thing,

Of friendship is good to sing,

For truly when a man shall end,

He lives in the memory of his friend".

Now it is clear that friendship is beneficial for the culture, civilization uplift of the world society and above all the spiritual evolution.

S.Asr:- Asar' means Time'. As all other religions, Islam has laid special emphasis on time consciousness which teaches us self-discipline in all walks of human life. This time schedule leads us to discharge our worldly duties and spiritual obligations, punctually and without wasting the precious factor Time. If we waste time, time will waste us. Allah has created human beings with rationality, so that they may play the role of dynamic activities which will justify our existence. Of course, rest is required for relaxation which enables us to get up again to continue our routine and regular activities. But over sleeping, inactive behavior and too much of rest take away our precious time. The expired time is gone and lost forever. It will never come back. We lose several advantages on account of our carelessness. The time consciousness is the worthy essence of human existence. This consciousness guaranties progressive socio-economic development, stable spiritual evolution and useful, pleasant and charmful human existence.

Time must be utilized to maintain both mental and bodily purity, for freedom from harboring evil thoughts and to increase our virtues.

S. Asr-103:1-3

وَالْعَصْرِ ۝ اِنَّ الْاِنْسَانَ لَفِى خُسْرٍ ۝ اِلَّا الَّذِيْنَ اٰمَنُوْا وَ عَمِلُوا الصّٰلِحٰتِ وَتَوَاصَوْا بِالْحَقِّ ۝ وَتَوَاصَوْا بِالصَّبْرِ ۝

Tr:-"By (the token) of time, through the ages, verily man is in loss, except such as have faith, and do righteous deeds, and (join together) in the mutual teaching of Truth and of patience and constancy".

This chapter of three small verses can be compared to a little pitcher which contains an ocean of matter. The following is the quotation of Moulana Yusuf Ali Sahib about this chapter.

"This Sura refers to the testimony of time through ages. All history shows that evil came to an evil end. But time is always in favour of those who have faith, live clear and pure lives and know how to wait in patience and constancy. Waste not, nor misuse your life. Time through the ages bears witness that nothing remains but Faith and Good Deeds and the teaching of Truth and the teaching of Patience and Constancy. But for these, man, against Time is in Loss".

This chapter conveys the importance of evaluating time consciousness and enjoins upon the believers to realize Truth, have faith and teach others righteousness, patience and constancy. This injunction means nothing but Taqwa, adherence to Divine Laws. These observances of Islamic tenets are different methods of worship. In order to avail the advantages of the short span of our life, four "Before" have to be observed:

1. Worship God when you are young "Before" you become old.
2. Worship God when you are wealthy "Before" you become poor.
3. Worship God when you are healthy "Before" you become sick.
4. Worship God when you are alive "Before" you die.

The disadvantages of losing time:

SPIRITUAL LOSS:

Cultivation of devotion and religious observances in prescribed time are the chief paths which lead a man to the goal of salvation. Avoiding worship entails spiritual loss which is in fact the greatest loss. Worship eradicates evil which some people do not consider to be important.

MATERIAL LOSS:

An idler does not understand the great value of time. Islam has enjoined upon us to strive hard for our livelihood and make best use of our time. One who wastes his time incurs economic loss which entails poverty. It leads him to stealing and cheating.

PHYSICAL LOSS

When a person consumes food but does not work, his metabolism will become unbalanced which is the cause for many ailments,

ORAL AND ETHICAL LOSS

One who likes idleness and avoids to work, gets indulged in all sorts of immoral conduct and vices

EDUCATIONAL LOSS

The person who does not know the worth of time, never cares to acquire and impart, knowledge. Illiterate people spoil the society.

SOCIAL LOSS

The dull people who do not activate the human faculties are condemned in the society. They do not mingle with the people and never promote brotherhood. They are the worst nationals of their country.

MENTAL LOSS

Those easy-going people who are not aware of the march of time, do not give exercise to their minds and become dull and they become incapable of attaining the ends of human life. Their reasoning, gifted by God becomes useless and inactive. They develop in their minds the complex of inferiority. "Take advantage of five things before five other things occur. 1. Your youth before you become old. 2. Your health before you become sick. 3. Your wealth before you become poor. 4. Your leisure before you become occupied and 5. Your life before you die". (Tirmizi)

Now we are convinced that an ocean of matter is contained in the Small Quranic Chapter "Asr". (Islamic concept of love, service, friendship and time).

CHAPTER - XXV

LIFE AFTER DEATH, REBIRTH, GOOD AND EVIL, EQUALITY, DEMOCRACY, OPPOSITE FORCES ETC

Stanza. 143

25۔حیات بعد الموت، تناسخ، خیروشر، اختلاف، مساوات، جمہوریت وغیرہ

143 ۔ جب نہ تھا واقف صفات رب سے ادراک بشر

روح ومادہ کی حقیقت سے تھا جب وہ بے خبر

نور وحدت رنگ کثرت میں نہ تھا جب وہ بے خبر

یک معما تھے جہاں میں جب رموز خیر شر

اختلافات مدارج کے نہاں جب راز تھے

خواب یک دیکھا تناسخ کا خیال خام نے

نوٹ، حیات بعدالموت۔

اسلامی عقیدے کے مطابق روز قیامت میں دنیا کے سارے لوگ مرجائیں گے۔ اس عقیدے کے مطابق انسان دوبارہ اپنی ماں کے پیٹ سے پیدا نہیں ہوگا ۔اسکے بعد ہر ایک آدمی کے اعمال کا حساب لینے کی خاطر پروردگار تمام مردوں کو یونہی زندا اٹھائیگاوہ دن یوم الحساب کہلاتا ہے۔ نیک اور بد عمل کا حساب ختم ہونے کے بعد جزا اور سزا دیکر لوگوں کو جنت اور دوزخ کو بھیج دےگا۔ موت کے بعد حیات ضروربہے۔اور اس پر ایمان لانانہایت ضروری ہے مگر صرف ایک دفعہ اور قیامت کے دن پروردگار تمام مردوں کو زندہ اٹھائیگا۔ لہذاتناسخ اورحیات بعدالموت میں فرق ہے۔

جی زیڈ رضیہ بیگم

تناسخ کے باب کے لیے دلیل صاحب کے نوٹس :

ہندو مذہب کا عقیدہ ہے کہ انسان مرنے کے بعد اس دنا میں دوبارہ پیدا ہوتا ہے۔ کئی دفعہ مرتا ہے اور کئی دفعہ پیدا ہوتا ہے۔ یہ عقیدہ اردو میں "تناسخ" کہلاتا ہے اور انگریزی میں Re Birth کہلاتا ہے۔ مگر اسلامی عقیدہ کے مطابق تناسخ کا نظریہ غلط ہے۔ سلسہ تناسخ پر تفصیلی بحث کے لیے صدہا صفحات درکار ہیں۔ یہ نظم اس کی متحمل نہیں ہوسکتی۔ لہذا اس نظم میں اس مسئلے کے بعض پہلوؤں کا ارادتا نظر انداز کردیا گیاہے۔ امید ہے کہ ناظرین کرام ان سے نا واقف نہ ہوں گے۔ یہ نظریہ چونکہ اختلافوں کی بنیاد پر قائم ہے۔ اس کی حقیقت پر روشنی ڈالنے کی کوشش کی گئی ہے۔ دلیلؔ

When the intellect of man was of no avail and he was not aware of the attributes of God; when he was unaware of the reality of matter and spirit; when he could not see the light of unity in the colors of diversities; when the factors of good and evil were a mystery for him; when the difference of real status was beyond his imagination, he dreamt of the unreal a notion of Rebirth.

Stanza:144.

144 ہے وہ باطل جس سے اخلاق بشر ہوں پائمال

ہے تقاضئہ حقیقت حسن فطرت میں کمال

گو ہلاہل سے تن فانی کو حاصل ہوں زوال

موت ہے دل کے لئے باطل خیالوں کا وبال

گر حقیقت سے شناسائی ہو بنیاد عمل

زندگی میں ہو نہیں سکتا کبھی پیدا خلل

نوٹ:

حیات بعد الموت : اسلامی عقیدے کے مطابق روز قیامت میں دنیا کے سارے لوگ مرجائیں گے۔ اس عقیدے کے مطابق انسان دوبارہ اپنی ماں کے پیٹ سے پیدا نہیں ہوگا ۔اسکے بعد ہر ایک آدمی کے اعمال کا حساب لینے کی خاطر پروردگارتمام مردوں کو یونہی زندا اٹھائیگاوہ دن یوم الحساب کہلاتا ہے نیک اور بد عمل کا حساب ختم ہونے کے بعد جزا اور سزا دیکر لوگوں کو جنت اور دوزخ کو بھیج دےگا۔ موت کے بعد **حیات** ضرورہے اور اس پر ایمان لانا نہایت ضروری ہے۔مگر صرف ایک

دفعہ اور قیامت کے دن پروردگار تمام مردوں کو زندہ اٹھائے گا۔ لہٰذا تناسخ اور
"حیات بعد الموت" میں بہت فرق ہے۔

جی زیڈ۔ رضیہ بیگم

Tr: The nature of man demands the importunity of reality because the false and fictitious notions are harmful for the character of man. Just as the poison is fatal for the perishable corporeal body, the vexation about the wrong conception has the paralitic influence on heart and mind. If the foundation of any action is based on real knowledge, life can never be defective.

Stanza. 145

ہے تناسخ کا عقیدہ آدمیت کا زوال

اسدادوالانتزائے جرم وآفت ہو محال

نفرت و ذلت غروروظلم ہو جائیں حلال

ہو مساوات اخوت ایک بے معنی خیال

ہرترقی کے لئےوہ چاردیواری بھی ہو

آدمی دنیا میں مجبور سیہ کاری بھی ہو

Tr. The Concept of Rebirth cannot serve as hindrance against committing crimes. The concepts of equality and brotherhood become meaningless, in case hatred, dishonor, vanity and oppression become lawful. In this world, there is scope for the promotion of goodness and at the same time, human being is bound to err.

Stanza. 146

146۔ جوہر اشیائ کا جس منزل میں ہوتا ہے گزر

دوربوسکتا ہے وہی اس کا ہر نقص ضرر

پچھلی منزل کی طرف ہوتا نہیں اس کا سفر

کس لئے کیونکر ہو خاک آلود پھر روح بشر

روح جوہر ہے سفر اسکا سوئے افلاک ہے

جسم خاکی ہے عرض انجام اسکا خاک ہے

developing stage of soul, the harmful and disadvantageous defect can be evaded. The soul never comes back to earth but advances towards heaven. It does not reenter the corporeal body. The end of corporeal body, made of mud, becomes mud again.

Stanza.147.

147 ۔ بزم قدرت میں ہیں سنگ و نسل ایوان و بشر

ارتقاء حسن کے آئینے پئے اہل نظر

جس نئے قالب میں ہوگی روح انساں جلوہ گر

لازمی ہے اس کا ہونا خوب تر حساس تر

چاہئے آباد تر بیدار تر ہو زندگی

چاہیے آزاد تر سرشار تر ہو زندگی

Tr: Among the Divine creations, whether they are stones or trees or irrational animals or human beings, are prone to develop. When a soul enters into the human body, it is essential for it to evolve and develop more than the other creations having no souls. In order to achieve this end, we must lead a free, prosperous life with full awareness about good and evil.

Stanza. 148

148۔ روح جو ہوتی ہے تن سے بطن مادر میں جدا

بالیقیں ہوتی ہے وہ بھی قابل نشونما

یوں تو ہوتی ہے جدا ہر روح کی شان بقا

وا مگر سب کے لئے یکساں ہے باب ارتقاء

ہیں ربوبیت نے وہ انداز اشیاء کو دئے

ہے قدم ہر چیز کا آگے تکامل کے لئے

Tr: As soon as the child is born with soul inside him, it certainly becomes capable for development. God has provided the same amount of scope for the evolution and perfection of all the souls which are eternal. But the degree of glory of eternity differs due to the nature of the deeds of the people in this world.

Stanza.149

149 ۔ منکشف تجھ پر تو ہے آزاد روحوں کی بقا

اختلاف ان سے تجھے بالواسطہ جو خوب تھا

جانتا تو ہے کہ وہ رجعت سے ہے ناآشنا

شامت اعمال کا احساس ہے انکو سوا

عرصہ محشر سے باہر گو نہیں اہل جہاں

روز آخر میں عمل کے سب نتائج ہوں عیاں

Tr. It is clearly known to you about the eternity of free souls because you are also united with the soul. The freed souls do not know the backward journey or retracing because they are deeply concerned with consequences of their deeds. The consequences will be experienced on the Day of Resurrection.

Stanza. 150

150 ۔ جسم خاکی سے نکل کر روح کرتی ہے ظہور

اپنے ہی اعمال کے جسم مثالی میں ضرور

خواب کے اسرار پر تجھ کو نہیں ہے کیا عبور

کیا نہیں حاصل تجھے پینا ٹزم سے یہ شعور

دیکھنے سننے کو چشم وگوش کی حاجت نہیں

روح کی قدرت ہے اس قالب میں حیرت آئیں

Tr. At the death of a person, the soul leaves his corporeal body and enters into the astral body. Don't you have any knowledge about the secrets of dream and hypnotism? For seeing and hearing, material eye and material ear are not at all required. The existence and power of the soul in our body are amazing.

Stanza.151

151 ۔ عالم ارواح کی منزل نہیں پنہا بہت

ارتقاء دل کے ہوتے ہیں وہاں ساماں بہت

رنگ لاتی ہے وہاں ہرقوت انساں بہت

معرفت ہر شئی کی ہوتی ہے وہاں آسان بہت

لائق پرواز ہے ہر روح کا جسم لطیف

پھر نہیں بنتا کبھی اس کا قفس جسم کثیف

Tr. The spiritual world is not beyond the scope of our knowledge. In the spiritual world. there are much provisions and equipment's for the evolution of the soul. The power or ability of man brings out its own color there and the mystic knowledge of everything is easily acquired. The soul becomes capable of flight and it does not become imprisoned in the impure body of mud.

Stanza.152

152۔ روح کے سازو صفا کو ہے وہاں سوز جحیم

اہتراز نفس کو ہے نکہت باغ نعیم

ارتکاب جرم کے قابل نہیں ہوتا اثیم

ہے عجب اک بارگاہ رحمت رب رحیم

ہیں جمال یار سے عاشق سوا محو سرور

جلوہ نو کی تمناؤں سے دل ہے ناصبور

Tr: For the pure soul, there is ample scope in the hereafter for comforts, the pleasant odour from the paradise and blessings for self-merriments. The realm of compassionate God is perplexing that no sinner can commit any more crime in the hereafter. The lover engrossed in the happiness due to the Beauty of God, and his impatient heart is full of desire to see the new Beauty in the hereafter.

Stanza.153

153۔ حکمت کامل کی رنگیں داستاں ہے اختلاف

حسن کی دنیا بہار بے خزاں ہے اختلاف

دعوت فکر و نظر تسکین جاں ہے اختلاف

اختلافوں میں نہاں ہے داستان زندگی

جادہ پیما ہے اسی سے کاروان زندگی

Tr: The divergence in the creations is the colorful account of the perfect wisdom of God. The eternal beauty depends upon the disparity in the objects. The dissimilarity objects invoke our interest to find out the truth and gives us feeling of comforts. The whole account of life is concealed in the dissimilarity of objects which induces the travelers to proceed in the march of their life (Philosophical Science).

Stanza.154

154۔ کچھ نہ ہوتا گر نہ ہوتے اختلاف جہاں

راز تکمیل بشر ہے اختلافوں میں نہاں

ہے انہیں کے دم سے حسن و عشق کی ہر داستاں

ارتقاء عقل و دل جوش جہاد جاوداں

ایک دنیا ئے عجائب جلوہ کثرت میں ہے

انتہا حیرت کی لیکن جلوہ وحدت میں ہے

Tr: Had there been no dissimilarity in the creations, the secret of the perfection of life will remain undisclosed. Only because of disparity, the impact of beauty, love, evolution of wisdom, the zealous and eternal fight with life is clearly understood. In this world of wonders. the unity in diversities is most puzzling (Spiritualism).

Stanza. 155

155۔ اختلافات مدارج کب نہیں تھے جلوہ گر

کیا نہیں ہے ان پہ تہذیب و تمدن منحصر

کیا تمدن ہے کہیں کردہ گناہوں کا ثمر

مٹ نہیں جائیں گے کیا ہوتے اگر یکساں بشر

دیکھتی ہے اختلافوں میں نگاہ دور میں

عدل اور خلاقیت کی شان حیرت آفرین

Tr: The civilization of the world depends upon the difference in grades and ranks of people. There is no society which has not experienced the consequences of the crimes of the people. If everything is uniform, it will become extinct. Those who can realize the truth is acquitted with the wonderful magnificence of God's justice and creative power.

Stanza.156

156 ۔ بزم قدرت کی ہم آہنگی ہے فیض اختلاف

منتشر ذروں میں ہمرنگی ہے وجہ انحراف

ہے تخالف سے جو پیدا ان میں جذب ایتلاف

یہ زمین مہر و ماہ و انجم ہے سر گرم طواف

اختلافوں سے زمانے کی روش ہے برقرار

زندگی پرور ہے ان سے گردش لیل و نہار

Tr:-Disparity is the cause for harmony in the creations of God. The scattered atoms of the factor of same nature are influenced by the factor of disparity.Due to their difference, connection is created between them.This world,Sun, Moon and Stars which are related to one another are always engaged in rotations and revolutions.The occurrences of night after day and day after night depend on the differences of their revolutions.

revolutions (Physical Science). on the

Stanza:157

157۔ اختلافوں کی ہوئی کیونکر جہاں میں ابتدا

اختلاف مردوزن کی اولیں کیا ہے بنا

آدم اول میں کیا جر ثومہ زندہ نہ تھا

ہیں نباتات اور حیوانات گوناگوں یہ کیا

حکمت خلاق عالم ہیں بنائے اختلاف

یاکہ خلق نوع آدم ہے بنائے اختلاف

خواہ وہ بے جان ہو یا جانور اللہ نے

Tr:-Who knows the origin of disparity, Don't you know the first foundation of the dissimilarity in the sex man and women? Didn't Adam the first human being on earth have the vital microscopic germ (Sperm) in himself. Don't you see the vegetations and animals of diStanza kinds, of different colours, of various shapes and of various sort or class? It is not humanity but it is the divine Wisdom which laid the foundation of dissimilarities (Biology and Genetic Engineering).

Stanza.158

158- سب کے جوڑے عرصہ ہستی میں ہیں پیدا کئے

بسکہ ہے نشونما ئے زندگی ترویج سے

جذب و الفت کے عناصر ہیں دویعت کردئے

اختلاف جنس میں پنہا ہے اسرار حیات

اختلافوں ہی سے قائم ہے نظام کائنات

بند 158 نوٹ : پاکی اور بزرگی اس ذات کے لئے ھے جس نے زمین کی پیداوار میں اور انساں میں اور ان تمام مخلوقات جنکا انسان کو علم نہیں دو اور مقابل چیزیں پیدا کیں یعنی جوڑے بنائےہیں۔ (یٰسن : 32-36)

Tr: Whether it is animate or inanimate things,God have created couples in them for the sake of their development,and have deposited in them the qualities of attraction and affectionThe secrets of life are concealed in the opposite sexe sand the universe is beautifully established and arranged by the opposite forces (Zoology and Physics).

Stanza.159

159- جب زمانے میں حیات نو کا یک عنوان وصال

آب و گل کے فیض سے وانے کی ہستی ہے نہال۔

برق کی ہے روشنی دو قوتوں کا اتصال

ارتقاء زندگی بے وصل ہے امر محال

ذات باری سے تعلق جب تلک حاصل نہ ہو

پوچھ اہل دل سے نفس آدمی کامل نہ ہو

Tr:-Just as a new life is the result of the union of two things, a grain develops, prospers and becomes a tree on account of the joint effect of soil and water. The light of the electricity is the result of two opposite forces (Protons and Electrons). The evolution of life is impossible without the co-existence of two opposite forces. Unless a man gets connection with God, spiritual perfection cannot be obtained. (Theory of evolution and spiritualism).

Stanza.160

160۔ زندگی بنتی ہے جو رنج و مصائب جھیل کر

غم ہے رحمت بھی جہاں میں یا بلا ہی سربسر۔

ہادیان قوم پر جور و ستم تھے کس قدر۔

کیا سیہ کاران بد انجام تھے یہ پیشتر

نیک ہوتے ہیں جو ارباب تناسخ بالیقیں

اس عقیدے پر عمل پیرا کبھی ہوتے نہیں

Tr: The really pious persons who wanted to guide their nation on the path of righteousness were mercilessly persecuted but they regarded the calamities of their life as blessings in Such noble personalities could never have been sinners. Those noble and pious individuals 'related to the people who believe in the concept of Rebirth, never have belief in this wrong notion.

Stanza.161

161۔ ہے عطا ہر چیز کو سامان حسب اقتضاء

ہر کسی میں ہے نہ شاں فضیلت یک جدا

ہے بشر کی زندگی سلسلہ بے انتہا

اور کچھ ہو جائیں گے کل آج کے شاہ و گدا

کس کو ہم بہتر کہیں جب تک نہ ہو پیش نظر

ابتدا سے انتہا تک داستان ہر بشر

Tr: Everything is blessed or bestowed with all the requisites according to its need Everything possesses in itself different digress of excellence and proficiency. The chain of successions of man's life is endless. God has the power to do whatever He wishes. He can bring about the change in the conditions of things in no time. He can degrade the king to the position of a beggar; and upgrade a beggar to the status of a king. We cannot assess the quality of the traits of man unless we scrutinize the accounts of his life from the beginning to end.

162۔ بہر ور عقل بشر سے ہو جو مخلوق دگر

غیر انساں کا عطا ہو جسم انساں کو اگر

گر بدل لیں اپنے عیش و غم کو آپس میں بشر

یا ہوں موجودات کل یکساں جہاں میں سر بسر

ہو جہاں ماتم کدہ برہم ہو دنیا کا نظام

مصلحت کے ماتحت ہیں بخششیں رب کی تمام

Tr: In case other creations are blessed with human prudence and human being is given the body of another animal; in case people exchange their happiness and grief among themselves or there is same level of uniformity in the creations, the whole administration of the universe will get upset and become a mess. Every lacking and beneficence is under the control of God's pleasure and prudence.

Stanza.163

163۔ ہے جدا ہر چیز کی قیمت ہر انساں کے لئے

اس کی فطرت ہے کہ ہر حالت کے سانچے میں ڈھلے

کون ورنہ اس مصاف زندگی میں جی سکے

چاہیے منزل سے اپنی ہر بشر آگے چلے

رحمت ربنے ولاو خدمت مجبور پر

اہل قدرت کی سعادت کو کیا ہے منحصر

Tr. The utility of a thing differs with different people. He gets accustomed to the condition, he is placed in. Otherwise, no person can lead the life in this battle field, the world. Every man is expected to advance in this field. The auspiciousness of prosperous people depends upon the service to needy community which is a Divine injunction.

Stanza. 164

164- ہے جنہیں راز قضاء و قدر کا حاصل شعور

ہو کمال حکمت رب بھی عیاں اُن پر ضرور

ہوں نہ وہ مرعوب دنیا سے نہ بندوں سے نفور

دور ہو کینہ حسد رنج و غضب یاس و غرور

دل مئے شکر و قرار و صبر سے مسرور ہو

جوش و استقلال ہمت سے عمل معمور ہو

Tr:- Those who are acquainted with future-destiny, the perfection of Divine Wisdom will be revealed to them.They should not be not be frightened or prevailed over by this hazardous world those who abhore or flee.The evil factors like malice,wrath, indignance, despair , frustration should be dispelled.Our minds should be frenzied with and full of the feeling of gratitude, contentment,patience, happiness, exuberance, perservance and constancy.

Stanza.165

165 - رنج و راحت ہیں زمانے کے اضافی بالیقیں

کیا مشیّت سے جدا ہوتی بھی ہے راحت کہیں

کیا کبھی راحت مصیبت کا سبب ہوتی نہیں

ہے سراپا مصلحت ناقص جو ہیں اہل زمیں

ہے عروج روز افزوں میں سرور لا زوال

ہے تنزل اور یکسانی میں اندوہ و ملال

Tr:-Both grief and comfort are certainly relative factors. Sometime by the will of God, comfort gets suspended orextinguished.Sometimes, comfort becomes the cause for calamities.It is the advisability of God for all sorts situations because people are imperfect.The day by day progress causes eternal happiness while lack of progress or demotion cause grief and sorrow.

Stanza.166

166۔ رنج و راحت کا اثر یکساں دلوں پر ہے کہاں

حادثہ اولاد قوت حسن دولت دل زبان

کونسی وہ چیز ہے جو ہو نہیں سکتی یہاں

باعث رنج و طرب و موجب سود و زیاں

پھر یہ موجودات جو انسان سے پہلے بھی تھے

ہیں نتائج کس جنم کے کونسے اعمال کے

Tr: Whether it is grief, or comfort or accident or progeny or power or beauty or riches or heart or tongue, they have no equal influence on our hearts. There is nothing here which cannot be the cause for sadness and happiness and which cannot be the reason for profit and loss. Before the creation of first man, the other creations required by man were present. Of which birth or of which deeds, these Divine bounties were the rewards?

Stanza.167

167۔ سارے موجودات میں پروردگار پاک نے

خیر و شر کے خاص اندازے ہیں قائم کر دیے

یہ بشر کے واسطے ہوتے ہیں اچھے یا برے

قصد و مقدار و محل سے طرز استعمال سے

خیر بھی ہوتی ہے شر جب حد سے جاتی ہے گزر

خیر بن جاتا ہے شر بھی حد میں ہوتا ہے اگر

Tr: All creations two aspects namely "Good" and "Evil". Their advantage and disavantage depend on the method of exploitation of of bounties, place, quantity and intention. If good exceeds the prescribed limit, it becomes evil and if evilsis within the limit it becomes good.

Stanza.168

168۔ عالم ایجاد پر فیض و حسین ہے کس قدر

خلق کی خدمت میں ہے مصروف یہ آٹھوں پہر

اس کا دل پاک ہے گرد گنہ سے سر بسر

اس میں اعمال بشر سے ہے نمود خیر و شر

یہ زمین و آسماں یہ نعمتیں ہے انتہا

ہیں عنایات خداوندی کہ محنت کا صلہ

Tr:-This world is full of beauty and beneficence. All the time, the creations are engaged in the service of humanity. Good and evil depend upon the conduct of man. The heavens and earth and the unlimited bounties of God are the remunerations for our strife.

Stanza.169

169۔ ہے حقیقت جلوہ رب یا کہ ایجاد بشر

واقفان راز دیتے ہیں فقط اس کی خبر

آشنا اسرار وحدت سے جو ہو جائے نظر

ہو مساوات و اخوت کی حقیقت جلوہ گر

نور وحدت سے زمانہ ہے ازل سے مستنیر

چشم ظاہر میں لیکن اختلاف وں کی اسیر

Tr: Is the truth, manifestation of God or invention of man? Only those who are acquainted with the secret can give the answer to this question. If we get acquainted with the secrets of unity of creations, the truth of equality and brotherhood will be manifested. From the beginning, the world is illuminated by the light of unity, but, for the outward eye, this light is confined in disunity.

Stanza.170

170جلوہ بے رنگ سے ہے سارے رنگوں کی نمود

پیش ارباب نظر ہے ایک ہی سبز و کبود

پر تو مہر ازل ہے یہ گلستان شہود

اس کی یك رنگیں کرن ہے ابن آدم کا وجود

ہے خدائے پاک کی توہین تحقیر بشر

ہے سراپا خاک ساری اہل ایمان و نظر

Tr: The existence of all the colours in this world is the result of the colourless Beauty, God. Those who have mystic knowledge, see no difference between green and blue, The Omni-potence of God is the source for the existence of the light of the sun, the time of origin of which is not known. The existence of man depends upon the coloured ray of the light of the sun. To ridicule or disdain a person is nothing but defamation, disgrace for and insult to God.

Stanza.171

171 - ہیں عیال اللہ کے افراد انسانی تمام

ایک ہی امت زمانے کے ہیں سارے خاص و عام

ایک ہی کل کے ہیں پرزے کل ہوں آقا یا غلام

اصلیت میں ایک ہی آبنائے عالم لا کلام

اہل تقوی کو فقط عزت خدا کے پاس ہے

رنگ و نسل مال و منصب کا شرف وسواس ہے

Tr: All people common or uncommon, high or low are all brothers and dependents of God. All are the small parts of a huge machine. The essence of all the people in this world is definitely the same, in other words equal. God respects only those people who are pious and God-fearing. The distinction in color, race, affluence and status is only distraction.

Stanza. 172

172۔ اہل کشور مواقع سے مساوی بہرہ ور

آدمی کی اہلیت پر ہوں مناسب منحصر

ہو نہ انساں پر کبھی انسان کی نیچی نظر

ہوں حقوق آدمی سارے نصیب ہر بشر

جلوہ وحدت سے روشن ہو فضائے زندگی

نغمہ درد و اخوت ہو نوائے زندگی

Tr: Spiritually successful people by chance comprehend the significance of equality. The different status of man depend upon his skill and capacity.The inferior person should not be looked down up. He must be entitled to enjoy the human rights just as his superiors have.May the atmosphere of life be enlightened with the Beauty of Unity.May the voice of life be musical and melodious with affinity and brotherhood.

Stanza.173

173۔ قوم ہی وہ کیا ہے جس میں آدمی بیکار ہوں

امتیاز بے حقیقت سے ذلیل و خوار ہوں

علم سے محروم ہوں بے دین ہوں بیمار ہوں

اہل دولت خود غرض اہل ہنر نادار ہوں

اقتصادی ہو سیاسی ہو سماجی ہو نظام

دین بر حق کی بناء پر چاہیے اُسکا قیام

Tr: It is not a good nation, inhabited by useless people who are the disgraceful and wretched ones due to their unreal discrimination among themselves. In this world there are all sorts of people some of whom are bereft of knowledge, some are ignorant about the religion, some are selfish and some are skilled and accomplished people.In some cases, the skilled and qualified people are desperate due to their misfortune.Whatever the quality of the nation may be, the functions of its government whether they are economic or political or social or administrative must be based on the sound principles of a true religion.

Stanza.174

174۔ دہر میں جمہوریت بسیار ناقص ہے ابھی

ہے مساوات و اخوت سے تمدّن جو تہی

فتنہ نسل و وطن میں مبتلا ہے زندگی

ہے زمانے میں غضب کا قرق محتاج و غنی

خلق پر چھائی ہوئی جمہوریت کے واسطے

سینہ جمہور میں احساس وحدت چاہیے

Tr: In the present world, the field of democracy is extremely defective, the civilization is devoid of the feeling of brother hood and equality. The life of the people is desperately immersed in hazards, because of the discrimination and feeling of inequality between rich and poor. But, for the sake of true democracy, the heart of the democrat must be full of the feelings of equality and unity of creations.

Stanza.175

175۔ دین ہی سے دل میں احساس وحدت جلوہ گر

ہے اسیر امتیاز اہل سیاست کی نظر

قوم و رنگ و نسل کے فتنے گراں جان پر ضرر

ایک ضرب لا الہ سے بے نشاں ہو سر بسر

دین حق سے ہے مساوات و اخوت کا ثبات

زندہ رکھتے ہیں انہیں روزہ نماز و حج زکوٰت

نوٹ : زکوۃ عربی زبان کا لفظ ہے قافیے کی موزونیت باقی رکھنے کے لیے اردو شاعری میں زکوۃ کی جگہ زکات لکھنا جائز ہے۔

Tr:- The true religion teaches the theory of Unity of Creations.But the politicians are captivated by the wrong concept of inequality which is highly detrimental, embarrassing disadvantageous and harmful.One Divine Blow is enough to erase the pride and prestige of the powerful,merciless and selfish people to the ground.True religion is the source to maintain the permanence and constancy of brotherhood and equality which are kept awakened by Faith, Fasting, Namaz, Hajj and Zakaat.

Stanza. 176

176- جلوہ وحدت شعور زیست کی بنیاد ہو

دل ہم آغوش حیات گلشن ایجاد ہو

زندگی جمہوریت کی روح سے آباد ہو

نخوت احساس ذلت سے بشر آزاد ہو

جلوہ توحید سے معمور ہو جمہوریت

بادہ تخلیق سے مخمور ہو جمہوریت

Tr: The foundation of intellectual life is the Beauty of Unity, May our heart embrace With that person who has made this world a paradise, May our life be prosperous with the true spirit of democracy. May people be free from the feeling of pride and dishonor. May the democracy be replete with Beauty of unity of God. May Democracy be frenzied by the Unity of God.

C: In this chapter the Poet has discussed religion, mysticism, spiritualism and social sciences together, which have been closely inter-woven. He has explained how the Anti-Islamic concept 'Rebirth" differs from the Islamic Concept 'Life After Death"

In view of the brevity of the poem, he has presented a few arguments to which I have supplemented by a few more ones. The following is the substance of the foot notes given by Daleel Sahib: - '"It is the belief of the Hindus that man dies repeatedly and is reborn repeatedly. In Urdu this notion of Rebirth is called "Tanasukh" and those who believe in this notion are called Ahl-e-Tanasukh. But according to Islam, this theory is wrong. Hundreds of pages are required for detailed discussion about Rebirth. But in this short poem detailed discussion is not possible. Hence, intentionally some arguments about this issue had to be overlooked. Hope the revered readers are aqcuinted with the omitted factors. As this theory is based on controversies, attempts have been made to bring the facts into light"….(Daleel)

According to Islamic concept, the whole population of the world will perish on the Day of the Doom. No person will be reborn in this world from his mother's womb after his first death. In due course, with the purpose of reckoning the good and evil deeds of the people, Almighty Allah will resurrect them in the hereafter. That day of reckoning is called Yaum-ul-Hisaab. After completing the reckoning, they will be awarded rewards or punishment and they will be sent to paradise or hell whichever they deserve.

The believers whose souls get purified by the heat and torment of the hell, will be sent to paradise. This is the last stage of sojourn of man's life. He cannot be reborn in this world and his soul cannot enter into another corporeal body. Hence, there is much difference between

Rebirth (anti-Islamic notion) and Life After Death i.e. Resurrection (Islamic Concept)

In the ancient times, man was ignorant about the reality of attributes of God, unity of God, unity of creations, soul and the real differences in real status. With advance of civilization, some people were blessed with some knowledge which they misused and instilled in the minds of their ignorant disciples some false and unsound notions with the purpose of elevating their own status in the ancient society. For the best and accomplished life, the foundation of the acquisition of correct knowledge, flawless acquaintance, capacity of comprehension and character are quite indispensable. The concept of Rebirth cannot prevent or eradicate,crime because this concept is the craft of the false sages. They themselves bluff and commit crime by the show of pride, vanity and superiority and by insulting and looking down upon This hamper and terminates the inculcation of the feeling of equality and brotherhood of course this world provides scope for the retraction or retrogression.

It is the pleasure and expediency of God that the souls enter the corporeal bodies only they cause them to find their journey towards heaven, because God wants the souls purified and become free from detrimental defects. When Allah is so compassionate, we must lead a chaste and noble life for the evolution of our soul. The soul cannot or retrogress because it has to experience the consequences of the deeds on the Day At the expiry of the person, his soul parts with its material body and enters into (Immaterial) body. According to Islamic concept, the souls in the immaterial bodies w, each other, can feel pain and pleasure and can hear and see what is happening in new spiritual world. Here, in order to convince the readers about the astonishing and operations of the souls, the poet has taken the examples of dream and hypnotism, The study of psychology has been broadly classified into three sub-topics; viz. (l) Norma! psychology in which the state of consciousness of the person is perfect (2) Sub-normal Psychology in which the mind of the normal person is in the state of sub-consciousness (3) In abnormal Psychology the mind is the state of retardedness and insanity.

Dream and hypnotism come under the classification of Sub-normalPsychology. The under the sub-normal state of mind when he is asleep or when he is hypnotized.In the dream, the person sees many objects when there are no such objects at all. These are objecting the immaterial objects seen by the immaterial eyes, in the dream. In the dream the person hears thundering sound when there is no sound at all in the material environmental area. There are all surprising, unimaginable and perplexing operations of the soul which is immaterial, the hypnotized person can read any page of the book when he is blind-folded. He does not see by the material eyes but by the spiritual eyes.

The poet has referred to dream and hypnotism to convince the readers about the life after death and the powers of the soul in the astral body after the demise of the person. The mystic knowledge about the mystic worlds, hell and heaven in the hereafter and the powers of the soul in the mystic astral bodies is the clue for the spiritual science, psychology.

The law in the realm of the merciful God is bewildering. The pure souls will be in ecstasy, delight andreveling at the sight of the highly illuminated world by the effulgence of God, and vicious persons can no more commit any crime in the hereafter.

Generally,the true preceptors who venture to guide their nations, were always suppressed and oppressed. They tolerated all sorts of afflictions with absolute patience and regard the adversities of their life as Divine Blessings in disguise. They could not have done evil dons in their previous births (wrong notion). This argument is the testimony for the invalidity of the wrong notion of Rebirth. In this context, the hazards of life endured by some Prophets is worth mentioning. For example, Prophet Nooh (A.S.) was bitterly ridiculed and insulted by his own kinsmen. Prophets Ibrahim (A.S.). Isa (A.S.) and Muhammed (SAVV) were severely persecuted. When Jerusalem was under the domination of Roman Emperor Herod Prophet Zakria (A.S.) and his son prophet Yehiya (AS.) were slain at the instruction of the Emperor. This does not mean that they were the sinners previously. It was the pleasure of God to test their faith and patience and then absorb them in himself.

Once Ibrahim (A.S.) requested Allah to demonstrate His powers as to how could he revive the dead persons when his body was consumed by the earth. In order to satisfy him. he revived four slautered birds with their corporeal bodies. It is a notable point that Allah selected the birds as they have no souls.

Q. Baqara - 2:260:

وَإِذْ قَالَ إِبْرَاهِمُ رَبِّ أَرِنِي كَيْفَ تُحْىِ الْمَوْتَى قَالَ أَوَلَمْ تُؤْمِنْ قَالَ بَلَى وَلَكِنْ لِيَطْمَئِنَّ قَلْبِي قَالَ فَخُذْ أَرْبَعَةً مِنَ الطَّيْرِ فَصُرْهُنَّ إِلَيْكَ ثُمَّ اجْعَلْ عَلَى كُلِّ جَبَلٍ مِنْهُنَّ جُزْءًا ثُمَّ ادْعُهُنَّ يَأْتِينَكَ سَعْيًا وَاعْلَمْ أَنَّ اللَّهَ عَزِيزٌ حَكِيمٌ

Tr: "And when Abraham said (unto his Lord) My Lord, show me how you givest life to the dead'. He said, Dost thou not believe?' Abraham said, 'Ye but, ask in order that my heart be at His Lord said, four of the birds and cause them to incline unto thee, then place a part of them on each hill, then call them. they will come to thee in haste. And know that Allah is Mighty, Wise".

The Persian Emperor conquered Jerusalem from the Romans and the city was erased to the ground. The Persian Emperor sent Azeez, a Zoroastrian priest of high piety to reconstruct Jerusalem and for bringing about social reforms. The Jude's (a sect Of Jews) call him Ezra and son of God and his Quranic name is Uzair. He wondered as to how this destructed city could be rebuilt. He was riding an ass with some hot meals. Allah caused him to die for hundred years. His corporeal body did not decay and was not consumed by earth because a soul cannot re-enter in another body The ass had died, his flesh was consumed by earth and only his skeleton was left beside Uzair. After hundred years, he was revived by Allah. But he thought that he slept for a few hours. Then Allah spoke to him and informed him that he was dead for hundred years and instructed him to see at the skeleton of his donkey. The meals he took with him was hot. The donkey was revived with flesh and blood. Then, he was given to understand and that by Divine Power Jerusalem could be reconstructed. Thus,Uzair was convinced about the omni-potence of Allah.

Once a Muslim contemporary of Muhammad (SAW) came to him and asked him to explain as to how Allah will resurrect a dead person. Our Prophet (SAW) began to interrogate him, 'Did you exist before your birth?" He said, "Not at all", Then Muhammed (SAW) asked him, "How did you come into existence?". He answered, "I came into existence by Allah's Divine Power". Again Muhammed (SAW) asked him. "Can't the same omni-potence of God resurrect you?" He said, 'Of course Allah can. I could not understand this issue before you explained". This conversation is clear evidence for life in the hereafter.

According to Quranic verses Jesus Christ was not crucified by the Jews. They crucified the man who chased him and resembled him. Allah took Isa (A.S.) up to the fourth firmament of heaven and he is there with his corporeal body adorn with Soul. As Islam is against Rebirth, Quran says that he will descend and reappear in this world with the same body and the same soul, He will reappear on the earth well in advance before the day Of the Doom. lead army against Dajjal (an avowed Jew enemy Of Muslims), kill him, eradicate evils from the Soc-jet", purify the world, die a natural death, will be buried and then he will be resurrected in the hereafter Birth is a warrant of death and death is a warrant of resurrection. Allah has kept Jesus Christ with his corporeal body and send him to the earth with the same body because it is the Divine Law and advisability that a soul should not enter in&) another body awn. This another argument against Rebirth. Ezra was only revived by God and was not reborn from his mother's womb as a child. Jesus Christ will reappear with same age and the same maturity and mind, he had when he was lifted up by

God. He will not be reborn from another woman's womb as a child with immatured mind.

God with his Supreme Power. can do whatever and whenever He wishes. He can change the condition of things and status of people in no time. The favorable and unfavorable happenings should not be connected with man's deeds in his previous birth (Arm-Islamic concept). The 162nd Stanza of the text consists of the substance of the essay, "man happy in any condition", written by an Urdu scholar, a reputed story and essay writer, Moulana Muhammed Hussain Azaad. In an interesting style, he interprets the philosophy of life in the form of a story. He personifies the aspects of life and makes them the characters of the story. In such a story, personified characters got fed up with their own fates and exchanged the pans and pleasures. But they could not tolerate the change of the beneficence of God. Consequently, the whole world got upset and became the field of mourning's and lamentations. Daleel Sahib also has explained the same idea and says, that everything is under the control of Gods advisability and prudence. Nothing should be connected with the past deeds of the previous birth. This world of hardships is habitable because people get accustomed to the conditions, they are placed in. Allah has commanded the rich and fortunate people to help the needy ones in this single span of life in this world and try to attain spiritual benefits.

Science and Quran prove that universe was created billions of years ago, before the advent of Adam, the father of humanity, having soul. All the bounties of God were present for the survival and progress of man before his birth. Ahl-e-Tanasukh believe that the present affluence and bounties are the consequences of piety and noble deeds of his previous births. But the wise and generous providence of God had procured every requirement before the advent of Adam. This scientific fact disproves the theory of Rebirth.

Islam believes in the Unity of God. He neither begets nor is He begotten. His not known and He is Eternal. But Ahl-e-Tanasukh worship numerous goddesses and gods,, They believe that some of their gods were the incarnations of their previous gods and some gods were the children of their older gods. According to this belief some gods were born from the wombs of ordinary women (other than goddesses). The begotten gods led the life of ordinary people, got married and begot children whose descendants are still present. If so, where is the dignity of Divinity ever humanity According to Islamic concept, all the creations are the manifestations of God, He will never appear on earth in the human form. We are not the children of God, but, the dependents and creations of God. The following Quranic verses prove the above-mentioned arguments.

S.Ikhlaas-112:1-4:-

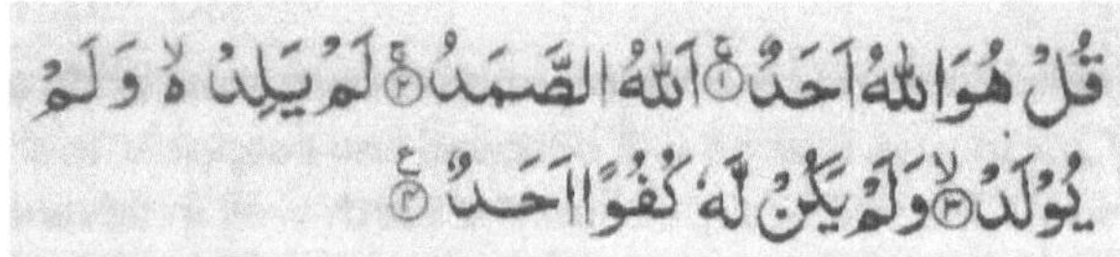

Tr: "Say. He is Allah. the One and Only: Allah. the Eternal, Absolute. He begetteth not, nor is He begotten, and there is none like unto Him"

These verses clearly imply that Allah is the Sovereign of the universe having Supreme Power. The wrong notion of Rebirth was instilled by false sages and it got spread. They did it purposely to elevate their own positions and status in the ancient society. The ignorant disciples accepted their exhortations. The stories, read in magazines and papers are all false ones to convince the people with this belief of Rebirth and spread it. The sages said that in their previous births, they were born as gods, or preceptors or kings. so far, no sage has said that he was born as a beggar or an ordinary man.

Many great Hindu theologians including E.V. Ramasami who have done research in their scriptures, have said that there is no mention of Rebirth at all in their Mantras, Puranas and Vedas. There are clear assertions in Quran that the dead persons will be resurrected in the hereafter with their souls in their astral (immaterial) bodies which will be awarded punishment or rewards, and they will be sent to hell or in heaven their deeds daring the only span of their life in this world. The believers Tanasukh contend to that cycle of rebirth a person will take place till his soul gets purified and attains liberation. His rebirth is a sort of punishment for his sins. Allah has created innumerable creations for the physical developments of living creatures whose life is short and transitory. Can't Allah make arrangements for the purification of soul which is eternal, in the hereafter? People of all the faiths believe in the existence of heaven and hell (Swargam and Nargam). If the person's punishment is over in this world and his soul gets purified here itself, there is no need for hell (Nargam). Heaven (Swargam) only is enough for him. According to Islamic belief, the stay of the believers in the hell is the stage of purification of the soul. After complete purification, the believers will enter into the paradise. Allah has created the mystic world, then for the punishment and purification of soul. Hence, persons need not be born again in this world. If the person can be born several times, he could have been born as a shudra in his past births, and can be born as a shudra in his future births. Then, the custom of untouchability is very absurd and insane. The greatest factors by which Islam has attracted the foreigners were the absence of caste system and the custom of untouchability. the believers in Tanasukh believe that human beings can be born as reptiles or beasts or any other living creatures on earth which have no souls as a sort of punishment. If so, a single person can be born as a human being with soul and many other different animals. which do not have souls, simultaneously. This absurdity is beyond imagination.

Now let us proceed to present the greatest and most convincing argument against the concept of Rebirth.

The believers in Tanasukh contend that one span of life is not enough to attain spiritual perfection. So. they are born again and again. Perfection can be attained only by evolution. A person dies with some amount of maturity and mental development. When, he is born again from another mother's womb, he is born with immature mind of a new born baby. and not with the maturity he had in his previous births. In the theory of evolution, backward journey and retracing is quite impossible (Scientific and Religious Philosophy).

GOOD AND EVIL: In the 17[th]Chapter "Struggle of Life". the poet has dealt with same topic "Good and Evil". but that aspect is quite different from the aspect he has dealt with in this chapter. In the 17[th]Chapter he has explained the consequences. pertaining to the good and evil deeds of human beings. In this chapter, he has explained the good and bad influences of things due to the method of exploitations Of Allah's bounties.

It is the magnanimity and glory of providence Of Almighty Allah. that whatever, he has created in this world, he has done it to satisfy the needs of other creations. As per his expediency, Allah has fixed a specified measure for everything, and has established two opposite facets for each and everything, namely good and evil, in other words, advantage and disadvantage. The poet explains chat the favorable effects and unfavorable effects of the bounties of Allah, depend on the method of usage, the intention of using. the place where it is used, time when it is used and the quantities of bounties, used. These can be explained by simple examples.

QUANTITY:

Nutrition is indispensable for survival. If it is consumed in the correct and balanced quantity, our metabolism will be balanced and it is advantageous for our health. If it is consumed beyond the required limit. It produces bad effect in our health. The nutrition which is helpful becomes harmful. The quantity of food and dosage of medicines required, must be correctly assessed. Otherwise, their excessive consumption will lead to indigestion and side effects.

INTENTION:

Intention counts much in the usage of things. When the house of the enemy is set ablaze with the fire. it is an Adverse thing. When the same fire is lit to prepare our food, it is a good thing for us. Money is absolutely necessary for all without which nothing can be purchased. The influence of this bounty of Allah is best for those people who spend it in the noble causes like giving charity to the needy community, spending it for the welfare of the common public and satisfy their own desirable needs, If people spend the money in vices and to attain their evil ends, it becomes the worst thing which invokes Allah's wrath.

PLACE :

Good and evil of the thing depends on the place where it is used. During the summer season, wearing the warm woollen clothes in the plains is harmful. while. the use of It gives us comfort in the high hilly places.

TIME:

Good and evil depend upon the time when something is consumed, or any activity is executed. Untimely consumption of food, untimely use of anything and untimely execution of any activity is harmful and disadvantageous to life,

young people and adults need highly nutritious food while small babies need only light and easily digestible food. If the baby is given hardlydigestible food, it will not be suitable for the child and he will become sick.

METHOD:

If anything is put to the correct use, it will be useful and if it is put to wrong use, we will have to incur loss. Especially in the case of mechanism. every machine should be operated properly and for specific purpose. Before executing any desirable activity, the best method should be determined and adopted.let us discuss the method of using chillie. If chillie is mixed in the curry in proper proportion with other ingredients, it produces a delicious taste. If chillie is chewed without the combination of other things. we feel an unbearable hot taste.

Further the poet says that if anything is used beyond limit, the good thing becomes an evil one and when a bad thing is used within the limit it becomes a good one. The first point is quite comprehensible. For example, nutrition is a good thing. but when it is used excessively, we have to suffer stomach disorder. Now, the question arises as to how an evil thing can become a good thing when it is under limit. It is an accepted fact, that poison is harmful for living beings. But with the advance of science, vaccines are prepared from the venom of poisonous creatures. A little amount of poison is mixed in the anti-biotic medicines. Of course, it also kills a small number of body cells and blood cells of the patient, but saves his life. After recovery, the devitalized cells are compensated by newly produced cells. Now, it is evident, that the use of a little amount of bad thing like poison becomes good and helpful. (Pathology & Pharmacology)

Now, it is proved that the five factors. namely method of usage, place, time, intention and quantity determine the nature of the thing viz, good or bad. Of course, intention counts much in Islam. No religious belief is entirely devoid of experience in its manifold practical aspect, namely the intention with which any act is done. Intention determines the test of its nature. Good or Evil. (Scientific argument and logical reasoning).

PAIRS OR OPPOSITE FORCES: -

When we consider God's wonderful creations, we see many mysteries, many opposites, many differences, the successions of nights and days and the creations of males and females.

God with His Perfect Wisdom created things with difference and disparity in order to make the world an ever-blooming beauty. This dissimilarity provokes our eternal quest of truth and activates human inherent faculties. This serves as the dynamo for the evolution and perfection of wisdom. The difference is not confined to the material objects only, but there is difference in all aspects of life like grades and status. This is due to Gods pleasure and justice. Otherwise, uniformity will lead to extinction. There is dissimilarity in the natural phenomena also. Night is opposite to day. The occurrences of night and day are the results of the rotations and revolutions of the planets in different axes and in different orbits. There are dissimilarities in plants and animals. God has created couples in both animate and inanimate things for their development and has imbibed in them the faculties of attraction, absorption and fusion.

It may be noted in the Quranic verses that the word "Pair" is used for propagation of plants, reproduction of all animals, procreation of human beings and existence of duality in all animate and inanimate objects. The Quranic exhortations of creation in pairs have been well comprehended and analyzed in almost all the sciences. The couplings by Divine even to the scientists. We are aware of the fact that two factors, a male and are absolutely necessary for sexual procreations. There is also asexual reproduction a multiplication according to the discoveries of the biological sciences, such as cell structure.The beauty of Allah's creations and his astounding deeds are really amazing.

S. Yasin-36:36: •

سُبْحَٰنَ الَّذِى خَلَقَ الْأَزْوَاجَ كُلَّهَا مِمَّا تُنبِتُ الْأَرْضُ وَمِنْ أَنفُسِهِمْ وَمِمَّا لَا يَعْلَمُونَ ﴿٣٦﴾

Tr: 'Glory to Allah. who created in pairs all things that the earth produces, as their own (human) kind and (other) things of which they have no knowledge"

In this Quranic verse. Almighty Allah has said that He created pairs in all his creations in the universe which include vegetation. animate and inanimate things about which human being have no knowledge. It means that the co-existence of two opposite factors i.e., sexes are necessary for procreations. The co-existence of two opposite factors is also for the inanimate things to generate energy and for all activities,

Plants and all matters, whether. they are solid, liquid or gas are composed of atoms and every atom consists of electrons and protons i.e. Negative and Positive electricity, proved the validity of this Quranic verse. (Biological science and physical science).

As usual. the poet has highlighted his sufistic philosophy in the 159th Stanza of the text. He says that though we are the manifestations of God, God and His creations are to be opposite to each other. We are other than God. If man does not have any connection or union with God. man can never attain perfection. Hence the existence of the pair and God is indispensable for attaining spiritual perfection. (Spritiualism).

The following brief notes explain how to merge with God and attain spiritual There are two kinds of people. Firstly, those who follow the dictates of their minds and by the glitter or glamour of world, are lost in sinful ways. Secondly, those who dictates of the scriptures. realize the true significance of life. Their endeavors are towards attaining union with God. Their minds turn away from the worldly activities come the five deadly foes, viz, ego, lust, anger, greed and attachment with undesirable things.

The All-Pervading God is the ultimate cause and the human soul is part of him. Our creed most be the loving devotion of God. Its objective must be the merger of human soul and Divinity. For attaining perfection in this case, is the union of the pair namely humanity and Divinity (Sufism)

Some Quranic o verses pertaining to pairs –

S. Hujuraat-49:13(Part of the verse

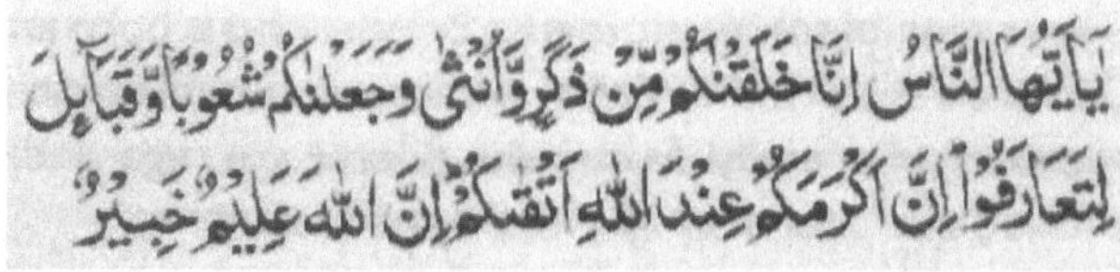

Tr:. "O mankind! we created you from a single pair of a male and female: and made you into nations and tribes, that ye may know each other not that ye may despise"

S. Ruum-30:21: -

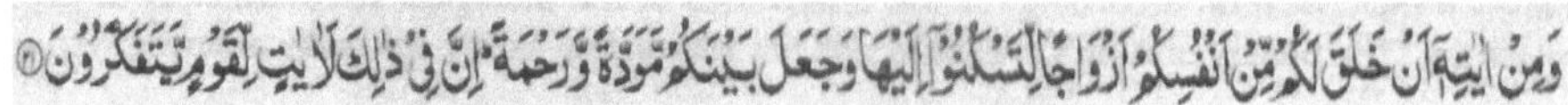

Tr:- And among His Signs, is this, that He created foryou mates from among yourselves, that ye may dwell in tranquility with them, and He has put love and mercy between your(hearts). Verily. in that are signs for those who reflect"

S. Ra'd-13:3:-

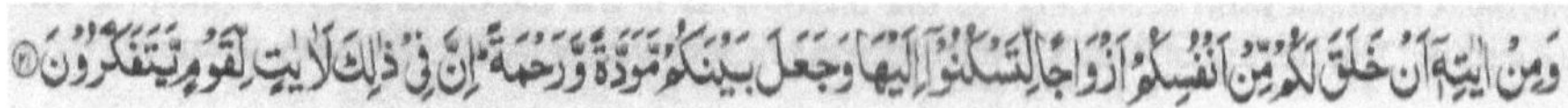

Tr:- "And, it is He who spread out the earth and set thereon mountains standing firm and flowing rivers; and fruit of every kind, He made in pairs, two and two. He draweth the night as a veil over the day. Behold. verily, in these things. there are signs for those who consider!"

S. Luqmaan - 31:10: -

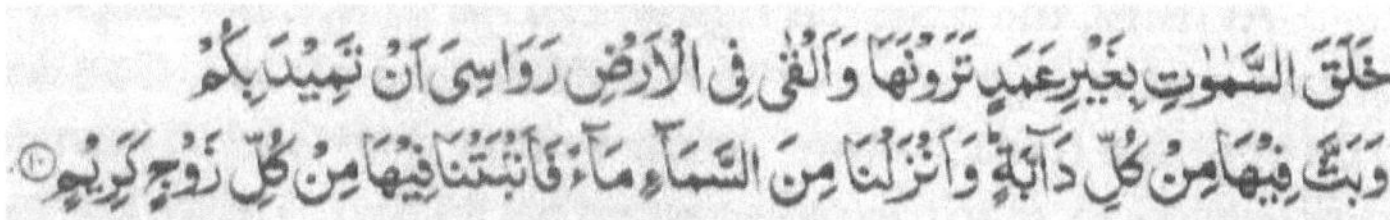

Tr:- "He created the heavens without any pillars that ye can see: He set on the earth mountains standing firm, lest it should shake with you; and He scattered, through it beasts of all kinds. We send down rain from the sky and produce on the earth every kind of noble creature in pairs".

The above-mentioned Quranic verses. have validated the assertions of Daleel Sahib. about the significance of pairs in his poem kayinath.

EQUALITY: -

Distinction based on status, bear no validity in the Kingdom of God, Divine grace does not depend on man's birth in any specified community. While conferring his boons and extending His Privileges, God chooses only those who proclaim their inability to maintain themselves, who are prepared to entrust themselves as well as the fruits of their belongings to God and wait for His directives.

God probes into the purity of their hearts, their sincerity and their stead-fast attitudes. Even a man of scholastic merits or one who is born amidst affluence cannot claim proximity to God if he is devoid of Faith, whereas a humble man of low birth, but of good principles can approach Him easily. Such pious people are regarded by God as His sincere devotees who are entitled to material or spiritual benefactions.

Those who are acquainted with the truth about the unity the importance of equality and brotherhood. Though this world is beet light of unity of creations. our narrow view is confined to the different appearances Here the unity of creations is dealt with in connection the aspect equality The beauty of God is the only source for all the colors in this world. The life of man is the highest creation of God is dependent on the rays of the sun, the inferior creation. It seems to us to be the irony of nature. But all Creations, including man are manifestations one God. Hence ridicule or scorn a man is equal to contempt and insult to God. Those who have mystichave experiences. Will feel that equality should prevail on all the creations of God. These believers will also give importance to the trait of humility. All the dependents of God equal one another. because their essence is same. namely, the effulgence of God. There is no factor which determines inequality in the estimation of God. God loves only persons are God- fearing and keenly interested in adhering His Laws. The wrong notion of inequality incolor. race, wealth and status is nothing but superstition.

The inferior and down-trodden people should not be looked down upon by superior and affluent people. All should enjoy the same human rights. Life should be Beauty Of unity and melody of affinity, brotherhood and equality.

Claiming no superiority is humility. Humility and sense of equality greatness and virtue. Of all religions, Islam has laid greatest emphasis on equality There custom of caste system and untouchability and priesthood and no differences social status. The Islamic equality is put into practice especially during prayer time when Muslims stand shoulder to shoulder in the Mosque or stand in the same line without minding their social status. Generally, in the Mosques, prayers are lead by very poor paid Imams.In the yearly days of the advent of Islam, when slavery was in vogue. the masters stood behind Prophet Muhammed (SAW) emphasized to the greatest extent that all human beings equal before God. irrespective of financial and social status. Many Prophets and spiritual leaders have been spreading the message of unity among all people of all faiths. They attempted bring about a transformation in the society and equality in the lives of the people. All of us must believe in the philosophy of one God. one caste and one reality All religions promise rewards for excellence of good heart and feeling of equality and punishment will be awarded for the proud people.

Before the advent of Islam, the world society was divided into several divisions' distinctions. The people of high ranks and status claimed superiority and condemned the unfortunate people to the position of their own animals of husbandry. As a result, the poor people became the victims of oppression and torment inspite of their hard labour.

During the period of the Caliphate of the second Khalifa. Hazrat Umar Khataab, after the expiry of Prophet Muhammad (SAW), the Islamic empire became unimaginably vast and expansive due to the numerous conquests by the valorous and enthusiastic Muslim Mujahideens. In his period Muslims conquered more than half the territory of the then known world. In his period Syria was the dominion of Roman Empire. Once when Muslims had to defend against the Roman invasion from Syria, Hazrath Abu Ubalda had to take the command of the Muslim army. When the Roman Commander In Syria, appealed for treaty, he agreed The Romans invited Abu Ubaida and arranged a very grand feast With numerous varieties of Roman dishes. When the Muslim Commander had a glance at the dishes, he asked, "'Is this sort of meals is being offered to the soldiers of your army?". The Roman Commander replied. "How can such food be provided for the soldiers?". Hazrat Abu Ubaida said. "By God, I cannot feast on such a luxurious food. According to Islamic principle, the true commander is that person who consumes the food what is provided for the soldiers". The Roman Commander was surprised at the principles of absolute simplicity and sense of equality of the Muslims.

There are several anecdotes in Islamic History when the valorous Negro Slaves and young slaves were given the assignments of Commanders-in-Chief of the Muslim army, during the Holy Wars called Jihad on the basis or equality the masters of the slaves and the great leaders of the tribes had to follow the slave commanders. Their pomp, pride and the sense of superiority were erazed to the ground by Islam. Only merit and bravery were given the first preference, and priority.

Human beings are equipped with the greatest potentialities. Islam teaches us the Sanctity of human personality and confers equal rights upon all Without any distinction of any sort. Hazrat Umar had employed a freed slave, Hazrat Nafi Bin Abd-al-Haris as the Collector of Makkah. That freed slave was employed as the collector, because he Was well- versed in Islamic Shariat and adhered to all the

Divine Laws. Claiming no superiority is humanity, Humanity and sense of equality are the hallmark of greatness and virtue.

S.Al. Baqara-2: 179: -

وَ لَكُمْ فِى الْقِصَاصِ حَيٰوةٌ يٰٓاُولِى الْاَلْبَابِ لَعَلَّكُمْ تَتَّقُوْنَ

Tr:- In the law of Equality, there is (saving of) life to you. O. ye men of understanding! That ye may restrain yourselves".

H:- "The Arab is not superior to Non-Arab; nor a non-Arab is superior to an Arab; neither the white to the black, nor black to the white. except on the basis of Taqwa or fear of God".

The above-mentioned Hadith has been extracted from the sermon delivered by Prophet Muhammed (SAW) on the occasion of his last pilgrimage, about equality.

BROTHERHOOD .

Though, Islam aimed-at Universal brotherhood, Islam in its initial stage introduced brotherhood after Hijrat Madinah among the Muhajirins(Refugees) of Makkah and Ansars (Helpers) of Madinah. Before the advent of Islam the whole world,especially Arabia was steeped in ignorance and the people were extremely uncompromising. Every clan claimed superiority Which 'led to hostility among the different tribes. The feeling of brotherhood was unknown.

As soon as Prophet Muhammed -(SAW) migrated from Makkah to Madinah, the three main and tough tasks which laid the foundations stone for brotherhood for the first time in the world; establishment of Islamic state through prudent diplomatic policies with Jews and Christians of Madinah and the Construction of Mosque; which is called Masjid-e-Nabvi for the congregational prayers.

The refugees of Makkah who left their homes. property and gave up their trades for the sake of Islam. were in dire need of establishment of a new fraternity.The new converts and (helpers) of Madinah generously. affectionately and gladly agreed to the idea of Prophet (SAW) of fostering brotherhood with the refugees. Each Ansar took one refugee as his own brother. The Ansars of Madinah gave the refugees, food, employments half of their income profits and produce and even half of their property. This sort of promotion of brother hood is indeed unique in the history of mankind. The brother hood and feelings of fellowship. created by Prophet Muhammed (SAW), produced a healthy and enjoyable atmosphere which was very beneficial to the establishment of Islamic State and propagation of Islam. The Introduction of Islamic brotherhood gradually had Its influence over other people to promote brotherhood in greater scale which actually resulted In the formation of universal brotherhood and international organizations, such as Lions International. Rotary Club, Round Table Club, Y's Man's Club, Round Table Club, Free Masons, Y.M.C.A. Junior Chamber, Red Cross Association and United Nation's Organization etc.

Allah is the universal guardian of the believers. They are the Universal Party of Allah where there are no exclusion of anyone. Islam has framed a code of conduct and discipline for both employers and employees and it is Islam which has bound the employers and employees relationship of brotherhood and equality. Equality and brotherhood are the bases for mutual love, regard and healthy industrial relationships.

S. Aal-e-Imran-3: 103: -

وَلَكُمْ فِى الْقِصَاصِ حَيٰوةٌ يّٰاُولِى الْاَلْبَابِ لَعَلَّكُمْ تَتَّقُوْنَ

Tr:-And hold fast all together by the Rope Which Allah (Stretches of for you), and be not divided among yourselves, and remember with gratitude, Allah's favor on you; for ye were enemies and He Joined your hearts in love, so that by HIS Grace ye became brothren; and you were on the brink of the pit of fire and He saved you from It. Thus, doth Allah make high signs clear to you; that ye may be guided."

S. Hu'uraat-49: 10: -

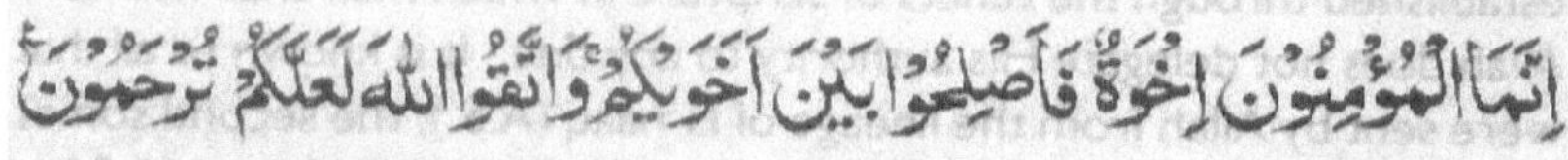

Tr:-The believers are but Single brotherhood; so make peace and reconciliation between your two (Contending) brothers, and fear Allah that he may receive mercy".

H:- "Islam demands united life for man Unity is bliss. Disunity misery. In loving devotion to Allah, live a united life as brothers unto each other"

H:- •Muslims being brothers to one another. A Muslim should not leave another Muslim helplessly nor speak untruth to him, nor oppress him. Surely each one of you the mirror for the other. If you see any short-coming in him, remove it". (Tirmizi, Mishkat).

H:- "A Muslim is the one who avoids harming other Muslim with tongue and hands. And a Mujahid is one who gives up all which Allah has forbidden".

H:- Say Salam to your brother Muslim whenever you meet him".

H:- "Eat together. not alone, for blessings come with Company". (Ibn-e-Maja)

H:- 'Help by stopping your brother when he commits a wrong or when a wrong is committed against him". (Bukhari)

Quranic.Verses and Ahadis-e-Nabvi have proved the importance of Islamic brotherhood which has led to universal brotherhood.

DEMOCRACY: -.

In this chapter. the poet has explained as to what the nature of Islamic democracy should be. Democracy is a system of Government which is for the people, of the people and by the people. But before the advent of Islam, monarchy was prevailing all over the world, with prince or princess having the right of inheritance of the throne. The lower classes of people suffered a lot under the tyranny. despotism and dictatorship of the monarchs. Of course. a supreme authority is indispensable for the good administration of a country. provided, the common public is benefited by the system of monarchy.

It was God Himself who formulated Islamic Laws which have been included in the Constitutions of the Islamic States. Thousands of years before the birth of our Prophet (SAW)

Prophet Ibrahim (A.S.) was given hint by Almighty Allah, about democracy.

S. Al-Baqara -2: 124:-

Tr:- "And (remember) when his Lord tried Abraham with (His) commands. and he fulfilled them. He said Lo! I have appointed you the leader for mankind. Abraham said, and of my offspring (will there be leaders)?' He said. "My covenant included not wrong doers".

From the above quoted Quranic verse, it is clearly revealed that government should be established through the tenets of scripture in which man shall not have any authority because Allah does not delegate His authority to anyone. It is known to all that a number of prophets were sent by Allah from the lineage of Is-haaq (A.S.), the second son of Ibrahim (A.S.) and our last Prophet Muhammad (SAW) was the descendent of Ismail (A.S.), the first son Of Ibrahim (A.S.). Some of the Prophets were also leaders of their tribes. But on that occasion Allah refused to promise Ibrahim (AS.) that He would make leaders among his descendants. He was given to understand that pious and meritorious persons should be awarded with leadership. This was a hint of democracy, one of the Divine Laws.

Daleel Sahib says that the nationals of a nation may be literate and illiterate. religious and irreligion's; healthy and sick; rich and poor, selfless and selfish; desperate and prosperous. At all circumstances, the diplomacy and policies of the Government of a nation such as economic policy, political policy, social policy and administrative policy must be based upon the sound Principals'comprehensible tenets of a true religion. The functions of the present democratic world is excessively defective and deficient; and the and culture are of the feeling of brotherhood and equality. Consequently. the public is desperately in distress. In a true democracy, the democrats must be generous, just, humble and treat the people as their equals. Prosperity of the nation lies in the true spirit of democracy Equality, brotherhood, justice, affinity, impartiality, selflessness and above all the unity of God and unity of creations must rule over the hearts of the democrats.

The system of Government must be based on consultations and not on autocratic manner of the state should not have arbitrary powers at any Situation. He should not change the constitutional laws without referring them to the public or a team of A writer has beautifully explained that the western world believes in the body of democracy. while believes in its soul; one believes in counting the heads while the other in weighing them". The most important aspect of democracy in Islam is that, the Will of the people is taken into account positively and effectively, rather than just fulfilling the standard custom.

A well-known scholar of Islamic studies. Sayed Abul Ala Maududi states. "The Islamic Government is a Divine Democratic Government, because the Muslims have been given a limited democratic popular sovereignty of God. Democratic state with strong foundation of absolute justice is one of the idealisms of Islam.

An eminent Kannada communist Mr. Bhaskar Rao spoke in a symposium held in Shimoga on 9th of January 1994 on the topic, "Threat to country through Communalism or Religion"At the outset he said, "Islam is a most democratic religion and teaches respect for other religions for bids imposition forcibly. It is not the religion which teaches communalism. but it is communalism which distorts and exploits religion in the country. We must fight communalism".

He quoted the Quranic verse "For you, your religion, and for me mine". This is the substance of Sur-a-e-Kafirurn: the 109th chapter of Quran. This verse clearly reveals that Islam is a democratic religion. Islam treats all religions with respect and does not try to impose itself on any one. A principle which is clearly stated in Quran is that, compulsion is inadmissible in matters of faith. What Muslims are required to do is to explain their faith to other people and to call on them to believe in it. The democratic aspects in Islam is obvious in the following Quranic verse .-

S.Al-Baqara-2:256: -

لَاۤ إِكْرَاهَ فِي الدِّيْنِ قَدْ تَّبَيَّنَ الرُّشْدُ مِنَ الْغَيِّ فَمَنْ يَّكْفُرْ بِالطَّاغُوْتِ وَيُؤْمِنْ بِاللهِ فَقَدِ اسْتَمْسَكَ بِالْعُرْوَةِ الْوُثْقٰى لَا انْفِصَامَ لَهَا وَاللهُ سَمِيْعٌ عَلِيْمٌ ۝

Tr:- "Let there be no compulsion in religion. Truth stands clear from Error: whoever evil and believes in Allah hath grasped the most trustworthy hand-hold that never breaks and Allah heareth and knoweth all things"

Islam urges the Muslims to assess the nobility of the people and hand over the leadership to the noblest and most trustworthy of them. This injuction is absolutely democratic.

S. Nisa-4:58: -

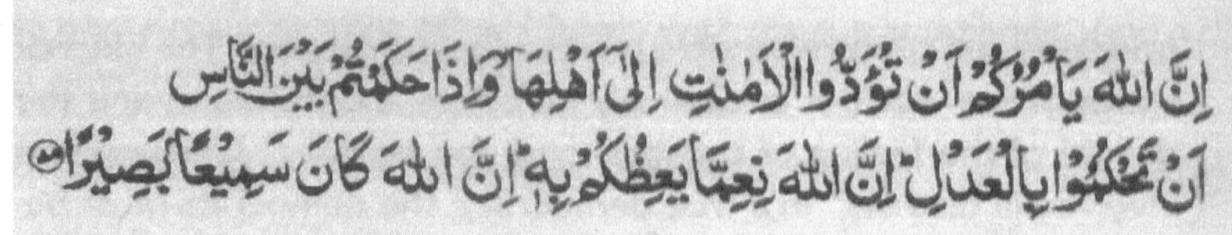

Tr:- 'Allah doth command you to render back your trusts to those to whom they are due and when ye judge between man and man and ye judge with justice; verily, how excellent is the teaching which He giveth you! For Allah is He who heareth and seeth all things"

This clearly indicates that Islam does not allow the right of inheritance of throne or leadership; but the head of a nation or community must be elected on the basis of his merit, Piety and prudence.

H:- "My Lord, beseech you to grant health, rectitude. trust worthiness. good manners and satisfaction with you". (Al-Mufrad, Baihaqi etc.)

Prophet Muhammad had always great fear of God. He frequently prayed God to guide him on the path of righteousness especially because the responsibilities of a religious preceptor and head of the Muslim State fell on his shoulders. The whole Muslim Community made him its monarch. But he always requested the people not to call him the King of the Muslim State. He behaved like a humble servant of God and sincere servant of the public.

Now, we should know the meaning of democracy the significance of democracy and the types of democratic procedures like (1) General Election (2) Referendum and (3) Plebiscite.

Democracy: Democracy is a form of government in which the supreme power vests in the people collectively and is administered by them or by officers appointed by the common people through elections. Hence, it is defined as the system of government "of the people, by the people and for the people". There is no much difference in the democracy and Republic, Republic is a form of government in which the supreme power vests in the representatives elected by the people.

Democracy: Election

Election is the act of selecting or choosing the administrators of the Government, through the votes of the whole common public or by a constituent body. In a democracy every adult (major) native is entitled with the right of franchise. Every native of the state can exercise his right of franchise with his free will, on the occasions of the general and public elections.

Democracy: Referendum

Referendum is a democratic principle or practice of submitting directly to the vote of the entire electorate, the legislative questions at issues of representative assemblies. Election pertains to the selection of the administrators while referendum pertains to the choice of the legislative issues.

Democracy:Plebiscite: -

This is a type of election which is confined to the district. This is a decree by the entirenation obtained by an appeal to universal suffrage. This is a democratic method of obtaining an express,on or option upon a certain point from the inhabitants of a district,

In the case of referendum, the legislative issues of the nation are directly submitted to the vote of the entire electorate in representative assemblies. In the case of plebiscite, the issues are referred to only inside the district.

Though democracy was hinted at. by Allah Almighty to Ibrahim (A.s.), it was put into practice, after the Hijrat of Prophet Muhammed (SAW) to Madinah. Now. it is time to discuss as to what type of democracy was being practised during the life time of Prophet Muhammad (SAW) and during the period of Khulafa-e-Rashideen after the expiry of our Prophet. Islam was the founder of democracy in the world. As the Zirnrnis (Non-Muslims in the Islamic empire) were the anti-islamic elements. they were not given the power to vote for the issues of Islamic State. General elections, referendum and plebiscite were held, but only Muslims had the right of franchise.

Plebiscite of the Battle of Uhad:-

When the army of the Quraish from Makkah was advancing towards Madinah in BAH with the intention Of attacking the Muslims of Madinah in order to avenge their loss in the battle of Badr in 2 A.H. our Prophet (SAW) received the following revelation:

S.A.al-e-lmran-3: 1 59 (Part of the stanza): -

Tr:- "It is the part of the Mercy of Allah that thou dost deal gently with them. Were thou severe or harsh-hearted they would have broken away from about thee: so, pass over (their faults), and ask for (Allah's) forgiveness for them; and consult them in affairs (of moment). Then, when thou hast taken a decision, put thy trust in Allah. For Allah loves those who put their trust (in Him)".

Though our Prophet (SAW) was a good politician and a prudent democrat, on this occasion, Allah instructed our Prophet (SAW) to place the issue for referendum whether to confront the enemies far from Madinah or to defend Madinah from within the city Prophet (SAW) and his elder companions were of opinion that defense should be put from the city; but the youngsters in the army suggested to move out of Madinah to keep the enemy away. It is a notable point that though our Prophet (SAW) was of opinion that the defense should be put from within the city, he agreed to move out of the city because the opinion of the youngsters turned out to be the majority view. He never minded that the majority of the people spoke against his opinion. This is what is called the real democracy, The 300 Munafiqeen (who pretended to be Muslim but actually, the spies of the Mushrikeens of Makkah) by their wicked strategy broke away from the army leaving only seven hundred Muslims to confront with three thousand strong and well-equipped enemies from Makkah. According to the results of the referendum, our Prophet, proceeded from Madinah and met the enemy in the place called Uhad.

H:- "Whomsoever consults others, finds guidance; and who does not, might fall on evil days"

How the different situations arose and how the principles of democracy were followed by the Muslims regarding the selections and elections of the Khalifas, after the expiry of our Prophet (SAW) are worth mentioning.

On the day of expiry of Prophet Muhammad (SAW). there was a serious tussle between the Muhajirin (Muslim refugees who migrated from Makkah to Madinah) and the Ansars of Madinah (those Muslims of Madinah who gave the refugees asylum and helped them in every possible way) over the issue of the appointment of the successor (khalifa of Islamic Empire) of our Prophet (SAW). In order to avert the bloodshed in the Masjid-e-Nabvi, Hazrat Abu Bakr Siddiq and Hazrat Umar Farooq hurried to the spot. According to the wish of our Prophet (SAW), Hazrat Ali had to remain at home in order to perform the duty of giving bath and shrouding his body, assisted by Hazrat Abbas and his two sons. Some Ansars of Madinah were power crazy, but at the same time, all of them had high regards for our Prophet (SAW), his ahadis and his prophecies.

At first, the Ansars expressed their wish that Sa'd Bin Ibada might by appointed as the Khalifa. Sad Bin Ibada said that the claim of the Ansars was lawful and just, as they gave protection to Prophet Muhammad and his companions. For all such things, the Muhajirin, kept quiet. Then the conservations among the Ansars, hurt the feelings and honor of the Muhajirin. Thus, the tussle began. Hazrat Abu Bakr pacified all, promising to ponder over the issue without prejudice, and appointing the Caliph at the earliest convenience. Hazrat Basheer bin Numan, inspite of his being an Ansar spoke in favor of Muhajirin who hailed from the Makka tribe Quraish (the tribe of our Prophet), and asked the Ansars, "Did we help the Muhajii-in with the aspiration of the Caliphate; or for the sake of Allah, His Apostle and Islam?" The supporters of Sa'd Bin Ibadagot angry with Hazrat Basheer Bin Numan. But when Hazrat Basheer reminded them of the prophecy of our Prophet (PBUH) that Khalifa would hail from Quraish, the Ansars withdrew their claim, who had great love and regard for Prophet Muhammad (SAW). It must be noted here that it was not his wish, but it was only the prophecy of our Prophet. Now Abu Bakr (RAA) sponsored two candidates for election who were present at that time. They were Hazrat I-Jmar Farooq and Hazrat Abu Ubaida (Quraishis). Both of them instantly said that they never liked to become Khalifa in the presence of Hazrat Abu Bakr Siddiq who was the most deserving personality. Saying so, both of them placed their hands on the hand of Abu Bakr as the sign of oath of allegiance. The third man to offer the oath was Basheer Bin Numan. His power of reasoning, broad-mindedness, good gesture and affectionate attitude towards the refugees were most applaudable. Soon after this magnanimous act of Basheer Bin Numan, the whole gathering of the Muslims clustered round Abu Bakr (RAA) to offer their oath With whole hearted willingness. The selection of the Khalifa started and ended with democratic process.

During his last ailment our Prophet (PBIJH) enlisted ten names of his deserving companions for candidature for the election of Khalifa after his expiry. He also said that Khalifa must be elected according to the choice of the people. This was the first election of the head of the Stace in the History of the world. Soon after the martyrdom of Hazrath Abu Bakr the whole population of the Muslims, enthroned Hazrat Omar (RAA) as the Khalifa.

Nobody wanted to consent withhim Thatwasthe case of consensus which was also a sort of democratic measure.

After the of Hazrath Umar Farooq, Hazrat Usman Osman and Hazrat Ali (RAA) the two candidates for election. Neither of them was thought that he would be able to serve Islam more than any other person because of the frights that the innocence of Hazrat Usman might entail difficulties to Islam and cause confusion 'n the Islamic empire. only in order to save Islam from treacherous people of whom Hazrat Osman would become the Victim. Hazarat Ali contested According to the last instructions of the dying Khalifa Hazrat Umar thaught of electing (ho Khalifa was not placed before the public and individual, suffrage was not exercised.HazratAbdur-Rahman Bin Auf had to hurriedly run about the streets of Madina for meeting the lenders of clans and for enquiring about their choice. The result of his enquiries was in favor of Hazrat Usman. Hence the election of Hazrat Osman could only be called half" democracy.

As feared by Hazrat Ali (RAA) the noble and innocent Khalifa Hazrat Usman became the victim of suspicion of a group of Muslims due to the mischief of his own cousin and personal secretary Marwaan Bin Hikam. That group of Muslims decided to murder the Khalifa In order to safeguard the life Of Hazrat Usman, Hazrat Ali (RAA) posted his sons Hazrat ImamHasan and Hazrat Imam Hussain at the door of Hazrat Osman (R) to protect his life at the risk of their lives. But the protestors of Khalifa Osman climbed up the roof of his house got down and murdered him while he was reciting Quran. Hazrat Ali was greatly worried and upset over this sorrowful incident. The warring group forced Hazrat Ali to accept be the fourth Khalifa, but he refused to accept the Caliphate, defining the throne of Caliphate as the throne of thorns. Under the threat of general massacre. Hazrat Ali had to accept the Caliphate quite unwillingly. In fact the Muslims of the Islamic empire except a few were in favor Hazrat Ali. The minds of those few Muslims were poisoned by the hypocrites who instigated them by saying that the murder of Hazrat Osman was due to the secret plot of Hazrat Ali', and he posted his sons at the door of the Khalifa for the eye wash of the public and to cover up his rebellious conspiracy against Hazrat Usman. Among those who believed the false allegations against Ali were the noble personalities and close companions of our Prophet (PBUH), Hazrat Zubair and Hazrat Talha. Later on, due to some events and prophecy of our Prophet (PBUH). Hazrat Ali's innocence was proved.

After ruling for five years. Hazrat Ali was murdered by Ibn-e-Muljam. Then, his son Imam Hasan was enthroned by the Muslims by force. So far, i.e., during the period of Khulafae-Rashideen, Khalifas were elected by different kinds of democratic processes, In Order to avoid the bloodshed among the Muslims, Imam Hasan had to enter into an agreement With Hazrat Ma'wia and resign his caliphate of his territory, The whole of Islamic empire came under the control. Of Hazrat Amir Ma'wia, the son of Abu Sufyan and Hinda. Amr Ma'Wia was the founder of Ummayad Dynasty It was actually a very sorrowful and painful of Islamic democracy Autocracy.

Even then the democracy introduced by our Prophet (PBUH) in the world did not go invain. It has been- having its effect through ages, The emergence of existing republics the Muslim world and rest-of the world are the results of the introduction of Islamic democracy.The political revolution in the despotic systems of governments such as the French Revolutionand Iranian Revolution and establishments of republics were due to the influence of democracy which has also been advocated in Quran.

Now let us discuss some systems of governments and find out which ones are acceptable to Islam.

REPUBLIC:

This is a form of government in which supreme power is vested in the representatives elected by the people. Common people have the voice for their demands through their respective political which have representations in the central governments . This system was put to practice due to the directives contained in Quran.

DEMOCRACY:

This is a system of government in which the supreme power is vested in the people collectively and is administered by them or by officers appointed by them. In this system human rights are being exercised to the extent possible. Democracy is defined as a form of government Of the people, by the people and for the people". just as in the Republic. There are many verses in Quran in which democratic processes are advocated.

BUREAUCRACY:

This is a system of government, centralized in graded series of officials. responsible only for their cheifs and controlling every detail of public and private life. In Islam merits of piety and capability are taken into account. Islam has no room for grading.

PLUTOCRACY:

This is a system of government by the wealthy. Islam does not discriminate between high and low; and poor and wealthy; and slave and master. Islam is dead against this system.

ARISTOCRACY:

Aristocracy is a form of government by the men of high birth and best conditions. where political powers vest in upper classes of people. This system was most prevalent in the world during the Feudal Age. As Islam does not distinguish between high birth and low birth; and high status or low status, it can never accept such a type of system. Islam has laid much emphasis on the principle of equality.

MONARCHY:

This is a system of government where the sovereignty and supremacy vest in a single person. Before the advent of Islam, monarchy was prevailing almost all over the world, of course, with a few contemporary Aristocratic Governments. In the tribal system. the leader was the sovereign of the tribe. In the Monarchial system which are still present in some of the countries, princes and princesses have the right of inheritance of the throne and the royal property Of course a superior authority is essential for efficient and good administration of a country. In the olden days, the lower classes of people suffered a lot, under the despotism and dictatorship of the monarchs. Islam permits monarchial system be benefited. Islam is quite opposed to the custom of Inheritance or appointment of crown ponce by the King. The Head of the state must be selected by the choice of the people in which the real democracylies. The monarchs which are prevalent now are different from the ancient ones. In some countries, the monarchs are prevalent now are different ministers and executive heads. The common public, the political parties appoint and the Parliamentarians have got the powers to elect the administrators. According to Islam. The prescribed punishments to the culprits and criminals. But now. for this portfolio have been established. In some monarchial system of governments democracy is not being practiced. Those monarchs are yet to be civilized.

Prophet Muhammad (SAW). was a monarch. Khalifa Hazrat Abu Bakr Siddiq, Hazrat Farooq. Hazrat Osman Ghani. Hazrat Ali (RAA), Imam Hasan (who ruled only for Six month) were the monarchs ofthe period of Khulafa-e-Rashideen. These monarchs and khajifa Bin Abdul Azeez who hailed from the Ummayad Dynasty, followed the footsteps of prophet Muhammad (SAW) by cent per cent. Monarchy with the democratic procedures was taught to the world by Islam.

FEUDALISM:

The Feudal system started about a century before the advent of Islam (Age of Ignorance) and was prevailing in most parts of the world till the beginning of the 16th century. In this system, during the Middle Ages vassals held lands from Lord Superior on condition of Military Service. Vassals are those people who render homage to their superiors.

Feudal System started in that period which is called in the History of the world, "The Age of Ignorance". In this age, the whole world was plunged into darkness which made the people the worst enemies of humanity. Islam came for the rescue of the world, to dispel darkness and to enlighten the minds of the people. After the advent of Islam. civilization and culture found their right path from darkness to light.

In the feudal age, the nobility exercised absolute powers over the common people who Wed in their estates. All the legislative, judicial and executive powers were in their hands. Their whims and fancies were the laws, by which, they ruled over the people. Since represented council were composed of members belonging to this class, it was but natural that the legislations they made would aim at protecting themselves, safeguarding their own privileges and interests. As for the common people, they had no privileges or any rights. They inherited poverty. slavery and humiliation and passed them on to their descendants. The significant economic development, which took place afterwards led the emergence of the Bourgeoisie, the new class of people which aspired to displace the nobility and to assume their privileges and prestige's. It was under the leadership of this emerging class, that the common people launched the tremendous and historical French Revolution in 1789. Unlike other nations the French Aristocrats continued feudalism till the 18[th]century. The royalties were called Aristocrats and the revolutionists were called the Republicans. Before the Revolution, numerous republicans were oppressed. persecuted and executed by the Aristocrats. At last justice triumphed and the Aristocrats were overpowered by the Republicans. Now the merciless executions of the Aristocrats was started by the Republicans. Even the King of France Louis XVI and his QueenMarie Antoinettewere slain under the guillotine. Those execution were the pleasant spectacles for the common people. By different wonderful strategy of the Britons. only a few Aristocrats could be saved, on humanitarian basis at the risk of their own lives, through the Strait of Dover which lies between France and England.

Such system of government without the principles of democracy cannot last long. Several revolutions took place from time to time including the recent Revolution of Iran. The revolutions and the establishments of Republics in the different parts of the world owe their origin to the Revolution of Islam. which brought the messages of equality, brotherhood, human rights and democracy. The Revolution of Islam awakened the consciousness of the world societies and made them fight for their lawful rights.

Daleel Sahib the poet, says that inspite of this much of progress and promotion of civilization 'n the world society, the democracy is still defective because Of the selfishness of the democrats. (Resurrection, rebirth, good and evil, pairs, psychology, hypnotism, dream.governments and revolutions).

CHAPTER – XXVI

PROVIDENCE AND RELIGION

Stanza. 177

26 /ربوبیت اور مذہب

177۔ ہے ربوبیت سے کیسا پرورش کا انتظام

ساتھ اندازوں کے موجودات عالم ہیں تمام

اسکی بخشائش میں ہے مقدار و ترتیب و نظام

ہر ضرورت اور حالت کا لحاظ اسکو ہے نام

ہر کسی کی پرورش میں آدمی ہو یا شجر

ہے برابر ایک ہی قانون قدرت جلوہ گر

نوٹ : اشیاء کے وجود پذیر ہونے سے پہلے انکی پرورش کے لیے سب ضروری

سامان موجود رہتے ہیں ----- دلیل

Tr: It is amazing how the providence of God has made arrangements for nourishing His creations and for their development with regulated system. Regarding His grants. His arrangement and system, the quantity is determined according to their need, In Divine Cherishing of every creation. whether it is man or tree, Divine law is ever active.

Stanza. 178

178 - ہے ربوبیت کی طولانی بہت ہی داستان

پرورش میں خلق کی مصروف ہے سارا جہاں

کر مک ناچیز بھی یہ کہ سکے بیشک یہاں

میری خدمت کے لیے ہیں یہ زمین و آسمان

جب ہے تن کی پرورش کے واسطے یہ اہتمام

روح انساں کے لیے کیا کچھ نہ ہوگا انتظام

Tr: The account of Providence is very lengthy, because the cherishing attribute of Allah Almighty, employs the whole universe in the service of His creations. Even a small worm, the existence of which is insignificant can say without any doubt that all the heavens and earth are at its service. When God has made such an elaborate arrangement for the development of the transitory body. He is sure to have much more vigilant supervision and arrangements for the evolution of soul which is eternal and worthier than the body.

Stanza. 179

179- ہے بہار زندگی مٹی کو آب آسمان

ہے وحی اللہ کی دل کو حیات جاوداں

یہ وہ بخشش ہے خدا کی جسکے آگے بے گماں

ہیچ ہے خود زندگی ناچیز ہر چیز گراں

یک نبی اللہ نے بھیجا ہر امت کے لئے

کی وحی اس پر کتاب اپنی ہدایت کے لئے

Tr: Just as the beauty of life on earth depends upon the water, showered from the sky the eternal life of man depends upon the Divine relations.Our very life and the most precious thing in this world is nothing when compared to the invaluable gift of Divine Revelations.

For every nation in the world, Almighty Allah has sent a Prophet (Preceptor for preaching) and revealed books on some of the Prophet for the guidance of humanity.

Stanza. 180

180- أن رسولوں میں کسی کی ہو جو منکر عقل خام

وہ سمجھ سکتی نہیں قدرت کا روحانی نظام

اس پر عالمگیر رحمت کا عقیدہ ہو حرام

وہ نفاق و جہل و فتنہ کا ہو سبب لا کلام

درس ایمان و عمل تھی جو ہوئی نازل کتاب

منکران بے خرد تھے مورد رنج و عذاب

Tr:- Those whose defective wisdom rejects faith in these prophets, it cannot understand the splendid Divine administration, established for the sake of the soul. The person Who is the cause for ignorance, enmity and mischief, can never hope or believe in world-conquering blessings. The unwise people who rejected the scriptures, which brought guidance for faith and endeavor became the victims of torment and trouble.

Stanza. 181

181۔ ہر صحیفہ آسمانی جب محرف ہو گیا

پڑ گئی اہل مزہب میں تخالف کی بنا

نوع آدم ہو گئی توحید سے نا آشنا

عقل انسان ہو گئی وہم و ہوس میں مبتلا

جونہی اقوام میں جہاں ربط قائم ہو گیا

دین عالمگیر کا محتاج عالم ہو گیا

Tr: When the scriptures underwent corruptions and adulteration, the people of different faiths began to have' different contentions, regarding their religions, Human beings lost their belief in the Unity of God, and they became the victims of apprehension misgiving and covetousness. When the nations of the world became closer to each other, they were unfortunate to be breft of the world-conquering true religion.

Stanza. 182

182 ۔ کون ہر مذہب میں تفریق حق و باطل کرے

کفر کی ظلمت کو پھونکے جلوہ توحید سے

وحدت ادیان کی خلق اللہ کو تعلیم دے

دین کو کامل بنائے ہر زمانے کے لیے

یہ فرائض کس طرح انجام دے عقل بشر

یہ مہم اسلام سے کی ہے ربوبیت نے سر

Tr: Who can distinguish between truth and falsehood and dispel the darkness of infidelity by means of beauty of the unity of God? Who can instill the belief of unity of Religions In the minds of people and the Religion of God a perfect one? This obligatory duty was undertaken by the Providence of Almighty Allah.

Stanza.183

183۔ زیر فرماں ہے ربوبیت کے قدرت کا نظام

ساتھ ہی تخلیق کی تکمیل کا بھی انتظام

ایک بہتر چیز ہوتی ہے بجائے چیز خام

تا رہے اشیاء انفع کا زمانے میں قیام

چیز ہو جاتی ہے جو بیکار دنیا میں کہیں

ارتقاء کے سیل میں قائم وہ رہ سکتی نہیں

Tr: The Divine Administration is under the command of His Providence. When God creates anything, He does it along with the arrangements for its perfection. Till the beneficial things exist in this world they are good, instead of being defective. A useless thing in this world cannot evolve.

Stanza. 184

184۔ نعمتیں اپنی خدائے پاک نے اتمام کیں

اس کی رحمت سے مکمل ہو گیا دیں مبین

آیتیں قرآن کی محفوظ ساری ہو گئیں

آشکار یکبارگی سب ہو گئے اسرار دیں

زندگی پیغمبر کامل کی اور اُم الکتاب

رہنمائی کے کافی ہیں تا یوم الحساب

Tr: Almighty Allah has showered all his blessings and bounties, among which the most precious one is the clear and accomplished religion, Islam. By the preservation of all the Quranic verses all the secrets of religion have been disclosed forever. The life of the ideal Prophet Muhammed (SAW) and Best Scripture Quran are enough for guidance till the Day of the Reckoning.

Stanza. 185

185۔ایک ہی حالت میں رہتی ہے کہاں بزم جہاں

ہر ادائے زندگی میں ہے تغیر ہر زماں

خلق پر یوں تو زمانے کا تلون ہے عیاں

یک حقیقت ہے نگاہ عام سے لیکن نہاں

ہیں اٹل سارے قوانین خدائے لم یزل

گو بدلتا ہے زمانہ یہ نہیں جاتے بدل

نوٹ: اللہ کا قانون ہے جو پہلے سے چکا آتا ہے اور تو اللہ کے قانون میں کوئی تبدیلی

نہیں پائے گا۔۔۔۔۔۔ قرآن ۔۔۔۔۔۔۔دلیل

Tr: The capriciousness and fickle-mindedness of the people are due to the change in the world society and its activities. Though there is change in everything with the passage of time, the Laws of the Eternal God are certain and unchanged.

Stanza. 186

186 یہ جہاں آئین بدلیں ہو وہیں برہم جہاں

ہے حقیقت اُن کی قرآن کے اصول جاوداں

جو انہیں توڑے کبھی خود ٹوٹ جائے ہے گماں

ہے ترقی وہ تغیر جو ہو طاعت سے عیاں

ہے جہاں اللہ کی ہے مثل یک فعلی کتاب

ہے کلام اللہ یک قولی کتاب لا جواب

Tr: If it is tried to change the law Of Quran, the universe will be upset. The promotion in the life of man and change in his life depend upon the submission to Divine Laws. If anybody disobeys them, they will be destructed because Quran is a matchless scripture which expounds the necessity of strife.

Stanza.187

187۔ کس ہدایت سے تہی ہے یہ کتاب لازوال

کس صداقت کے لئے اس میں نہیں حسن کمال

حکمت رب پر نہ ہو عقل بشر کا احتمال

حکم باری کا کبھی ہے سود ہوتا ہے محال

دین برحق کو سمجھنا قابل اتمام ہے

احمقانہ حکمت کامل پہ ایک الزام ہے

Tr:-'The Eternal Book Quran is neither devoid of any guidance, nor void of perfect beauty of truth. The human wisdom should not doubt about Devine Wisdom, as the command of God is never disadvantageous. It is our stupidity to accuse the perfect Wisdom of God.

Stanza. 188

188 ۔ ہادی دنیا و دیں تنویر ذات لا یزال

سپہر علم و عمل کے آفتاب لا زوال

حسن ہر خلق نکو کی انتہا انکا جمال

کس نبی کے حسن کو حاصل نہیں انمیں کمال

پیر و صادق جہاں میں رہبر کامل بنے

زندگی کے یہ سفر میں صاحب منزل بنے

Tr:- Prophet Muhammad (SAW). the brightest light of the effulgence of External God the best preceptor for this world and the hereafter. He is the Eternal Sun which induces Co acqul.re knowledge and to make endeavors Our Prophet's personal beauty is which reveals the beauty of his piety. His handsome personality has attained the perfection of the beauty of all other prophets. The true follower of his example, may become the perfect in every walk of human life and succeed by reaching the destination. Guide

Stanza. 189

189۔ جانتے ہو جن کو ہے تاریخ عالم پر عبور

بے نظیر اس مصلح اعظم کی ہستی ہے ضرور

اس حقیقت سے نہیں نا آشنا اہل شعور

پھر کبھی ایسے بشر کا ہو نہیں سکتا ظہور

رحمت عالم جو سالار نبی آدم نہو

ظلمت اوہام سے باہر کبھی عالم نہو

Tr:- Those who have perfect knowledge about the History of the world, will definitely know about the life of the matchless and eminent reformer, Prophet Muhammad (SAW). They also know that this sort of human being will never appear again.

Had he not become the leader of entire humanity, the darkness of superstitions would not have been expelled from this world.

Stanza. 190

190۔ در حقیقت ایک ہی اب تک ہوا ہے انقلاب

زندگی کا جس سے ہر شعبہ ہوا ہو باریاب

کھل چکی ہے جس سے دنیا پر ہر یک راہ ثواب

خلق پر جاری ہو جس کا فیض تا روز حساب

وہ رسول اللہ کا دنیا پہ فیض عام ہو

وہ خدا کی خاص رحمت خلق پر اسلام ہو

Tr:- In fact, there had been only one revolution in the real sense by which every aspect of human life was benefited, which has showed every method of acquiring piety and the benefactions till the Day of Judgement. God sent Prophet Muhammad (SAW) as a common beneficence for all, and the religion of Islam as His special bounty for humanity,

C: The poet has entitled this chapter as 'Providence and Religion "He has discussed allied subjects such as need of the guide (Quran), preceptors (Prophets and Saints), unity of religions, praise of Quran, Islam, aims and objectives of Islam , praise of Prophet Muhammad(SAW) and revaluation of Islam which played a vital role for the evolution of Islam and establishing and permanent religion and Islamic State a perfect.

By God's benevolence, He has created human beings in the best and highest form. Man's creation is higher than the creations of the angels. Another benevolence of Aliah is that He has gifted human beings with soul which has not been gifted to other living creatures of world. Because of His benevolence. His creative power became active. Out Of His mercy: He created all other things needed by the living creatures for their physical development. As Allah has gifted human beings with soul, it is also, His responsibility to provide necessities for spiritual elevation, spiritual perfection and for attaining our goal (Allah) by our piety and fear of God Allah has revealed scriptures for our guidance and has sent preceptors in all nations.

Providence is one of the Attributes of God which means cherishing, fostering, developing and evolving. For His creations, through His splendid and regulated administration, He keeps the sustenance ready before creating a thing. Every requirement was provided on earth and sky, well in advance before the advent of Adam (A.S.). For elucidation one simple example is enough. God provides milk in mother's breasts before the birth of the child. The Law of Divine Bounties for the development Of His creations is always active.

The account of God's providence is lengthy and interesting. He does not overlook even a minute insect but fosters it with all considerations. Though God creates things and makes arrangements for their evolution before hand. some useless things do not enter the field and scope of evolution. God has provided sustenance for the growth of man and animal in rain, in milk, in fruits. in honey, in heavenly bodies and in whole of the nature. In the case of man's life, Almighty Allah, provides opportunities for Social, Moral and Spiritual growth.

S.Al.Baqara -2:29 (Already quoted)

Tr: "It is He who has created for you all things that are on earth. Moreover, His designs comprehended the heavens, for

He gave order and perfection to the seven firmaments and of all things. He has perfect knowledge'

S. An-'am-6:97:

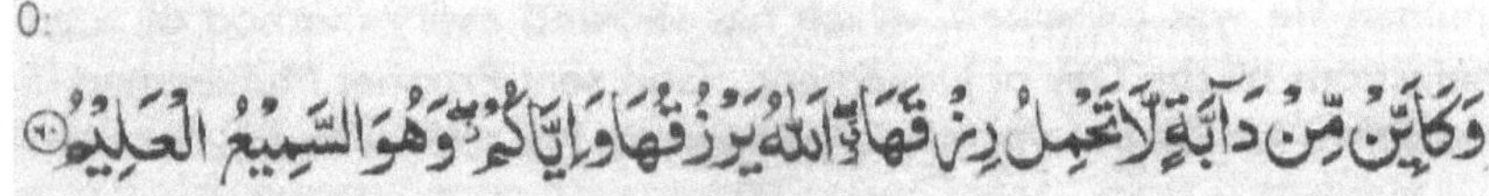

Tr: 'It is He Who maketh the stars (as beacons) for you. That ye may guide yourselves, with their help. through the dark spaces of land and sea; we detail our signs for people who know.

S. Ankabut-29:60:

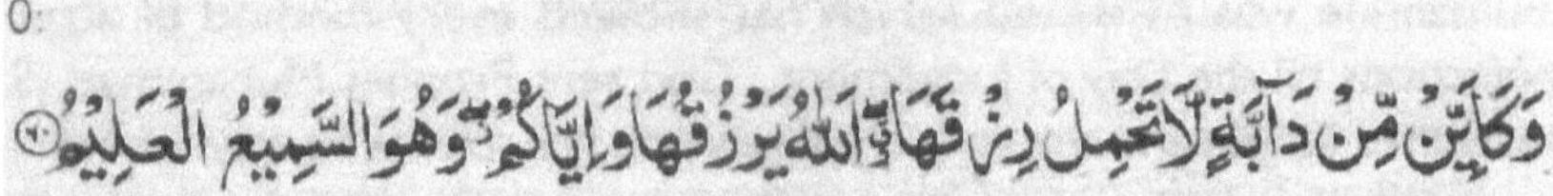

Tr: 'How many are the creatures that carry not their own sustenance? It is Allah Who feeds (both) them and you: for He hears and knows (All things)".

S. Ta-Ha- 20:132

Tr: -Enjoin prayer on thy people, and be constant therein. We ask thee not to provide sustenance. We provide it for thee. But the (fruit of the hereafter is for righteousness".

S. Hud-11:16:

Tr:- There is no moving creature on earth, but its sustenance dependeth on Allah. He knoweth the time and place of its definite abode and its temporary deposit. All is in a clear record".

God has provided us with wisdom and has given guidance against yielding to the influence immoral senses for obtaining spiritual perfection. A life of justice and righteousness is enjoined by God.

Now, let us discuss the importance of the guide (The Holy Quran) and the preceptors (Prophets and Saints) required for the spiritual perfection.

QURAN: MOTHER OF BOOKS:

The poet has called our Holy Quran "The Mother of Books", which is full of guidance for entire humanity at all times till the Day of Judgement. All of us know that the existence of mother is most precious and there can be no equal substitute for a mother. The importance of mother can be understood by the usage of the words such as "Mother Land" and "Mother Tongue". The poet has given the prefix "Mother" to the Holy Quran in order to explain that this is the most precious scripture, ever revealed, and there can be no book which is equal to this.

The improvement in prosperity and promotion in the life of man depend upon the eternal fundamental principles of Islam and obedience to Quranic Laws, because this is an unparalleled scripture of decisive pronouncement and expounder of endeavor and action. Quran is a scripture which is replete with perfect beauty of Truth and full of guidance for all walks of life. It is our own idiotic actions which doubt about the Divine Wisdom and remark it with Adverse allegations. The command of God and the tenets of Islam contained in Quran are always favorable and advantageous.

Quran is the only existing interpolated scripture, its original text being the same as it was at the time of its revelation, with cent per cent precision.

S.AL.Bagara -2:2

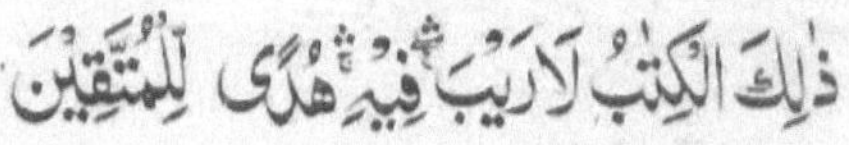

Tr: "This is the Book, in it is guidance, sure without doubt, to those who fear Allah".

H:- "The best mannered among you are dearest to me and have the nearest position to me on the day of Judgement".

The poet is justified in calling the Holy Quran, 'The Mother of Books".

PRAISE OF PROPHET MUHAMMAD AND NEED FOR PRECEPTOR

Next to prophets, saints also show the ways to realise God. Caught up inextricably in the web of worldly activities, a human being feels helpless and hence desires to get rid of the miseries and enjoys happiness. But he is baffled as how to put an end to his grief. Can he avoid sufferings by dominating over others as he is keen to experience joy somehow? prophets and saints gifted with spiritual wisdom have left us various directives to seek bliss. Spiritual knowledge reveals God's nature. The acquisition of spiritual knowledge alone can reveal the real nature that God creates and sustains the universe. The development of devotion together with the performance of the ordained religious duties is essential to enable a person who aspires to reach the goal of salvation and to get the objective fulfilled. The knowledge so secured through intense study under a proper guide will make him realise who the ultimate Reality is; what His Powers are; how He safeguards the interest of all the beings and in what manner. He provides opportunities for them to get their blemishes wiped out. They should serve God through worship. Spiritual preceptors train their disciples to chant God's name right from their childhood and advise them not to deviate from the high moral standard and not to accept the wrong notions. All the scriptures, revealed by Almighty Allah are in consonance with codes of ethics. Scriptural texts urge people to have faith in God, respect and obey their parents and preceptors who are but Divine emissaries.

Every human being has innate Divine qualities and potential to attain salvation sooner or later. In whichever, field a person will be placed in life. there is need for assistance from external forces. This will be all the truer when he desires to pursue the spiritual path or to take a disciplined way of life. For this purpose, the chastening and nurturing of a spiritual guide is necessary to put him on the safe and easy path.

People who cannot understand the significance of the missions of the Prophets and those who reject their guidance, contained in the scriptures, and those who do not tread the path of righteousness are sure to become the victims of trials and tribulations. They are ignorant and stupid people with wrong temptations. Hence, they are bereft of Divine grace. There are several anecdotes in the pre-Islamic history about the Divine wrath and the destruction of many a nation, which rejected the message of Allah through His Holy Prophets.

S. Baqara.2: 151

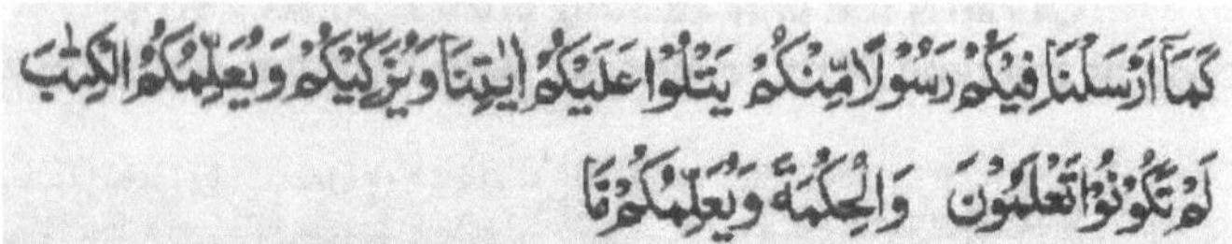

Tr: "A similar (favour, you have already received) in that we have sent among you an Apostle of your own, rehearsing to you our Signs and sanctifying you, and instructing you in Scripture and wisdom and in new knowledge".

S. Hadid-57:25   (Already quitted inChapter-17)

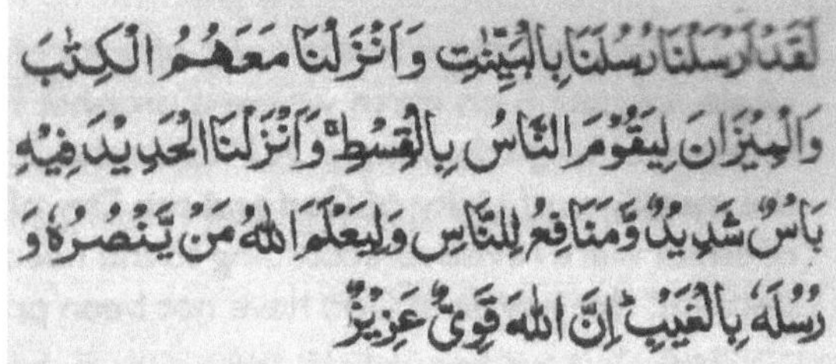

Tr: -'We sent aforetime our Apostles With clear signs and sent down with them the Book and the Balance of (Right and Wrong) that men may stand forth in justice; and we sent down in which is (material for) mighty war, as many benefits for mankind, that Allah may test. who it is that will help. unseen. Him and His Apostles; for Allah is full of strength, exalted in might (and able to enforce his will")

In the realm of spiritual field, the relationship between the spiritual leader and his disciple is a sacred and enduring one. The teacher has the utmost concern for the spiritual progress of his disciple.

UNITY OF RELIGIONS:

It is true that Almighty Allah sent prophets to all the nations for the guidance of humanity. Allah revealed some scriptures to the prophets through the angels. But when the scriptures were interpolated. the people were divided into different religious sects with mutual oppositions, difference of opinions and different concepts of mythology, Thus, this difference caused them to get involved in lust, greed, Adverse and absurd superstitions.

They lost faith in the Unity of God and their religions were no more inspired. In the classified and divided sects of the same religions, no person can squander or dispel the darkness of superstitious religion, by means of the initially inspired religion which advocated the unity of God. It is true that all the religions were descended from one and the same God. The advocacy of unity Of Religions requires to be taught and interpreted. Islam undertook this strenuous venture and solved the problem,

Quranic verses assert that God sent prophets in all the nations of the world but, the later generations adulterated their own religions according to their own inventions, whims, fancies and needs. Hence God sent Prophet Muhammad (SAW) with missions of purifying and completing the true religion. Islam is the most comprehensive religion which provides a complete way of equilibrium. The name of the prophets mentioned in Quran are the names of the ancestors of Ibrahim (A.S.) and his descendants. The Judaic tradition was started by Is-haq (A.S.) the second son of Ibrahim (A.S.). The descendants of Yaqub (A.S.) and Is-haq (A.S.) were called the tribes of Bani

Isra'il. Except Prophet Muhammad (SAW) all other prophets, mentioned in Quran hailed from Bani Israi'l.

The Judaic tradition was ended with Jesus Christ whose mother Bibi Maryam (St. Mary) hailed from Bani Israil. The last Prophet Muhammad (SAW) was the descendant of Ismail(A.S.) the first son of Ibrahim Alaihis Salam. Now, it is clear that the names of prophets mentioned in Quran are the ancestors of Ibrahim (A.S) such as Nuh (A.S.) and Adam and the descendants of Ibrahim (A.S.). Prophet Lut (A.S) was the nephew of Ibrahim (A.S).

Now, we come to the point of unity of religions. Quran clearly states that there is not a single habitation on earth where a prophet has not emerged and where God has not a messenger to guide people. A Muslim should believe in the Unity of Religions which brought the messages of unity of God and the Day of Resurrection and Reckoning. The Islamic of ethics were revealed according to the need of the Period. we do not follow other religions. because. the words of God have not been preserved in their original form.

As Islam advocates the unity of religions, it respects all true faiths. According to principle, the peace of the society is paramount consideration. Religions should be directed towards maintenance of peace, harmony, cohesion, amity, and religious tolerance.

H: "The Jews and Christians are referred to, as religious groups."

"Prophet Muhammad (SAW) allowed the Christians to pray in Masjid-e-Nabvi" (Baihaqi).

"Prophet Muhammad (SAW) stood in reverence when a fier of a Jew passed by". (Bukhari)

We must accept the Quranic verses which explain that the followers of other earlier Prophets who maintained the basic principle of belief that there is no God other than Allah. and followed the teachings of their prophets, will be admitted into paradise in the hereafter.

S. Maida-

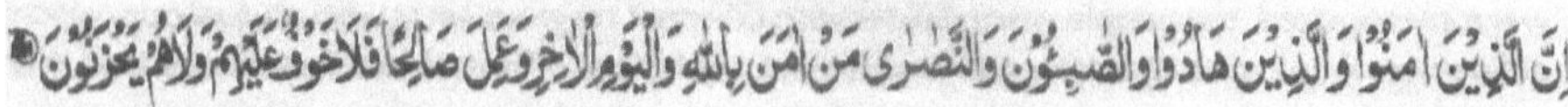

Tr: "Those who believe (in the Quran), those who follow the Jewish (scriptures), and the Sabians and the Christians, -any who believe in Allah and the Last Day and work righteousness, -on them shall be no fear, nor shall they grieve".

S. Ankabut-29:46.

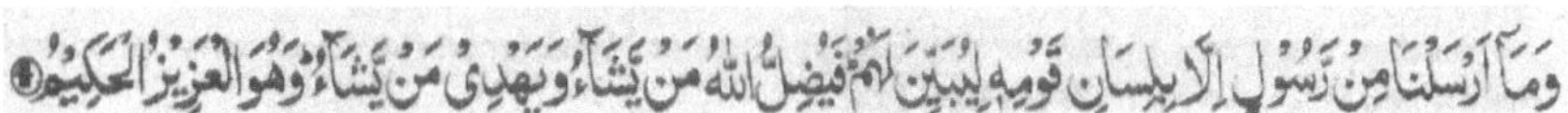

Tr: 'And dispute ye not with the people of the book, except with means better (than mere disputation), unless it be with those of them who inflict wrong (and injury); but say "We believe in the Revelation which has come down to us and in that which came down to you: and our Allah and your Allah is one and it is to Him, we bow (in Islam)".

S. Ibrahim –

Tr: 'We sent an Apostle except (to teach) in the language of his (own) people in order to make (things) clear to them. Now

Allah leaves straying those whom He pleases and He is exalted in Power, full of Wisdom".

S. Yunus. 10:47:

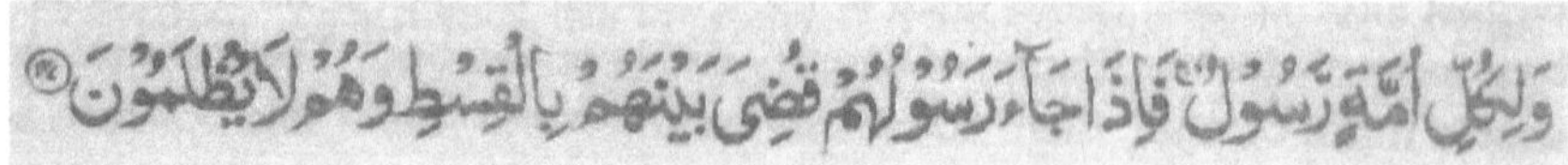

Tr: "To every people (was sent) an Apostle. when their Apostlecomes (before them), the matter will be judged between them With, Justice. and they not be wronged.

S.Ra'ad – 13.7:-

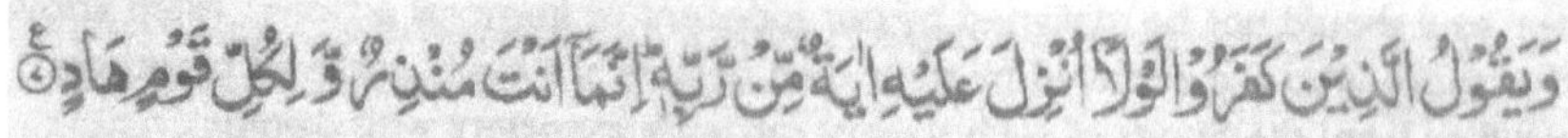

Tr: "And the unbelievers say! "Why is not a Sign sent down to him from his Lore but Orthodoxy, meditation and religious tolerance are equally important. As Muslims, we must adhere to all the sound doctrines of Islam. At the same time, we must respect all religions.

ISLAM - ITS MESSAGE AND OBJECTIVES:

Islam literally means "Surrender to the will ofGod" as well as 'Peace'. Islam is the name ofthe religion. preached by Prophet Muhammad (SAW) who attained Prophethood in Makkah more than 14 1/4 centuries ago. This religion is as wide in its conception as humanity Itself, because it aimed at universal reformation. Islam finds its origin right from the advent of Prophet Adam (A.S.), the father of humanity. Almighty Allah sent prophets to all the nations of the world, from time to time for the rehearsal of Islamic doctrines. Islam can be defined as the league of nations as it is the religion of all prophets, Adam, Nuh. Ibrahim, Moosa. Dawood. Isa. Muhammad (SAW) and the hosts of other prophets who preached the unity of God and laws of God. in various parts of the world from time to time.

Islam is not meant for one people or one age or one country. In Islam whole-heartedendeavors are as essential component part of religion as the belief Teachings of Islam are not shrouded in myths and stories. The subjects are some what comprehensive such as brotherhood, service to humanity, freedom of conscience, reverence to authority, elevation of the position of women. Islam's attitude towards gambling, drinking, promiscuity, usury, charity. labour, peace. prosperity and above all belief in monotheism and the Day of Judgement.

At times when human society is largely sunk to its lowest depths spiritually and morally; when the human society is hopelessly degraded, when the horizon of life is surcharged with dark cloud of corruptions, dishonesty. moral depravity; want of trust and confidence: the immediate propagation Of Islam is the only remedy with a view to serve humanity. As the spiritt of universal brotherhood and equality are recognized by Islam, their feasibility in the social life ofthe Muslim community is a practical idea and the great achievement of Islam. No distinction among people regarding race, class and ranks is recognized by Islam. The whole world is attracted and enticed by the real universal brotherhood of Islam as it is dead against the custom of untouchability. Islamic brotherhood is one which binds man to man, family to family, society to society, nation to nation state to state and finally country to country. Hajj pilgrimage is the biggest international conference of the Muslims, where no status is taken into account, is the best example for elucidation of equality and brotherhood. The spiritual idealism of all religions should make us one. Islam advocates common and favorable concern and inspires sense of obligation to one another.

According to Islam a human being is the combination of a body, a mind and a soul. The Physical, Mental and Spiritual aspects should be utilized in the balanced and lawful way so that our soul should not be maligned by our indecent or immoral actions. Islam knows fully Well that those who are enslaved by their own desires are easily enslaved by others. Those who are free from the bonds of such slavery can walk in society with dignity.

PURITY OF ISLAMIC SOCIETY AND ITS TEACHINGS:

Can any person find out a single flaw in the codes of ethics of Islam? Islam is a peace_ loving. pure and flawless religion. The very word "Islam" means "Peace". It is dead against offensive and aggressive use of sword. Our last scripture, the Holy Quran. revealed to our last Prophet Muhammad (SAW) is full of. verses breathing the spirit of peace, good-will and love. Quran has strongly advocated religious tolerance at all times and at every situation.

At the same time the early Muslims had to resort to the use of sword, because in the early days of Islam. the Muslims were subjected to the Most torturous persecutions.

They were flayed alive, burnt alive, stoned to death and all sorts of cruelties were inflicted on them. When they found that their enemies were bent on exterminating them, there was no other go than to resort to the use of sword in self-defense. The real sword which spread the message of Islam far and wide was the medium of Quranic tenets. According to the Islamic doctrine, the use of sword for self-defense is lawful. Offensive attacks are tersely prohibited.

The first cousin and the youngest son-in-law of Prophet Muhammad (SAW) and the fourth khalifa of Islam Hazrat Ali was walking along his way unarmed when an enemy of Islam came from the opposite direction with a sword in his hand and wanted to kill him. He asked Hazrat Ali (RAA) "Ali! say. who can save you now? Can your Allah come for your rescue? "Hazrat Ali said, "Of course, my Allah can save me". As soon as he heard Hazrat Ali's reply with so much of confidence in Allah's grace, he began to tremble and his sword fell down from his hand. Instantly Hazrat Ali (RAA) picked up the sword, threw his enemy on the ground, sat on his chest and when he was about to kill him, he asked him, "Tell me, who can save you now?" The enemy was sure that he was about to die. Instead of giving any reply, he spat on the face of Hazrat Ali. Hazrat Ali immediately got up from his chest and spared his life. 'His enemy was wonderstruck and asked him, "which factor made you release and pardon me?". Hazrat Ali said, 'When you ridiculed my Allah and attempted offensive it became lawful for me to kill you. But when you spat on my face, it aroused my anger. Had I killed you the purpose of killing would have been different. According to Islamic teachings, Muslims are not allowed to satisfy their anger by wreaking avenge". on hearing this reply, he felt greatly ashamed at his awkward action, caught hold of Hazrat Ali's hand with repentance, embraced Islam immediately with all appreciations for the purity and teachings of Islam.

The teachings of Islam are pure sound and simple behind its rigid monotheism. It has removed the causes of friction.

"Which spoil the very Vitals of the people and adds to thew miseries and sufferings. National progress is impossible where communal troubles originate. It can only be promoted with inter-communal solidarity. Islam condemns all sorts of harmful practices and immoral activities. Islam created a new era of mutual good Will and fraternity and absolving their differences, so that people might live on God's earth in prosperity and peace with pure soul, which is the goal of Islam.

H: "If you have four characteristics you need not bother about what has been dented you of in this world; good manners. Observing integrity with what you have to eat, maintaining the truth with what you have to say, and being faithful to your trust". (Ahmed, Bakhan, AliAdab, Al-Mufrad)

H: "One who speaks indecency and one who spreads it commit equal offences". (Bukhari. Al-Adab, Al-Mufrad, Baihaqi)

The Islamic framework is constructed on the universality of its principles. A Muslim carries the moral obligation to order that which is right and to forbid that which is wrong. Purity of Islam lies on the acceptance on one Allah, Holy Quran, the only uncorrupted scripture and one Qibla for all the Muslims.

WORLD SOCIETY BEFORE ISLAM.

When Ibrahim (A.S.) was still a nomad, several Monorchial states were established. Despotism was the culture of the members of the royal families. The royal families and privileged classes of people did not know the meaning of humanity. The unfortunate and unprivileged classes of people were severely tortured, poorly fed and treated as the animals of labour. The age of feudalism started one century before the advent of Islam. Tyrannical and monarchial systems, feudalism and despotism prevailed all over the known world.

EGYPT:

The Egyptians were very proud of their most ancient civilization. We know very little about the pre-dynasty or pre-historic period. The recent researches and excavations in Egypt have thrown a good deal of light on the culture of the pre-historic period. We have come to know many more detail: about the arts, tools and ways of life of the Egyptians of the prehistoric age. Their art of constructing the pyramids and the devices of preservation of the dead bodies(Mummies) of the kings of Egypt are quite appreciable. Some four years back a great treasure was obtained during the excavation. It was the Holy Book Zaboor, revealed to Prophet Dawood (A.s.) which could not be preserved by the people of those days. It is intact in an undamaged container. Though evil dominated in the world, the light of truth shone in some parts of the world at all ages. Several dynasties of Pharoahs were cruel and infidels. There were some noble Pharoahs who believed in the unity of God. Ibrahim (A.S.) performed some miracles in the court of a Pharoah, and he came into the fold of the religion of Ibrahim (A.S.) before it was given the name as Islam by Allah in compliance with the request of Ibrahim (A.S.) and his son Isma'il (A.S.). The noble Pharoah admired Ibrahim (A.S.) to that extent that he gifted him his own daughter Hajra as his slave girl. Later he married his slave girl, the Egyptian princess andIsma'il (A.S.) was born to them who was the ancestor of Prophet Muhammed (SAW).

The Pharoah of Hyksis dynasty was extremely noble and compassionate towards subjects. He appointed Yusuf (A.S.) as his Prime Minister. embraced his religion and after some time. he handed over the reins of whole administration of his state to Yusuf (AS.). He was unmindful of his powers and got indulged in meditation.

The Pharoah who confronted with Moosa Alaihis Salam hailed from the 18[th]generation of Thothmes Dynasty, claimed Divinity, chased Moosa (A.S.) and his followers and was drowned in River Nile along with his huge army. He was infidel, but his wife Aasia who adopted Moosa (AS.) was a believer and pious woman:

GREECE:

The Greek society was highly advanced in philosophy even before the birth Of Isa (As.). Socrates, Plato and Aristotle were among the famous philosophers Of Greece belonging to the period of B.C. All these philosophers believed in the unity of God and preached against the religion of the Greeks which was called Pantheism. The Pantheists worshipped nature and had numerous gods. Aristotle was the disciple of Plato and Minister of Alexander the Great. the Greek Emperor. On the change of their belief in Monotheism. Socrates and Aristotle were severely persecuted, but they never minded the torture. They stuck to their belief in the unity of God till the last breath of their life and said that nature was only the creation of the one Supreme power God. At last,Socrates was imprisoned, given poison and was asked to take it by his own hand. Without any hesitation, he gladly drank the poison and attained martyrdom quite peacefully. In accordance with the royal command of

Alexander, Aristotle also was executed. Those great philosophers wrote about religious philosophy. democracy and codes of ethics. The following is one of the quotations of Plato and Aristotle, "Justice is a virtue which gives everyone his right dues. From this point of view, justice becomes the master virtue which includes most other virtues".

They had very few disciples. As the Greek Government did not recognize their philosophy in their life time, their philosophy was confined to the theoretical knowledge and could not be put into practical applications. It was Islam which translated all the theoretical philosophy into practical ethics for the first time in the world in all aspects of life. Islam is the natural and dynamic religion which refined the world society.

FRANCE:

In France, the common people suffered a lot under the Feudal System of the Aristocrats till the French Revolution took place in 1789 A.D.

THE ROMAN AND PERSIAN EMPIRES:

The Roman empire of the Christians and the Persian empire of the Zoroastrians were always engaged in religious wars and also the wars regarding territorial ambitions. When Prophet Muhammad (SAW) was born, the Persian and the Roman empires were the greatest ones with numerous dominions. Iraq was the dominion of Persia and Syria was the dominion of Rome. The Syrian state under Roman domination was called the Byzantine Empire.

America was founded by Crystopher Columbus only few centuries ago. In the pr. Islamic, society. America was unknown to the rest of the world. The then known world was full of Persian and Roman dominions. spread all over it, including Africa.

INVASION AGAINST MAKKAH:

Yemen Which lies in the south of Arabia was ruled over by Abraha, a Christian governor, under the Egyptian king before the birth of Prophet Muhammad (SAW). Makkah being the commercial and pilgrimage center was attracted by the surrounding tribes and Abraha. the Christian ruler of Yemen. But in the frequent invastions. the Quraish tribes of Makkah (The descendants of Ismail (A.s.)), miraculously emerged victorious. Just forty days before the birth of Prophet Muhammad, Abraha the Christian Governor of Yemen, mounted on an elephant and led a large army to invade Makkah with the intention of destructing Kabathullah and taking away the Black Stone (Hajr-e-Aswad). The scanty population of Makkah was desperately defenseless. Abdul Mutallib, the grand father of Muhammad (SAW) prayed Allah to save His Sanctuary. At this crucial juncture, a miracle took place. When Abraha reached the vicinity of Makkah, his elephant refused to walk forward. All a sudden a large host of lakhs of birds called Ababil appeared high above Abrahas army. Every bird brought three stones. one in its beak and two in its two paws. The birds killed the whole armyof Abrahaby showering these stones and then disappeared. You can read this parable in Sura-e-hl (No. 105) which means elephant.

In the history of the world. this period including the Fuedal age was called "The Age of Ignorance". The whole world was steeped into the darkness of apostasy, seduction. selfishness and ignorance. The darkest part of the world was Arabia. The world was badly in need of a universal reformer.

PRE-ISLAMIC SOCIETY OF ARABIA:

In the aga of ignorance, there were many tribes ruling independently in and around the Arabian territories: Irv that Age of darkness, Arabia was the worst part of the world. The Arabs were divided in two main classes. called the Ahl-Hadr which means the people of the town or village, settled in particular places, and Ahl-Badhu (Beduins), the nomads who roamed from place to place in the deserts in search of pastures and water and lived in the tents. These Ahl-Badhu constituted the major part of the population of Arabia. They loved free life and nomadism. Most of them were Heathens (Atheists). Even the settled people were devoid of culture and civilization. They were called by the people of other advanced countries as Arab savages. The population of Arab nation was divided into thousands of tribes and sub-tribes under the domination of hot-headed and proud chieftains. Those tribes consisted of Christians, jews, Zoroastrians (fire worshippers) Sabeans (worshippers of heavenly bodies) and idolators (Politheists).

Even a trifle thing would provoke the wrath of the Arabs and spark fire of wars against one another. For a slight gesture of contempt, they would draw their swords out of their sheaths and it will end in a grave bloodshed. Moulana Abdur Rahim says, to offend an Arab was very easy, but to befriend him was very difficult". Women were considered to be commercial commodities. They were sold from hand to hand, Women had no status at all . Adultery, drinking, gambling. debauchery. female infanticide and human sacrifices were their common practices. They married the widows of their fathers, Old and disabled mothers were condemned and left to die of hunger on the roads. No woman had the right of inheritance Of property as the nation was divided into tribes and clans, an organized state with a sovereign was impossible. It was a mess everywhere. According to them might was right, their crude law was opposed to the emancipation of slaves. They beat the slaves mercilessly for trifle offence or no offence. In fact, they were considered to be worse than the brutes. So far, we have been enumerating their vices and disqualifications. Those Arabs, especially the idolators Of Makkah were possessed of several virtues also. Moulana M.R.M. Abdur-Rahim enumerates their virtues in the following words. "In liberality and hospitality; in simplicity and self-respect; in freedom of thought and keeping words; in intellectual development and eloquence of tongue in bravery in battle and patience in misfortune; in persistence in endeavor and painstaking in labour, in the protection of the weak and defiance of the strong. the people of Arabia were foremost and far advanced than others of the world and even evoked the admiration of Nepoleon in later day". The Arabs had considerably advanced in Arabic literature both in the fields of poetry and prose. It is said that Nepoleon Bonapart was enticed by the doctrines of Islam and he was a secret Muslim by heart, though he was the Emperor of a Christian country, France.

Abd-e-Munaf was the grandfather of Abdul Mutallib, the grandfather Of Prophet Muhammad (SAW). For clearer understanding. Prophet Muhammad was the son of Amina and Abdullah bin Abdul Mutallib Bin Hashim Bin Abd-e-Munaf.

Abd-e-Munaf had four sons by name I . Qusyy 2. Hashim 3. Abd-e-Shams and 4. Nufil. The descendants of these four brothers belonged to the tribe of Quraish which was subdivided into several clans. Our Prophet (SAW) and Hazrat Ali were the descendants of Hashim. Bi Bi Amina (Mother of our Prophet), Hazrat Abu Bakr Siddiq. Hazrat Umar Faroq and Hazrat Usman Ghani were the descendants of the other three brothers i.e.. the other three sons of Abd-e-Munaf. Now, it is clear that our Prophet (SAN) and the khalifa•s who succeeded him were distant cousins, having the same ancestor Abd-e-Munaf,

The religious set up of Makkah was a strange one. The descendants of Isma'il (A.S.). son of Ibrahim (AS.) were badly steeped in idolatry and superstitions. His descendants had converted the Kabathullah into a temple and had installed 360 idols for their worship. At the same time, they had belief in Allah from Whom Ibrahim (A.S,) brought the message, as the Supreme Being. They had the foolish belief that they could reach Allah only through their false dieties. Avery few members of Quraish did not worship the idols among whom were Prophet Muhammad (SAW), Hazrat Abu Bakr Siddiq, Hazrat Usman etc. The second Khalifa of Islam.Hazrat Umar was the great and staunch idolator of Makkah, and wash an awoved enemy of Islam. One day, he held the unsheathed sward in his hand and went out with the intention of killing Prophet Muhammad. On his way, he called on his sister and her husband. He beat them, harshly for having embraced Islam. His sister began to bleed but was 'determined to stick to her faith. Hazrat Umar kept silent for some time and then asked his sister to recite some verses of Quran. When he heard the musical recitation of Sura-e-Taha, tears rolled along his cheeks and he realized his folly. He felt ashamed and repented over his cruel behavior with his sister and brother-in-law. 'He went straight to Prophet Muhammed (SAW) and embraced Islam. The previous night, he had prayed Allah, that either Omar or Abu Jehal might come into the fold Of Islam who could strengthen it. Hazrat Umar was so brave that he was a terror 'n Makkah just as his contemporary Rustum was a terror in Porsia. Rustum was killed by a Muslim in the battle field during the Khilafat of Hazrat Omar. After Hazrat Omar's conversion. the Muslims could perform namaz in Kabathullah.

Arabian society as well as the world society were purely materialistic. They had nothing to do with humanity. They did not believe in and unmindful of hereafter. The Arabs believed in the existence of Demons and attributed diseases with the influence of evil spirits Dung the prolonged Age of Ignorance which the world was passing through with silly superstitions, a universal preceptor and reformer was urgently needed. Hence Allah sent the brightest light in the darkest part of the world Arabia. Allah assigned Prophet Muhammad (SAW) with universal mission of reformation, Now, we will have some discussion about the Revolution of Islam.

REVOLUTION OF ISLAM:

According to Daleel Sahib, the Revolution of Islam is worthy to be called the only Revolution in the real sense in the history of the world as this was the multi-dimensional revolution by which both the religion and all the social aspects of life were benefited are being benefited and will be benefited till the Day of the Doom. It was the ever-lasting revolution This revolution was brought about by the common beneficence of the Prophethood of Muhammad (SAW) and the special Divine bounty of Islam.

H: "Every Prophet was sent for his own people, but I have been sent for all of mankind-. (Bukhari. Muslim).

H: "The difference between myself and the other Prophets is that of a building, which is complete except for one brick. Observers were wondering to note the missing brick. It is I who filled the gap. No new messenger will come after me, for the building is now accomplished (Bukhari Muslim).

H: "Allah has sent me to complete the excellence of virtues and perfect all good actions* (Sharh-al-Sunnah).

The whole world was submerged in the ocean of selfishness and all Hijrat. the migration of our Prophet (SAW) from Makkah to Madinah was to change the fate and the course of world history through Islamic Revolution which has its roots when our Prophet (SAW) attained Prophethood twelve years before Hijrat.

The objective of all the religion is to establish a balanced social life with justice. nobility. morality and all sorts of virtues. In the Age of Ignorance, it was not possible for anybody to set right the world regarding spiritualism through inspired religions and regarding all the aspects of life. Even in that age there were some reformers in different parts of the world. In Makkah there were four brothers or who were the a organization by name "Halaful In his young age our Prophet the Members of the association. Their objectives were to help the needy. help the travelers. safeguard the caravans from decoity and to eradicate the evils from the society. It was by the contributions of such reformers through the ages that religion brought by Adam (AS.) evolved gradually.

The success of such organizations are nothing when compared to the multifaceted Revolution of Islam. Our Prophet (SAW) was the greatest Revolutionist ever born in the world. Such an example of personality can never be seen again in the future. The example set by our Prophet (SAW) shows us how the Revolution has to be brought about by love, affinity, brotherhood. equality. compassion and concern for humanity. The greatest revolution brought about by our Holy Prophet was unique in nature in the sense that, we do not find the play of negative emotions like hatred, revenge or anger in its process. Love, affection. justice, harmony, forgiveness towards enemies and fair play to the entire humanity were the hallmarks of Islamic Revolution. The world history is the best witness to prove that the Revolution was the revolution of reformations both spiritual and social while other revolutions were the revolutions of executions:

Thousands of people were executed during French Revolution and Iranian revolution. How much human blood was shed when Hitler was executed in Germany? It is the responsibility of Muslims to follow the foot-steps of our Prophet (SAW) while safeguarding and propagating Islam.

The advent of Islam was the mightiest movement and its revaluation was greatest. Though the early converts were suppressed and mercilessly persecuted by the idolators a new world was unknowingly being created through Islam which changed the history of the older world.

At the outset Islamic State came into the contact of its contemporary Roman Empire and Persian Empire. The internal disturbances were numerous. The revolution of Islam had not only a political significance but a deep spiritual significance also. The effect of the Islamic Revolution still exists and will continue to exist till the Day of the Doom.

Islamic Revolution aims at ideal man an idea' society, an ideal servant of Allah who can refine the world society, leading to an ideal and successful human life. The members of an ideal society obey Allah's commands, make best use of halal (Lawful things) and strictly avoid haram (unlawful things), control their passions and emotion, not to fall pray to lust, greed and unlawful desires. An ideal servant of Allah does not transgress the limits prescribed by Allah and always fears him. This is the idealism of Islamic Revolution.

SOCIAL REFORMS:

The revolutionary movement of Islam includes moral, religious, economical, ethical, judicial. educational. political and all the social reforms. The changing attitude and whimsical aspect of people are due to the law of changes with march of time. Nothing will stagnate but undergo evolutionary processes. The common and popular assessments cannot realise the facts. The ignorant man may deviate the path of righteousness. The poet has explained the law of changes in connection with the certainty of unchanged laws of God. Islam is a great boon for humanity as this religion is perfect and its laws are unchanged.

Q: 'From the beginning, the Divine Laws have been continuing uniformly. You can never find out a change in them",

Islam's message to the world is peace, love. progress and spiritual advancement. Spiritualism is the greatest ally Of Islam.Islamic Revolution has given individuality to every man. Almighty Allah caused this revolution by sending Prophet Muhammad (SAW) who was very simple. unassuming, obliging, affectionate, intensely zealous extremely selfless and compassionate. The revolution brought universal reformation which all other systems of governments and religions failed to do.

Revolution means a sudden change aiming at reformations. Evolution means changes by gradual means. Both revolutionary and evolutionary aspects are essential for the reformation of the world society. Islam has both the aspects. We have discussed much about the Revolution of Islam. A small glimpse is enough to understand the Evolutionary aspect of Islam. Prophet Muhammad attained prophethood twelve years before Hijrat. He received the first revelation through Angel Jibra'il, when our Prophet (SAW) was meditating in the cave of Hira in the vicinity of Makkah on the 27th night of Ramzan 6 IQ A.D. He received the last revelation on the 10th Of the Month of Hajj on the occasion of his last pilgrimage (Hajjatul-wida'ay 1 0 AH i.e., 632 A.D. Now it is easy to calculate that he received revelations for twenty-two years and three months, which have been.recorded in Quran. The injunctions and prohibitions were being revealed one after the other, when the previous ones had been firmly established. This was the evolutionary aspect in the revolution of Islam which brought reforms in every aspect of life.

RELIGIOUS REFORM:

Cultivation Of religious belief, sentiments and fear Of God can help to boldly face the calamities and solve the problems easily. Man has been created by God in the best form, showered His choicest blessings and has provided with plenty of opportunities for enabling him to raise the excellence of humanity. The role of religion is very great in human life, as it has prescribed religious codes which take him to the Realm of God. From the date of the advent of Adam (A.S.), the religion has enabled man to uphold the traditional values and lead a pious and civilized life, with absolute discipline. Any community which loses its religion will gradually degenerate and then get destructed.

EDUCATIONAL REVOLUTION:

The Age of Ignorance when Islam was born was followed by the Golden Age after the revolution of Islam. The educational movement emerged from the teachings of our Prophet (SAW) in Arabia, gave up a whip to research and development in the intellectual sphere in the entire world. Data for all branches of arts and sciences are available in Quran and their impact is ever lasting. Especially the Europeans are amply benefited by these data. They went on, are going on and will go on doing researches and making discoveries on the basis of data given in Quran.

The Muslims of the revolutionary period and the Muslims of Middle Ages contributed a great deal which is noteworthy in the history of the world. This period is called "The Golden Age" in the world history. It was a miracle, that before our Prophet (SAW) could bind the Arabs in a common bond and even before he conquered Makkah, and before he could abolish the tribal system and establish Islamic state, the lead in the educational sphere was given by the nomadic Arabs. They took with them and spread Islamic teachings in other parts of the world.

This educational reform started from the 27th night of Ramzan twelve years before Hijrat. The first call of Allah gave the first importance for reading, writing and acquisition of knowledge. The very first message brought' by Angel Jibra'il was, "Read in the name of the Lord, the Cherisher, who created man out of (mere) a clot of congealed blood". Several Ahadis and Quranic -verses urged the Arabs to pursue knowledge which gave them the head Start in education. Education was not confined to the men folk. Women had the equal rights to acquire education. The Arab women substantially contributed with the men folk especially in the field of education. The Arab women acquired knowledge in medicine. literature, mysticism and religion. They taught both men and women and helped the men in social, political and economic spheres and even rendered military service during the Abbasi Khilafat. During the life time of our Prophet (SAW), the Ashab-e-Suffa dedicated their whole lives in memorizing the then revealed Quranic Stanza before their compilation; writing Ahadis and giving religious education to others. Hazrat Abu Huraira was the eminent personality among the Ashab-eSuffa. The third wife of our Prophet (SAW) and daughter of Abu Bakr Siddiq. Bibi Asha who became the widow at her early age, was an extraordinarily intelligent woman. She was well in Ahadis. All the companions of Our Prophet (SAW) took her help for clarifications of their doubts. The present books of Ahadis woe much to the contribution of Bi Bi Aisha. In the Golden Age of Islamic

Education i.e., the 8th and 9th century A.D, the Jews and Christians began to write their scientific subjects in Arabic language. In the Golden Age, religious sciences, the study of Quran. Ahadis. Islamic jurisprudence. grammar, astronomy, physics. music, mathematics and intellectual sciences and arts were taught. It is known to all that the Islamic empire became very vast due to the conquest of many countries during the Khalifat of Hazrat Omar. During the Khalifat of Hazrat Usman, he had the Quran calligraphed and sent it throughout the Islamic empire. The Islamic governments and private organizations played a vital role in establishing educational institutions. During the Umayyad Dynasty and Abbasi Dynasty all branches of Arts. Sciences and Technology were patronized by the then Khalifa's in all the countries under the Islamic empire. This era when the maximum efforts were mobilized by the Muslims in promoting educational and intellectual field, is called the Golden Age. With the expansion of Islamic Empire, Arabic became the international vehicle for educational promotion.

SOCIAL REFORMS:

The Reformations in all fields. brought by the Islamic Revolution were in consonance with Ahadis and Quranic tenets. As human beings. we should follow some guidelines for a social order. Islam has laid certain guidelines for a good and effective social administration. We must form organizations for consultations for the welfare of the public. For the first time in the history of the world. Islam brought the legislative revolution in all social fields which is beneficial

HUMAN RIGHTS:

Human rights include all social reformations. The United Nations Organization has got a special charter for Human Rights. Was there any provision for such a charter in the pre-Islamic days? In fact, the movement of human rights was initiated by Human Rights argentations are the results Of Islamic Revolution which effects. The following passage has been extracted from "Radiant Weekly",

'The Universal declaration of Human Rights was endorsed Naoons General Assembly. In 1980 A.D, the International Commission

University of Kuwait together with the union of Arab lawyers. Organized Human Rights. One very significant purpose of this seminar was to refute the idea and the continued development of the concept of Human Rights must be to western culture. The practical exercises of Human Rights was first The important conclusions are:

1. "Islam was the first to recognize the basic Human Rights and to safeguarding the Human Rights some 1425 years ago, These guarantees in Universal Declaration of Human Rights only recently.

2. Islam was the founder religion to realize and safeguard personal irrespective of caste and creed.

3. The Islamic codification of Human Rights continues a solid foundation exercise of Human Rights. freedom and protection against injustice,

4. Islam recommends that economic, social and cultural rights as well as civil political rights must be honestly and faithfully guaranteed to all human beings. Thus, in

Islam, God given human rights are seen as the means of assuring human dignity to preserve human dignity of man. It is necessary that society guarantees him drink, employment as well as the right to express his opinion, participation in and to be assured of his own security and that of his kin.

5. Poor people, children and crippled Zimmis (Non-Muslims in Islamic Empire) were exempted from Jizya, whereas no sick Muslim or child was exempted from Zakaat and Sadaqatul-fitr Those who can afford, Zakaat and Sadaqatul-Fitr they are Obligatory on them. In the case of young children, their parents or guardians must do it on their behalf.

There are hundreds of Ahadis, pertaining to social reform which is been presented in the following:

H: "Allah will not look upon him who trails his garments out of Pride(Muslim).

H: "A Muslim who lives in the midst of society and bears with patience the afflictions that came to him is better than the one who shuns society and cannot bear any wrong done to him".

H: "The best among you is the one who is best towards his wife".

H: "The perfect believer is one who has a perfect character and is kind to (Ibn-e-Maja).

H: "Even paradise lies under the feet of your mother".

H: "If a man, possessing a female slave was to provide her an excellent education and teach her the best etiquette and then free her and take her as his wife. he would get recompense". (Bukhari).

H: "Whoever will have pride in his heart, even at the weight of an atom. shall not enter heaven". (Bukhari, Muslim)

H: "Whoever will wear a dress for display or fame in the world, God will make him wear the dress of ignominy in the hereafter". (Abu-Dawood, Masnad-e-Ahmed. Ibn-e-Maja).

H: "On removing the distress of every living being, including animals, that can feel the pangs of hunger and thirst will fetch reward". (Bukhari. Muslim)

H: 'When a person goes to enquire after the health Of a Muslim brother or just pays a call on him, a caller from the heavens pronounces. You have done well, your walking is propitious, you have earned a dwelling place in paradise". (Tirmizi)

H: "Three persons shall not enter paradise, the one who is disobedient to his parents, the pimp, and the woman who imitates man". (Al-Hakim, Nisai)

H: "He is not conceited who allows his servant to eat with him, rides a donkey in the markets and ties up his sheep and milk it" (Bukhari).

H: "He who does not thank men is ungrateful to Allah". (Al-Bukhari, Al-Adab, Al-Mufrad, Ahmed. Abu-Dawood, Tirmizi, Ibn-e-Maja).

H: "Avoid seven harmful things, setting up a partner with Allah, sorcery, unlawfully killing a soul, involving yourself in usury. exploiting the property of an orphan, keeping behind on the day of the fight and slandering chaste and innocent believing woman". (Bukhari, Muslim).

During his exemplary life our Prophet (SAW), counselled gently and firmly to subdue evil and he solved the most befalling mysteries by scaling heights of heavens, and prohibiting wayward life, lust and greed. Through Sura-e-Falaq, Islam urges the believers to seek refuge with God from outer ills and through Sura-e-Nas, to seek refuge with God from inner evils. These two exhortations are contained in the form of supplications in the first chapter, Sura-eFatiha. The 114th Chapter Sura-e-Nas is the last Sura in Quran. We can conclude that the Holy Quran begins and ends with the exhortations of social reform. Some more Ahadis:-

H: "One who reciprocates in doing good is not the one who upholds the ties of kinship. If is the one who' is kind to them when they are hostile to them". (Bukhari)

H: 'The best of social actions, is to love and hate for the cause of Allah". (Abu Dawood) H: 'One Whose neighbor is not safe from his mischief shall not enter paradise". (Muslim).

H: "Shall not teach you the best form of charity? Taking care of your daughter Who has been returned to you and who has no earning member except you". (Ibn-e-Maja).

ACHIEVEMENTS OF ISLAMIC REVOLUTIONS:

The true and inspired religion has been accomplished by Allah which is choicest blessing. The secrets and tenets of religion were revealed altogether by the preservation Of Quranic verses without any interpolation.

Unlike other scriptures. Quran is the permanent guide and the life of our last Prophet (SAY" is the best example for humanity to follow till the Day of the Doom. Soon after Hijrat, a systematic Islamic State. with dynamic governing rules, constitution for Law and Order and team of councilors was established.

Besides numerous conquests and territorial achievements. spiritual achievements were greater even during the life time of our Holy Prophet (SAW) as well as after his expiry. For example, the King of Abyssinia (now called Ethiopia), Negus and Raja Bhoj Of Madhya Pradesh embraced Islam in the life time of Muhammad (SAW) without seeing him. Islam was most welcomed by India. The lists of early Hindu rulers who embraced Islam, the Hindu kings who welcomed Islam and the Prophet's companions who visited India have been extracted from "Radient Weekly".

EARLY HINDU RULERS WHO EMBRACED ISLAM:

1. Raja Jai Siya, son of Raja Dahir of Sindh.

2. The Queen of Sindh and mother of Raja Jai Siya and Raja Chuch.

3. Raja Chuch. the Son fo Raja Dahir of Sindh.

4. Raja Bhoj of Madhya Pradesh.

Even during the life time of our Prophet, Negus the Christian king of Abyssinia and large number of kings, leaders and common people of different countries embraced Islam. During the caliphate of Hazrat Umar. more than half of the then known world was conquered and Islam spread far and wide.

EARLY HINDU KINGS WHO WELCOMED ISLAM·

1. Raja Rasil of Kutch (Sourashtra and Gujarat).

2. Raja Rutbail of Northern Baluchistan.

3. Raja Qaiqan of Upper Sindh.

4. Raja Ashtradribid of Sourasthra.

5. Raja Kakakatak of Upper India.

6. Raja Harchand of Kannauj.

7. Raja Rai of Punjab.

8. The great Rashrakutas ofWest, Central and south India.

9. The Maitrakas of Vallabhi.

10. The Cheras of Keral.

11. I I . The king of Tushar.

12. The kings of Darad, Northern Kashmir

13. The kings of Bhutan.

14. The kings of Tibet (Buddhists)

Some Hindu kings sent gifts to the Muslim rulers as their recognition of Islam.

EARLY MUSLIMS (COMPANIONS OF PROPHET (SAW) WHO VISITED INDIA:

1. Hazrat Usman Bin Abu Saqafi. He was one of the distinguished companions of Holy Prophet

2. Hazrat Hakam Bin Abdul Aasi Saqafi, one of the great Muhaddis

3. Hazrat Rafi Bin Zaid Harasi

4. Hazrat Hakam Bin Aman Thababi

5. Hazrat Sahhar Bin Abbas Anadi

6. Hazrat Abdullah Bin Omar Ashjaie

7. Hazrat Ubaidullah Macemar Taini

8. Hazrat Mushaje Bin Masood Salami

9. Hazrat Sinan Bin Salma Huzali

10. Hazrat Abdur Rahman Bin Sumrah

11. Hazrat Munzia Bin Jar-ood (He died in India and was buried at Qusdar).

Scores of the followers of the companions of Muhammad (SAW) visited India grabbing opportunities for propagation of Islam. The descendants of Hazrat Ali (RAA) and Bi Bi Fathima (youngest daughter of our Prophet), Saint Khaja Moinuddin chishti of Ajmir and Saint Shahul Hameed Baba of Nagoor were among those who came to India for propagation Of Islam. The everlasting effects of the Revolution of Islam have been appreciably active throughout centuries.The world society accepts that now-a-days, the fastest spreading religion is Islam. During the periods of Umayyad and Abbasi dynasties the Muslim rulers patronized all branches of arts and sciences and there was an appreciable advance in every field.

IDEAL PROPHET:

In this chapter, the poet Daleel Sahib has called our Holy Prophet (SAW). the "Perfect Prophet" who in other words is called "ideal prophet". In two of the Stanza of this chapter, he has praised him in the following words: -

"Prophet Muhammad (SAW) is the brightest and Eternal Light. created by Almighty which leads us it' the righteous path this world which in Its turn facilities to enjoycomforts and eternal bliss in the hereafter his eminent personality and his sayings (Ahadis) impart knowledge and persuade us to make hard endeavors. The continuous we avail from his preaching's can be compared to the rays of the sun being emitted by it. Those who have consciousness and intellect have perfect knowledge of the history of the world and are fully aware of the fact that such a grand and noble person as Muhammad (SAW) can never be born again. He the leader of entire humanity who dissipated the darkness of superstitions from the world'.

In this commentary, I have dealt with topics. such as a brief sketch of the life of Muhammad (SAW) the confirmation of his prophethood, the purpose of Allah in sending the prophets , the different missions of different prophets, the universal mission of our Prophet (SAW), his character, his merits and his special prestige's over other prophets and a few Ahadis.

Prophet Muhammad (SAW) lost his father bore he was born. He lost his mother Bi Bi Anna and his grand father Abdul Mutallib, who was his guardian in his young age. Then he was brought up by his compassionate uncle Abu Talib (Hazrath Ali's Father) who was very poor and had no means to educate him. Though he was brought up in the society of Pagan Arabs, he did not worship any idol even before he obtained his prophethood. This illiterate prophet became the greatest and world-famous figure in the history of mankind and excelled the wisest and the learned. He lived with his pasture folk, worked with them and won their affection. He wandered about in the hills , valleys, caves and deserts, but never deviated from his path of righteousness or the ways of truth. In his young age, he went to Syria with his uncle for commercial purpose. Then he became the servant in the business of Bi Bi Khadiia, a widow whom he married later, when he was twenty-five years old and she was forty years old. He was born in Makkah in 570 A.D., brought up in Makkah got married in Makkah obtained Prophethood in the cave of Hira in the vicinity of Makkah, embarrassed and persecuted in Makkah and Taif till Hijrat. He experienced the mystic and prestigious event of Me'rai two years before Hijrat. He was born in the sacred city of Makkah. he received revelations and was forced by the circumstances to migrate to Madina with his companions in 622 A.D. where they were offered asylum. Hazrat Ali placed without any reserve, his chivalry, his powers, his Wit. learning and his sword at the disposal and service of the Mighty Messenger of God and even staked his own life to safeguard the life of his beloved cousin and would be father-in-law (Prophet Muhammad SAW).

The Quranic verses were revealed to him as the need arose on different occasions and in different places, they were recorded by the pen by his literate companions. They were imprinted on his heart and mind and in the memory of his loving disciples. These revealed and inspired verses constituted the Holy Quran. During his exemplary life, he counselled gently and firmly, subdued evils and solved the most baffling mysteries.

As the Pagan Arabs doubted about the Prophethood of Muhammad (SAW), Holy Quran confirms his Prophethood and praises him as the best example and most beautiful pattern among human beings, bringer of good tidings, lamp of spreading light, a prophet of tremendous nature and the last prophet to whom was revealed the last scripture. the HOW Quran. has described him in different verses and in different words. He claimed to be the Prophet and proved to be the true messenger of God by performing some surprising and amazing miracles.All the Arabs and foreigners were wonder-struck to witness the miracle of splitting up of the moon.

When the Religion of Islam was perfected, when the Holy Quran was carefully preserved, when it began to be recited with cent percent precision and clarity, when the Divine Law had prescribed the limits of activities, when Divine injunctions and prohibitions were established: when the sunnat and Ahadis-e-Nabvi began to command high esteem and when the Islamic Government had been established permanently, there was no need of a new prophet or a new scripture. He was the perfect exemplar, endowed with excellent moral character. He confirmed the Prophethood of the past prophets and their messages. He said that neither did he bring any new religion, nor did he claim to possess supernatural powers. When all his specific duties were discharged by him faithfully, fully, finally and to the complete satisfaction of Almighty Allah, the chain of succession of Apostles also ceased with him. He was called the best exemplar because he practiced what all he preached. Through Prophet Muhammad (SAW). Almighty Allah sanctified the souls of men. cleansed their character, changed their life style of sinful attitudes and eradicated all wicked customs and evil ways. Thus, Allah perfected the religion and completed his favors unto mankind. Islam does not accept pessimism. It advocates optimism and hope. With this optimistic ideology our Prophet (SAW) strived hard for the prosperity of entire humanity and eternal bliss in the spiritual world. He fought for human freedom. women's emancipation. secularism. democratic principles and human rights. He effectively roused up the dormant human faculties and awakened them to fight for social freedom and national ascendancy.

The Quranic verses quoted below contain the following subject matter:

The people of Makkah doubted about the Prophethood of Muhammad (SAW). Almighty Allah challenges the Mushrikin to present a like Sura. He confirms that Muhammad (SAW) is the last Prophet and the Holy Quran is the last scripture. He praises His Holy Messenger in different words in many verse from which I am presenting a few ones:

S. Ankabut - 29:48:

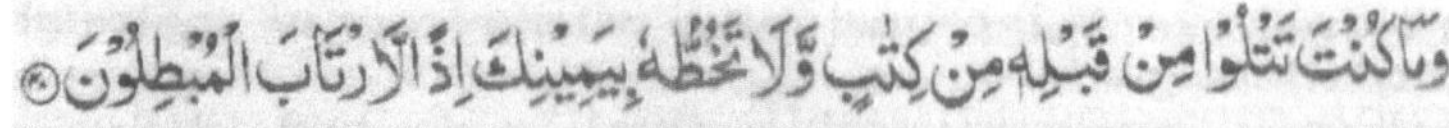

Tr.-And thou was not (able) to recite a book before this (Book came), nor art though (able) to transcribe it with their right hands. In that case. indeed, would the talkers of Vanities have doubted".

S. Aa'araf - 7:58:

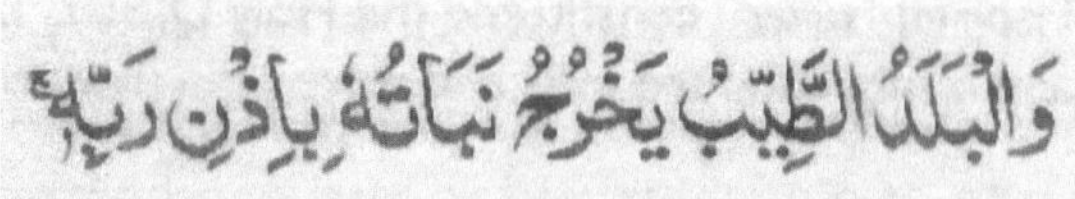

Tr:- "From the land that is clean and good by the Will of its Cherisher, springs up produce, (rice) after its kind, but from the land that is bad, springs up nothing, but that which is niggardly Thus do We explain the Signs by various (symbols) to those who are grateful".

S. Al-Baqara - 2:23: (Quoted in Chapter 12):

"And if you are in doubt as to what We have revealed from time to time to our servant, them produce Sura like thereunto; and call your Witness or helpers (if there are any)

S. Ma'ida -5:21

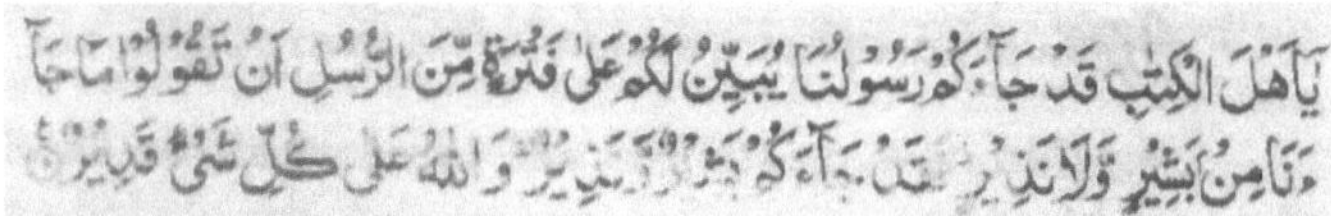

Tr:- "O! People of the Book! Now hath come to you many things clear unto you,Our Apostle, after the break (in the series of) our Apostles lest Ye should say, there came unto us, no bringer of glad tidings and no Warner from (evil)'. But no harm come unto you a bringer of glad tidings and no warner from (evil); and Allah hath power over all things"

S. Ahzab - 33:21: (Already quoted in chapters 14 and 7):

Tr: 'Ye have indeed in the Apostle of Allah, a beautiful pattern of Conduct for any one whose hope is in Allah and the Final Day; and who engages much in the praise of Allah"

S. Aaraf - 7: 188

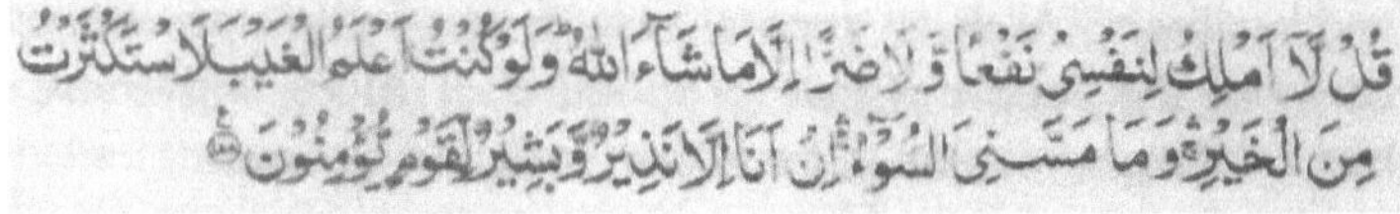

Tr:- 'Say, ᴶ I have no power over any good or harm to myself except as Aliah Willeth. If, I had knowledge of the unseen, I should have multiplied all good, and no evil should have touched me. I am but a warner and a bringer of glad tidings to those who faith'

S. Ahzab - 33:45: (quoted in Chapter 1 4)

Tr: "O Prophet! Truly we have sent thee as a witness, as a bearer of glad tidings and a warner",

S. Najim - 53:2-3:

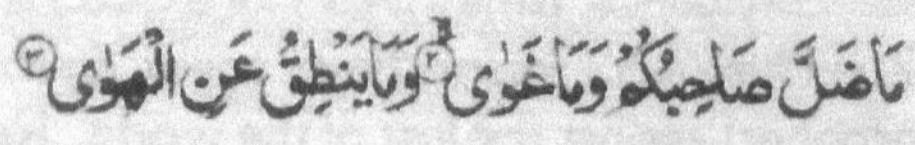

Tr:- "Your companion is neither astray, nor being misled, nor does he say (aught) of (his own) Desire"

S. Qalam - 68:4:

Tr:- "And thou (standest) on an exalted standard of character"

S. Aal-e-Imran - 3: 164:

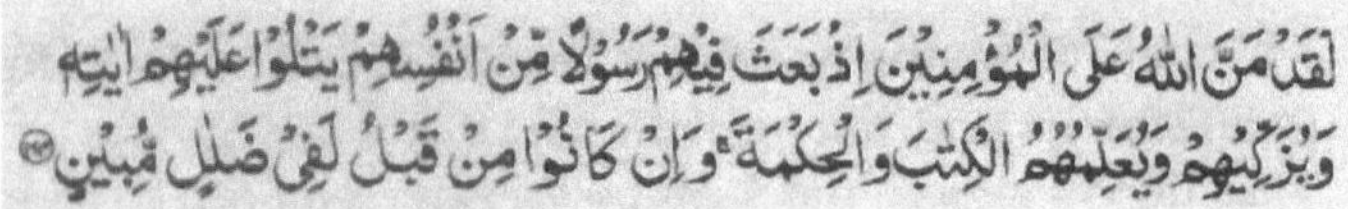

Tr:- 'Allah did confer a great favor on the believers when He sent among them an Apostle from among themselves, rehearsing unto them the Signs of Allah, sanctifying them and instructing them in Scripture and Wisdom. while before that, they had been in manifest error"

H:- Give On oath of allegiance to me that you shall not set up anything equal with Allah, nor shall you steel, nor shall you fornicate. nor shall you kill your children nor shall you commit slander. nor shall you neglect virtuous acts". (Bukhari. Muslim).

H: - "Every prophet was sent for his own people, but. I have been sent for all of mankind"

H: - "NO new messenger will come after me for the building is now accomplished" (Bukhari, Muslim)

H: - "Allah has sent me to complete the excellence of virtues and to perfect all good actions (Sharh-al-Sunnah)".

H: -"Whoever Obeys me, obeys Allah and whoever disobeys me, disobeys Allah". (Bukhari)

DIFFERENT MISSIONS OF DIFFERENT PROPHETS:

Every prophet was sent by Allah for the renewal of His message of unity of God, unity of creations and certainty of Resurrection in the hereafter. All the prophets brought the same Divine messages of warnings against evil, and enjoinments to purify the soul through prayers and praises to Allah, in general. He granted them powers to perform different miracles to convince the people of their prophethood. Along with these same messages, every prophet had a different mission in particular, assigned by God.

Mention of a few prophets have been made in the following

Ibrahim (A.S.) fought against idolatry and worshipping Namrood. the ruler for Iraq. Lut (A.S.) fought against unnatural wickedness and homo-sexual sins. Nuh (A.S.) warned against Atheism. Dawood (AS.) and his son Sulaiman (A.S.) fought against injustice and warned against failure to proclaim Gods glory whole-heartedly by making use of faculties and powers gifted by God. Ayyub (AS.) set an example of patience and warned against impatience and want of self-confidence. Isma'il

(A.S.) Idris (A.S.) and Zulkifl (A.S.) warned against want of perseverance; Zun Nun (AS.) against hasty angerZakriya (A.S.) against spiritual isolation, Bi Bi Maryam (not prophet) against the lust of the world. Isa (A.S.) preached how to be merciful towards others. Yehiya (A.S.), the son of Zakriya (A.S,) was the fore-runner of Jesus Christ and spread Christianity,till he was slain by the Romans at the instance of the Roman Emperor Herod.

The King of Egypt was called Pharoah. Several dynasties ruled over Egypt for several centuries. After the release of Yusuf (A.S.) from the prison, his contemporary Pharoah made him his Prime Minister, reposed confidence in him and gradually handed over to him the reins of administration, because the believer and noble Pharoah preferred to spend rest of his life in meditation. It was at this time when Yusuf (A.S.) invited to Egypt, Yaqoob (A.S.) and his eleven brothers from Canaan, the famine-stricken place Thus the twelve tribes of Bani Israi'l flourished in Egypt. led a royal life and got settled there peacefully. They lost their pomp, pride and glory and gradually became theslaves of the succeeding" pharaohs They were mercilessly maltreated tortured. They suffered pain and humiliation under the despotism and autocracy of many pharaohs. Moreover, the contemporary Pharoah of Moosa (A.S.) claimed. The unbeliever Pharoah and his Wife Aasia who believed in one God adopted Moosa (AS.) as their son and brought him up in their palace. By Allah's unaccountable bounties. He granted him prophet hood in order to fight against the claim of his Divinity and to liberate his people. the twelve tribes of Bani Isra'il from the proud and adamant Pharaoh. After the Pharoah and his army were swallowed by

River Nile and Moosa (A.S.) and his followers emerged victorious the throne was passed on to a better Pharoah. Moosa (A.S.) never aspired to ascend the throne though it was possible for him to do it. He went on with his mission of eradicating evils and propagating the religion of Allah. In the absence of Moosa (A.S.), a man by name Saamari who was practicing witchcraft made a golden calf and was successful in persuading the people to worship the calf. Again he was commanded by Allah to go there with the difficult mission of abolishing calf-worship. By Allah's grace, he Was successful in all his missions in his life time itself .Haroon (A.S.). brother Of Moosa (A.S.) was granted prophethood to support and help in all the missions of Moosa (A.S.).

Prophet Sikandar Zulqurnain who was a great ruler also, was very humble affectionate and compassionate towards human race. When he was travelling far and wide, he came across a nation the people of which were always in terror and distress owing to the presence of the pre-historic tribals called Yajooj, Majooj. They were cannibals. They used to Come from the mountains, eat up all the fields and devour human beings. When Prophet Zulquarnain reached that territory the inhabitants lodged a complaint against Yajooj, Majooj. Hence, he started the tedious task of constructing a very strong wall with hard stones and molten iron between two summits of the mountains and blocked the passage of Yajooj and Majooj. His mission was to relieve humanity from the cannibals.

In all the above-mentioned aspects and missions of the past prophets, there is a special purification of soul. But Prophet Muhammed (SAW) is called an ideal Prophet, because he brought about universal revolution and universal reforms in all aspects of life. He refined the Pagan Arabs, savage tribes and the entire humanity in all walks of life. He dispelled the darkness of the age of ignorance from the world society and brought the light of Golden Age. Allah offered him every opportunity to practice what all he preached. His mission was all-faceted and universal when that of the past prophets were tribal. Their message revealed from God was confined to their respective tribes. Our Prophet (SAW) was the embodiment of all the beautiful faculties and all the noble traits of all the prophets. Now let us examine the greatest merits and prudent deeds of Muhammed (SAW) one by one: -

IDEAL RELIGIOUS PRECEPTOR AND BEST EDUCATIONIST

Though, our prophet (SAW), was illiterate, his teachings are pregnant of complete codes of life. The essence of Quran and Ahadis are inter-related, especially regarding codes of ethics.

We can observe Quranic essence in Ahadis and Ahadis containing injunctions and prohibitions. incorporated in Quran. There are many Ahadis not contained in Quran. His teachings have been briefly summarized in his last sermon. he delivered on the occasion of his last pilgrimage (Haijatul-Wtda'a) which has been quoted in the previous chapters. Allah sent revelations to our Prophet (SAW) through the Arch Angel Jibra'il, and his responsibility of preaching and convincing the people about the good in them, was very tough. A child is born innocent with human potentialities to develop, and the religion of Allah, Islam. According to Moulana Khaia Kamaluddin. " The objective of the religion of Muhammed (SAW) Islam was not salvation from the fall, but the upliftment of the development of that potentiality which is latent in man, in other words, evolution of humanity. Like everything in nature, man possesses certain aptitudes or capabilities and hidden faculties. It is to work them out to bring them to development to the best of advantage. that religion has been vouch safed to him. Religion as Muhammed (SAW) taught a theory of life a thing to live upon, in order to bring to prominence that which novel and good in us"

Our Prophet (SAW) was the best teacher of discipline, manner and etiquette. Once Bi B' Asha (R) rebuked at a man for having scolded our Prophet (SAW). He taught her the etiquette of life and admonished her by saying, " I have been sent to give comfort to the people and not to trouble them ". The believer disciples who sought his advice and teachings were amply benefited by him. He used to preach them with all patience and untiringly.

As soon as Prophet (SAW) reached Madinah, he established an Islamic State and after gaining some amount of stability, and after constructing Masjid-e-Nabvi, he established the first Islamic University in the varandah hall of Masjid-e-Nabvi where some of his companions were lodged who were called Ashab-e-Suffah. They were the guests of the Prophet (SAW) With whom he partook his meals, obtained as gifts from the Muslims of Madinah. He never ate anything leaving them hungry. Several occasions occurred when our Prophet (SAW) and his quests went Without food as long as two or three consecutive days. They suffered the pangs of hunger with all patience. These Ashab-e-Suffa had no families. Hence they could dedicate the remaining part of life in acquiring and imparting religious knowledge to others, memorizing the already revealed Quranic verse and recording Ahadis. The most popular Sahabi of this Islamic University was Abu Huraira who very often called on Bi Bi Aisha. who was well versed in Ahadis. in order to clarify doubts. There are scores of books of Ahadis. The first contributors of these books were Bi B' Aisha and the Ashab-e-Suffah. Though our unlettered Messenger of God was the founder of that Islamic University, we consider him as the first and best Educationist of Islam.

Here it is necessary to quote a few short and easily comprehensible Ahadis to describe his teachings.

H:- "Allah has sent me to complete the excellence of virtues and perfect all good actions (Shrah-al-Sunnah).

When asked to invoke course upon the polytheists. our Prophet (SAW) said

H:-" I have not been sent to invoke curse. but I have been sent as mercy". (Muslim)

H:-'When Iman enters the heart. it opens it for Islam"(Baihaqi).

H:- "Modesty is the distinctive quality of Islam"(Moatha)

H:- " Gentleness adorns everything while lack of gentleness makes things defective (Muslim)

H:- "the man who does not have tender feeling for his fellowmen, lack goodness" (Muslim)

H:- Wealth is not riches but in contentment" (Bukhari)

H:- One who is able to act calmly in composed manner gets blessing from Allah, while one who acts is haste, entangled in the mischief of Satan" (Tirmizi).

H:- One has Imam is simple and beneficent; and the sinner is cunning and cowardly" (Abu Dawood).

H: -" Charity does not in any way decrease the wealth and he who forgives the servant Of Allah, adds to his own respect. Allah elevates his position of the person in the estimation of the people who show humility " (Muslim)

H " By him, in whose hand is my soul no one is a perfect believer until he wishes for his Muslim brothers, what he wishes for himself ". (Bukhari. Muslim).

H :- " The best social action is to love and hate for the cause of Allah L' (Abu Dawood)

H IV-The cleanest food is that which a man earns by his own hands " (Baihaqui)

H 'i If Allah pleases, he can forgive all the sins of a sinner, except his disobedience to his parents. Allah punishes in this life for one who disobeys his parents" (Baihaqi).

H i" Stay close to your mother to serve her well, because paradise lies at her feet V" (Ahmed, Baihaqi, Nasai).

H :- "If you find a person who is blessed with abstension from worldly possessions and avoids vain talks, then be close to him, for such a person is blessed with Divine Wisdom" (Baihaqi).

H :- Whoever failed to thank a person, who did a favour to him, actually, failed to thank Allah " (Ahmed, Tirmizi).

H - " The worst among the people is the double faced one. He comes to some people with one face and to others with the other face (Muslim).

H:- Who makes hoarding is sinner" (Al-Mun-Taqa)

H:- He who wrongly took a span of land, Allah shall make him carry around his neck seven earths on the day of resurrection"(Muslim)

H:- The charity to the needy; being with your near relatives" (Abu Dawwod).

H:- Pay to the worker, his wages, before, sweat from his labour dries on his body"

Ibn-e-Maja)

H:- The first thing that will be decided among the people on the Day of Resurrection will pertain to bloodshed " (Muslim)

H:- None of you should judge between two persons when they are angry " (Muslim).

H:- " Kindness to every living being has reward " (Bukhari, Muslim)

H:- Whoever guides someone towards goodwill receives the reward of the one who acts upon it (Muslim)

H :- It the greatest Jihad to speak out truth in front of a tyrant ruler (Muslim)

H:- He who loves to meet Allah, Allah also loves to meet him and one who dislikes to meet Allah. He also abhors to meet him" (Muslim)

H:-The world is a prison-house for a believer and a paradise for a non-believer"(Muslim).

BEST PROPAGATOR OF ISLAM:

For the propagation of Islam. our Prophet (SAW) sent 300 letters to kings of different countries, tribal chiefs. religious heads including Pope Paul of Rome, through the Muslim emissaries, inviting them to come into the fold of Islam. It is believed that his letters reached as far as China. Besides. he sent his companions far and wide to preach the tenets and objectives of Islam. The letter of Mohammed (SAW) addressed to the Christian King of Egypt has been discovered and preserved in Istanbul. Shaikh Falah Zaki. who is the member Of Cultural Foundation. Abu Dhabi. has compiled one hundred letters of Mohammed (SAW). addressed to his contemporary heads of States and Tribes. He has said that this compilation would be published in chronological! order.

As our Prophet (SAW) was unlettered. his companions wrote the letters on his behalf in compliance With his request. The seal of his silver ring bearing his name "Mohammed" was used as his Signature. Even after his death. this seal was used by his successors in documents, agreements. letters and orders from Islamic State. During the period of the third Khalifa Hazrat Usman Zun-Nurain (R), he was wearing this ring in his finger. When he was drawing water from the well, the ring slipped from his finger and fell into the well. The water was emptied from the well for its recovery. For the dismay and disappointment of all the Muslims. It could not be recovered. It was nothing but the expediency of Almighty Allah that it was lost forever. His letters are being recovered one by one with his seal some of which have been published in different magazines- As examples. I am presenting in the following his letter with his seal discovered in Tunisia address to the ruler of Omen: a letter with his seal addressed to Mundhir Governor of Bahrain: English translation of two letters. addressed to the Pope of Rome and Jews of Khaiber.

Letters of the Holy Prophet

Letter to the Pope of Rome

In the name of Allah, the Compassionate, the Merciful.

Peace be upon him, who believes in Allah. I am of the faith that Isa (Jesus A.S) son of Mariam (Mary) was the spirit of Allah and His World. Allah infused him in the pious Mariam.

I believe in Allah, all His Books and His commands which he sent to Ibrahim, Ismail, in what was given to Musa and Isa (A.S), and other prophets by Allah. In faith and belief, we do not differentiate in accepting any of the prophets. We are Muslims (meaning obedient to Allah) peace be upon him who follows the guidance (Tabar.'s History Vol.3, p88)

Allah's Seal Prophet Muhammed

Note: Alongwith the letter to Caesar, the Holy Prophet (pbuh) had also sent a letter to the Pope. The letter testified to his Prophethood and observed, **No doubt, he is a true Prophet**". Thereafter he addressed a congregation in the cathedral and informed the people and he had recieved a letter from the Arabian Prophet Ahmed (pbuh) who had then testified that there is no god save Allah and that Ahmed (pbuh) was the servant and Prophet of Allah. The people were highly infuriated to hear this truthful declaration and they beat him so much (Ibn a-S'ad. Vol.3 p20)

Letter to the Jews of Khyber

In the name of Allah, the compassionate, the Merciful

From Muhammed, the Prophet of Allah who is like Moosa (Moses A.S) a prophet and messenger and he testified to what Moosa (A.S) had brought.

O people of Torah, has Allah not stated in the Torah people who will be with him, shall be harsh towards the enemies of Allah. And amongst themselves, they shall be kind and loving. They shall bow and prostrate before Allah and they shall seek his bounty and goodwill"

I ask you to swear by Allah, who sent Torah for you and made your forefathers eat 'mann' and 'Salva' dried sea for them and rid them of the tyranny of Pharaoh. Is it not written in Torah that you should believe in me?

After the explanation about me in the Torah, do guidance and transgression become apparent?

Therefore I invite you towards Allah and His prophet (Kanz ul-Ummal, Vol. p285)

Allah's Seal Prophet Muhammed

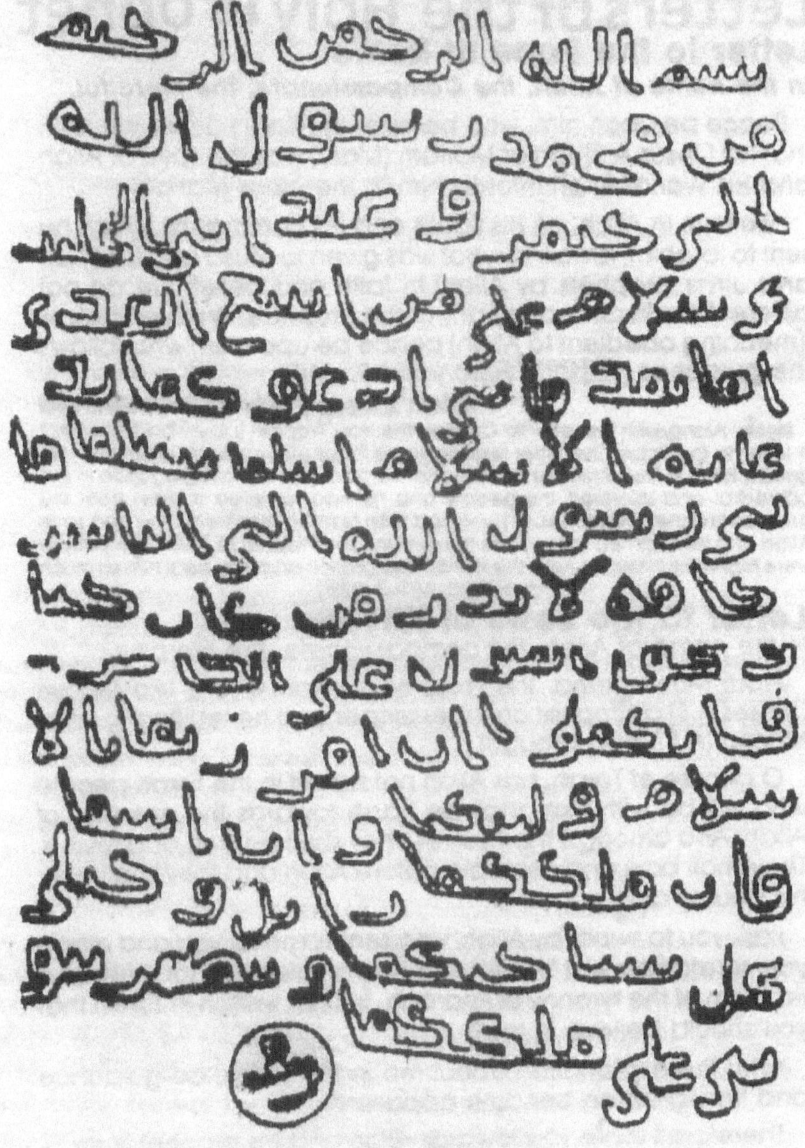

(Courtesy, Weekly Magazine " Rani " Dated 13.03.1994)

The Prophet Muhammad's Letter to Mundhir, Governor of Baharain

In the Name of Allah Most Gracius Most Merciful

From Muhammad messenger of Allah to Mundhir Governor of Bahrain Peace be upon you. I praise Allah to you than Whom there is no other Allah. And I bear witness that there is no deity except Allah and that Muhammad is His servant and messenger — I remind you of Allah The Mighty Sublime. Whoever accepts admonition accepts it for his own soul. And whoever obeys my envoys and follows their guidance, he has, in fact, obeyed me and who ever accepts their admonition he has, in fact accepted my admonition. My envoys have praised your conduct and I have recommended you to your people Therefore leave the Muslims (and all others) in what they believe in I have pardoned the criminals, so accept their excuses So long as you keep on the right We will not remove you from your office Whoever is firm on his (old religion of) Christianity or Judaism must pay Jizyah (tax).

(Courtesy " Islamic Voice " Dated October 1988)

Original Sanskrit Text

एतस्मिन्नन्तरे म्लेच्छ आचार्येण समन्वितः ।
महामद इति ख्यातः शिष्यशाखासमन्वितः ॥ ५ ॥
नृपश्चैव महादेवं मरुस्थलनिवासिनम् ।
गंगाजलैश्च संस्नाप्य पंचगव्यसमन्वितैः ।
चंदनादिभिरभ्यर्च्य तुष्टाव मनसा हरम् ॥ ६ ॥
भोजराज उवाच—नमस्ते गिरिजानाथ मरुस्थलनिवासिने ।
त्रिपुरासुरनाशाय बहुमायाप्रवर्तिने ॥ ७ ॥
म्लेच्छैर्गुप्ताय शुद्धाय सच्चिदानन्दरूपिणे ।
त्वं मां हि किंकरं विद्धि शरणार्थमुपागतम् ॥ ८ ॥

(Bhavishya Purana, part 3, Khand 3, Adhya 3, Shalok 5-8)

ORIGINAL SANSKRIT TEXT.

॥ अथर्ववेदे २०।१२७ ॥

॥ अथ कुन्तापसूक्तानि ॥

इदं जना उप श्रुत नराशंस स्तविष्यते । ॥ १२७ ॥
षष्टिं सहस्रा नवतिं च कौरम आ रुशमेषु दद्महे ॥ १ ॥

उष्ट्रा यस्य प्रवाहणो वधूमन्तो द्विर्दश ।
वर्ष्मा रथस्य नि जिहीडते दिव ईषमाणा उपस्पृशः ॥ २ ॥
एष इषाय मामहे शतं निष्कान्दश स्रजः ।
त्रीणि शतान्यर्वतां सहस्रा दश गोनाम् ॥ ३ ॥ (५)

(Atharva veda. In its 20th Kanda, 127th Sukta, the Mantra 1-3)

(Courtesy " Islamic Voice " Dated, November 1988)

The letters of Mohammed (SAW), addressed to different heads of states, prove, as to how he carried out the divine command regarding the execution of his mission in propagating Islam.

BEST SOCIAL REFORMER-

Islamic Revolution brought about by Prophet Mohammed (SAW) was religious as well as social because it aimed at revolutionary concepts. such as unity of God, human rights etc. its objectives were social reforms in every aspect of life. The theories of reformations Of Our Prophet (SAW) were coupled with practice which attracted the other nations of the world during his life time. This was the reason for the fast spreading Of Islam in other Countries. After the lapse Of the Age of Ignorance and advent of Golden Age which started after the Islamic reformations. The preamble of the constitution of every country provides for securityJustice, personal liberty, equality, fraternity, freedom of speech and human rights It was our Prophet (SAW) who Introduced all reforms and laid certain norms for the welfare of the weaker sects of the societies. His democratic spirit brought him grand success and achievements.

Before the advent Of Islam. women were considered to be the commercial commodity and domestic animals having the worst or no Status in the society. The Islamic principles emancipated women from the bondage of man. Islam teaches that man and woman were created from the same soil, equipped with equal capabilities for intellectual. spiritual and moral attainments. Our Prophet was the first person in the world who worked for the emancipation of women. He introduced significant reforms to improve the status of women which led the whole world to recognize the equal status and rights of men and women. Before the advent of Islam old and disabled parents and relatives were mercilessly driven away to suffer till their last breath. Islam imposed religious dunes on every Muslim to maintain the aged parents' relatives and children.

Our Prophet was the first person to prescribe the guidelines for the welfare of the labourers. According to his principles, the daily wages of the labourers must be pad reasonably and soon after the work is done. Every child is born with his own human rights. Our Prophet (SAVV) was against child labour. because he has got rights to be educated. Inspite of their rights for the education they were and are being exploited in labour in pitiable conditions in their tender age. Our Prophet (SAW) laid guidelines for the welfare of the children and to safeguard their rights as he did in every aspect of life.

H :- "Of all that the father can give to his children, the best in their good educational training" (Muslim)

THE GREATEST FORGIVE: -

As Prophet Mohammed (SAW) was the Prophet for entire humanity. it was against his nature and below his dignity to invoke curse or take revenge on his enemies and the enemies of Islam. Some instances will prove that he was the greatest forgiver ever born in the world.

After the conversion of Hazrat Umar (R) and at the time of infancy of Islam. our Prophet (SAW) was praying in Kabathullah. An enemy of Islam poured a basket full of filth and stool on him. Some Muslims caught hold of him and wanted to punish him. But. this afflicted noble personality dissuaded them to punish him and persuaded them to pray for him that God might lead him on the path of righteousness. The mother of Hazrat Abu Huraira. the most prominent personality of the Ashab-e-Suffah. was a polithetst (Mushrik). There had been always exchange of words between the son and the mother regarding the difference of opinions about their faiths, once she rebuked against and spoke ill of our Prophet (SAW), On hearing this. he prayed Allah that He might bless her with Islam. When her son returned home, he found her as a Muslim.

In spite of the maximum efforts of Muslim emissaries who went to convey the message of Islam, many nations remained infidel. But he refused to invoke curse on them but only prayed for them that they might be benefited by the Divine Guidance. Once one of the greatest enemies of our Prophet (SAW) was arrested and tied to the pillar of Masjid-e-Nabvi. He pleaded for clemency and to spare his life by accepting ransom. But he released him without taking ransom. Highly impressed by his noble gesture and act of forgiveness, he immediately embraced Islam and pronounced that nothing was dearer to him than the Apostle of God. I-abid Bin A'Sam. a Jew of Madina practiced sorcery upon our Prophet (SAW) which affected his health and he suffered for a certain period. But. he never thought of revenging on the sorcerer. Abdullah Bin Ubal was the ring-leader of the hypocrites (Munafiqin) who applied and made use of all his strategy to crush the Islamic common wealth, and cast a false and unjust slander on the character of Bi Bi Aisha, the chaste wife of Mohammed (SAW). On the day of his demise, he offered his own sheet to cover his dead body and extended his pardon.

At the instance of Hinda, the wife of Abu Sufyan the arch enemy of Islam, Hazrat Hamza the uncle of our Prophet (SAW) was killed by a Negro by name Wahshi, in the Battle of Uhad in 3 A.H. Later. Our Prophet (SAVV) extended his forgiveness. The inhabitants Of Taif who persecuted him, Hazrat Bilal and Hazrat Zaid, most cruelly and brutally, were also the recipients of his forgiveness. A Jew accused and rebuked at him for not repaying the loan, before lapsing the time of agreement. Hazrat Omar (R) spoke angrily with him. But, our Prophet never got angry but arranged to repay the dues, along with some gifts in addition. in order to remove from the creditor's heart any hard feelings against the rude behavior of Hazrat Umar (R) The main mission of Abu Sufyan was to kill our Prophet (SAW) and to destruct Islam totally. On 8 A.H. our Prophet (SAW) entered Makkah as its conqueror In this bloodless conquest. the people of Makkah including its Chief, Abu Safyan surrendered and expected to be executed. Out of fear. some of the people of Makkah fled to Jeddah and other countries. Instead, our Prophet (SAW) proclaimed general amnesty and Sufyan is safe in his home and those who take shelter in his home. have special security". Abu Sufyans wife. Hinda who chewed the liver of his uncle Hazrat Hamza (R) also received generous pardon. On receiving the Information of general amnesty. Akramah, the son of Abu Jehl, the enemy returned from Yemen and met our Prophet (SAW) in Madinah who received him with smiling face and welcomed him warmly. Habbar Bin Aswad beat Bl Zainab, the daughter of Mohammed (SAW) mercilessly. while she was migrating to Madinah. She was pregnant the assault of her enemy resulted in her death after a few days. He was forgiven. When Makkah was conquered. Safwan Bin ummya fled to Jeddah. The Apostle of God sent his turban to him through his companions as a Sign of assurance of security.

It was the habit of our Prophet (SAW) to invoke blessings on his enemies. Instead of invoking curse or imprecations on them. whenever they did wrong to him. His heart was so pure that was free from ugly, impure and unholy spirit of revenge. In his character one of the lustrous jewels was his quality of forgiveness.

BEST POLITICIAN, DIPLOMAT AND DEMOCRAT

The two traits of Prophet Mohammed (SAW) may seem to be quite contradictory to each other But the contradiction was meaningful and lawful. He was the great hero and military commander, the world has ever witnessed. At the same time, he was the efficient peacemaker and peace-lover. He laid down certain norms for securing peace with God. peace with people of various religion and peace with irrational animals. A good politician in the purest sense is one whose polices and activities are most beneficial to his nation and all its citizens. Our Prophet (SAW) was a politician par excellence, who was the best example for other politicians of every age and in every place.

As soon as he entered Madinah, he created relationship and cemented brotherhood between the refugees of Makkah and the helpers Of Madinah to the full satisfaction and pleasure of the people concerned. The system of Islamic Government was republic consisting of Muslims and Non-

Muslims on the basis of equality and equal status with an elected chief as its head. Automatically, all the Muslims accepted our Prophet (SAW) as the head of the State and religious Preceptor. As a shrewd politician, first of all he wanted to safeguard the Muslim minority community from the Non-Muslim tribes. He invited the powerful Jewish chieftains of the tribes of Banu Qainuqa, Banu Nazir and Banu Quraiza and concluded with them a pact of friendship, affinity and mutual help.

This was the first political victory of Islam. According to the pact, the following conditions were prescribed.

1. The Muslims and the Jews should live as one people and citizens of Islamic State.

2. The two parties could follow their own faiths and one should not interfere with the religion of the other.

3. In the event of a war with a third party, each was bound to come to the assistance of the other, provided, the latter was the aggrieved and inflicted party.

4. In the event of attack on Muslims, all the three parties must join hands in defence,

5. Madinah should be regarded sacred by the population of Madinah, all bloodshed being prohibited therein.

Through this pact and sagacity of Mohammed (SAW), the whole population of Madinah was safeguarded from even internal bloodsheds and to some extent calmness prevailed. Prophet (SAW) was a lover of democracy and he was the first to introduce it in the history of the world. He was the head of the Commonwealth and gave special importance to the doctrines of democracy. As a true and perfect democrat, he did not nominate his successor, but only suggested some candidates for election. which was purely a democratic procedure. The administration of his government was always with "Shura"or consultative assembly with representatives of people like our present democratic legislatures. He decreed a norm that: nobody should be appointed or elected who seeks or canvasses for the post. He fought against undue favoritism. nepotism, prejudice or corruption, because, these are the factors which spoil the administration of the state. The noble, unique and sagacious introduction of democracy of our Prophet (SAW) opened the eyes of the people and several republics emerged in the world.

Before the advent of Islam, prisoners were treated most harshly and persecuted in an uncivilized manner. Our Prophet was the first person who tried humanize law. According to his directives, his companions did not kill or illtreat the prisoners of war.After the victory in the Battle of Badr 2 A.H., ail the prisoners of war were released hope over the prospects that they would come into the fold of Islam.

As the Muslims were badly in need of money and the Baitul-Mal (State Treasury' empty, they were forced by the circumstances to take ransom for the prisoner's war during the event of Badr. Throughout the life of Mohammed (SAW). Several battles were fought several thousands of war captives were brought to Madinah. Highly impressed by the honourable and kind treatment by the Muslims, most of the captives embraced Islam. and rest of them were released without taking any amount for ransom. Among the captives of in Badr, were two uncles and one cousin (Hazrat Ali's Brother) of Prophet (SAW).Hazrat Abbas, Hazrat (name) and Ageei, who embraced Islam later. Ageel was the son of Abu Talib and father of Muslim who attained martyrdom in Kufa. Muslim was the first cousin of Imam Hussain the martyre of Karbala. The people of Madinah strongly refused except for all the three persons as they were closely related to our Prophet (SAW).

Tribe of Banu Khuraiza had signed a pact of friendship with the Islamic State But. they broke the diplomatic ties with Islamic State, joined hands with other Jewish tribe and Invaded against Islam. They were defeated and captivated. They lawfully deserved punishment for their treason and rebellion. The destruction of their tribe and their execution became indispensable because they posed a great threat to Islam. There were few execution of criminals on special situations which were unavoidable. Several thousand captives were fortunate to receive pardon from our Prophet as he was a great diplomat, and efficient politician. The efficiency of his compassion and peace-loving nature was beyond description. The Muslims had to fight wars only after migration to Madinah for self-defense against the of their enemies. Prophet Mohammed (SAW) Instructed the Muslims to fight only with the culprits and aggressors, leaving all others in peace and sparing their lives and properties. Those who surrendered were treated most honourably and were assured full protection, security and peace. The Islamic State ensured amity and peace between different countries.

BEST ECONOMIST-

It has already been said that Zakaat and Zakaatul-Fitr are obligatory charity on the assets of all Muslims including sick people, crippled people and children. In addition to these, our

Prophet (SAW) advocated voluntary charities as Sadaqa etc. Zimmi means the Non-Musiim citizens of Islamic state. Our Prophet (SAW) imposed a very little and nominal tax called Jizya on the Zimmis as the compensation for the exemption from participating in the wars and for safeguarding their interests by the Islamic State. He exempted from paying Jizya. the poor, the unemployed, the sick, the old, the crippled and children of the Non-Muslims. But, the Islamic State shouldered the responsibility of the safety of life, property and honour of every memberof Non-Muslim community including those who were exempted from paying Jizya .Thus the Revered Islamic Sovereign maintained peace and tranquility in the state, The Zimmis were highly pleased with his economic policies.

Before the Hijrat. the plight of the slaves was unimaginable. They were poorly fed, poorly clothed and harshly beat. They were sent to work in the enterprises of other masters and their own masters swallowed their whole wages. our Prophet (SAW) laid some principles according to which the slaves would be maintained in the same standard in which the masters lived. Certain percentage of his wages should be given to him.

He could not completely abolish the system of slavery, because of the presence of the in the Islamic State. The principles, he advocated were favorable for these slaves and unfavorable for the masters. Hence, even Muslims began to dislike to possess slaves. For the sake of Allah's pleasure thousands of slaves were bought and liberated by the Muslims. The slaves Of the Muslims were treated as their own family members..

When Madinah was flooding with gold and silver and the State Treasury was full, the house of our Prophet (SAVV) was empty. According to Quranic injunction, he distributed 4/5 of the war booties among the participants of war. One fifth of the booty went to him, which he distributed among his relatives, poor and needy communities. He kept nothing for himself. Through his recommendations, the unemployed refugees of Makkah were given employments by the Ansars of Madinah. As the best economist, he brought about better distribution of wealth by his prudent economic policies which are the salient features of Islamic Socialism.

BEST HOST: -

All the Muslims are aware of the generosity, hospitality and patience of our Prophet (SAW). No needy person went away empty handed who approached him for help. He used to barrow money and help others in genuine cases, Sometimes. he wished to invite his friends in order to enjoy and promote brotherhood. For example. he held the tonsuring ceremony (Head - Shaving function) of his son, Ibrahim and invited all his friends. The child died at the age of 1 1/2 years. On behalf of Hazrat Ali (R), he hosted a Valima feast on the occasion of his wedding with Bi Bi Fatima (R) (Prophet's youngest daughter). He used to forego his meals whenever he received hungry guests. Ashab-e-Suffah were his permanent guests. The goodness of his hospitality reached its pinnacle when he received a Jew guest. One night, a Jew came to him and sought his permission to stay in the night at his home. He offered his palm-leaves mattress to sleep on. At early morning he saw that the Jew had absconded, after passing stool on his bed. In haste, he left his travelling bag absent-mindedly. The news spread in the neighborhood. The Muslims wanted to catch hold of him and punish him. But, our noble Prophet (SAW) prevented them to wreak avenge. saying that his bowels might have been upset and he ran away due to frights. When other Muslims offered to clean his bed, he did not allow them to do so, saying that the Jew was his guest and he was his host. This Supreme host himself cleaned his bed. Trembling with fear, the Jew came back to recover his bag. Our Prophet (SAW) got up. made kind enquiries about his health and handed over his bag most politely with smiling face. Has anybody heard of such hospitality of any Sovereign of a State?

BEST JUDGE: -

Our Prophet had the greatest sense of justice and equality irrespective of caste, creed race or status. He never discriminated between friends and foes and Muslims and Non-Muslims, in matter of law and justice. He never showed partiality towards his relatives, the rich or the people of high birth. Regarding justice, equality was his prime basis and he maintained a very high standard of justice. As no separate judiciary was established at that time, he had to the duties of the judge, and he was the final authority for appeal. He did it most fearlessly, not minding the hostility, enmity, malice or rancor. Once, in a trial between a Jew and a Muslim, he pronounced his verdict in favor of the Jew. Once. a well-to-do woman of the highly respected clan of Makhzum from which Hazrat Umar (R) also hailed, committed theft and the theft was proved. The people of the tribe approached him to procure pardon for her. He refused to distinguish between rich and poor, and relative and non-relative; and ordered that her hand should be cut off. He said, " Had it been my own daughter, Fatima, I would certainly have cut her hand". Whenever, he got any case without witness, he did not use to settle the matter, but used to help the loser by offering the reasonable compensation from the State Treasury, in case, both the opponent parties were Jews, he used to decide the case, according to the law Of Torah.

When both the parties were Christians, he decided the matter according to the Gospels of Bible. As the best judge, he respected the religions and the Laws of their scriptures.

BEST LEGISLATOR -

There are four sources for Islamic Laws (Shariat) namely

1. Divine Laws contained in Quran.

2. Sunnat-e-Rasool

3. Qiyas which means legislation by referring the analytical cases in order to solve the new problems.

4. Ijma'a which means legislation through consensus on the basis of indirect exhortations of Quranic Laws, for example, the Muslim law has legalized the blood-transfusion and donations of organs on the basis of Quranic verse in which Almighty Allah commands the believers to share His bounties with the needy ones.

Qiyas and Ijma'a constitute the science of Islamic Jurisprudence, because Islam should not be incapable of solving new problems. The codes laid by our Prophet (SAW), the greatest legislator of the world, embrace all the spheres of human life, The holy Quran and Ahadis-eNabvi give us the codes, pertaining to religion, society, administration, morality, international brotherhood, organization of military and war ethics. The Divine law has left scope for legislation to solve the new problems. After consulting the members of the "Shura'

'(Parliament). our Prophet (SAW), the greatest legislator, so easily and pleasantly solved the new cases and pronounced his verdict to the happiness and satisfaction of the concerned parties, preserving

GREATEST MILITARY COMMANDER AND GALLANT WARRIOR:-

First of all. we must know what kind of military commander our Prophet (SAW) Was. Allah chose him as His last Apostle, assigning him with the universal missions of spreading the true religion, refining the world society and fighting for the rights of the weak, downtrodden and the oppressed. He never had territorial ambitions or craze for power. The wars, he fought were truth verses falsehood; light verses darkness; peace Stanzas aggression; humanity verses brutality and Islam verses infidelity. His wars were sacred which were meant for the service to humanity and permanent peace.

In the opinion of the common people. a great commander was one who had a great and well-equipped army. emerges victorious in battles by the help of numerical strength of the army, conquers territory after territory, executes the prisoners of war and loves general massacre. But our Prophet (SAW) was a different type of commander who was supreme by his nature. After Hijrat 27 great battles were fought, during his life besides the small invasions of the Arabian tribes. The Islamic capital was surrounded by the enemies such as the Christians and Jews of Arab, the Romans. the Zoroastrians of Persia and the Quraish of Makkah. The Islamic army was always numerically weak and ill-equipped when compared to the armies of the foes. But, miraculously, the Muslims achieved triumphant victories, because truth prevailed over those small armies. Our Prophet (SAW) was such a type of commander who treated the prisoners of war with affection, humility and applaudable generosity. He led the Muslim armies in several battles such as first Battle of Badr, Battle of Uhad, second Battle of Badr, Battle of Muraisi, Battle of Trench. Battle of Khaiber, bloodless conquest of Makkah, Battle of Hunain etc. Though our Prophet (SAW) and the Muslims were untrained in warfare, they won several battles as great warriors do. Though he was untrained and unlettered, but, as the greatest war-nor, tackled splendidly. the most perilous and difficult situations in the battle field. In the battle of Uhad and Hunain, he was trapped and surrounded by his enemies, Many of the Muslims attained martyrdom in order to save his life. He tactfully got out of the dangerous spots and fought till he won the battles. In several battles especially in the Battle of Uhad, he was seriously wounded. He received eighty-three wounds, bled profusely and was more dead than alive. But, his gallantry and chivalry did not stop him from participating in wars. The Quraish of Makkah had to defend their city against the invasions of the surrounding tribes for forty years, when our Holy Prophet was young. This untrained but greatest warrior was brave right from his boyhood. When he was ten years old. the Quraish had to defend Makkah twice from the aggressive Invasions of the surrounding tribes. in the history of Makkah, those two battles were called the Battles of Fijar. Those two battles were fought between the tribe of Qajse and the tribe of Quraish of Makkah. As a lover of peace, our Prophet (SAW) never used to interfere in the internal feuds, unless, he was called for. During the two battles of Fijar. he was young in age (only ten years old), but old in wisdom. As he felt that justice was with the Quraish (his own tribe), he wished to help the army of Makkah, unrequested, Who would take this young warrior to confront with the hostile army ? He voluntarily ran to the battle field and helped the Makkan army by picking up the arrows and spears of the enemies and supplying them to the Makkan solders. He helped them as much as possible in both the battles of Fijar. Any number of arrows might have struck him and caused his death. This valiant and chivalrous young lad staked his own life fearlessly and undauntedly for the sake of Makkah. Atlast he became the greatest military commander; the world has ever witnessed.

PRUDENT PEACE MAKER: -

Though our Prophet (SAW) became the head of the Islamic State, who did not in the internal affairs of the Christians and the Jewish societies of Madinah, they were to decide all matters among themselves by referring their scriptures, revealed to their prophets, whenever he was approached to settle any controversial issues, he used to refer their scriptures and settle the matters beautifully to the full satisfaction of the concerned opponent parties, in his young age and long before he obtained prophethood, he was the active member of an association, called "Halaful-Fuzool". It was an oath, taken by four Fazal brothers. whose names ended with the name "Fazal", The objectives of the association founded by these four brothers were to eschew violence, pursue peace, help the needy and safeguard the travelers from decoity and help those travelers who became the victims of the plunder of the decoits, Through this information we can come to know that there were reformers and social-minded people in Arabia, the darkest part of the world, during the age of Ignorance. We can imagine, how much our Prophet was fond of maintaining peace and service to humanity.

There was an occurrence of an incident when our Prophet (SAW) averted a great bloodshed and established peace among the four main clans of Quraish which was his great contribution to the stability and safety for Kabathullah. It has already been stated that the people of the four distinguished tribes Of Quraish Were the descendants of the four sons Of Abd-e-Munaf. Those tribes had their own sub-tribes and sub-clans. Those four main tribes were the custodians of Kabathullah, who were always hostile to each other, At the same time, all the members of all the tribes admired and loved our Prophet dearly, held him in high esteem, reposed confidence in him and called him "Al-Ameen" which means the trust-worthy. Whatever he said, it was agreeable to all of them. Before he became the Prophet, there was a prolonged torrential rain and sudden flood which cracked the walls of Kabathullah. The four walls of the Kaba had to be pulled down and rebuilt. The members of the four tribes, including Mohammed (SAW) unitedly worked in rebuilding the Kabathullah. The sacred Black Stone (Hajr-e-Aswad) had to be placed again in the Eastern wall of the Kaba. At this issue, the dispute arose as to who should have the honour of placing the Sacred Stone in its original place, there was about to be a great bloodshed over this issue. Abu Umayyad. a great influential, respected and powerful personality of Makkah wanted to avert the bloodshed and tabled a proposal to which all the tribes agreed. He said, 'Let the first person who passes through the gate of the Haram (Precincts of Holy Kaba), be our arbitrator Fortunately, it was our Prophet (SAW) who passed through the gate. The joy of the highly elated people knew no bounds and they cried together. "It IS AlAmeen! We will accept his verdict. He asked for a mantle to be brought. He placed the Black Stone in the middle of the mantle and asked the representatives of four tribes to hold the four corners of the mantle, lift it up and take it inside the Kabah. On reaching the Eastern wall of the Kaba, he lifted the Stone from the mantle and placed it in the wall to the full satisfaction of the disputing clans. With his sagacity and prudence, he brought about reconciliation and peace among the fiery people of Makkah. Such was the appreciable deed of the greatest peace-maker..

It was the ancient custom of Arabia, that any Arab. whether he was friend or foe or Christian or Jew or idolator, should not be prevented from performing Hajj or Omrah. When Makkah was in the hands of the Autocratic pagans, our Prophet (SAW), left Madinah for Makkah with his 1,400 companions and camels for sacrifice, With the intention of performing Umrah in zul-Qaada 6 A.H. (February 628). They wore Ihram (Two Pieces of unstitched cloth), meant pilgrimage. The people of Makkah got frightened at the news, did not believe the noble intention and took it for granted that they were coming with the intention of offensive attack, they assembled their allies to put on the defensive. After some time, though they were convinced about their genuine purpose, they feared to allow them to enter Makkah. Hence the Makkhans stipulated a treaty through their emissary, With the Muslims in place called Hudaibiya near Makkah. In Islamic history it is called "Treaty of Most of the terms of the treaty were humiliated and disadvantageous to the Muslims, who disliked them in heart, AS a peace-loving prophet, he agreed to all their terms to avert bloodshed and to diminish hostility. This one point is enough to explain as to which extent, he was humiliated by Suhail the representative of Makkhans. As our Prophet was illiterate, Hazrat Ali (R) wrote on his behalf. When, he wrote on the paper, the words "Mohammadur-Rasoolullah" (Mohammad. the Apostle of God), Suhail objected saying that the Makkans did not believe in the Prophethood of Mohammed (SAW). Immediately, Prophet instructed Hazrat Ali(R) to rub off the words and to write "Mohammed Bin Abdullah". Noticing his peace-loving nature and leniency, Suhail embarrassed the Muslims to the extent, possible. The conditions of the idolators for the treaty were as follows..

1. The Muslims should go back to Madinah, without performing the pilgrimage that year.

2. They could perform Hajj, the next year. They should not bring with them any weapons of war, except a sheathed sword each. They could stay in Makkah only for three days.

3. There was to be peace between the idolators of Makkah and Muslims of Madinah for ten years.

4. Any tribe or person was free to join any party or make alliance with it.

5. Both the parties should take action against their own allies in case any ally of a party harmed the ally of other party.

6. In case, a person from Quraish Of Makkah, under guardianship joined the Prophet without the permission, he or she should be sent back to the

guardian, but in contrary, the Muslims would not be sent back to Madinah.

The last term was quite disagreeable and humiliating to the Muslims. As they were restless, Almighty Allah revealed some -verses to Mohammed (SAW), promising and assuring the Muslims, of the victory, which will be the consequence of the terms, He also promised them to pardon their past faults.

S. Fat-h-48 1-3.-

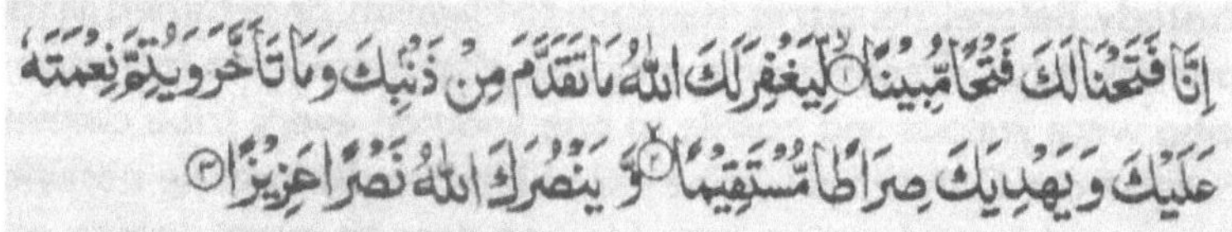

Tr "Verily, we have granted thee a manifest victory; that Allah may forgive thee, thy faults of the past and those who follow, fulfil His favor to and guide thee the Straight-way: and that Allah may help thee with powerful help".

At last what happened? The idolator Suhail who stipulated the treaty and humiliated the Muslims. had his own son Abu Jandal, imprisoned for having embraced Islam,, Somehow, he escaped. reached Hudaibya and requested our Prophet to take him under his Protection, in the presence of his father Suhail. Soon after the treaty was signed. Can anybody imagine, as to how much Almighty Alah humiliated Suhail How can a true Prophet commit a breach treaty ? He refused to take Abu Jandal bin Suhail; but comforted, consoled. and blessed him and prayed for his prosperity Abu Jandal proved to be a great contributor, regarding the conquest of Makkah. Abu Jandal and his friends had formed a network and got settled on the route Of Makkan caravans of merchandise. They broke the backbones of the idolators by plundering their caravans. The Makkans desperately approached our Prophet to Call Abu Jandal to Madinah. He replied that the treaty was signed for ten years, and he would not deviate the terms of the treaty Because of Abu Jandal and his party, the Makkans lost much of their strength.

Another incidence took place which facilitated the Muslims to march against Makkah just after two years of the signining of the treaty and to conquer Makkah in 8 A.H. The tribe Banu Bakr, the ally of the idolators attacked the tribe of Banu Khuza'a the ally of the Muslims. But, the Makkans refused to take action against it which was a great breach of agreement. Thus, it became lawful for the Muslims to invade Makkah in 8 A.H., when all the idolators surrendered and came into the fold Of Islam.

The treaty of Hudaibiya with the people of Makkah, was an agreement which consisted of the purport of peace. The concessions made by our Prophet were attracted by all the nations of the world. The unpleasant, unfavorable and humiliating terms turned out to be beneficial to the Muslims and embarrassing to their adversaries. At last the terms of the treaty of Hudaibiya brought grand victory to the Muslims which was moral, social, political and spiritual, because of the trait of peaceability of our Prophet (SAW). The significant events of migration to Madinah and signing the Treaty of Hudaibiya changed the course of Islamic history, Allah fulfilled his promise of granting victory. The patient dealings, lenience and peace-loving nature of our Prophet (SAW) resulted in the peaceful conquest of Makkah

ASSEMBLAGE OF ALL VIRTUES: -

The Islamic ideology is the source of ending all the conflicts which are corrupting the modern societies. It has enabled to solve many social problems. It must be the ideal of every Muslim to ponder over the life and ideals of our Prophet Mohammed (SAW), scrutinize his personal excellence, merit, moral character and God-fearing quality.

Our Prophet was so trust worthy that people generally left their valuables in his safe custody. Before, his secret migration to Madinah, he returned all the valuables to the respective owners. It has already been mentioned, that there were four main tribes of Quraish in Makkah who were jealous and hostile to one another, every tribe claiming superiority. Our Prophet hailed from Quraishi sub-tribe called Has-him. Before. he obtained prophethood, no person harbored hatred against him. He was dear to every person of Makkah, on account of his refined traits, especially honesty. They were highly pleased to see him and so affectionately gave him the title Al-Ameen which means the trustworthy.

In his daily activities, he adhered to all the injunctions of Quran, presenting a true picture Of Islamic teachings. His unassuming nature was characterized by Simplicity, humility, unparalleled excellence of chastity, exuberance and desire lessness of material temptations. He was the grateful servant Of God, a faithful companion of his companions, compassionate politician for the weaker sects of people. an elegant reformer of world society and above all a service minded, a generous and humblest monarch of Islamic State. He did not like haste, indecency, turmoil and turbulence. He preferred to be calm, cool and dignified even at odd situations.

He used to calmly pray at nights till his legs got swollen and till he got completely exhausted. As he was the lover of democracy. he used to consult his Companions, before he settled matters. He was very kind towards the slaves and even irrational animals. In order to help the slaves, he used to milk the goats, mend his clothing's which were full of patches. He liked to be self-sufficient and never liked to trouble others. He used to help his wives in the household work. In those days slaves were looked down upon. Our Holy Quran has enjoined on the Muslim man to marry the believing-slave girl in Sura-e-Nisa, and has enjoined the Muslim woman to marry the believing male slave in Sura-e-Naml. The purposes of most of his weddings were for political reasons, raising the status of slave girls and captives of war and for giving protection for the widows. He laid such norms in favor of the slave, that the system of slavery gradually got abolished after his expiry. He was the humblest sovereign. He departed from the world leaving nothing behind him. His attitude was unchangeable in adversity and prosperity, he was humble in his ways and was Averse to display of pomp and splendour. He remained hungry, feeding others and kept his promises to every letter. His unassuming nature is a fit model for the entire humanity.

Daleel Sahib has praised our Prophet (SAVV) in many places in his poem, "Nazm-e-Kayinat". In fact, no words are adequate or appropriate to portray his character. With my little capacity, I have tried to prove that he was the "Ideal Prophet"

SOME SPECIAL PRESTIGES OVER OTHER PROPHETS

Besides all the exemplary qualities of Prophet Mohammed (SAW), he was fortunate to have some special prestige's over other prophets, bestowed upon him by Allah. Firstly, he was the promised Prophet, mentioned in previous scriptures. Secondly, he ascended to the Holy Abode Of God which is called Meiraj-e-Nabi. Thirdly he had the seal of Prophethood on his back. Lastly, he performed the miracle of splitting the moon which is still being witnessed by the Astronauts.

It is well known to all that missions of all other past Prophets were tribal and the spreading of the messages of Allah were confined to their own tribes, while, our prophet's multi-dimensional missions were universal. As kings, Prophet Sikander Zulqarnain (PBIJH), Dawood (A.S.) and Sulaiman (A.S.) ruled over larger territories, propagated Allah' religion and refined the respective societies. Dawood (A.S.) had the prestige of establishing Jewish Monarchy

I. PROMISED PROPHET: -

No other Prophets were promised in the past scripture. The earlier scripture torah, revealed to Moosa(A.S) and the scripture Bible revealed to Isa (A.S), predicted the coming of Prophet Mohammed (SAW) his messages his description and miracles.

S. Saff-61 :6: -

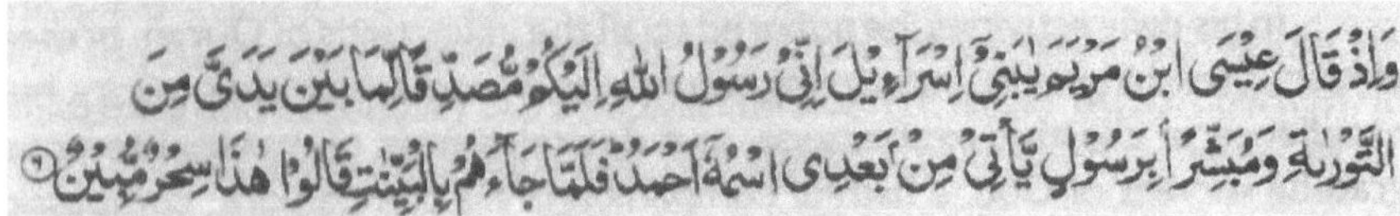

Tr:- "And remember the son of Mary had said," O Children of Isra'i! I am the Apostle of Allah, sent to you confirming the Law (Which Came) before me and giving glad tidings of an Apostle to come after me. whose name shall be Ahmed But, when he

came to them with dear signs, they said, "This is evident sorcery".

Out of His great love for our prophet and owing to his qualities, Allah has called him by 99 names. One of his names is Ahmed. mentioned in Quran. Whenever, he performed miracles. The Jews and the idolators used to say that he did them by means of his tactics of sorcery:

The translated quotations of Bible are available in the verses of Holy Quran. The prophetic traditions and foretelling's of Bible regarding the birth of Ahmed (Mohammed SAW), the praised one that the messenger of Islam. after Jesus Christ, clearly establishes a pretext for amicable relationship between the true followers of Jesus and the community of the Muslims. In order to become a true Muslim, we must accept Jesus as a Prophet from Allah and He revealed Injeel (Bible) to him.

Once Jesus Christ said, that the last prophet would be born, who would have control over the moon. He had hinted at the miracle of our Prophet, of splitting up of the moon into two halves and then joining them together.

The translated descriptions of our Prophet in Torah. revealed to Moosa (A.S.) are also available in Quran. The translated quotation is as follows

"He is the guardian of the illiterate. He is one who is neither rude nor unkind, nor quarrelsome in the markets. He does not repel on bad deed with another, but he forgives and pardons. Allah will not cause him to die until he has caused the faith which had become crooked, to be straightened with his efforts, so that his followers will declare that there is no diet)'. Save

Allah; and open with statements blind eyes, deaf years and hardened hearts.

S. Maida-5:72:-(Already Quoted): -

Tr: -Those who believe (In Quran)those who follow the Jew (Scripture) and the Sabians and the Christians, Any who believe in Allah and the last day, and work righteousness: on them, shall have no fear. nor shall they grieve".

In the above-mentioned verses, Allah has exhorted the Muslims to believe in the scriptures, revealed to Moosa (A.S.) and Jesus Christ and establish our relationship with them. How beautifully and justly Allah has foretold in the Torah and Bible, the birth of our prophet, as well as has confirmed the prophethood of Moosa (A.S.) and Isa (A.S.) and their scriptures in the in the Holy Quran, revealed to Mohammed (SAW)?

I am a staunch Muslim. Readers need not suspect about the firmness of my faith Islam, if I mention about other scriptures, not mentioned in Quran, in which Allah has promised birth of Muhammad (SAW) and has given descriptions about his character, personality, miracles and birth place. A deep and concentrated study of the following Quranic verse convince the readers that all great religions descended from Almighty Allah, and he sent to the nations without any exception. True Muslims must have undisputed belief in every word of Holy Quran.

S. Yunus- 10 : 47 (Already quoted in Chapter-26)

Tr:- "In every people (was sent) an Apostle; when their Apostle comes (before them) the matter will be judged between them with Justice and they will not be wroned".

S.Ra'd-13:7 (Already quoted in Chapter-26)

Tr:- "And, the unbelievers say! Why is not a sign sent from their Lord? But thou art truly a warner and to every people a guide".

S. Ibrahim-14 : 4 (Already quoted in Chapter-26)

Tr:- "We sent an Apostle, except (to teach) in the language of (his own) people in order to make (things) clear to them. Now Allah leaves staying those whom he pleases' and He is Exalted in Power, full of Wisdom".

Now it is clear that Allah has sent Apostles to all the nations and has revealed scriptures in their folk languages.

Raja Bhoj of Madhya Pradesh embraced Islam after witnessing the miracle of splitting of the moon performed by Prophet Muhammad (SAW) and after referring the Vedas in which this miracle has clearly been mentioned. Due to unavoidable circumstance he could act satisfy his intense desire to meet him.

Mahamat of Mahabharat: -

Maharishi Viyasa had compiled the great epic Mahabharat. In its Kaliyuga Kanda; he has mentioned, the birth of the final prophet, his name and events of his life.

Ahmed in Sama Veda: -

There are many references to the expected great prophet in Sama Veda. The Veda says, "Ahmed will get religious laws from God'.

Buddhist Scriptures: -

Buddha said. "Do not think that, I am the only Buddha (Enlightened one). There have been many Buddhas before me and mere are going to be many after me. In due course a great

Buddha is to come. He will be Lord of humanity and all other creatures- He would see universe as if he saw it in front of him. Like me, he would preach men a perfect and pure religion"

The quotation of Buddha confirms the advent of past prophets, his succeeding Prophets and the miracle of the event of Me'raj-e-Nabi and has given the descriptions Of Muhammad (SAW).

I hereby present some extracts from "Islamic Voice" in order to acquaint the readers that Allah had promised to send the last Prophet (SAVV) in different ancient scriptures and in different languages. such as Vedas and Bhavishya Puranas of the Hindus, Zoroastrian scriptures. Dasatir and Zand Avasta, Bible of the Christians, Torah of the Jews, The Gospel Of Barnabas. Ishaiah Of the Hebrews etc.

The following passages have been extracted from Islamic Voice dated November, 1988

"The Advent of Hazrath Muhammed (peace be upon him) the holy prophet of Islam was predicted in the earliest scriptures. These scriptures range from the ancient Vedic Sources of Hindus from India to Christian and Parsi scriptures like Bible, Dasatir and Zand Avasta.

Last month we published the definite references to such predictions from Bhavishya Purana and Atharv Veda, equally authentic are the references from the Gospel of Barnabas and the Parsi scriptures.

The Gospel of Barnabas is maintained as the True Gospel without being distorted in anyway. There is a direct reference to the advent of the Holy Prophet Muhammed (PBUH) in this Gospel. This along with references from other old and new testaments confirm the Prophethood of Prophet Muhammed (PBUH). The -verses 15-18 from Deut XVIII reproduced here clearly indicate that the promised prophet from the Isma'ilites is only Hazrath Muhammed (PBIJH) and none else.

Deute XVIII, 15 and 18

"The Lord thy God will raise up unto thee a prophet from the midst of thee of thy brethren, like unto me; unto him ye shall hearken".

"I will raise them up a prophet from among their brethren, like unto thee, and I will put my words in his mouth, and he shall speak unto them all I shall command him"

Equally authentic and important are the scriptures of the Zand Avasta which are as old as those of the Hindu religion. In Dasatir no. 14, associated - with the name Of Sasanil, there is a corroboration of the doctrines and the teachings of Islam as well as clear prophecy about the advent of the Prophet Muhammed (PBUH). The prophecy is in very clear terms. It is preceded by a vision of a state of extreme disorder and demoralization in Persia. The original Pahlavi and the modern Persian versions and the English translations are reproduced herein.

"When the Persians should sink so low in morality, a man will be born in Arabia whose followers will upset their throne, religion and everything. The mighty stiff-necked ones of Persia will be overpowered. The house which was built (referring to Abraham's building the Kaaba) and where many Idols have been placed will be purged of idols, and people will say their prayers facing towards it. His followers will capture the towns of the Parsis Tus and Balkand other big places round about.

People will embroil with one another. The wise men of Persia and others will join his followers"

"As can be seen the prophecy present in the book which is read by the Parsis even to this day has a reference to a person hailing from Arab. It is also enjoined that the Persians would accept his faith and that the fire temples would be destroyed and idols removed. That people will pray turning towards the Kaaba is also referred to in very clear terms".

Thus if, on the one hand, the holy Prophet Muhammed (PBUH) testified to the truth of all the different nations of the world, and made it a part of his religion, on the other hand, the scriptures of these previous Prophets are found to contain clear prophecies about the advent of our holy Prophet Muhammed (PBUH). This mutual corroboration, by furnishing great evidence of the spiritual providence of God for humanity, strengthens people's faith in religion in general, and in the religion of Islam in particular and accept Islam as the final undistorted message of God to be followed by mankind replacing old scriptures which suffered tragic fate at the hands of those whom the Holy Quran described as follows

'Therefore, woe be unto those who write the Scripture with their hands and then say,

"This is from Allah," that they may purchase a small gain therewith"

'Woe unto them for that their hands have written, and woe unto them for that they earn thereby". (Quran 2: 79)

"Lo those who hide aught of the Scripture which Allah hath revealed and purchased a small gain therewith, they eat into their bellies nothing else than fire."

Courtesy:Islamic Voice dated November 1988.

The following passages have been extracted from Islamic Voice dated November 1988

Courtesy : Islamic Voice dated November 988

The following passages have been extracted from Islamic Voice dated November 1988

"Islam is, comparatively. a young religion, although it is also the oldest religion. Being path leading to the worship of One Eternal God following virtues that have indisputable values for ever is (he oldest of religions. Revealed as the concluding religion through the last of the prophets. it is the youngest religion. Being so, it is but natural to expect a reference to such a fact earlier scripture, Even the Holy Quran refers to such reference. wherein the advent of our Prophet Muhammed (PBOH) has been expressly foretold. Aal-e-Imran is the third chapter Of Quran, the 81st of this chapter reads, "Call to mind what God said when He entered into a covenant with you (the Israelites) regarding the Prophets. (He had said): "This is the Book and the wisdom which I give you, Hereafter, should a Prophet come to you confirming is already with you, ye shall surely believe in him and ye shall surely aid him. Are you and do you accept the covenant on these terms? They said, "We are resolved"

Thus, it has been claimed that there will be a Prophet who will verify the truth of all the prophets who had preceded him in the world.

Equally true is the claim that there has been a pointed reference to the advent of Prophet Islam in many Old scriptures-be they belong to West Asian countries like Palestine, Iran. etc. Or the mid-Asian countries like India. Although references can be cited from the old and new testaments of the Bible alike and the Dasatir and the Zand Avasta of Parsi religion. We are publishing here such of the prophecies that were made in Hindu scriptures. The strange fact country and the person have been referred to by name in some of these prophecies. One such clear prophecy is in the Bhavishya Purana which according to Sanathana Pandits is considered to be very authentic. The original Sanskrit Text as in part 3 of the above Purana, Khand 3, Adhya 3, Shalok 5-8.

Its English translation reads; -

Malecha (belonging to a foreign country and speaking foreign language) spiritual teacher appear with his companions. His name will be Muhammed. Raja Bhoj offered him tie presents of his sincere devotion and showing him all reverence said. "I make obeisance to Ye the pride of mankind, the dweller in Arabia, Ye have collected a great force to kill the Devil and you yourself have been protected from the Malecha opponents". "O Ye ! the image of the Most pious God. the biggest Lord, I am a slave to thee, take me as one lying on thy feet.

In this eulogy of the Holy Prophet, Maharishi Vyasa has enumerated the following points.

1. The name of the Prophet is clearly stated as Mohammed.

2. He said to be belonging to Arabia. The sanskrit world MARUTHAL used in the Prophecy means a sandy treat of land or a dessert.

3. 3, Special mention is made of the companions of the Prophet. There has any other prophet in the world who had such a host of companions all resembling.

4. He will be immune from sins, having an angelic disposition.

5. The Raja of India will show him his heart felt reverence.

6. The Prophet will be given protection against his enemies.

7. He will kill Devil, root out idol worship and will do away with all sorts of vices,

8. He will be in image of the All-Powerful God.

9. The Maharishi claims to be lying at his feet and

10. He is regarded as the pride of mankind (Parbatis Nath)

A second of such prophecy appears in Atharva Veda. In its 20th Kands, 127th Sukta, the Mantra 1-3 reads.

Translated, it gives the mean

"O people, listen this emphatically the man of praise (Muhammed) will be raised among the people. We take the emigrant in our shelter from sixty thousand and ninety enemies whose conveyance are twenty camels and she camels, whose loftiness of position touches and heavens and lowers it.

As can be seen from the above prophecies, there is clear evidence about the advent of our holy Prophet Muhammed (PBUH) even in Hindu scriptures. Equally significant is the fact that believing in all religions propagated through Prophets preceding our Holy Prophet (PBIJH) constitutes an essential pillar of the Islamic faith. These facts furnish great evidence of the spiritual providence of God for humanity, strengthens people's faith in religion in general, and in the religion of Islam in particular, and accept Islam as the final undistorted message of God to be followed by mankind replacing old scriptures which suffered tragic fate of distortion.

It also bears ample testimony to the unquestionable fact that all revealed religion, in their original and pristinely pure form, were one and the same i.e "Islam the first and final religion".

MAHATMA GANDHI'S TRIBUTE TO THE HOLY PROPHET

"In its glorious days Islam was not intolerant. It commanded the admiration of the world. When the West was sunk in darkness, a bright star rose in the Eastern firmament and gave light and comfort to a groaning world. Islam was not a false religion."

"I passed from the companions to the Prophet himself. When I closed the second volume, I was sorry there was no more for me to read of that great life. I became more than ever convinced that it was not the sword that won a place for Islam in those days in the scheme of life. It was the rigid simplicity, the utter self effacement of the Prophet, the scrupulous regard for pledges, his intense devotion to his friends and followers, his intrepidity, his fearlessness, his absolute trust in God and in his own mission. These and not the sword carried anything before them and surmounted every obstacle"....

Courtesy : Islamic Voice dated November, 1988

Fish Testifies

"Muhammad is God's Servant and Messenger"

BEIRUT: George Wehbi, a Christian Lebanese, caught along with other fishes, a strange, 50 cms long fish. His wife, noticed some arabic writing on the head, body and tail of the fish.

The fish was taken and shown to Sheikh al-Zein and to other religious scholars, who read the writing on the fish. After a careful examination, they said that the writing is by nature and could not be done by any human being, its God's creation which the fish was born with. It read: "God's servant", on its belly and "Muhammad" on its head, and "His Messenger" on its tail.

The senegall, Lebanese and other daily papers carried the story in detail.

The fish is preserved and kept by Sheikh, Al Zein, the President of the Islamic Social & Charit Institution in Senegal. This report is sent by Noor Al-Islan Publication, POB 25/156, Beirut Lebanon.

Courtesy : Islamic Voice; September 1988.

Several scientists and people of different nations and religions, including Mahathma Gandhi have appreciated the religion of Islam and have spoken very high of Prophet Muhammed (SAW). Even the aquatic animal fish has testified his prophethood.

"Muhammad is God's servant and messenger"

Beirut: George Wehbi, a Christian Lebanese, caught along with other fishes, a strange, 50 cm long fish. His wife, noticed some Arabic writing on the head, body and tail of the fish.

The fish was taken and shown to Sheikh-Al-Zein and to other religious scholars, who read the writing on the fish. After a careful examination, they said the writing is by nature and could not be done by any human being, it is God's creation which the fish was born with. It read: " God Servant" on its belly and "Muhammad" on his head, and "His Messenger" on its tail.

The Senagali, Lebanese and other daily papers carried the story in detail.

The fish is presented and kept by Sheikh-al-Zein, the President of the Islamic Social &Charity Institution in Senegal. This report is sent by Noor Al-Islan Publication, POB 25/156. Beirut Lebanon.

GANDHI'S TRIBUTE TO THE HOLY PROPHET

"In its glorious days Islam was not intolerant. It commanded the admiration of the world. When the West was sunk in darkness, a bright star rose in the Eastern firmament and gave light and comfort to a groaning world. Islam was not a false religion."

"I passed from the companions to the Prophet himself. Vs/hen I closed the second volume. I was sorry there was no more for me to read of that great life. I became more than ever convinced that it was not the sword that won a place for Islam in those days in the scheme of life. It was the rigid simplicity, the utter self-effacement of the Prophet. the scrupulous regard for pledges. his intense devotion to his friends and followers. his intrepidity, his fearlessness, his absolute trust in God and in his own mission. These and not the sword carried anything before them and surmounted every obstacle"

ME'RAJ-E-NABI: -

The event of Meraj-e-Nabi has already been described in detail in the 14th Chapter.Sura-e-Najm is full of verses confirming the event of Mei'raj-e-Nabi which took place on the 27th night of Rajab, the 7th month of lunar calendar, two years before Hijrat and after returning from Taif which is called the 2nd Hijrat in Islamic history. The greatest boon our Prophet received during his Ascension (Mei'raj) to the Holy Abode of Allah (Arsh) that He promised him, that He would pardon every member of his Ummat(follower) and admit him into the paradise after punishment or pardon of his sins, in case, he does not commit Shirk. ie. Associate anybody or anything in the Divine worship. The event of Mei'raj was a matter of special privilege, prestige and distinction over all prophets.

MIRACLE OF SPLITTING OF MOON.

The Mushrikeen of Makkah asked Mohammed (SAW) to perform a miracle in order to convince them of his prophethood. They demanded that the moon must be bifurcated in two halves. This demand was received on 8th of Rajab when the moon was not full. He asked the Mushrikeen of Makkah to assemble in a large square to witness the miracle on the 14th night of Rajab, when the moon would be fully round. This fantastic occurrence of splitting the moon was witnessed on the 14th of Rajab, in the 8th year of prophethood, on Friday night i.e. three hours after sunset, on Thursday in 6 1 7 A.D. The following Quranic Stanza confirms the event.

S.Qamar - 54: l

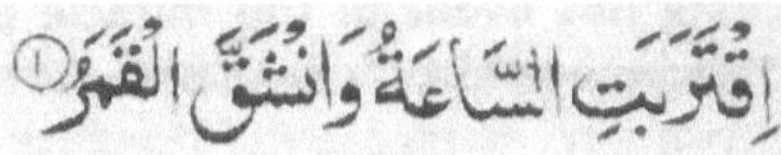

Tr:- "The hour of Judgement is nigh, and the moon is cleft asunder"

The bifurcation of moon into two equal halves was visible for six to eight hours. The two halves of the moon moved far apart leaving a gap of several miles in between. The bifurcation of the moon was witnessed by thousands of people of different countries from the East to West. As soon as our Prophet commanded those two halves by his signs to come and join they joined together and formed a full moon again. There is one distinguishing feature in miracles of our prophet and the miracles of past prophets. The past prophets could perform miracles on earth while Muhammad (SAW) performed on the sky.

Jesus Christ had foretold, that, "The comforter, the promised Prophet would disclose himself to the world by a miracle that would be done by him in 617 C.E. and it would be simultaneously seen over large areas of the world. The prophecy of Jesus Christ about the miracle was evidently, the splitting of moon into two halves. He also added that, ['The moon Shall minister sleep to him (Mohammed SAW) in his boyhood and when he shall be grown up, it will come under his control. Let the world beware of casting him out, because he will slay the idolators"

In India Raja Bhoj of Dhar (Madhya Pradesh) and the king of Malabar witnessed the unnatural and surprising phenomenon when they were relaxing and enjoying the cool breeze in the open space. The King of Malabar is said to have recorded the perplexing and unusual phenomenon of nature in his diary and it is said to have been preserved in the museum, After Witnessing this wonderful miracle, Raja Bhoj became a Muslim and was eagerly yearning to meet our Prophet. but Adverse circumstances did not allow him to go to Arabia. He sent his Prime Minister to him .with precious gifts and sent his good wishes. Highly pleased with his affectionate gesture, he informed the prime minister that the king Raja Bhoj had embraced Islam. On his own behalf, our Prophet sent for him through the prime minister, the name "Abdullah". It was the name of the father of our Prophet. Abdullah means the worshipper of God. It is said that a shrine is still standing bearing the name 'Abdullah Bhoj".

Space Science also reveals the truth of the miracle of splitting of the moon by Prophet. Theorbiter 4 photographed the hidden side of the moon which shows a straight or diametrical crack on the surface of the moon. Cracks by natural causes are always irregular and never in straight line. But this crack is in a perfectly straight line which indicates that it must have come about owing to something unnatural or miraculous performance. Thus, the Scientific achievement of Orbiter 4, has proved by photograph, the miracle of our Holy Prophet (SAW) of splitting the moon in exactly two equal parts in 6 1 7 A.D. Later, some Astronauts have confirmed this miracle. (Space Science and Technology).

Almighty Allah sent prophets with different miracles. They are recorded in Holy Quran and history. They can be read and spoken of by us and can never be seen again. But, the miracle of our Ideal Prophet can still be seen in the diametrical crack on the surface of the moon and will be seen by several space scientists till the Day of the Doom. The purpose of citing this event of the miracle is to explain the prestigious distinction of Ideal Prophet Mohammed (SAW) over other prophets.

SEAL OF PROPHETHOOD:

The presence of the seal of Prophethood on the back of our Prophet Mohammed (SAW) was one of the greatest bounties of God for the sure and certain confirmation of his Prophethood , an astounding distinguishing feature of his prestige and privilege over other prophets. It is said that this seal, a red growth was present on his back. right from his birth'. But only a few people had seen it with some words inscribed on it because, he always used to cover his body with a mantle. His contemporaries have given different descriptions of the Seal,which have been recorded on the books of Ahadis.

Sa'ib Bin Yazid said."I saw the seal of prophethood, which was like a canopied bed. it was of the size of the egg of a dove" (Tirmizi).

Yaqoob Bin Hasan said, "This sign was present right from his birth, (There is controversy whether something was written on it at the time. Of his birth). Ibn-e-Hasan said, that. "Mohammed-ur-Rasoolullah" was written on the words mean that Mohammed the Apostle of Allah.

Some scholars said that some Arabic words were written which meant, "Wherever you go, you will be helped (Tirmizi).

Jabir Bin Samra (R) said, "I saw the seal of Prophethood. It was read and thick and between his two shoulders. It was of the size and of the shape of the egg of a dove (Tirmizi)

There was much controversy about the size and colour of the seal, some scholars have said that it was changing in size and colour. (Tirmizi).

Hazrat Ali said. "There was the seal of Prophethood at his back, between his two shoulders, and he was the last Prophet" (Tirmizi).

Umar Bin Akhtab while speaking to his friend, 11ba Bin Ahmar. said that when he was pressing the body of the Prophet, he touched the seal of Prophethood by chance. He described it a collection of hair.

About the Seal of Prophethood. Abu Sayeed Qadri said that there was a fleshy growth on his back (Tirmizi).

Abdullah Bin Sarjes has said. "Once, I saw Prophet Mohammed in an assembly. I was walking here and there repeatedly in the hope of having a glance at the seal of Prophethood He understood my desire and pulled down his wrapper (Coverlet) and exposed it for some time. It was between his shoulders. Its shape resembled a fist. in all the four sides of which there were moles" (Tirmizi).

One of the companions of our Prophet said." The Prophet's back was broad; and near his right shoulder blade, there was a black mole some what yellowish, around which. there was some thick hair " (Bukhari).

In order to arrive at the conclusion about the correct description of the Seal of Prophethood. it is necessary for us to study a brief outline of the life of Hazrat Salman Farsi and his research done on the Seal of Prophethood

Hazrat Salman Farsi(R) was a Zoroastrian of Persia and the son of a leader of jay, a place in the Province of Isfahan. His father made him the trustee of the fire-temple. He was a learned man and had read in the previous scriptures, that the last Prophet would be born in Arabia, Who would not accept any charity or propitiatory offering (Sadaqa) but, would accept presents and gifts (Hadyah). Hazrat Salman had these things in his mind. Noticing some changes in his faith, his father had chained and imprisoned him at home. He some how managed to escape from home and embraced Christianity. His ill-luck overtook him and he became a slave. A man of high birth who was in quest of a true religion had to serve under ten masters. Some of them were cruel and some were kind. Before arriving at Arabia, he was serving under a very noble and learned Bishop In Syria who was ailing for several years. Hazrat Salman used to seek advice as to where he could go. He replied. "The birth of the last Prophet is approaching, who will follow the religion of Ibrahim. He will be born in Arabia. He will migrate to that place where the product of dates will be abundant. On both the sides of the place, there will be lands full of pebbles. He will accept gifts (Hadyah) and refuse propitiatory charity (Sadaqah). There will be a seal of Prophethood at his back between the two shoulders. If it is possible. you go there".

Hazrat Salman served the Bishop till he died. With great interest, he had listened to the Bishop's predictions. He decided to do research in the signs of the last Prophet and wanted to go to Arabia. By his hard-earned money, he had bought some sheep and cattle. He made agreement with merchants of the tribe of Banu Kulb, to take his herd from him and escort him to Arabia. When they reached Makkah the treacherous merchants owned all his herds and sold him as a slave to a Jew of Banu Quraiza, his last master who hailed from Madinah. It was the astounding deed of Allah that he got settled in Madinah. When he reached Madinah, he felt that this was the place, described by the Bishop. He purposely saved money in order to start his research. When he heard about our Prophet's migration to Madinah he became very impatient and anxious. He could not wait till he entered Madinah. Before entering Madinah our Prophet had stationed in a place called Qaba. From this time onwards. Hazrat Salman started his research anx.ously_ He bought some dates and hurried to Qaba where our Prophet was staying. He offered the dates to him as a propitiatory offering (Sadaqah). Our Prophet refused to accept this charity After his arrival at Madinah. Hazrat Salman bought dates again and offered them to Prophet Mohammed (SAW) as a gift (Hadyah). He accepted to have the dates and ate them with his companions. Hazrat Salman felt highly elated that he had heard from the Bishop about the signs and descriptions of the last Prophet. mentioned in the previous scriptures. Now he grew more anxious and impatient about the last stage of the research Of the Said of Prophethood. He met the Prophet near the graveyard, Baq'i where he had gone for the burial of one of this friends.

Hazrat Salman was turning round our Prophet back repeatedly with his anxious eyes at back. He understood the reason of anxiety and silently exposed his seal. To his surprise. he saw and read the Seal, completely exposed with letters "Mohammed-ur-Rasoolullah* written on it and black hair around. As soon as he succeeded in his last research, he fell on his back, kissed the Seal of Prophethood and immediately embraced Islam. On hearing the account of his life, research and ambition Prophet (SAW) tolled and labored hard to earn money for the Sake of his liberation from his Jew Master It said Salman(R) lived long and served Islam devotedly till his death. It was his suggestion to dig a trench around the City of Madinah on the occasion of the Battle of Trench. Previously the Arabs were not aware of such stratagem of As Salman Farsi (R) saw the Seal of Prophethood completely exposed. Ulamas explain that his description of the Seal Was accepted to be the most authentic one by his Contemporaries. (Purity of Islamic Society, Arabian and world society before Islam, Islamic Revolution. achievements and Ideal Prophet).

CHAPTER - XXVII

FOUNDATION OF HOPE

Stanza. 191

27/اساس امید

191۔ ہے ابھی انسان طریق زندگی سے با خبر

زندگانی خود وبال زندگی ہے کسقدر

زر پرست اقوام ہوں کیونکر جہاں میں معتبر

بد گمانی سے نہیں اُن کے لیے کوئی مفر

آہ یہ خونریزیاں بربادیاں غارت گری

آہ یہ بے دردیاں نا داریاں دولت گری

Tr: Life in this world has become a nuisance for man because, he is not still aware of the correct way of life. Those nations which are materialists can never be trust-worthy nor can they escape from the suspicions of others. Love for wealth and lack of feelings for others. lead to raid, wastage, ravage and despair,which are really sorrowful.

Stanza. 192

192 ۔ ہیں بہت آگاہ انسان کے فساد و شر سے ہم

اے کہ بزدل ہے بہت ہے کشتہ جور و ستم

زندگی کو دیکھتا ہے تو جو وقف آہ و غم

ہو نہ کا نومید انساں سے تُجھے رب کی قسم

فطرت آدم کی ہے گر کوئی بنیاد خام

آج تک قائم نہ رہتا بزم انساں کا نظام

Tr:- We are well-informed of the disturbance and wickedness of man. The weak community is the victim of its mischief. But, do not lose hope of the goodness in man, because your grief-stricken life is not permanent. In case the foundation of human nature is defective, the administration of human life cannot be stable.

Stanza. 193

193۔ بہتریں ہیّت میں ہے پیدا ہوا بیشک بشر

مصلحت کے ماتحت پستی سے ہے اس کا سفر

نور ایمان ہے ازل سے اس کے دل میں جلوہ گر

لعنت الحاد سے ہے اس کی فطرت ہے خبر

نفس انساں گر نہ ہوتا قابل نقص و زوال

آدمی ہرگز نہ ہوتا قابل اوج و کمال

Tr:- It is doubtless that man has been created in the best form. Under the Divine expediency, his journey of life, originates from the lowest position. From the beginning, he is blessed with the enlightenment of faith. His nature is unaware of the disgrace and curse of atheism. If man's self-have no blemishment and decay, he would never become capable of attaining higher position and perfection.

Stanza. 194

194۔ وہ پئے اہل و عیال انسان کی قربانیاں

اس کی گرد شر میں بھی ہیں خیر کے ذرہ نہاں

خیر کا پلہ ہے اس شر کے پلے سے گراں

چشم ظاہر پر نہیں کل خوبیاں اس کی عیاں

کارہائے خیر سے اس کے جہاں معمور ہیں

بو الہوس بھی خدمت و ایثار پر مجبور ہے

Tr:- A man sacrifices his whole lot for the welfare Of his family members. His mischief is manifest when his goodness is concealed. Man has more goodness than mischief in his nature, but all his good qualities are not being realised. This world is full of and benefited by the noble deeds of man. Even the lustful and greedy person feels that he is bound to make sacrifices and render service to others.

Stanza. 195

195 ۔ نفس کے جذبات اسفل بھی ہیں بالکل لازمی

ہے جہاد اُن سے عروج دل فروغ زندگی

ہے اُنہیں کے دم سے مسجود ملائک آدمی

خود وہی تہذیب سے ہوتے ہیں شان ایزدی

حاجت ابلیس ہے شان خلافت کے لئے

اس کے ہنگامے ہیں زینے بام رفعت کے لیے

Tr.- The mean emotions of some people are also essential, because the fight for self-control, the exaltation and good development of another man can be realised. The controlling of carnal emotions of men has made them superior to the angels. The civilized and chaste people add pride to the splendour of God. The existence of Iblis enhances the dignity of vicegerency of man and his disturbances actually serve as the steps for the chaste people to reach the higher position.

Stanza. 196

196۔ یہ وہی ہے جو بشر کی شان سے واقف نہ تھا

سجدہ آدم کے جو انکار سے غارت ہوا

پیش ہر مومن سدا رہتا ہے سر جس کا جھکا

کافر و کمزور پر کرتا ہے جو حملے سدا

اہل طاعت کا وہ یک طبع فرماں غلام

اُن کی عظمت کے لیے ہے قوتیں اس کی تمام

Tr:- As he was not aware of the greatness of man, Iblis refused to prostrate before Adam and got himself ruined. He always bows down his head before every believer but grabs every opportunity to attack and mislead the infidels and weak-minded people. He is an obedient slave of the believers who worship Allah. He has been granted the power of mischief in order to enhance the greatness of man.

Stanza. 197

197۔ حالت اصلی میں سیدھی راہ چلتا ہے بشر

جلوہ حاضر سے ہو جاتی جو خیرہ نظر

جہل و مجبوری سے وہ جاتا بھی ہے حد سے گزر

خیر پنہان اس کی فطرت میں ہمیشہ ہے مگر

جب فساد و شر کے ہوتے ہیں بپا طوفان کہیں

نیکیاں بے ساختہ اٹھکر دباتی ہیں وہیں

Tr:- When a man is in the natural condition, he treads on the right path. But, when he becomes immodest, the appearance of the present beauty allures him. His ignorance and lack of goodness make him incapable of controlling his emotions. Even then goodness is always concealed in his nature. When there are uproars of mischiefs, the Piety of noble people suppressed and crushes them by natural extempore.

Stanza.198

198۔ جلوہ گر سو رنگ میں ہے اس کی رحمت کا نظام

اہل شر سے بھی فلاح و خیر کا لیتا ہے کام

ہے نہاں شر بھی یک ابطا ے شر کا احتمام

ہے نہاں تہذیب میں تعمیر کا بھی اہتمام

دشمن جاں کو وہ مجبور مسیحائی کرے

شو رہ پشت اقوام کی محو جبیں سائی کرے

Tr:- Every way the Divine administration is evident. God makes even the culprits to perform good deeds. When the culprits intend to make mischief, he hesitates and interposes delay in doing so. There is arrangement for construction in the destructive attitude.

Stanza -199

199 ۔ کار فرما عدل ہے اللہ کا آٹھوں پہر

قوم جاتی ہیں رہ عصیاں میں جو حد سے گزر

قوم دیگر سے مٹا دیتا ہے اس کہ زور و شر

ہے خداوندی حکومت کے جہاں زیر اثر

ہے گناہوں کی سزا بھی عدل و رحمت کی ادا

زندگی کا پاسبان ہے اس کا قانون جزاء

Tr:- The justice of Almighty Allah is always active. When any nation which indulges in breach of moral laws and committing vices, another nation comes forward to crush or totally destroy their perverted powers and qualities and efface their mischief under the influence of Divine act of blessings. It is the Divine act of justice that Allah punishes the sinners and the Divine Law rewards the pious persons as Allah is the guardian of man's life,

Stanza -200

200۔ ہے خدا کے ہاتھ میں سارے زمانے کی عنان

اصلیت میں نیک ہے فطرت بشر کی بے گماں

مبتلا ہو گو قیامت خیز فتنوں میں جہاں

مٹ نہ جائیگی کبھی انساں سے بزم کن فکاں

آدمی کی فطرت اصلی بدل سکتی نہیں

قبضہ حق سے کبھی دنیا نکل سکتی نہیں

نوٹ: اللہ کی بنائی ہوئی فطرت پر قائم رہو جس نے لوگوں کو اصلی حالات پر پیدا کیا

اللہ کی پیدا کی ہوئی حالت کو کوئی بدل نہیں سکتا۔۔۔ قرآن ۔۔۔۔۔۔۔ دلیل

Tr:- The rein of whole administration of the world is under the control Of God. It is doubtless that the natural faculty of man is noble. Even though the world is immersed in dreadful adversities, the world cannot be destroyed by man. Neither the natural faculty can be altered nor can the world get out of Divine control.

C:- In the 27th chapter of the text 'Foundation of Hope". the poet exhorts us to repose full confidence in Allah's expediency, adopt optimistic policy, advocated by Islam, even at the most critical situations and worst calamities and to avoid pessimism. The main topics he has dealt with in this chapter are: the foundation of hope, ignominy of materialism, necessity of the existence of Iblis, wreckage of Iblis, superiority of man over angels, Divine justice and Divine administration.

This world is a mixture of contradictory aspects, such as sorrow and happiness, poverty and prosperity, calamities and comforts, and good and evil, but we should not lose heart at any odd situation, but hope for the good. This is the main idea, incorporated in this chapter the poet has presented arguments in favour of optimism and confidence in Divine Justice which is always active.

Materialism prevailing in some nations leads to vexation, nuisance, bloodsheds and lack of tender feelings for others. Those nations have lost their individuality, reliability and credibility as well as the scope to escape suspicion.

We must not feel desperate due to the wickedness, tyranny and oppression of others because, there is Divine advisability hidden in every act of God. We must hope that our dark days will be followed by our prosperity. Hope affords us patience, we must not assume that all human beings are evil-minded. In case the foundation of human nature is defective, the administration of the world would have become impossible. The original and natural faculties created by God are good. It is the expediency of God, that the sojourn of man's life starts from lowness, inspite of his best form and figure. From the beginning he is enlightened with faith and is unaware of imprecation of Atheism.

Physical development and spiritual evolution are indispensable to activate the creations of God. In case the self of man is flawless and devoid of decline, he cannot have scope to attain elevation and perfection. Generally, the lustful and lascivious person possesses noble qualities and feels bound to shoulder his responsibilities. He makes all sorts of sacrifices for the sake of the welfare of his family. Mean and lustful emotions of people are essential as they make us realise the restraint and control of carnal emotions of other ones. The contrast in the qualities of different people enables us to distinguish between good and evil, the purity of character enables us to understand the excellence of exaltation. and the enlightened mind of the chaste people.

Angels have no corporeal body nor any sex. They have no need to fight with or control any emotion. This is the distinctive factor which proclaims the superiority of man over the angels, to whom Allah made prostrate before Adam (A.S,). Through the noble fights of man, he has become the pride for Divinity. Allah felt the necessity of the existence of Ibis in order to display the splendour of vicegerency of man. His mischief leads the pious people to higher postion by rejecting the temptations caused by him. He got himself ruined and wrecked because of his disobedience to Allah to prostrate before Adam (A.S.). He disobeyed Allah because, he was not aware of the greatness of man.

Allah has granted him power in order to enhance human excellence by granting the pious people more power. Whenever evil is prevalent the inherent noble qualities of human beings spontaneously crush and efface them. The rein of administration of the world is under the Divine control. Any number of tremendous calamities will to alter the original quintessence of man created by God nor can the world get out of His control.

Q:- Be firm and stable in the natural condition in which Allah has created you. No person can alter the original condition created by God,'"

DIVINE ADMINISTRATION:

Destiny has an extraordinary hold over man. Because of its operation, no one can stall its function nor can he defy it, nor can he bring about any reversal in its events. Destiny is controlled by God which cannot be altered.

Quran naturally interprets that some sort of government is essential for the maintenance of a Civilized Man. The real and greatest sovereignty vests on Almighty Allah alone. The entire humanity is being benefited by Divine Administration,

S. An'am-6 : 115:-

وَتَمَّتْ كَلِمَتُ رَبِّكَ صِدْقًا وَّعَدْلًا لَا مُبَدِّلَ لِكَلِمَاتِه وَهُوَ السَّمِيعُ الْعَلِيمُ ۞

Tr:- 'The word of thy Lord doth find its fulfilment in truth and justice. None can change His words for He is the One Who heareth and knoweth all".

S. An'am-6: 57

قُلْ اِنِّى عَلى بَيِّنَةٍ مِّنْ رَّبِّى وَكَذَّبْتُمْ بِه مَا عِنْدِى مَا تَسْتَعْجِلُوْنَ بِه اِنِ الْحُكْمُ اِلَّا لِلّٰهِ يَقُصُّ الْحَقَّ وَ هُوَ خَيْرُ الْفٰصِلِيْنَ ۞

Tr:- •Say for me, I have an obvious sign from my Lord, but ye reject it. What ye would see hastened is not in my power. The command rests with none but Allah. He declares the Truth and He is the best of Judges".

S. Yusuf-12: 40

مَا تَعْبُدُوْنَ مِنْ دُوْنِه اِلَّا اَسْمَاءً سَمَّيْتُمُوْهَا اَنْتُمْ وَاٰبَاؤُكُمْ مَّا اَنْزَلَ اللّٰهُ بِهَا مِنْ سُلْطٰنٍ اِنِ الْحُكْمُ اِلَّا لِلّٰهِ اَمَرَ اَلَّا تَعْبُدُوْا اِلَّا اِيَّاهُ ذٰلِكَ الدِّيْنُ الْقَيِّمُ وَلٰكِنَّ اَكْثَرَ النَّاسِ لَا يَعْلَمُوْنَ ۞

Tr:- 'If not Him ye worship nothing but names, which ye have named, ye and your fathers for which Allah hath sent you no authority; the command is from none but Allah. He hath commanded that ye worship none but Him; that is the right religion, but most men understand not".

S. Baqara-2 : 286:- (First part of the Stanza)

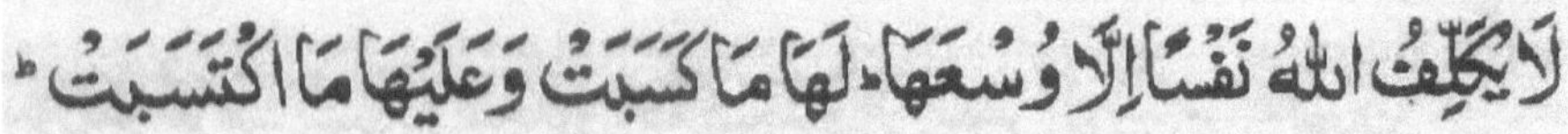

لَا يُكَلِّفُ اللّٰهُ نَفْسًا اِلَّا وُسْعَهَا لَهَا مَا كَسَبَتْ وَعَلَيْهَا مَا اكْتَسَبَتْ

Tr.- "On no soul doth Allah place a burden greater than it can bear".

O! By the careful study of Divine administration, we must avail the advantage of acquiring knowledge about the qualities of a good administrator such as stability, accessibility and justice.

IBLIS:

Allah created Iblis from fire and Adam (A.S.) from clay. He made the angels and Iblis to bow down to Adam in order to convince them about their inferiority and superiority of man. All the angels obeyed Allah's command immediately, but Iblis refused to bow down saying that he was superior to Adam who was created from clay and he himself from fire. Hence, Allah commanded him to get down. He asked Allah respite for punishment till the Day of Resurrection. Allah granted him respite but Iblis got angry that he was thrown out of the way and said that he would deviate human beings from the path of righteousness, deceive them assault from all directions and lead them astray. Thus, he became the avowed enemy of human.

Allah asked Adam and Eve to reside in the paradise and enjoy all the good things and not to eat the fruit of particular tree iblis convinced the couple that he was their friend. He whispered to them that Allah forbade them to enjoy the fruit of the tree because it would make them angels who would live forever. They became the victims of his deceit and tasted the fruit of tree. This disobedience to Allah brought about their fall. Allah threw them on the earth separately Due to their sincere repentance, they were forgiven by Allah and they were united again to procreate human beings.

Iblis fell due to his pride, jealousy and arrogance and Adam fell because he listened to his deceit. Allah has given respite to Iblis to be punished, till the Day of Resurrection. Out of His mercy God, forgave the couple. granted them gifts and guidance and taught them moderation and justice. Above all He granted Prophethood to Adam (A.S.), the father of humanity. The details about the conversation between Iblis and Allah can be studied in the 7th chapter of Quran. A'raf

S.Kahf-18:50:-

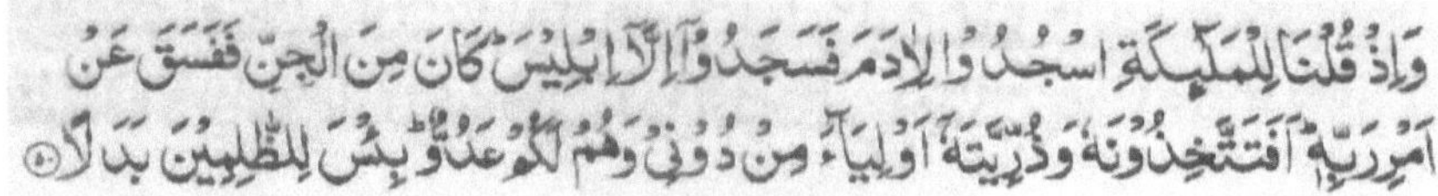

Tr:- "Behold ! We said to the angels. 'Bow down to Adam; they bowed except Iblis. He was one ofthe Jinns, and he broke the command of his Lord'. Will ye take him and his progeny as protectors rather than Me? And they are enemies to you! Evil would be the exchange for the wrong doers".

S. A'araf-7: 1 1-12:-

Tr:- "It is We Who created you and gave you shape; then We made the angels 'Bow down to Adam and they bowed down: not so Iblis. he refused to be of those who bowed down and not so Iblis. Allah said What prevented thee from bowing down. when I commanded thee?' He said, 'I am better than he: Thou didst create me from fire and him from clay'".

S.A'araf-7 : 14-15

Tr: - "He said, 'Give me respite. till the day they are raised up', Allah said. 'Be thou among those who have respite'".

H: "Satan sets some traps and snares. His traps and snares include ingratitude for Allah's grace, boasting about Allah's gifts, arrogant behavior towards Allah's servant and following vain desires in what displeases Allah" (Bukhari).

By the above explanation, it is evident that Iblis was a jinn. jinns were created before the creation of Adam. They live in a material world and procreate. Iblis has been granted by Alan the power of deception and mischief-making. But his deception, corruption and seduction can never have influence over the pure souls of devotees of Allah, who seek His refuge. Believers must love and obey Allah and beware of the trap of Iblis.

FOUNDATION OF HOPE:

The Holy Quran is the best evidence for all of us to believe that God exists. Holy Quran is the best Book of hope and optimism in the sense that our Creator forgives us and protects us against our follies as well as the follies of others.

S. Baqara-2:269:

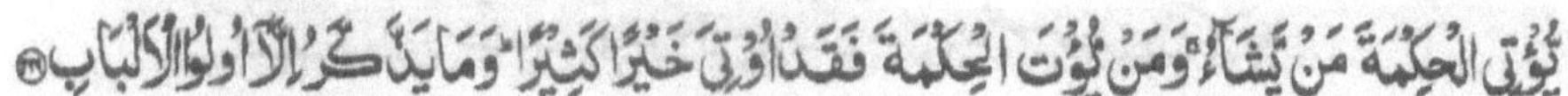

"Tr:- "He granteth wisdom to whom He pleaseth, and he to whom wisdom is granted receiveth indeed a benefit, overflowing, but none will grasp the message, but men of understanding"

S - Ahzab - 33:45-46 (Quoted in the 14th Chapter)

Tr:- "O Prophet! Truly we have sent thee as a witness, a Bearer of Glad Tidings and a Warner - And as one who invites to Allah's (Grace) by His leave, and as a lamp spreading light.

Any noble venture like public good is bound to face many hurdles and hardships Wisdom lies in trying to surmount these impediments and complete the task, instead of getting demoralized or losing heart. Personal efforts, coupled with reliance on Drine blessings are bound to help the man to achieve success in projects to be accomplished. The gospel of hope and good tidings was a revolutionary message of Islam to the despondent humanity, condemned for ever. God gives hopes to us as we give help to others. God is the sanctuary for worthy devotees. His chief aim is to fulfil the aspirations of those who beseech His help. Believers must avoid the feeling of despair but be hopeful of God's redemptive grace. Almighty Alah and his Messengers have laid golden rules, governing pious conduct. Those people who adhere to the scriptural dictates and Divine directives with almost sincerity are sure to reach Almighty Allah and attain spiritual perfection. Grateful servants of Allah are those who appreciate fully his blessings. He has informed us through scriptures and Prophets, that there is a limitless life in the hereafter, beyond the limited life of this world. The consequences of the actions of this life will certainly continue in the life after death.

H:- "No Muslim is afflicted by difficulty, continuous pain, anxiety grief, injury or even by a thorn with which, he is pierced, without Allah, thereby, making an atonement for his sins (Muslims, Bukhari, Mishkat).

As Muslims, let us follow the optimistic policy and hope for the best in this life as well as the life in the hereafter. (Philosophy of life. pessimism and optimism. materialism. Iblis. Divine Justice).

CHAPTER - XXVLLL

RELIGION AND POLITICS

Stanza-201

27/دین و سیاست

201۔ کشتہ وہم و ہوس پروردہ سودائے خام

دور ہے جس سے بہت عشق الٰہی کا مقام

ہوں زمانے میں جو دنیائے سیاست کے امام

وہم ہے امن و مساوات و محبت کا قیام

شیطنت دل کی سیاست سے نکل سکتی نہیں

جب نہیں بدلیں گے ہم دنیا بدل سکتی نہیں

Tr:- Those who are trained by or influenced by defective ambition are lovers of superstition, pseudo passion and covetousness. Dignity and love for God is very far from them. The stable establishment of affection, equality, peace and genuine leadership in the political sphere have become imaginary. The evil genius of wickedness, the devilish schemes and political tactics cannot alter the administration of the world unless we ourselves change our attitude.

Stanza-202

202 ۔ بندگان زر کو بھی ہے جنگ سے نفرت کمال

باعث امن و حفاظت بھی ہو خوف جان و مال

ہے قیام امن کا اہل ہوس کو بھی خیال

ہے مگر خوف و ہوس ہی باعث جنگ و جدال

جذبہ ایثار و اُلفت امن کی بنیاد ہو

جلوہ ایمان سے پہلے مگر آباد ہو

Tr:- Even the materialists and lovers of wealth have hatred for conflict. The fear of losing their own life and wealth is the sole cause for their desire for peace and safety. The greedy and covetous people also desire the firm and stable establishment of peace, but now-a-days the conflict and armed clash are the consequences of fear and covetousness. Enthusiasm for sacrifice and love may be the foundation of peace, but our mind must be amply enlightened with faith.

Stanza-203

203- یہ زمانے کے مدبر حکمراں سرمایہ دار

جنکے ہاتھوں میں بظاہر ہیں جہاں کے کاروبار

گو نگاہ خلق میں ہو لاکھ صاحب اختیار

دست قدرت کے کھلونوں کا شمار

دیدہ بینا کی ہوتی ہے مشیّت پر نظر

ہو عیاں اس پر ہے کس جانب زمانے کا سفر

Tr:- All administrations of the world seem to be under the control and command of capitalists and statesmen, who are considered to be the sovereign ruler. Though, the common public consider them to be all powerful, in reality, they are nothing, but the toys for the Divine hand. The devotees of God submit themselves to the will and pleasure of God. who leads them on the path of righteousness.

Stanza-204

204- ہے دل انسان پہ جب تک حرص و بے دینی کا راج

ہو سکوں نا آشنا یونہی زمانے کا مزاج

ہو تہ و بالا جہاں میں نوع انساں کی سماج

ہے خدا کا عشق ہی بیماری دل کا علاج

دولت دل سے بشر ہوتا ہے جتنا سرفراز

دولت دنیا سے ہوتا ہے وہ اتنا بے نیاز

Tr:- The people do not feel contented till they continue to be ruled over by greed and Atheism. God's love is the only remedy for all the social ills and social evils which have made the present societies a mess. The more a man is bestowed with the spiritual purity, the more, he becomes desireless of worldly wealth.

Stanza-205

205 ۔ جب الٰہی صرف مقصود بنی آدم نہ ہو
وحدت دامن و اخوت کا کبھی عالم نہ ہو
نغمہ ہستی میں ہم آہنگ زیر و بم نہ ہو
دہر میں ایک سلطنت اقوام کی قائم نہ ہو
دونوں عالم کی سعادت ہے خدا کے عشق میں
دین و دنیا کی مسرت ہے خدا کے عشق میں

Tr:- The concept of unity of God, Unity of Creations, peace and brotherhood, never exists, when the achievement of Allah's pleasure and nearness is not the objective of human life. There can be no melody in the song of life, nor can there be any harmony in the human life, nor can a good kingdom be established when people have no love for God. The auspiciousness, felicity, fortune, pity, and happiness depend on the love for God.

C: - In this chapter, the poet has discussed the relationship between Religion and Politics, selfishness and corruption of the politicians, the reasons for their hatred for conflicts, the evils of covetousness and Atheism and the great and real advantages of love for God, our Goal.

A Republic or democratic government advocated by Islam is expected to be administered by consultations with the representatives of different political parties, elected by the people. In case the political activities are in consonance with religious laws, their significance is great. But 'now-a-days, the politicians have been influenced by pseudo passion, covetousness and superstitions. In the political spheres, the leaders have the undesirable and covetous ambitions. The evil of wickedness cannot establish real love. The politicians, the elected parliamentarians and ministers carry out their portfolios, but not with the sincerity for the welfare of the public. Their devilish intention is to obtain material benefit for themselves. They prevent conflicts not to safeguard the nation, but in order to safeguard their own lives and wealth, in fact, their selfish motive is the greatest cause for the conflicts and terrorism. Whatever they do, they do with the demonish attitude of achieving their own ends. The powerful capitalists who act according to their own whims and fancies, are nothing but the toys in the Divine hand. The Divine advisability is sure to be hidden behind their power, granted by Allah. As long as the politicians are greedy and Atheists, the society cannot be lifted up and refined. As the Atheists have no religion and no fear of God, they have made a mess of society with awkward ups and downs. The poet expresses his wish that the zeal and enthusiasm of the politicians may be the foundation of peace, and they may be enlightened with the effulgence, lustre and beauty of Faith (Religion). The poet concludes by enumerating the Divine blessings which are the consequences of love for God. The love for God is the only remedy for all the ills of the society. It makes the enlightened man desireless of worldly wealth and fame. It fetches good fortune, felicity, auspiciousness and happiness to the lover of God.

For the civilization of a nation, a good government is necessary which in its turn needs good politicians. The politicians must be enlightened by religion for the efficient and just executions of their duties and responsibilities. Islamic society is clean, chaste and peaceful. It is a society of perfect purity.

H " Everything which belongs to a Muslim is forbidden to other Muslims, his blood money and honour"

It is clearly revealed in Quran that government should be established through the Book of Allah, in which man shall not have any say, for Allah does not assign His authority to anyone.

S.Ma'ida - 5:47 (Last part of the verse)

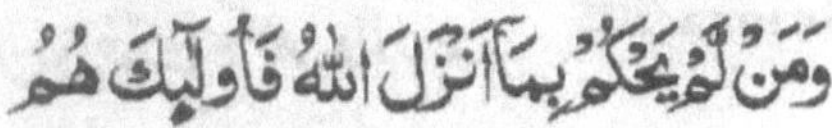

Tr:- If any do fail to judge (by the light of) what Allah hath revealed, they are (No better than) unbelievers.

S. Ma'ida- 5 : 49:

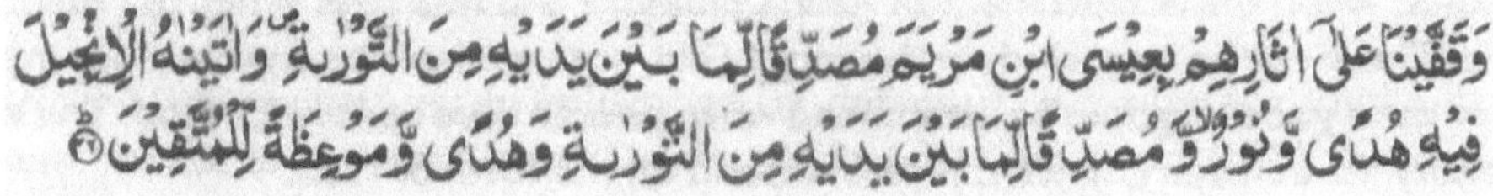

Tr:- "And, in their footsteps, we sent Jesus, the son of Mary, confirming the Law, that had come before him. We sent the Gospel; there in was guidance and light, and confirmation of the Law that had come before him, a guidance and admonition to those who fear".

Canvassing and bribing for votes at the times of election is not permitted by religion. Allah refused to promise Ibrahim (A.S.) to make his progeny leaders of their respective tribes. It means that one should come up by dint of his merit and it is the duty of the public to judge the qualities of the candidate without any prejudice or partiality. Mohammed (SAW) did not appoint his successor. No person should be elected or given the authority of a politician who is power crazy, and arrogant and who seeks dominance.

S. Luquman - 3 1:18: -

Tr:- 'Swell not thy cheek (for pride) at men nor walk in insolence through the earth, for Allah loveth not arrogant boaster".

H :- "Two hungry wolves, let loose in the herd of goats will not create that much of tumult as the desire for wealth and power causes " (Tirmizi).

H :- " The best ruler among the rulers, is he who may love you and you may love him; who may pray for you and you may pray for him. The worst ruler is he who may have grudge against you and you may have grudge against him, and he may invoke curse on you and you may invoke curse on him." (Muslim)

H:- "Gentleness adorns everything while lack of gentleness makes things defective.•

This chapter is not meant to attack on, or criticize the politicians. Of course, goodness prevails over evil in this world, there are numerous politicians who are selfless and discharge their duties with the true spirit of sacrifice and service to humanity. The general discussion of the poet in this chapter aims at eradicating the existing evils in the society and bring about reformation to the extent possible. A sincere politician should not transgress the limits, prescribed by religion. Our goal is God, all of us including the politicians must pursue His pleasure, because He is the Supreme authority over all of us. Hence, like other social science, politics also is closely related to religion. (Social Science, Politics, Religion, Divine administration).

CHAPTER - XXIX

FAITH AND LOVE

Stanza-206

29/ ایمان و محبت

206- کس کی رحمت کا ہے جلوہ خلق پر چھایا ہوا

کار فرما ہے جہاں کس کا قانون جزاء

ہے مشیت کس کی ہر قانون قدرت کی بنا

مصلحت کس کی ہے ہر یک چیز میں جلوہ نما

حکمت کامل ہے کس کی ذرہ ذرہ سے عیاں

ماتحت کس کی ربوبیت کے چلتا ہے جہاں

Tr:- Whose lustre and effulgence of blessings are prevailing over the creations ? whose law of rewarding is operating in this world? Whose decision is the foundation of Divine Law? Whose perfect prudence and skill are hidden in every molecule? Under whose providence is the world existing?

Stanza-207

207- عاشقان نے پاک طینت صاحب صدق و یقیں

جلوہ حق سے ہے سینہ جنکا فردوس بریں

کیا اٹھا سکتے ہیں اس کے آستانے سے جبیں

ہے ربوبیت بھی مربوب بھی کیا رب نہیں

یک قدم جاتا ہے بندہ جب سوئے پروردگار

سو قدم آتا ہے وہ بندہ کی جانب بے قرار

نوٹ : (اے پیغمبر) جب کوئی میرا بندہ میری نسبت تم سے دریافت کرے تو میں اس کے پاس ہوں وہ جب پکارتا ہے تو میں اس کی پکار سنتا ہوں اور اسے قبول کرتا ہوں۔۔۔قرآن۔۔۔۔۔۔ دلیل

Tr:- The selves of those people have become the highest paradise by the lustre of truth and by those who are lovers of pure character and pure knowledge. When Almighty Allah, our Creator, His creations and His Providence are nothing but one and the same thing. Can the people avoid prostration before Allah? If a worshipper advances by one step towards Allah He becomes anxious to meet His devotee and advances to meet him by hundred steps.

Stanza.208

208۔ حیطہ منطق سے باہر ہیں بہت اسرار دیں

عقل کو حاصل ہو جس سے رفعت عرش بریں

جنکا ہو وجدان اور الہام کو عین الیقین

منکروں پر منکشف اسرار یہ ہوتے نہیں

کفر تقلید و گماں سے دل جو مردہ ہو گئے

حق پزیری کی لیاقت ہی وہ اپنی کھو گئے

Tr:- The secrets of religion are beyond the scope of logical arguments or human comprehension. The height of Empyrean Throne of God (Arsh) cannot be reached by wisdom and through logical reasoning. The intuition and inspiration are not received by the infidels. Those selves which have lost vitality due to infidelity and heathenism have lost the power of recognizing the truth.

Stanza.209

209۔ غیب پر انساں کو ایماں نہ ہو گر استوار

زندگانی کے مسائل حل نہ ہوں گے ذینہار

ہو نہیں سکتے کبھی اسرار پنہان آشکار

آدمی ہو کر رہے ہیں حیوانیت کا ہی کا شکار

یک معمہ ہی رہے انساں کو مقصود حیات

ہر بت حرص و ہوا ہو اس کا معبود حیات

Tr:- If human beings do not have firm and resolute faith in the unseen God. the problems of life will remain unsolved. The hidden secrets can never be disclosed to such persons and they will become victims of beastliness. The purpose of life (God) will remain a mystery to those whose deities are greed, lust and worldly desires.

Stanza-210

210- نور ایماں سے ہے دل انساں میں اخلاق عظیم

عفت قلب و نظر عشق خداوند کریم

قوت رب عشرت جاوید الطاف عمیم

خوف حق پاس امانت درد دل عقل سلیم

ضبط نور معرفت صبر و حیا صوم و صلوٰت

سوز اُلفت راستی تسلیم ایثار و زکات

Tr:- The bright light of faith is the cause for magnificent character, spiritual vision, chastity and love for God. The effulgence of firm faith in human beings is the cause for Divine strength. eternal bliss and all-embracing favors. The beauty of faith is the cause for fear of God, protection of entrusted thing, feeling for others, self-control, Divine knowledge, perfect wisdom, patience. modesty, passionate love, righteousness, love for worships such as Namaz and Fasting and attitude for giving charity and offer sacrifices.

Stanza-211

211- شان ہے مومن کی اخلاص و توکل انکسار

عدل استقلال تقوی صدق شکر کردگار

اعتدال امید آزادی وفا ذکر و قرار

حق پرستی علم خود داری و عزم استوار

انہماک جاوداں سوز یقین و اعتماد

بے نیازی ہمت بے باک و بے پروا جہاد

Tr:- The pride of a believer is based on sincerity, resignation to God's will, humility. justice, perseverance. fear of God, piety, truthfulness, thankfulness to God. moderation. hopefulness. freedom, faithfulness, repeated invocation of Allah's name, contentment. recognition of truth, literacy, self-respect, firm determination, devoted and repeated attempts, love for precise knowledge, confidence, desire lessness, daring valour and fearless struggle.

Stanza. 212

212- دین و دنیا میں سدا ہوتے ہیں مومن کامیاب

گو مزاہم انکے آفات جہاں ہوں بے حساب

غیب کی تائید سے ہے اُن کی قوت باریاب

جلوہ ایماں سے بن جاتے ہیں ذرہ آفتاب

ہائے وہ مومن کہ ص ید گردش ایام ہے

دہر میں بے دین کی ہر کامیابی خام ہے

Though the countless adversities become the impediments of life, the believersemerge successful in this world and in the hereafter. Their strength is empowered by mysterious help. Just as individual atoms have assembled together to make a sun, mysterious helps from all directions empower the strength of the believers. It is a real plight of those believers who become the victims of vicissitude of misfortunes and lose their hearts. Those who have no proper faith in God, their success if any. is defective.

Stanza.213

213- ہر گنہ میں کفر اور الحاد کی یک شان دیکھ

حکمراں ہے ہر دل کافر میں یک شیطان دیکھ

حرص دنیا سے بشر کو بد تر از حیوان دیکھ

کیا سے ہوجاتا ہے کیا انکار سے انسان دیکھ

در حقیقت مبتلائے شرک ہیں وہ اہل دیں

گرد شر سے پاک جنکا دامن ہستی نہیں

Tr:- It is wonderful to see that infidelity and atheism is involved in every vice. In the heart of every infidel, evil spirit (Satan) is dominating. The greed for worldly desires makes a man worse than the beast. What a change occurs in humanity when he becomes a Satan and worse than the brute by refusing to believe in God and disobeying Him In fact the believers are now involved in polytheism due to their own mischief.

Stanza-214

214۔ بستہ سود و زیاں ہوتا نہیں مرد فقیر

غیب کے منکر ہوس کے دلدلوں میں ہیں اسیر

قوبی فطرت سے بھی خالی جو ہو انکا ضمیر

ہے زمانے کے لیے خطرہ وہ برنا ہوں کہ پیر

صاحب اخلاق ہیں یوں بھی اگر دہری کہیں

اور ہیں اسباب اسکے کفر کی لعنت نہیں

Tr:- A devotee of God is free from the influence of profit and gain. Those Who do not believe in the unseen God, have become victims of worldly desires and lust. Whether, his young or old, he is very dangerous for the people, if his conscience is unoccupied with natural goodness. When there are people of virtuous disposition and ethical morality, the causes for their worldly desires are not the anathema or execration of infidelity,

Stanza.215

215۔ اُلفت اہل ہوس مطلب پرستی ہے گماں

ایک جوش عارضی سوز بہیمی کا دھواں

جوہر ایماں سے ہوتی ہے محبت جاوداں

روح پرور باغ جنت کی بہار بے خزاں

اُلفت ارباب دیں رحمت کی ہے جلوہ گری

بندہ دنیا کی اُلفت ہے فقط سوداگری

Tr:- It is doubtless, that the outward affection of covetous people is meant for their selfies purpose. Their temporary emotion is nothing but brutalinstincts. The merit of faith, in fact, promotes the eternity of love, causes spiritual evaluation and becomes the eternal beauty of the garden of paradise. The true affection of the religious people is the very manifestation of God's blessing. The false affection of those who worship the worldly desires is nothing but trade through which they wanted to extract material profit.

Stanza-216

216۔ نخل ایمان و کا محبت کا ثمر انسانیت

درد مند عشق کا سوز جگر انسانیت

سینہ عارف میں جنت کی سحر انسانیت

قلب انسانی پہ رحمت کا اثر انسانیت

مہرباں ایمان سے انسان بنتا ہے بشر

کونسی انسانیت الحاد پر ہے منحصر

Tr:- Humanity is the fruit of faith and love. Perfection of sincere love is humanity. The pleasantness of morning of the paradise, contained in man, possessing Divine knowledge is humanity. A man converts into human being because of sincere faith. Which type of humanity is based on Atheism?

Stanza-217

217۔ وہ شب خلوت میں یاد یار سے تسکین جاں

وہ نزول معنی قرآن کا سینے میں سماں

آہ وہ اعماق دل میں عرش اعظم کا نشاں

وہ زمین قلب پر باران رحمت ہر زماں

اکتسابی علم کی یوں تو ضرورت عام ہے

علم ہے لیکن وہی جو بخشش الہام ہے

What a contentment due to the remembrance of God during the auspicious night of solitude! What a pleasant atmosphere during the reception of revelation Of Quran! How beautiful the Emblem of the Abode of God, impressed in the depth of the heart! What a permanent rain of Divine favours on human beings! Though we generally need the knowledge, acquired by our efforts, but the real knowledge comes of God's beneficence and generosity.

Stanza-218

218۔ ہے دل مومن کی وسعت رو کش کون و مکاں

اسکی عالمگیر ہے اُلفت محیط بیکراں

اہل ایماں کا ہے سرمایہ خداوند جہاں

اپنی خلوت میں وہ خود ہوتے ہیں بزم کن فکاں

شخصیت انکی ہے دنیا کے لیے مہر مبیں

جاگتی ہے اُن کے دم سے قسمت اہل زمیں

T:- The believer's heart is so vast that the boundless universe is embarrassed. The universal love of the believers is an Ocean without shore. The whole stock of wealth of the believers, is

God Who created the world. In their solitude, they enjoy the company of God. Such personalities of the world are a bright sun, which enlightens minds of others and their fortune exists because of the existence of these personalities.

Stanza-219

219۔ کس طرح عاشق کا دل ہے   ہے نیاز دو جہاں

کس طرح اڑ جاتی ہے دل سے ہوس بن کر دھواں

عشق میں موجود ہیں دونوں جہاں کی خوبیاں

وہ مسرت جس کے آگے ہیچ ہے کون و مکاں

تابش حسن ازل ہے عشق کا سوز نفس

ہے خیال ماسوا سے عشق بیگانہ زبس

Tr: - To which extent, the heart of the true lover is desireless of both the worlds i.e. this world and the world hereafter? How, the lust vanquishes like a smoke from the heart of the lover? This world is nothing when compared to the happiness of excellence and elegance of both the worlds, contained in the true love for God. The perfect love for God in one's self is the beauty of the effulgence of God. If one thinks or desires for anything other than God, he has no knowledge as to what the real love is.

Stanza-220

220۔ ہے خدا کا عشق ہی انسان کے شایان شاں

ہے اسی آتش میں جنت دین و دنیا کی نہاں

ہے اسی کا ایک جلوہ برتر از وہم و گماں

ایک تصویر خیالی ہے زماں ہو یا مکاں

دیدہ حق بیں میں ہے اول وہی آخر

اے شہید جستجو بطن وہی ظاہر وہی

Tr:- The aspect of love for God is the worthiest one and suitable for the high status of man. The paradise of both the worlds is concealed in the love for God_ The splendid manifestation of God's love is beyond imagination. Those who acknowledge the truth and who are in quest of true knowledge must know that God is the first and God is the last and He is the In-Dweller and He is the Out-Dweller.

C:- In order to enlighten the minds of the readers and convince them about the existence of Almighty Allah, the poet started composing the poem by describing a landscape which speaks out the manifestations of God who is All-Pervading. In order to strengthen their Faith. the poet, has struggled a lot throughout the poem by mentioning the physical phenomena in nature. and by discussing the Islamic tenets and religious aspects such as Realization of Truth and Goal of our life, God. In the concluding chapter of the poem, he has slightly touched some aspects of life. which have already been discussed in the previous chapters, with the main purpose of creating indelible impressions on the minds of the readers. that the prime bases for the success in this life and the life in the hereafter, are the love for and fear of God called spiritualism. These are the factors which purify our souls, evolve our souls and bring about concordance with God which is called spiritual perfection. In this chapter, the poet has dealt with the topics, Faith and Love ', Human Dignity". "Mysticism", "Love for God" and All-Pervading Attribute and Eternity of God.

The poet explains that it is only the blessing of Almighty God which is the root cause of every Divine Law of rewarding which is always active, His prudence and advisability are concealed in every happening, His perfect wisdom is concealed in every atom and His Providence prevails over whole of the world.

Those lovers of chastity, who have true knowledge, enjoy the beauty of truth, always bow down in the threshold of Divine Abode, because they realise that there is unity among the Cherisher, the cherished and the act of cherishing. If the sincere worshipper loves God, develops his self and evolves his soul. If he goes one step forward to meet God, He anxiously comes towards his devotee by hundred steps.

Q:- "Oh Prophet! If any of my worshippers enquires about Me, tell him that I am close to him and when he supplicates, I hear his supplication and accept it"

Though, the secrets of religion are beyond the Scope of logical arguments, the intimate knowledge about God and adherence to Divine Law can take us to the sublime Abode of Allah. Those people who have lost their tenacity and capability of realizing the truth, have ruined themselves by their emulation and by following the footsteps of the infidels. If we do not have strong faith in the unseen, our problems of life can never be solved, nor can we be acquainted with the secrets, revealed in the scriptures. If we do not have steady, resolute and firm faith in the unseen, we will remain as irrational animals. The Goal of life (God) will remain a mystery for us and our deities will be greed, avidity and lust.

In the 210th Stanza of the poem, the poet has enumerated the benefactions of the light of Faith. By virtue of Faith, we are benefited by magnificent chastity, self-respect. love for God, Divine help and power, Divine favour and grace, fear of God, honesty regarding entrusted things, feelings for others, healthy and perfect wisdom, light of Divine knowledge, morality,patience, passionate love for humanity. righteousness, submission to Gods will motive of sacrifice and Divine benedictions through Namaz, Fasting and Zakaat,

Now the poet proceeds to describe the exaltation of the believer by enumerating Some of his qualities. These qualities are sincerity, loyalty, complete resignation and total submission to God, humility. modesty, perseverance, justice. constancy, fear of God, piety, abstemiousness, sincerity of thankfulness. moderation, temperance, balance, evenness. repeated invocations and supplications to God. love for truth, self-respect. self-dignity, firm determination, definite purpose. eternal concentration and absorption in endeavors, sincere belief, confidence. trust, assurance, certainty, definiteness, positiveness, reliance, desire lessness, fearless gallantry and careless fight.

Inspite of the several misfortunes, adversities, impediments and hindrances in the life of the believers, they emerge successful in this world and in the hereafter as they are blessed with the beauty of Faith. It is a great plight that sometimes, the sincere believers also become the victims of misfortunes and vicissitudes. Sometimes the Atheists achieve great success, but it is sure to be defective.

Every sin is imbibed with infidelity and Atheism, because the Satan (Iblis) rules over the hearts of the Pagans and Heathens, Greed and covetousness make the human being worse than the beast. There is an ugly stain in the life of a non-Atheist who is steeped in Paganism and idolatry. The real devotee is not influenced by materialism. He never cares about profit and loss. Those who reject belief in the unseen, are bound by the mundane things. Whether they are young or Old, whose conscience is empty and unoccupied, they are dangerous for the society. In some cases. the people have manners, good disposition, virtues and morality, but, at the same time, love materialism. The causes of their materialistic view are different ones and not the imprecation of infidelity and Atheism.

It is doubtless that the show of affection of those people who have undesirable passions, is nothing, but their own benefits. Their temporary emotions are nothing but brutal instincts. The quintessence of Faith evolves the soul, makes the garden of paradise an eternal beauty Without autumn and makes the love an eternal one. The real love of the religious people is the beauty or splendid gift of God. Contrary to this. the love of those who worship the worldly enjoyments, is nothing but trade or Commerce. The poet has described all sorts and categories of people and their qualities in this chapter.

Now the poet supposes to explain the significance of human dignity and presents some definitions for humanity. He says that humanity is the fruit of Faith and Love, the title of this chapter. It is the real love and passionate feeling for others. It is the mystic or intimate knowledge about God, of the devout. It is the influence of Divine bounty on the pious. It is the evening of paradise for the learned. By the virtue of the beneficence of Faith, the man becomes a human being. The poet means to say that a man without humanity, cannot be called a human being. Humanity is alien to Atheism.

Now the poet appreciates the spiritual bliss and expresses his joy over the remembrance of God which gives him consolation; imagines the pleasant atmosphere when the Holy

Quran was revealed to Prophet Mohammed (SAW); and imagines the elegant emblem or the sign ofthe high Abode of God in the heart and the continuous Divine blessings on us. Acquiring knowledge is a general necessity. but it is the real knowledge which is the beneficence of inspiration.

While realizing the vast expanse of the believer's heart, the world seems to be shrinking or contracting. The world-conquering love of the believer is a shoreless ocean. The only wealth and treasure of the believer is Almighty Allah. When the believers are lost or engrossed in devotion in the solitude. they enjoy the company of all the creations Of God. These personalities are certainly auspicious, and sure guiding lights for the rest of the world. world is a mixture of good and evil, inhabited by pious and impious people. The impious people also enjoy the Divine blessings, showered on this world for the sake of pious people. As the love for God goes on increasing the lover of God becomes more and more desireless of worldly enjoyments. The merriments and retellings of this World are worthless and nothing, when compared to the virtues, elegances and excellences of true love for God. The love for the Eternal Beauty of God is the greatest interest of our life. Those, who think of other things, i.e., other than God, are quite unaware of the true love.

The last Stanza of the text implies the poet's purpose for composing this poem. The conclusive and exhaustive purpose of the poet is to enlighten the minds of the people with love for God, show the right path to reach Him and to attain spiritual perfection. He says that it is love for God which is worthy and suitable to enhance human dignity and status. We find all the pleasures and comforts of paradise in the love for God.

Whether, it is time or place, they are only imaginary factors but, the beauty of love for God is beyond human imagination. In the concluding couplet of this poem, the poet has addressed those people who are eagerly in quest of the intimate knowledge about God. While interpreting, the poet enlists four of the unique attributes of Allah, which imply and cannot that Almighty Allah is Eternal and All Pervading. While explaining His Eternity, he says, Allah is the First and He is the Last. The origin and end of Allah is not known which means that He is Eternal. While describing His presence, every-where, he says, "Allah is the In-Dweller and Out-Dweller in all His creations. It means He is pervading in whole of the universe.

It is the salient feature of my father's works that they end with his marvelous Sufistic Philosophy.

FAITH AND LOVE

Love for God and faith in Divine dispensation will enable the ardent devotees to overcome the obstacles and surmount their difficulties which may appear to be unsurmountable. The devotional fervor of such extraordinary persons is imbibed both by firm faith and true love. On some occasions, even such beloved devotees are put to severe test. As they have strong confidence in God's favor and grace and stand steady. unaverred, Almighty Allah comes for their help. There may be certain limit to the acquisition of knowledge, but there is no bounds with regard to the services, rendered to God and humanity. Service should be spontaneous and extended without expecting any return. This will help the aspirants to merge with God can be approached by selfless, unflagging and unswerving love. God's love and blessings are not confined to one section or one group of humanity His love transcends all humanboundaries. It spreads beyond limitations of time and place, because. Allah is always concerned with the needs of his creations. He protects aid sustains them. He guides human beings and leads them to the higher life in the hereafter.

The spiritual love arises from the soul which gets tranquility from the fear of God (Taqwa). It is only rational that Allah loves man for his good deeds and fervor for his bad deeds. By giving the glad tidings and warnings He wants to show the right path to entire humanity. The love of God for humanity is greater in magnitude than the love of human beings for God.

H:- "None among you can be Momin. unless, I am endeared to him more than his parents and children and all others combined". (Bukhari).

H:- " You cannot enter paradise unless you become a believe You cannot be a believer unless you love others " (Muslim)

H:- " He who loves to meet Allah, He also loves to meet him. One who dislikes to meet Him, Allah also abhors to meet him." (Muslim).

H:- "He realized the flavor of Faith (Iman) who became pleased with Allah as his Lord, with Islam as the code of life and with Mohammed as the messenger of

H:- I' Remember Allah very often, so that you will be most prominent among the servants of Allah"

H:- " One who has Iman is simple and beneficent and the sinner is cunning and cowardly/' (Abu Dawood).

S. Mumin- 40:60: -

وَقَالَ رَبُّكُمُ ادْعُونِي أَسْتَجِبْ لَكُمْ ۚ إِنَّ الَّذِينَ يَسْتَكْبِرُونَ عَنْ عِبَادَتِي سَيَدْخُلُونَ جَهَنَّمَ دَاخِرِينَ ۝

Tr:- "And your Lord says : 'call Me; I will answer your (prayer), but those who are too arrogant to serve me will surely find themselves

S. Baqara: 2:152: -

فَاذْكُرُونِي أَذْكُرْكُمْ وَاشْكُرُوا لِي وَلَا تَكْفُرُونِ ۝

Tr:- "Then do ye remember Me. Be grateful to Me and reject not Faith".

S. Ma'ida- 5: 57:-

يَا أَيُّهَا الَّذِينَ آمَنُوا لَا تَتَّخِذُوا الَّذِينَ اتَّخَذُوا دِينَكُمْ
هُزُوًا وَلَعِبًا مِنَ الَّذِينَ أُوتُوا الْكِتَابَ مِنْ قَبْلِكُمْ
وَالْكُفَّارَ أَوْلِيَاءَ ۚ وَاتَّقُوا اللَّهَ إِنْ كُنْتُمْ مُؤْمِنِينَ

Tr:- 'O ! ye who believe ! If any from among you turn back from his Faith. soon will Allah produce a people whom He will love and they will love Him"Remembrance to Allah results in physical stability. Physical stability depends on spiritual power which in its turn depends on complete and continuous Faith, Now, it is evident that spring of love is Iman.

HUMAN DIGNITY

The magnificence of human dignity can be assessed by the story of Adam (A.S.), the father of humanity. related in the Holy Quran. The greatest value of human life, his significant role on earth, the position he occupies in the system of existence. the standard of human excellence, his Covenant made With Almighty Allah, his vicegerency on earth and prostration of angels before him have established human dignity. Except man, no other creature on this world has rationality, nor can it understand spiritual values. Hence, man is called the Crown of Allah's creations. He is also Called Masjood-e-Malaik (Adored by the Angels). It is man's bounden duty to make use of his rationality in the best possible way and to avoid perversion and hypocrisy After the lapse of the Age of Ignorance and Advent of Islam, people began to appreciate the fact that human beings are the glorious creations of God, and entitled to much more love. regard and honour Our Prophet (SAW) accorded to man the rank only next to God. God himself has declared in Quran that man is the highest of His Creations with best form.

S-Al-Baqara - 2:29 (Quoted in Chapter - I)

Tr:- " He it is who created for you all that is in the earth"

H:- " Allah has revealed to me that you must show your humility so that no one deals unjustly with another and no one treats another with disdain" (Bukhari)

H:- The best among you are those whose appearance reminds you of Allah" (Bukhari. A-Adab, Al-Mufrad, Ahmed, Bathaqi).

H:- The first (thing) that will be decided among people on the Day of Judgement. Will pertain to bloodshed" (Muslim)

The human race is distinguished from the brute creation, by the family set up which is the primary unit in human civilization. The cohesive force and affinity of family owes its existence to the feeing of love wich Allah has kindled in the hearts of the family members. Man's inherited potentials like intelligence aptitude and craze for endeavors, inventing skill, sacrificing motive and aspiration for achieving spiritual perfection (In case of pious man) are some of the constituent factors of human dignity.

Mr.R.Meganathan, B.Sc.B.L. who hails from Udamalpet has written a marvellous article,entitled, "Integral Development of Human Personality" , in which he has dealt with the subjects "What is Development "What is personality? Learning", "Physical Development", "Mental Development". "Emotional Development", "Social Development", "Moral and "Spiritual Development" and "Talent Development", As Almighty Allah has been generous and compassionate to bless man with soul and his mental development is the highest one with discriminating power. I am presenting in the following Mr.Meganathan's idea about mental development in his own words.

"The mind is the complex entity, performing innumerable functions, The mind includes the conscious, sub-conscious and unconscious area, The conscious mind perceives knowledge through the five sensory organs and develops intellect, The sub-conscious mind controls the involuntary functions of the body organs and is the store-house for roar Sarnskaras, instinctsand emotions. The unconscious mind forms the largest part of the brain which ought to be tapped for unfoldment of brilliancy. The human brain has two hemispheres; the right side known as intuitive brain, responsible for inventions, creative ideas, expression of artistic talents etc, and the left side known as analytical brain responsible for reading, discriminating, calculating etc, the unification of two sides of the brain should be the aim of real education, Mental development takes place through constant mental exercises, memorization, concentration, meditation,

Mantra recitation etc. Mental powers are unlimited, and only through training and disciplined life, those powers can be brought out,"

Nothing is richer and more complex than the human personality Its all sided-development and moral perfection should be the goal of human dignity.

MYSTICISM:

To believe in the unseen is mysticism. Anything which involves mysteries is called mysticism, there is no need for scientific proof or logical arguments to fathom all the mysteries of the universe, which Allah does not wish to acquaint us with. By the permission Of Allah, man can fathom the mysteries only to a very small extent. If acquisition of our knowledge is equal to the knowledge of Allah. There can be no dignity of Divinity over humanity, there can be no religion Without mysticism and mysticism without religion is defective. Mysticism Without true religion is nothing but myth. Religion is a way of understanding God Which seeks to enhance the excellence of the entire humanity, while mysticism aims at elevating the position of the chosen individuals above the common herd of humanity.

The Holy Quran is full Of Mysticism, which the true Muslims should believe in, The physical eyes see by the light of the sun While the spiritual eyes see by the Revelations of Holy Quran Mysticism includes, the Existence of God and His Attributes, the creation of the universe; creation of Adam (A,S.) from clay; existence of several worlds in the universe; the amazing; phenomena Of nature; the existence ofJinns and Angels, creation of seven firmaments of heavens and earth, descriptions of the Day of Doom, Resurrection, Reckoning, pleasantness of paradise, torments of the hell, Recreation of the universe etc. There are mystic events, mystic worlds, mystic time, mystic animal, and miracles of saints and prophets.

We are not required to tax our mind about the physical concept of Divinity which is beyond human imagination. What all is demanded of us is to appreciate the grand creative art, so prominently displayed as signs on an enormous canvas of nature. Our maxim should be, "Realize Allah through His creations."

The word, "Seven" means several in the plural sense. The mention of seven firmaments may mean that there are several heavens and earths, similar to ours, existing in the universe, which is a mystery for us. It is logical to assume that other earths having the same environments as ours, capable of supporting similar lives exist. But we are not aware of the physical structure, culture and civilization and the religious beliefs of the people inhabiting the other earths. In other Quranic verses Allah has said that He has created several moons and several suns in the universe. In the first Quranic verse the words, " Cherisher of the Worlds". confirm the existence of many worlds. It is clearly stated in the Quran that there is a world for Jinns and a separate world for the Scientists have discovered some planets having protoplasm in them which is the essential and primal requisite for life. But the correct number of worlds existing in the vast expanse of the universe will ever remain a mystery for the greatest scientists. Mei'raj-e-Nabi is the glorious mystic event in Islamic History, of the journey of Prophet Mohammed (SA\N) to Holy Abode of God above all the heavens and his audience there With Allah Himself. We must believe in this mystic journey Isra (From

Kabathullah to Masiid-e-Aqsa in Jerusalem) and our Prophet's ascension to Arsh (Mei 'raj) as there are confirmations in the Quran. In fact, this mystery is a challenge for humanity. The white beautiful mystic animal with the body of a horse and two wings called Buraaq was the steed of our Prophet (SAW) which transported him to the highest heaven on the occasion of Mei'raj. Quran says that Allah lifted up Isa (AS.) and he is alive in the heavens; and that he will reap in the world with his corporeal body, before the Day of Doom. This also is a great mystery for the Muslims. There is mystic information in Quran that a mighty Jinn was at the disposal and service of Sulaiman (A.S.). History says that the name of the mighty Jinn was frit.

In Quran two frames of time have been hinted. One is the time frame of this world and the other belongs to God. We calculate the time with the help of the rotations and revolutions of the planets. This calculation was possible only after the creation of the universe and after the advent of Adam (A.S.) on the earth. As Allah is an Eternal Being, He existed before the creation of the universe and He has His own time frame which has no relativity with the time of this world. The subject 'Relativity of Time is Included in Mysticism because the mystery of the two frames of time is involved in it, the following Quranic verses will reveal the two frames of time.

S. Hajj-22 : 47

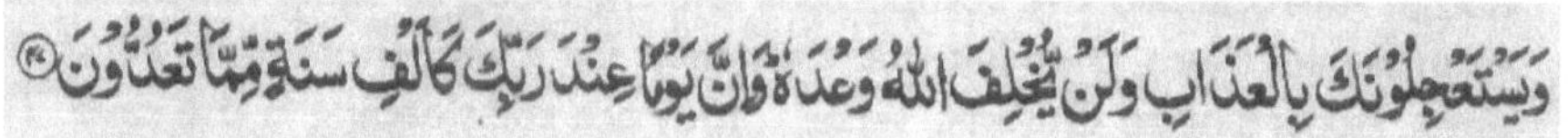

T:- "Yet they ask thee to hasten on the punishment ! But Allah Will not fail in His promise. Verily, a day in the sight of thy Lord is like a thousand years of your reckoning".

S: Ma'arij-70 : 6-7

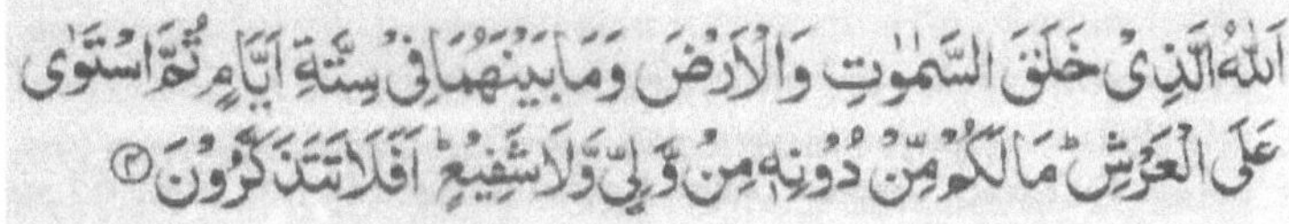

Tr:- "They see the (day) indeed as a far-off event. But we see it very near"

S. Sajdah-32-5:-

Tr:- "He rules all affairs from the heavens to the earth: in the end will (all affairs) go up toHim, on a day, the space whereof will be (A.S.) a thousand years of your reckoning"

S. Sajdah-32 : 4:-

Tr:- "It is Allah Who has created the heavens and the earth, and all between them, in six Days, and is firmly established on the Throne (Of Authority); ye have none besides Him. to protect or to intercede (for you); will ye not then receive admonition?".

In the Quranic verse 32:4, Allah has said that He created the universe in six days. Those six days might have been billions of years. In 22:47 and 32:5, Allah has said that a single day of His time frame is reckoned to be a thousand years according to the time frame of this world. Contrary to this statement. Allah has said in 70:6-7, that the event expected to be a far-off one by the people very near to Him.

Our idea of time is defective as we are incapable of calculating both the time frames. The event Of Mei'raj and the stories of Uzair and the companions of the cave (Ashab-e-Kahaf) who had patience and all other virtues and believed in a true Faith are quite amazing for us. The prolonged happenings on the occasion of the events of Isra and Mei'raj were accomplished in less than a second of this world on the 27th night of Rajab. Uzair Was caused to die in Jerusalem for hundred years, by Allah. But, when he was revived by Allah, he felt as if he slept for a few hours. Allah wanted to prove the validity of His statement that he was dead for hundred years. He instructed him to look at the hundred years old skeleton of his ass on which he rode. In order to display His wonders and the time frame of this world, Allah caused his food to remain hot. The King of Persia had sent uzair to reconstruct the ruined Jerusalem. When he saw the totally destructed Jerusalem, erased to the ground, he thought that it was impossible for him to reconstruct Jerusalem. But Allah wanted to hint him, that it was possible to reconstruct Jerusalem and nothing was impossible for Allah. So, he revived his ass with a fresh body in the wink of an eye in the presence of Uzair, encouraged by these events, he started reconstructing Jerusalem. Terrified by the massacre, performed by the then King of Rome, the believer companions, along with a dog, hid themselves in the cave of (Kahaf) in Rome. Allah caused the companions and their dog to sleep for three hundred years. When Allah awoke them, they felt that they slept for a very short time. Again, Allah caused them to sleep. According to Quranic verses, they are still sleeping in the cave. This event took place after the period of Jesus Christ and before the advent of Islam. According to our approximate calculation, they have been sleeping since more than sixteen centuries. They will be caused to wake up before the Day of the Doom and then die.

The relativity of time is the sub-branch of the study of Mysticism which in its turn is a branch of study of religion. All knowledge is for God. Mystery can be fathomed only to a small extent by human beings. God works wonders beyond fathoming and imagination.

The following passages have been extracted from the commentary of Moulana Yusuf Ali Sahib about mysticism. These are the parts of the essence of Sura-e-Sajdah (Adoration), Surae-Fatir (Creator), Sura-e-Suffat etc,

"The theme of the short Sura (Sajdah) is the mystery of creations, the mystery of time and mysteries as viewed through the revelations of God. In contemplation of these, mysteries should lead to Faith and adoration of God. These mysteries of creations, the mysteries of time and mysteries of end of things are but known by external symbols to man. Revelations bring Faith and humble adoration and blessings like rains, which bring life to dead soil. Man can experience, what infinite shades and grades of colour there are in nature. So, there are grades in the spiritual world. The good and truthful understands God who knows and watches over all the creatures. The good will reach the eternal bliss while the evil will find no helper. Gods promises have mystic meanings.

The mysteries of spiritual world are manifested in different ways. Through all the mysteries of the heavens and earth, there is sorting out of the evil against the good, their final destination, contrasted.

Our heaven is independent of time and space or feeling circumstances, No one can know precisely, how the spiritual delights, hidden in reserve for him. But we must necessarily use terms that imply all these three conditions, for they can be expressed by allegory or imagery. The righteous soul enters the regions of bliss and is given to drink of a cup (Sharaab-e-Tuhoor) from the mystic fountain of Kafur literally means camphor. In mystic language, it stands for all that is wholesome, cooling, soothing, refreshing and agreeable. Zanianbil which typifies warmth and zest to taste is given from the mystic fountain called Sal-Sabil. In heaven, people have whatever they call for. The musicians of the heaven will be full of music".

Sura-e-Kausar sums up in the mystic world (Abundace), the doctrine of spiritual riches through devotion and sacrifice. To the men of God, rich in Divine blessings is granted a Fountain unfailing, that will quench the spiritual thirst of millions. Turn them in devotion and sacrifice to God. Nor heed the venom of hatred which destroys hopes about the present and the future. Kausar is the heavenly fountain of unbounded grace and knowledge, mercy and goodness, truth and wisdom, spiritual power and insight which was granted to the Holy Prophet, the man of God, and in some degree or other to all men and women who are sincere devotees of God. That Fountain quenches the highest spiritual thirst of man. It confers over flowing benefits of all kinds And, he to whom wisdom is granted receives indeed a benefit, overflowing. Such a person wants for nothing. Worldly pomp and wealth are as dust beneath his feet"

In order to explain the Islamic concept of hell, only two verses have been quoted in the following

S.Ibrahim - 14: 16- 17.

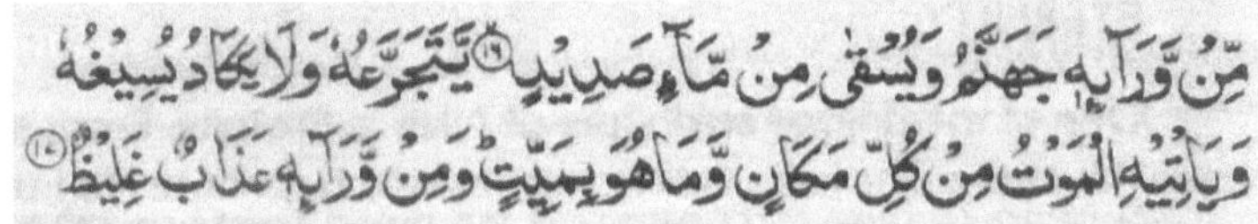

Tr:- "In front of such a one is Hell', and he is given for drink boiling fetid water; in gulps will he sip it, but, never will he be near swallowing it down his throat: Death will come to him from every quarter, yet will he not die; and in front of him will be a chastisement, unrelenting"

S. Waaqui-ah-56 :42-44: -

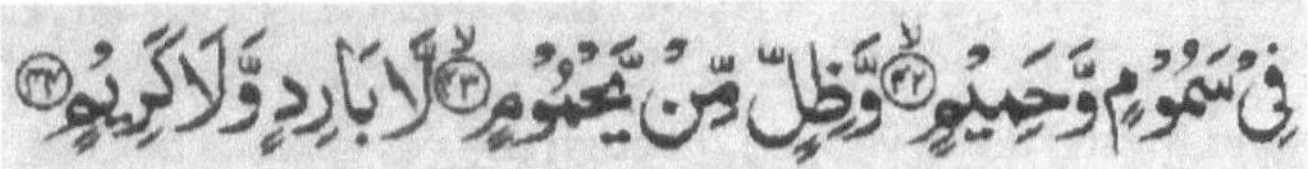

Tr.'- "(They will be) in the midst of a fierce blast of fire and 'n boiling water. and in the shades of black smoke: Nothing (Will there be) to refresh, nor to please*

Immaterial worlds. Paradise, Hell and Barzakh, the entering of souls into the astral (immaterial) body. the pleasures. comforts and eternal bliss of heaven. and the pains and torments of hell are extremely amazing. The immaterial worlds do not require space to occupy, it is not a matter of location, nor a matter of time, The amenities of pleasure and articles of pain are also immaterial i.e., immaterial creations for immaterial worlds, Another argument. supporting this statement is that Allah has said in the Holy Quran that He would create a universe, soon after the destruction of the present universe, and this world would be transformed into another world, which would require space. The Divine Omnipotence of creating immaterial worlds. Human astral body with soul inside and the immaterial articles of pleasure and pain, is extremely amazing mystery for us, which true Muslims should believe in.

Miracle is the sub-branch of the study of mysticism. What Allah does beyond the law of nature is called a miracle. Miracles were performed by saints and prophets with the help and permission of Allah. For example, Isa (AS,) gave life to a bird, made of clay, revived dead people, healed the leper and gave sight to the inborn blind. Moosa (A.S.) had a glittering hand, who stopped the course of River Nile to create a dry path to cross the river, converted the water of River Nile into blood, transformed his rod to a big crawling snake etc. Prophet Mohammed (SAW) ascended to Arsh and had audience with Allah. He split the moon into two equal halves, I have mentioned a very few miracles of the above mentioned three Prophets. But the Prophets never claimed authority on their miracles, but attributed the credit only to Almighty Allah. Allah's interference is the main cause for the change in the natural phenomena and the miracles remain mysteries for us. Hence, the miracles are called a branch of study of Mysticism, Allah will not permit every human being to perform miracles. It is the great privilege of men of God to see the sublimest mysteries of the spiritual world and instruct the common people in righteousness and warn against evil Hence, it is justified to say that Mysticism aims at elevating the excellence of a few chosen noble and magnificent personalities.

ISHQ-E-ILAHI or LOVE FOR GOD: -

The poet Daleel Sahib has so affectionately entitled the concluding Stanza of his poem as Ishq-e-Ilahi in which he has dealt, with favor of his love for God, His Eternity and Al-pervading Attribute.

ETERNITY:

One of the unique attributes of Allah is Eternity From all the beautiful names of Allah (Asma'-Ul-Husna), he has used two names which connote His Eternity. Allah is the First (Awwal) and He is the Last (Aakhir). Time is not His accomplice. His being precedes time and his Eternity transcends all beginning.

His Existence is not confined to any duration of period, nor can we ponder over His origin while He Himself is the Originator of all His Creations. We have past, present and future and the factor of time brings about decline and decay. But. Almighty Allah has neither past not' future; neither decline nor decay. His Existence cannot be influenced by time. His Existence and Eternity is beyond human imagination, intellect, estimation and conception. Hence. we need not tax our mind and ponder over the ultimate cause (God) of the long chain of causes and effects. Allah will annihilate the universe and terminate its existence. But He Will continue to exist as He existed before the creation of this universe. We must be satisfied with the Quranic verses which interprets His Eternity.

S.Al-Baqara - 2•.255 (Quoted in the 14th chapter- Top most part of the verses)

Tr:- Allah ! There is no God but He the Living! The self-subsisting, Eternal. No slumber can seize Him nor sleep"

S-Ar-Rahman – 55:26-27

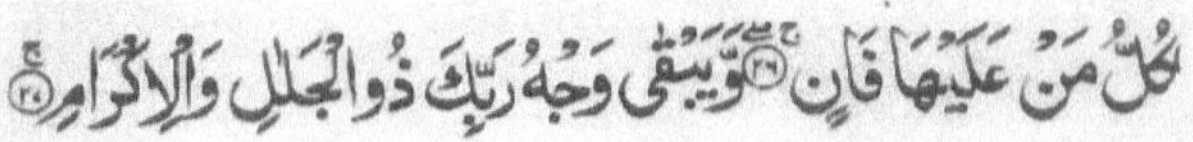

Tr.'- "All that is on earth will perish. But will abide (Forever) the Face of Thy Lord. full of majesty, Bounty and Honour"

OMNI-PRESENCE: -

Allah is All-Pervading. In order to interpret His Omni Presence, the poet has used two of His names. Allah is In-Dweller (Baatin) and Allah is Out Dweller (Zaahir). Allah is unseen but his manifestations can be seen in all His Creations, because, He is the In-Dweller and OutDweller in all His creations.

S-An'am - 6:3:- (Already quoted in Chapters 3 & 9)

Tr:- And, He is Allah in the heavens and on earth. He knoweth what ye hide. and what ye reveal, and He knoweth the (recompense) which ye earn (by your deeds)"

The whole of the poem Kayinat and especially its last Stanza, entitled "Ishq-e-Ilahi, are replete with spiritual philosophy. The poet has shown us the perfect way to redemption and has taken us through all the possible channels of Love for God, which facilitates merging with Almighty Allah. The poet has written in his foreword that he would consider as a grand remuneration for his endeavor, even if a single believer would be enlightened through the study of his poem, Kayinat. Daleel Sahib has taken us through all channels of love for God in order to achieve his goal of enlightening the minds of the readers. He has concluded the poem by mentioning the four beautiful names of Allah, viz: "Awwal", "Aukhir", "Baatin" and "Zaahir".

In his foreword, my late father Daleel Sahib has entreated the readers of his poem to pray for him. May his soul rest in peace. Ameen! (Faith and love, mysticism, meditation, human dignity, All -pervading attribute and Eternity of Allah).